INDIAN AFFAIRS IN COLONIAL NEW YORK:

The Seventeenth Century

New Amsterdam, ca. 1650. (Original in General Government Archives, The Hague; facsimile in Museum of the City of New York.)

INDIAN AFFAIRS IN COLONIAL NEW YORK

The Seventeenth Century

ALLEN W. TRELEASE

FALL CREEK BOOKS

AN IMPRINT OF

CORNELL UNIVERSITY PRESS

ITHACA AND LONDON

First published 1960 by Cornell University Press
First printing, Fall Creek Books, 2009
Printed in the United States of America

To Karin

Preface

WHEN Europeans first took up homes on the North American seaboard, they encountered an Indian culture which was not only old and
well established but even dynamic within a Stone Age context. By
European standards the American Indian was unquestionably primitive and barbarous; few colonists ever doubted that his way of life
was inferior in every important respect to their own. The Indian by
no means agreed, but he was willing and eager nevertheless to modify
his own material culture by plentiful adoptions from that of the newcomers. Seventeenth-century Europeans brought with them tools,
skills, and luxury goods of every description which led the Indian
overnight to regard much of his previous existence as drab, laborious,
and unprofitable. The means of gratifying new appetites were close
at hand, for the Indian had at least a temporary bargaining power.
Aside from the fact that he kept early colonists from starving while
they adjusted to the new environment, the Indian possessed a major
economic resource in the peltry supply of the surrounding forest.
Beaver skins in particular brought a high price in Europe, where they
were manufactured into hats, coats, and other items of apparel. This
Old World demand gave rise to a flourishing commerce in the New,
and the American Indian became a factor in world trade. The things
that he got in return ranged all the way from ribbons and beads to
firearms and firewater. In differing degrees each of them brought re-

markable changes in his accustomed way of life. Guns and ammunition revolutionized the methods of warfare and hunting; iron hoes, axes, kettles, and knives lightened and simplified the domestic burdens of both sexes, young and old; woolen cloth altered clothing habits; and liquor wrought havoc in tribal discipline and morale.

European trading goods might only have modified Indian civilization by transforming its material basis. The white man's land hunger and diseases were another matter. Traders required little or no land, and the Indians usually welcomed them for the goods they brought. Even farmers were tolerated at first because the land was plentiful, but it did not remain so for long. As settlement expanded, the hunting, planting, and fishing resources of the Indian shrank correspondingly. Just as drastic, even if undocumented in most cases, was the decimation of native population by epidemics of smallpox and other European maladies for which the Indian had developed no immunity and no cure. Within a generation of the original contact, therefore, Indian civilization was on the road to extinction. It was a bitter pill to swallow, and many tribes fought back blindly to avoid it. Others sought refuge in flight, often losing their separate identity in the process, but the pursuit was remorseless. The two cultures were incompatible, and that of the Indian, being the weaker, had eventually to succumb. Kinder treatment and more understanding on the part of the settler would have eliminated part of the friction and eased the consciences of later generations, but would hardly have eliminated the alternatives. Full respect for Indian rights would have entailed rolling back the tide of European settlement and leaving America as Columbus found it. As it happened, most colonists chose to stay, and most Indians were sooner or later overwhelmed.

The purpose of this book is to retrace in one corner of North America the early steps of that European expansion which later became worldwide in scope. It was not an insignificant corner, if only for the examples that it offers of interracial contact under diverse conditions. The history of Indian affairs in seventeenth-century New York falls into two main divisions, corresponding roughly (and to some extent coincidentally) with the periods of Dutch and English rule, before and after 1664. New Netherland was a large province, extending from southern Delaware to western Long Island and up the Hudson as far as Albany and Schenectady. Within that compass or adjacent to it were found "valuable" Indians, who controlled the peltry supply, and "expendable" Indians, whose economic value as consumers of European trading goods failed to outweigh their destructive capacity. This dichotomy was not noticeable in the earliest years, but it became increasingly apparent as intensive trading brought exhaustion of the seaboard fur supply. The inland tribes were strong to begin with, and the Dutch found it profitable to appease them and even to increase their initial advantages. The weaker coastal bands, on the other hand, bore the brunt of European invasion, receiving only transitory benefits in return. Although the Dutch embarked only briefly on a deliberate policy of subjugating these Indians by force, they were the expendables, with whom war was always a possibility and sometimes a reality.

When the Dutch gave way to the English, the coastal bands had already begun to decline rapidly in power and prestige. As this process was running its course, the new rulers gradually acquired political aspirations in the west and an imperial rivalry with the French in Canada. Both factors led, by the 1680's, to an increasing emphasis on relations with the Iroquois confederacy and other tribes farther west. A new dimension was added to New York Indian affairs as the economic importance of the Iroquois was subordinated to their political and military value as buffers and allies—even mercenaries—against the French. This policy carried disastrous implications for the Indians themselves, but at the opening of the new century they managed to establish a position of neutrality between the two European powers. In so doing they helped to prolong their independence for another two or three generations.

Several words may be appropriate at this point concerning mechanical or procedural details in the pages which follow. The variant spellings of Indian names are almost infinite in number and complexity. To avoid confusion I have adhered, except in direct quotations, to the forms sanctioned in Frederick W. Hodge's *Handbook of American Indians, North of Mexico.* I have also taken the liberty, when quoting from the *New York Colonial Documents,* of removing the italics from all proper names unless there is a positive reason for retaining them. In the matter of dating I have followed the New Style, in use among the Dutch and French, for all events prior to the English conquest. The old calendar, as observed by the English until 1752, was ten days behind the new in the seventeenth century, and the year began on March 25. For events after 1664 I have followed the Old Style in computing the month and day, but have kept January as the first month of the year.

I wish to thank Barnes & Noble, Inc., publishers of the Original Narratives of Early American History, for permission to quote from two volumes in that series, the *Journal of Jasper Danckaerts*, edited by Bartlett B. James and J. Franklin Jameson, and the *Narratives of New Netherland*, edited by J. Franklin Jameson. I am happy to acknowledge similar permission from the editor of the *Mississippi Valley Historical Review* to reprint a passage from Arthur H. Buffinton's article, "The Policy of Albany and English Westward Expansion," which appeared in volume VIII, page 235, of that journal.

My greatest debt of gratitude in preparing this study is to four men who have been dead for many years now—Edmund B. O'Callaghan, John R. Brodhead, Berthold Fernow, and A. J. F. Van Laer. Without their magnificent work in collecting, editing, translating, and interpreting the source materials of early New York history none of these pages could have been written. For more personal assistance I am indebted to Dr. William N. Fenton of the New York State Museum and Dr. Anthony F. C. Wallace of the Eastern Pennsylvania Psychiatric Institute, who were kind enough to read and criticize the first chapter, and to Professors Samuel Eliot Morison and Frederick Merk of Harvard University, Raymond de Roover of Boston College, and Lawrence H. Leder of Brandeis University, who have been very helpful in sharing with me their time and advice. I am also grateful for the cooperation of Miss Edna L. Jacobsen and the staff of the Manuscripts and History Section of the New York State Library, as well as the librarians at Harvard University, Wells College, Cornell University, the Massachusetts Historical Society, the Connecticut State Library, and the New York Public Library. Above all I am indebted to my wife, Karin Enebuske Trelease, who has gladly shared the burden of preparing this manuscript at every stage of its development.

A. W. T.

Aurora, New York
September 1959

Contents

Maps

Illustrations

Abbreviations

ARSCM   A. J. F. Van Laer, ed., *Minutes of the Court of Albany, Rensselaerswyck and Schenectady, 1668–1685* (Albany, 1926–1932).

CSP   *Calendar of State Papers, Colonial Series, America and the West Indies* (London, 1860–).

FOBCM   A. J. F. Van Laer, ed., *Minutes of the Court of Fort Orange and Beverwyck, 1652–1660* (Albany, 1920–1923).

LIR   Lawrence H. Leder, ed., *The Livingston Indian Records, 1666–1723* (Gettysburg, Pa., 1956).

LONN   Edmund B. O'Callaghan, ed., *Laws and Ordinances of New Netherlands, 1636–74* (Albany, 1868).

NNN   J. Franklin Jameson, ed., *Narratives of New Netherland, 1609–1664* (New York, 1909).

NYCD   Edmund B. O'Callaghan and Berthold Fernow, eds., *Documents Relative to the Colonial History of the State of New York* (Albany, 1856–1887).

NYDH   Edmund B. O'Callaghan, ed., *Documentary History of the State of New York* (Albany, 1849–1851).

NYHSC   New-York Historical Society, *Collections.*

RCM   A. J. F. Van Laer, ed., *Minutes of the Court of Rensselaerswyck, 1648–1652* (Albany, 1922).

VRBM   A. J. F. Van Laer, ed., *Van Rensselaer Bowier Manuscripts* (Albany, 1908).

INDIAN AFFAIRS IN COLONIAL NEW YORK:

The Seventeenth Century

I

The Indians of New Netherland

THE Indians of New Netherland fell into two linguistic stocks, the Algonquian and the Iroquoian. The Algonquian was by far the larger, both in population and in territorial extent. Occupying the Atlantic seaboard from the Gulf of St. Lawrence to North Carolina, Algonquian tribes could also be found as far west as the northern plains and the Rocky Mountains. Completely surrounded by them was the greater part of the Iroquoian stock. These tribes, the most famous of which were the Iroquois proper or Five Nations of New York State, occupied the bulk of present-day New York, Pennsylvania, Ohio, and southern Ontario as well as the lower Appalachian region. Although membership in one of these linguistic stocks implied related dialects, customs, and social institutions and a common ancestry among its respective tribes, it by no means reflected unity of purpose or action or even friendship among them. Some of the bitterest wars of the Iroquois were fought with their kinsmen the Huron, Erie, and Susquehanna.

The tribe is accepted as the major unit of classification within the linguistic stock, but its role in Indian society seems to have been less important than was once supposed. More and more in recent years ethnologists have discovered that tribal divisions in many parts of aboriginal America were less significant as social and political units than the smaller village communities or bands of which they were composed. In modified form this principle has been applied to the New York Iroquois, but it seems to have been especially true of the seaboard Algonquian. At least one writer has gone so far as to say that the Delaware tribe, one of the largest groups in the region, was in fact no tribe at all for most purposes until well along in the eighteenth century.[1] My own research in purely historical sources has led to the same conclusion, which I would extend in large, but varying, measure to the other Algonquian groups in New Netherland. Among them the tribe was chiefly important as an ethnic and geographical subdivision of the linguistic stock, whose members retained a closer cultural (but not necessarily political) relationship among themselves than with more distant Algonquian groups. Thus the dialectical differences which may or may not have existed in the language of a given tribe were less marked than those occurring within the Algonquian stock as a whole. Other aspects of their culture bore a corresponding relationship.

A significant feature of Algonquian organization was, therefore, its fragmentation. For the individual the primary unit of society, apart from his family and clan, was his own band, usually composed of from fifty to three hundred persons living in one or more villages. Each band was independent of the rest, though this rule is subject to variations, and united action between two or more of them, while common in times of emergency, was not the general rule. Just as the band was the principal object of allegiance on the part of individual tribesmen, so it was also the political unit which was known to Europeans and with which they had to deal.

The coastal position of the Algonquian put them first in the line of European expansion. The southernmost groups encountered immediately by the Dutch were those whom the English later called the Delaware, but who referred to themselves as the Lenni Lenape. Delaware bands occupied the Atlantic seaboard from Cape Henlopen to western Long Island and extended inland to include the Delaware

[1] A. L. Kroeber, "Nature of the Land-holding Group," *Ethnohistory*, II (1955), 303–314; William N. Fenton, "Locality as a Basic Factor in the Development of Iroquois Social Structure," in W. N. Fenton, ed., *Symposium on Local Diversity in Iroquois Culture* (Bureau of American Ethnology Bulletin no. 149; Washington, 1951), 35–54; William W. Newcomb, Jr., *The Culture and Acculturation of the Delaware Indians* (University of Michigan Museum of Anthropology, Anthropological Papers no. 10; Ann Arbor, 1956), 9; review of preceding by Anthony F. C. Wallace in *Ethnohistory*, IV (1957), 322–323; Anthony F. C. Wallace, "Political Organization and Land Tenure among the Northeastern Indians," *Southwestern Journal of Anthropology*, XIII (1957), 301–321.

River valley. If Delaware tradition be true—and there seems good reason to accept its substance—the tribe reached its historic location only after a long trek eastward from beyond the Mississippi. Also according to tradition the Delaware were a parent stock, of which neighboring tribes had once been a part. This is substantiated by the peculiar respect in which they were held by such tribes as the Nanticoke to the south and the Mahican to the north, who referred to the Delaware as "grandfathers" while using the term "brother" among themselves. Like ancient Gaul, as a modern authority on the Delaware has pointed out, that tribe was divided into three parts by the classical writers on American ethnology.[2] These subtribes, each of them forming a clan or totem as well as a political subdivision, were said to have been the Unalachtigo (Turkey), the Unami (Turtle), and the Munsee or Minsi (Wolf).[3] Within the last few years the traditional threefold division has been seriously questioned; instead the tribe seems to have been composed of thirty to forty autonomous communities. It also appears—although this point is contested—that the clans of the Turkey, the Turtle, and the Wolf existed side by side in many of these communities and were primarily social rather than political divisions. Anthony F. C. Wallace, the chief critic of the older interpretation, asserts that the Unami were but a single village band occupying lands on the upper Schuylkill River. The Munsee did not exist as such until about 1694, when a group of Shawnee combined with remnants of local bands on the upper Delaware under that name. The Unalachtigo did not survive at all, and they have been identified with various tribal remnants of the Delaware Bay region.[4]

Long before the white man arrived on the scene, a branch of the Delaware probably split off from the parent stock and migrated northward and eastward, most of them crossing the Hudson. Some reached a point north of Albany, and others spread into Connecticut and western Massachusetts. Either in the process of migration or at later dates this hypothetical offshoot itself underwent further divisions re-

[2] Anthony F. C. Wallace, "Woman, Land, and Society: Three Aspects of Aboriginal Delaware Life," *Pennsylvania Archaeologist*, XVII (1947), 15.

[3] Daniel G. Brinton, *The Lenape and Their Legends* (Philadelphia, 1885), 36–38.

[4] Wallace, "Woman, Land, and Society," 14–16; cf. Newcomb, *Culture and Acculturation of the Delaware*, 10.

3

sulting in the subsequent Mahican, Munsee, and Wappinger tribal groups, among others.[5]

The Mahican tribe, occupying eastern New York and adjacent portions of Massachusetts and Connecticut in historic times, is not to be confused with the Mohegan of eastern Connecticut although they probably had a common origin and their names are variations of the same word—Algonquian for "wolf." In the colonial period their territories were not contiguous, and they had no common history. Despite the fact that the Mahican were in existence and available for observation for at least three generations after colonization had begun, comparatively little is known of them today. Far more than the Delaware, they seem to have been classed as a single power by contemporary observers and officials. They were distributed among some forty villages according to a modern estimate, although the number of bands was much smaller.

Even less is known of their southern neighbors, the Wappinger, who were subjected earlier to the disintegration attending European settlement. The Wappinger seem to have resembled the Delaware more than the Mahican, at least in the absence of any effective tribal organization, and probably the tribal designation itself is a misnomer. As nearly as can be ascertained, there were about eighteen Wappinger bands, living between the Hudson and Connecticut Rivers and back into the interior from Long Island Sound. Seven of these bands were primarily in New York, occupying lands from Manhattan Island northward into Dutchess County. Their name was derived from an Algonquian word meaning "easterners," other variants being found in the names of the Abnaki tribe in Maine and the Wampanoag in Massachusetts.

Fully thirteen bands lived on Long Island at the time of the white man's first arrival. Except for one or two of them at the western end these bands were very closely related to the Indians of southern New England. Their social and political organization was similar to that of the groups already discussed, but several variations are more suggestive of New England than of Delaware practice. Here, for example, are encountered chief sachems with limited authority over more than one band. The eastern groups were confederated for a time under the leadership of the Montauk at the island's eastern tip, and on at least

[5] Alanson Skinner, "The Manhattan Indians," in New York State Museum, *Bulletin*, no. 158 (1912), 199.

one occasion the younger brothers of the sachem at Montauk acted as chiefs of neighboring bands. For a long time there was a similar official over some if not all of the island's western bands. Although the individual communities seem to have acted on their own initiative as often as not, there is some justification for referring to them as the Montauk tribe.

Throughout most of aboriginal America population bore no comparison to that of the whites in the same areas once colonization had gotten well underway. But apart from this generalization the problem of determining actual numbers is very difficult. Although natives and colonists alike were concerned with Indian population and distribution, usually neither possessed the opportunity or motivation to enumerate them in detail. Most Indian population figures for the seventeenth century are based upon rough estimates which must be balanced with other factors like archaeological findings, the availability of economic resources, and historical references to tribal activity. The problem has plagued observers from the beginning, and in many cases they are still far from agreement. The best authority, despite criticism that he erred too often on the side of conservatism, is the anthropologist James C. Mooney, who a generation ago estimated the tribal populations along the eastern seaboard as of about 1600—the eve of the European invasion. Including the so-called Munsee bands, Mooney's figure for the Delaware is 8,000. No breakdown is possible, and the total number itself is uncertain in view of the lack of knowledge about the very existence of some communities. With the same reservation, his estimates for the Mahican and Wappinger were 3,000 persons each, slightly less than half of the latter living in what is now New York. The Indian population of Long Island at this time was about 6,000, a comparatively heavy concentration.[6]

The identification and location of individual Algonquian bands in New Netherland are largely dependent on the degree to which the Dutch and their English successors made contact with them. Those groups living nearest to colonial settlements therefore are usually the best known today.

The best known of the Delaware bands were those living in the

[6] James Mooney, "The Aboriginal Population of America North of Mexico," in Smithsonian Institution, *Miscellaneous Collections*, LXXX, no. 7 (Washington, 1928), 4.

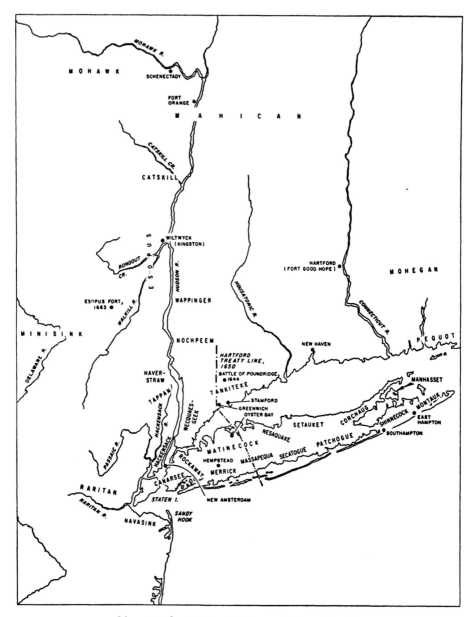

Map 1. The Hudson Valley and Long Island

vicinity of New Amsterdam. The first of these to meet Henry Hudson in 1609 were the Navasink, who occupied the Atlantic Highlands below Sandy Hook. The Raritan lived in the valley of the Raritan River, and their domain also included the lower end of Staten Island. The Hackensack were among the closest neighbors of New Amsterdam, controlling the present Jersey City–Bayonne area as well as another part of Staten Island. North of them, straddling the New York–New Jersey line as it intersects the Hudson, was the Tappan band. Just beyond were the Haverstraw, living around the later town of that name. Still another band, which was more closely related to the Delaware than to its more immediate neighbors, was the Canarsee of Long Island. Living in what is now Brooklyn and along Jamaica Bay, they also controlled Governors Island, the east end of Staten Island, and probably the lower tip of Manhattan.[7]

On the west side of the Hudson and beyond the Haverstraw were the six bands whom later authorities have classed as the Munsee branch of the Delaware. It appears, however, that they spoke a dialect more closely related to Mahican than to the Lenape dialect of the Delaware proper. Since the Munsee category is dubious as a Delaware subdivision and since the colonists did not include them among the Mahican, these bands might better be considered as a separate group. About four of them, occupying the bulk of Ulster and Orange Counties, were lumped together by the Dutch as the Esopus Indians and were to figure prominently in the last days of Dutch control. A fifth band was the Catskill, who lived farther north along the Hudson, between Saugerties and Catskill Creek. South and west of the Esopus was a final "Munsee" community, the Minisink. Occupying the headwaters of the Delaware River and extending southward into New Jersey and Pennsylvania, it apparently controlled a large area and was relatively populous. Its comparatively remote position in mountainous terrain prevented disastrous contact with Europeans for many years, but the band was subject, on the other hand, to forays from the western Iroquois.[8]

[7] E. M. Ruttenber, *History of the Indian Tribes of Hudson's River* (Albany, 1872), 89–92. Ruttenber omits the Canarsee from this group, classing them as a Montauk band. Cf. Reginald P. Bolton, "New York City in Indian Possession," in Heye Foundation, *Indian Notes and Monographs,* II (1920), 280–287; John R. Swanton, *The Indian Tribes of North America* (Bureau of American Ethnology Bulletin no. 145; Washington, 1953), 49–50.

[8] Ruttenber, *Indian Tribes of Hudson's River,* 93–96.

Identification of the Mahican bands is more difficult, but apparently there were five divisions. The first of these, the Mahican proper, lived in the vicinity of Albany and controlled territories extending from about thirty miles west of that point (where they abutted on the Mohawk) to Lake Champlain. The others were the Mechkentowoon, on the west bank of the Hudson above Catskill Creek; the Wawyachtonoc, in Dutchess and Columbia Counties and eastward to the Housatonic River; the Westenhuck, near Great Barrington, Massachusetts; and the Wiekagjoc, on the east bank of the Hudson River near the town of Hudson.[9]

The southernmost of the Wappinger bands was the Rechgawawanc or Manhattan, who occupied the major part of Manhattan Island, the western half of the Bronx, and part of Westchester.[10] Because of this vulnerable location they disappeared quite early. The Wecquaesgeek, whom the English referred to simply as the Westchester Indians, were one of the most important of the Wappinger bands and controlled the region between the Hudson, Bronx, and Pocantico Rivers. The Sintsink held lands around Ossining, New York, and gave their name to the town as well as to its most famous institution. The Kitchawank lived in the northern part of Westchester and had a village at the site of Peekskill. The Nochpeem occupied Putnam and lower Dutchess Counties, and the Siwanoy, another large band, held the north shore of Long Island Sound from Norwalk to Hell Gate. Back of them, and also straddling the New York–Connecticut line, lived the Tankiteke, sometimes called the Pachamis after the name of their sachem. Only one other band needs to be mentioned here, the Wappinger proper, who were sometimes included with their neighbors under the name of Highland Indians. Occupying part of the highlands along the Hudson, they lived in the vicinity of Poughkeepsie.[11]

Of the thirteen Long Island bands the Canarsee in modern Brooklyn

[9] *Ibid.*, 85.

[10] The identity and affiliation of the Manhattan Indians are a source of considerable confusion. I have followed Bolton, "New York City in Indian Possession," 239, who further believes that this band might have been subordinate to the Wecquaesgeek to the north. Cf. Ruttenber, *Indian Tribes of Hudson's River*, 77–78; Skinner, "Manhattan Indians," 199; Swanton, *Indian Tribes of North America*, 49.

[11] Bolton, "New York City in Indian Possession," 259–260; Ruttenber, *Indian Tribes of Hudson's River*, 78–84; Skinner, "Manhattan Indians," 199; Swanton, *Indian Tribes of North America*, 45.

have already been mentioned. Next, and perhaps closely related to them, were the Rockaway in Queens and southern Nassau Counties. The remaining bands lived on either the north or the south side of the island, with the separating boundary running along its center to Peconic Bay. On the north shore, moving from west to east, were the Matinecoc (one of the largest groups on the island), the Nesaquake, the Setauket, and the Corchaug, who occupied the northern branch of the island to Orient Point. On Shelter Island, nearby, was the Manhasset band. Next to the Rockaway on the south shore, and in the same order, were the Merric, the Massapequa (another important band), the Secatoag, the Patchoag, the Shinnecock, and finally the Montauk at the eastern tip.[12]

Each Algonquian band seems to have been governed by a sachem, or chief, and a council of lesser chiefs. The latter were commonly chosen on account of age and experience, warlike exploits, or some other service rendered the community whether of a peaceful or military nature. The sachem, on the other hand, was chosen through a combination of hereditary descent and appointment. Among the Delaware and Mahican at least, descent passed through the female line. A sachem therefore could normally be succeeded only by a brother or by the son of a sister. As this system provided a number of hereditary claimants, some of whom were usually unfit for the post by reason of age, inexperience, or incapacity, a further choice was necessary. This power was exercised by the oldest capable woman of the lineage in which the sachemship descended. Although women performed a great part of the manual labor in Indian society, they wielded considerable power in certain questions of public concern.[13] Most of the Long Island bands differed from this description only in that they allowed the sachemship to pass from father to son and permitted women to hold the office in the absence of a suitable male heir.[14]

Government was by persuasion, since there was no adequate pro-

[12] Benjamin F. Thompson, *History of Long Island* (3d ed., ed. by Charles J. Werner; New York, 1918), I, 125–129; Ruttenber, *Indian Tribes of Hudson's River*, 73–75; Frederic H. Douglas, "Long Island Indian Tribes" (Denver Art Museum, Dept. of Indian Art, Leaflet no. 49; 1932); Bolton, "New York City in Indian Possession," 270–279.

[13] Wallace, "Woman, Land, and Society," 6, 11; cf. A. C. Flick, ed., *History of the State of New York* (New York, 1933–1937), I, 78.

[14] Frederic H. Douglas, "Long Island Indian Cultures" (Denver Art Museum, Dept. of Indian Art, Leaflet no. 50; 1932).

vision to enforce the will of the chieftains against contrary tribal opinion. The sachem had the duties, both ceremonial and substantial, which usually pertain to executive office, including the responsibility for keeping order and settling minor disputes and the conduct of "foreign relations." Because of the absence of any effective police power, his own strength of character and personal influence were the measure of his success or failure. Policy decisions were shared by the council, and in peacetime no important action could be taken without a unanimous vote of that body. If the sachem departed from these ground rules, he was subject to deposition at any time, though normally he was treated with deference even if unpopular. In wartime all the powers of civil government were suspended. No sachem had the power to declare war without the consent of his war captains, who held office by virtue of military distinction. They might or might not be members of the peacetime council, but in wartime they took over the government completely from the sachem and his advisers. If peace negotiations were afoot during wartime, the captains could present the enemy's proposals to the sachem for his acceptance or rejection. If he accepted them, by that act he formally resumed authority, and ambassadors were appointed to conclude the peace.[15] Such is the present-day idea of Algonquian government, much of it deduced from later practice; but how fully applicable it is to the seventeenth century or how often special circumstances led to extraordinary action can never be known.

In the absence of political ties the Algonquian clan structure provided a social bond which was almost the only force making for tribal unity. For certain purposes the individual tribesman's primary affiliation was with his clan rather than his band or community. As these groups cut across community lines—and probably tribal divisions too, such as they were—a member of the Wolf clan, for instance, like a Rotarian or a Sigma Chi, was received as a kinsman by his brethren throughout the tribal domain. If he never ventured beyond the precincts of his own community, much of his private life was regulated by the clan as distinguished from the village band. One of

[15] Brinton, *Lenape and Their Legends*, 46–48; William Nelson, *The Indians of New Jersey* (Paterson, 1894), 91–93; Anthony F. C. Wallace, *King of the Delawares: Teedyuscung, 1700–1763* (Philadelphia, 1949), 9; Newcomb, *Culture and Acculturation of the Delaware*, 51–53; Ruttenber, *Indian Tribes of Hudson's River*, 42–43, 47–49; cf. Flick, *History of New York*, I, 78–79.

the most binding rules of Algonquian society forbade marriage within the clan, and violations were regarded as akin to incest.[16]

All the Indians with whom this study is concerned were comparatively sedentary and subsisted more by agriculture or large-scale fishing than by hunting and trapping, although the latter were important. Differing locations, of course, imposed different ways of life upon the individual communities. Thus fishing was more important for those living along the seacoast than it was for the bands farther inland. But if generalizations can be made, the raising of crops was paramount for all of them. In the summer they cultivated maize, the great Indian staple, as well as beans, squash, and other vegetables, the surplus of which was dried and stored up for winter or emergency use in large underground pits. In the winter the communities frequently broke up, and each family group traveled up the streams to inland hunting territories.[17] The economy was almost entirely self-sufficient, and commerce among bands, although it existed, was of comparatively slight importance.

Indian and colonist alike drew their livelihood from the land, and questions of its use and ownership had corresponding importance in the relations between them. The Indians did not, of course, roam at will through unlimited tracts of wilderness. Each tribe or subtribe occupied a specific territory, the bounds of which were well known and usually well marked by geographical features. Among the Algonquian, the lands of each community were further divided into family hunting units. These varied in size but normally contained one or more streams and, like the tribal and subtribal domains, were bounded by recognizable landmarks. As New Jersey, for instance, apparently contained no more than eighty or a hundred of these territories, the family group in possession was considerably more than a single household. What constituted a family for this purpose is not fully known, and the requirements probably varied from time to time and place to place. The largest known Delaware "family" hunting territory— measuring two hundred square miles—was located in east-central New Jersey, but those in the more densely populated regions around the Delaware River were much smaller. European purchase deeds of the

---

[16] Wallace, *Teedyuscung*, 10; Newcomb, *Culture and Acculturation of the Delaware*, 49–52.
[17] Wallace, *Teedyuscung*, 7–8, and "Woman, Land, and Society," 17.

seventeenth century often gave specific names to the hunting territories and associated them with individual "owners," who in reality were probably the heads of the families possessing them. Although the family had exclusive hunting and fishing rights in its own preserve, it probably lacked the right to dispose of this land in any way that it saw fit. As the village or band made the original allotment, it presumably retained the right of ultimate disposal. Therefore the consent of the sachem or other local chiefs was a usual prerequisite before an Indian could legitimately sell his land to the white man.[18]

Land was a product of nature which the Indian appropriated to his own use. It was not considered a commodity to be bought and sold. It could pass from one generation to another through normal hereditary processes, but when a family or an individual ceased to use it the land was regranted to someone else. The advent of the white man modified these ideas, but the transition period was long and painful. Indians readily accepted gifts for their land from the colonists, and the deeds often specified that the original "owners" should retain their hunting rights. Trouble ensued when the Indian discovered not only that hunting was destroyed by extensive settlement and the fencing of fields, but that the transaction was considered to be permanent. Land purchases, according to Indian jurisprudence, were merely conveyances of residence and subsistence for as long a time as the interested parties were satisfied with the terms. Only in this light can the repeated Indian demands for repayment or retrocession of lands they had already deeded away be fully explained. The white man occasionally took lands by fraud and the Indian sometimes knowingly conveyed tracts to which he had no right, but more often both parties acted in good faith. Unfortunately they proceeded on different principles, and neither was able to recognize, much less concede, those of the other.

During the seventeenth century this problem was less pressing for

[18] Wallace, "Woman, Land, and Society," 3–5; John M. Cooper, "Land Tenure among the Indians of Eastern and Northern North America," *Pennsylvania Archaeologist*, VIII (1938), 55–59; Melvin R. Gilmore, "Some Indian Ideas of Property," in Heye Foundation, *Indian Notes and Monographs*, V (1928), 137; William C. MacLeod, "Family Hunting Territory and Lenape Political Organization," *American Anthropologist*, n.s. XXIV (1922), 448–463; Frank G. Speck, "The Wapanachki Delawares and the English," *Pennsylvania Magazine of History and Biography*, LXVII (1943), 340–341.

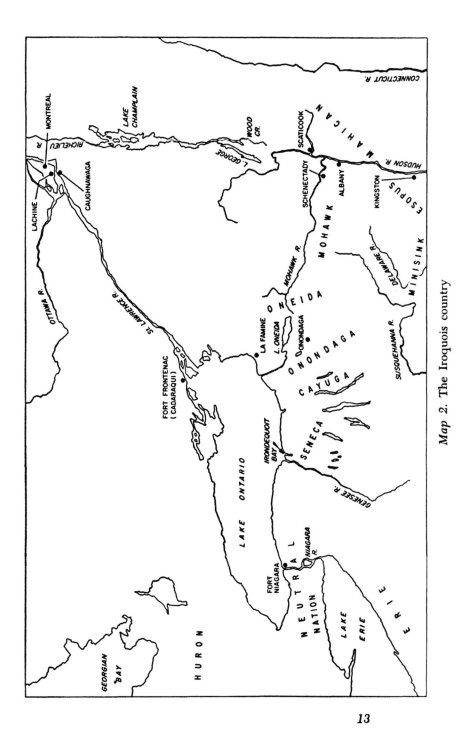

Map 2. The Iroquois country

13

the Iroquois tribes than it was for their Algonquian neighbors. The Iroquois confederacy in this time was the most powerful Indian combination east of the Mississippi and a vital factor in the North American rivalry of France and England. The Five Nations, later expanded to six by adoption of the Tuscarora after 1712, occupied the greater part of upstate New York as their home territory, and Iroquois war parties ranged as far afield as Illinois, Maine, and South Carolina. Their most common type of dwelling, the multifamily long house, was allegorically applied by the Iroquois to represent their confederacy.[19] Living at the eastern end of the long house and acting as keepers of its eastern door were the Mohawk, with whom the white man made first contact. The name Mohawk is derived from an Algonquian word meaning "man-eaters"—a literal and figurative epithet which gives a fair idea of the tribe's reputation among its neighbors. They called themselves the Kaniengehaga, or "people of the place of the flint." The eastern boundary of the Mohawk, coinciding with that of the league, extended from the lower part of Lake Champlain to a point west of Schenectady and then southward near Schoharie Creek. On the south they touched the Minisink near the northern line of Delaware County. Their western boundary, separating them from the Oneida, lay just west of Herkimer. Mohawk hunting lands extended as far north as the St. Lawrence and as far east as Lake Champlain, but the upper portions of this territory were also ranged by the hunters of other tribes. In connection with these and other tribal boundaries it must be remembered that, although specific territorial limits were known and recognized by the tribes concerned, the boundaries were provisional and, especially among the Iroquois, were altered frequently as villages changed locations. Among the Iroquois these changes were amicably arranged, but boundary alterations with outside tribes usually accompanied the vicissitudes of intertribal warfare. The Mohawk dwelt in several villages, called castles by the Europeans since they were usually fortified, the exact number and positions of which varied from time to time. There seem to have been from three to seven villages during the historic period occupying sites on both

---

[19] The following résumé of Iroquois boundaries and village sites is based on William N. Fenton, "Problems Arising from the Historic Northeastern Position of the Iroquois," in Smithsonian Institution, *Miscellaneous Collections*, C (Washington, 1940), 199–231.

sides of, but never very far from, the Mohawk River, mostly in Fulton and Montgomery Counties. About 1640 the Mohawk castles were moved downstream toward Schenectady, possibly to enjoy more easily the delights of civilization at Albany. This was made possible by the steady pressure that the Mohawk exerted on the retreating Mahican, who occupied the territory before them.

The Oneida were the second fire of the long house. In the historic period they possessed but one village, which gradually moved from the high hills at the headwaters of Oneida and Oriskany Creeks, in Madison and Oneida Counties, down into the valley toward Oneida Lake. Smallest of the Five Nations in population, the Oneida claimed a large territory extending from that of the Mohawk to a line drawn roughly north and south through the middle of the lake that bears their name. Their northern hunting territory extended to the St. Lawrence, and to the south they reached the east branch of the Susquehanna River.

The central fire of the long house, protected by two friendly tribes on either side, was in the keeping of the Onondaga. Their western boundary ran slightly to the east of Owasco Lake and its inlet, then northward to Lake Ontario. The Onondaga hunting lands lay at the eastern end of Lake Ontario, chiefly within Oswego and Jefferson Counties. Their southern limit was probably the Susquehanna River. The Onondaga seldom possessed more than one town, which also served as capital of the confederacy. During the seventeenth century it occupied a number of successive hilltop sites west of Cazenovia Lake, later moving to locations in the Onondaga valley, slightly farther west.

The next tribe was the Cayuga, whose villages were located between Lakes Owasco and Cayuga or at points a little to the north and south of that area. In 1677 three Cayuga villages were reported, but this figure undoubtedly varied from time to time. Cayuga territory was embraced within a relatively narrow strip of land, including the two lakes mentioned above and extending from Lake Ontario on the north to the Susquehanna on the south.

The Seneca were the fifth—or, from their own point of view, the first—fire of the long house and keepers of the western door. The Seneca name, like that of the Mohawk, was not of the tribe's own choosing, nor was it a result of European classicism. Rather it was "an Anglicized form of the Dutch enunciation of the Mohegan

[Mahican] rendering" of the Iroquoian term for the Oneida.[20] The Dutch commonly applied the term "Sinnekens" or some variation of it to any or all of the four farther nations. Since Dutch relations were almost entirely with the Mohawk, no further refinement was necessary. As the other tribes became better known to those at Albany, the name seemingly moved westward and attached to the farthest tribe. The southern boundary of the Seneca skirted the headwaters of the western Finger Lakes, and when the white man first knew them, they extended little beyond the Genesee River on the west. In 1651, however, they expelled their Iroquoian neighbors, the Neutral Nation, from the land east of the Niagara and four years later destroyed their relatives the Erie, who lived between the Genesee and Lake Erie. After 1655, therefore, the Seneca domain included all the territory between Lakes Seneca and Erie. Still later, after the defeat of the Susquehanna tribe, Seneca settlements were to be found along the Allegheny River in Pennsylvania. The tribe inhabited a number of towns, most of them clustered above the western Finger Lakes; each of them moved its location several times within the historic period.

The tremendous military power of the Iroquois and the widespread influence which resulted from it were out of all proportion to the league's population. Although Mooney's estimated total of 5,500 for 1600 is probably too small, it can be said that from the coming of the white man until very recent times their combined population never exceeded 15,000 persons. They never had a fighting force of more than 2,500 men, and at no time did they put this number in the field at once. An estimate of 1660 gave the Mohawk no more than 500 warriors, the Oneida less than 100, the Onondaga 300, the Cayuga 300, and the Seneca no more than 1,000—a total of 2,200 men.[21] These figures are perhaps as accurate as any available for a fairly early period, and they reflect the relative size of the member tribes. Iroquois population was never constant during historic times. The ravages of disease or warfare could wipe out hundreds within a single year, and the adop-

[20] J. N. B. Hewitt, in Frederick W. Hodge, ed., *Handbook of American Indians North of Mexico* (Bureau of American Ethnology Bulletin no. 30; Washington, 1907–1910), II, 502.

[21] These figures are given by Father Jerome Lalement, in Reuben G. Thwaites, ed., *The Jesuit Relations* (Cleveland, 1896–1901), XLV, 207. J. N. B. Hewitt, in his articles on each tribe in Hodge's *Handbook*, has multiplied each of these figures by five to reach an approximate total population for the league of 11,000.

tion of new members was practiced regularly, in the case of both individual prisoners and entire tribal groups.[22]

The Iroquois depended greatly on the wild fowl, deer, bear, and other animals they could hunt or trap in their own hunting territories or, occasionally, farther afield. During the seventeenth century they conquered additional lands beyond Lakes Erie and Ontario, which were particularly valuable for beaver hunting. This animal, however, had been relatively unimportant until the advent of the white man and the fur trade. The main hunting season occupied the winter months; the fishing season, when salmon and eel were especially sought after, lasted from the middle of March until late fall. Primary dependence, however, was placed on the raising of crops. As with the Algonquian this task occupied the whole summer and was carried on by the women. Much of the territory was densely forested, and clearing the land was often a prerequisite to its cultivation. Occasional riverbank sites, where clearing was unnecessary, were much in demand. On the other hand, hilly positions were more easily defensible, and the possibility of enemy attack was for many groups an ever-present danger. Furthermore, the primitive methods in use among the Indians resulted in soil exhaustion every ten or twelve years. This was the main cause of the frequent removal of Iroquois townsites, and it meant that the village must start all over the process of clearing and breaking the land.[23] Maize, always the chief crop, was supplemented by beans, pumpkins, melons, and even orchard fruits. The first two could be planted in the same field, with the cornstalks serving as supports for the bean vines. The relative importance of agriculture over hunting and fishing varied from one locality to another. The Seneca lived in a more densely wooded area than the Cayuga, for example, with the result that more game was available to the Seneca and farming was harder.[24]

Land tenure was simpler than among the neighboring Algonquian tribes. In the vicinity of Iroquois villages small garden plots were often held in severalty, each family having the exclusive right to cultivate

[22] The best discussion of Iroquois population is given in George S. Snyderman, "Behind the Tree of Peace," *Pennsylvania Archaeologist*, XVIII (1948), 38–43.

[23] Fenton, "Locality," 42. By contrast, the New England tribes and perhaps the Delaware of New Jersey had developed methods of soil fertilization which made periodic removals unnecessary. See Wallace, "Woman, Land, and Society," 18.

[24] Sara H. Stites, *Economics of the Iroquois* (Lancaster, Pa., 1905), 20–26.

the bit of ground allotted to it. Hunting lands, on the other hand—by far the larger part of the tribal domain—were held by the nation as a whole for the use of all its members. The acquisition, use, and disposal of these lands were matters of tribal concern and, so far as it is known, no individual pretended to exclusive jurisdiction over any part of them. Occasionally in the 1690's and afterward small groups would convey tribal lands to the white man, but the pretext of purchaser and seller alike was that these Indians acted on behalf of the whole tribe. In so doing they incurred the wrath of the sachems, who sometimes prevailed upon English officials to nullify the transactions.

The origin of the Iroquois tribes has been a subject of controversy for many years. The Seneca and Cayuga very likely entered their historic seats after a long migration from the southwest. The most reasonable theory is that they were a single offshoot of the Erie, or of a tribe from which the Erie were also descended. After this offshoot had worked its way north and east into New York State, a further division resulted in the separation of the Cayuga.[25] The origins of the other three tribes present quite a detective problem, with the earliest clues being furnished by Jacques Cartier in 1534–1541. During his three voyages to the St. Lawrence, Cartier encountered an Iroquoian people dwelling on both sides of the river between Quebec and Montreal. But when Champlain entered the scene in 1603, this territory was completely deserted. One guess is that these Laurentian Iroquois migrated southward sometime in the interim. Themselves probably an offshoot of the Huron tribe or its ancestors, they formed at least two bands which may be called for convenience' sake the Onondaga and the Mohawk. The Onondaga traveled to their historic position, stopping for a while in what is now Jefferson County, New York. This theory accords with Onondaga tradition. The second group also migrated southward, perhaps by the Richelieu River–Lake Champlain route, later dividing to form the separate tribes of Mohawk and Oneida. This theory, too, accords with the best evidence available, for the Mohawk and Oneida resemble each other more closely than they do any

[25] Frederick Houghton, "The Migrations of the Seneca Nation," *American Anthropologist*, n.s. XXIX (1927), 245–250; Arthur C. Parker, "An Analytical History of the Seneca Indians," in New York State Archaeological Association, *Researches and Transactions*, VI (1926), 18–19.

of their other confederates.[26] It is possible, on the other hand, that all five tribes were in their historic homes longer than this explanation would allow. The Laurentian Iroquois may only have been a "frontier" group while the main center of Iroquoia was then, as later, in New York State.

The testimony of Cartier seems additionally to show that the Laurentian Iroquois were politically disorganized, with the respective bands engaged in nearly constant warfare with one another. Yet when the earliest Jesuit missionaries and Dutch traders encountered the New York Iroquois, they observed an offensive and defensive alliance more effective than anything to be found north of Mexico. The conclusion seems, therefore, to be—and again, this has been a controversial problem for many years—that the league of the Iroquois dates from a time not far anterior to the beginning of the seventeenth century. The most convincing hypothesis places the date somewhere between 1559 and 1570. Earlier dates, in the fifteenth century and before—although still widely held—appear inconsonant with the theory of tribal migration traced above.[27] The actual process of confederation appears to have been shrouded in mythology almost from the time it occurred. According to the legend the inspiration for unity was provided by Deganawidah, a deified figure of Huron birth but Mohawk by adoption. Much practical assistance was provided by a disciple in the person of Hiawatha, who resembles in name only the figure celebrated by Longfellow. Also according to tradition the Mohawk were the first to take up the covenant chain, followed in order by the Oneida, Onondaga, Cayuga, and Seneca. The basic objective of the league appears to have been peace—peace, that is, between the warring Iroquois so that they might better take up the hatchet against their common enemies. This objective once attained, it was but a short step to the proposition that all tribes who refused to enter the Iroquois orbit were *ipso facto* enemies. What began as a defensive alliance became, if not a positive instrument of conquest, at least a covering device for aggression of the bloodiest variety.[28]

[26] The best discussion of this problem is in Fenton, "Northeastern Position of the Iroquois," 167–177.

[27] Cf. J. N. B. Hewitt, "Era of the Formation of the Historic League of the Iroquois," *American Anthropologist*, VII (1894), 61–67; Paul A. W. Wallace, "The Return of Hiawatha," *New York History*, XXIX (1948), 397–400.

[28] The best popular account of the league's formation is Paul A. W. Wallace's

At the institution of the league a council of forty-nine permanent sachemships was created, each with its appropriate name.[29] These offices corresponded with those already in existence within the constituent tribes. They were both hereditary and appointive along the lines already observed among the Algonquian, and the sachems themselves were equal in rank and authority. When he had been formally installed in office, a sachem dropped his own name and assumed that of the office itself, which passed from generation to generation like a title of nobility. As the respective nations had differing numbers of sachems when the league was founded, the unequal numbers were perpetuated in its council. This had no practical effect, however, since each nation spoke with only one voice and had but one vote.

As the Mohawk, Onondaga, and Seneca were and continued to be more powerful than the other two members, they were assigned primary roles in administering the league. These pertained chiefly to the conduct of war and relations with other tribes, but the machinery was so hedged about with checks and balances that none of the three, individually or collectively, could abuse their power. The Onondaga, by virtue of their central position, were appointed keepers of the fire and the archival wampum. To one of their sachemships was attached the role of permanent moderator. Insofar as the league had a presiding officer, this was he, although his powers were closely circumscribed.

The council of the league met regularly, and extraordinary meetings might be called at any time by any one of the member nations. The councils were normally held at Onondaga, but this rule too was flexible. The functions of the council were essentially twofold. In the realm of internal affairs it adjusted differences between the member nations and invested the sachems with office. More important was its conduct of foreign affairs: "It declared war and made peace, sent and received embassies, entered into treaties of alliance, regulated the affairs of subjugated nations, received new members into the League, extended its protection [*sic*] over feeble tribes, in a word, took all

---

The White Roots of Peace (Philadelphia, 1946), in which the variant forms of the legend are woven together.

[29] Written a century ago, the classic work on the Iroquois is still Lewis H. Morgan's *League of the Ho-De-No-Sau-Nee or Iroquois* (new ed.; New York, 1901). My own discussion of Iroquois political structure is based on Morgan, I, 59 ff.; Fenton, "Locality," 50–52; Wallace, *White Roots of Peace*, 32 ff.; and Stites, *Economics of the Iroquois*, 114–115.

needful measures to promote their prosperity, and enlarge their dominion." [30] There was no particular machinery for enforcing the council's decisions. These were carried out either by special agents appointed for the purpose or by each of the tribes.

It has already been noted that among the Algonquian the clan system was the only real force for tribal unity. In the case of the Iroquois it supplemented the political structure of the league and provided the best device for holding it together in the face of intertribal jealousies. "The relationship between members of a given clan was as binding as that between the members of a family. Yet these clans were intertribal." The rule against marriage within one's own clan was equally strict among the Iroquois, and affiliation was similarly transmitted through the mother. The number of clans differed among the five nations. The Mohawk and Oneida had three (the Turtle, Bear, and Wolf), which were found in the other tribes as well. The Onondaga, Cayuga, and Seneca had additional clans, the Cayuga possessing ten, "including the three Bears: Big Bear, Younger Bear and Suckling Bear." [31]

In addition to self-defense the original motivation for forming the league may have included a sincere aspiration for universal peace. This ideal was, however, firmly grounded in a tribal superiority complex. The Iroquois were convinced that they constituted a master race, and if universal peace were to be achieved, it must be done within their fold. As time passed, the eventual aim became less apparent than the actual process of reducing the gentiles to submission. One of the basic principles of the league was that its members were at war with all tribes not positively allied to it. Thus throughout their history the Iroquois engaged in warfare for the partial purpose of adding new nations to their confederacy. If this were not the only cause for war, at least it helps to explain the bitterness with which they harried their Iroquoian kinsmen—these people had the divine spark but resolutely refused to see the light. Some tribes did indeed enter the *pax Iroquoia* —the Tuscarora became a sixth nation and the Mahican, Scaticook, Nanticoke, Tuteloe, and Delaware among others were either adopted by one of the members or extended Iroquois protection—but most of this was done at gunpoint, both figuratively and literally. The cause

[30] Morgan, *League of the Iroquois*, I, 63.
[31] Wallace, *White Roots of Peace*, 39.

for so little enthusiasm on the part of outsiders is not hard to find. Real membership in the league, on a basis of equality with the original nations, was never extended. Even the Tuscarora were as much an adjunct to the Oneida as they were an equal member of the confederacy, and the others lost much of their independence and in some cases their separate identity and culture in the process.

The role of the league must not be overestimated in explaining Iroquois development; nor must its theoretical mechanics as outlined above be taken as the constant method of conducting business. In practice things did not go so smoothly. Whereas the league provided a constant shield for its member nations, each of them was completely free to make war or peace, negotiate treaties, and regulate its own domestic affairs without interference from above. Fundamentally the members had different interests to pursue most of the time, and the records in fact show far more cases of war conducted by one nation alone, or by a combination of two or three of them, than of such conflicts maintained by the confederacy itself. This is also true of "foreign relations" as a whole.

The same sachems who administered league affairs when they met briefly in council governed their respective nations during the rest of the year. "The nine Mohawk sachems," for instance, "administered the affairs of that nation with joint authority, precisely in the same manner as they did, in connection with their colleagues, the affairs of the League at large." [32] These officials by no means possessed absolute authority. A constant factor in Iroquois as in Algonquian polity was the strong current of public opinion. Many writers have waxed eloquent over this "forest democracy," but it might as easily be termed anarchy. If the voice of the warriors (and the women) prevented absolute rule by the oligarchic body of sachems, it also prevented the tribe from pursuing a resolute policy for any length of time. Tribal effectiveness was all too often diffused at the expense of factionalism or personal whim.

Nowhere did private initiative nullify tribal policy more than in the conduct of war. The powers of the sachems and their assistants were entirely civil and confined to the affairs of peace. The Iroquois sachems apparently retained their civil authority in wartime, however, and there was no distinct class of war chiefs. "All military operations," on

[32] Morgan, *League of the Iroquois*, I, 65.

the contrary, "were left entirely to private enterprise, and to the system of voluntary service, the sachems seeking rather to repress and restrain, than to encourage the martial ardor of the people." The principle of divided authority was applied to military as well as to civil organization:

Small bands were, in the first instance, organized by individual leaders, each of which, if they were afterwards united upon the same enterprise, continued under its own captain, and the whole force, as well as the conduct of the expedition, was under their joint management. They appointed no one of their number to absolute command, but the general direction was left open to the strongest will, or the most persuasive voice. As they were at war with all nations not in their actual alliance, it was lawful for any warrior to organize a party, and seek adventures wherever he pleased to direct his steps. . . . It is believed that a great part of the warlike transactions of the Iroquois were nothing more than personal adventures, or the daring deeds of inconsiderable war-parties.[33]

In the event that the several nations conducted a joint war in which their forces were united, the two war chieftains—always assigned to the Seneca—were entrusted with over-all supervision in the interests of unanimity.

When the traders of New Netherland first established themselves on the Hudson, they found the Iroquois beset on all sides and busy with subduing their closest neighbors. Thus their rise to a position of continental eminence was the product of historic times. The problem of accounting for this eminence has occupied the attention of successive observers from that day to this. A greater natural ferocity, superior institutions, easier access to firearms, and, more recently, an economic interpretation have all been advanced. Iroquois ferocity was never questioned by those who fell into their hands, but neighboring tribes were capable of equally impressive exploits and atrocities. At any rate this trait could not have been hereditary, for Iroquois blood was well diluted by adoption before, during, and after the league's ascendancy. Superior institutions the Iroquois undoubtedly possessed, and the fact is of great importance although institutions generally reflect more than they determine the character of a society. Both as individual tribes and as a confederacy they were more united than most of their neighbors. They were not always able to bring greater numbers to bear against an

[33] *Ibid.*, 68–69.

enemy, but even as a defensive device the league brought a degree of unity which multiplied their strength. The Five Nations were, moreover, plentifully supplied with arms and ammunition from Albany. This favor was not exclusively theirs, for many of their rivals got armaments elsewhere; yet the Iroquois were better furnished as a general rule, and they enjoyed superior firepower in most of their contests. A final advantage was the strategic Iroquois location, offering access to both the western fur supply and the eastern market at Albany. Their resultant buying power helps to explain the supply of firearms, which in turn caused the English after 1664 to propitiate them with still more arms in order to prevent their defection to the French. Iroquois power therefore depended upon several factors, no one of which is sufficient to explain the phenomenon by itself. Pure chance put them athwart the only "water-level route" between the English (or Dutch) and the Great Lakes and enabled them to acquire so much armament by means of the western fur trade; superior organization enabled them to use this strength more effectively; and, finally, a reputation for success bred further success. Two vital links in this chain, the fur trade and firearms, were not present in aboriginal America. Without European intrusion the Iroquois' geographical location would have signified nothing, the economic factor would not have existed, and superior organization alone would have produced fewer and less spectacular victories. The trade and aid from Albany therefore were indispensable components of Iroquois greatness.[34]

[34] Cf. George T. Hunt, *The Wars of the Iroquois* (Madison, 1940), 6–12, and Wallace, "Return of Hiawatha," 387–390.

II

The Beginnings of New Netherland

NEW NETHERLAND, like the rest of the Atlantic seaboard, was discovered and explored in the interests of an expanding European economy. At the dawn of the seventeenth century the United Dutch Provinces, along with most of maritime western Europe, were intensely interested in tapping the partly real and partly fabled riches of Cathay and the Indies. In an effort to avoid the long and hazardous route around Africa which Portugal had already pre-empted, English, Dutch, and French navigators searched eagerly for a shorter way—a northeast or a northwest passage—to the Orient. In this quest the North American continent represented, not an end to be sought in itself, but rather a giant roadblock placed by nature in the path of European commercial expansion.

Henry Hudson was English by birth, but it was under the colors of the Dutch East India Company that he earned his greatest fame as a pioneer in search of a new route to Asia. Setting out from Amsterdam in the *Half Moon* in April 1609, he determined to follow up two previous attempts at finding a northeast passage through the Arctic Ocean. Hudson doubled the cape of Norway in May, but was soon confronted with impassable ice and a mutinous crew who demanded that he find his route to the Orient somewhere else. Accordingly the ship turned round, and Hudson decided to seek a western passage through North America. It was the view of most informed persons that an inlet, at least, of the great Western Sea, or Pacific Ocean, extended to within a few miles of the Atlantic coast. This misconception, surviving well into the eighteenth century, was responsible for most of the efforts wasted on the search for a northwest passage. Hudson undoubtedly shared it, and, already familiar with fruitless explorations for an interocean waterway south of the Chesapeake, he determined to pursue the search north of that point. Touching the capes of the Chesapeake, the *Half Moon* turned northward and sailed into Delaware Bay on August 28. As shallow waters at the mouth of the river prevented his entrance, Hudson coasted northward as far as New York Bay, which he entered early in September. Verrazano had been here in 1524 in the employ of the king of France, but French claims and interest had lapsed, and it remained for Hudson to explore the river that he found here and to plant the claims of the United Netherlands to the adjacent territory. Having spent a month on the river, vainly probing for an outlet to the Western Sea, Hudson returned to Europe to report his failure.

As the great navigator's exploration of the Hudson River provided the basis for later Dutch claims to New Netherland, so his encounters with the native inhabitants foreshadowed the course of Indian relations in the years to come. Hudson's initial reception, like that of most of the early seamen, was entirely cordial. As the *Half Moon* lay at anchor on September 4 in the protected waters behind Sandy Hook, some Indians came aboard for the first time, welcomed the strangers, and exchanged tobacco for knives and beads. The next day the process was repeated, but on September 6 a small boat returning from an exploration of the Narrows between Long Island and Staten Island was set upon by two canoes of Indians, who with bows and arrows shot and killed one of the crewmen and wounded two others. Very likely the attackers were Canarsee, whereas the friendly natives belonged to the Navasink band. The latter, at any rate, boarded the ship again two days later, bringing tobacco and maize, as if no fight had occurred. On September 9 two large canoes came alongside the *Half Moon,* and the Indians, some of whom were armed, climbed aboard. The crew distrusted this show of force after the recent attack and forcibly detained three Indians as hostages, all of whom managed to escape within a few days by jumping overboard. At night the ship moved away and anchored at the Narrows. In the following days it traversed the upper bay and began working up the river. Only once more in this region did Hudson allow the seemingly friendly natives to come aboard.

Otherwise they had to remain content with trading over the side.[1]

By the night of September 15 Hudson had reached the Catskill vicinity, where his crew met a "loving people" interspersed with "very old men." Relaxing his discipline, the captain allowed them aboard the next day, when they sold fresh vegetables and tobacco to the crew. As the *Half Moon* sailed upstream, these peaceful meetings continued and Robert Juet, the master's mate, was entertained at the wigwam of an old Mahican sachem near Albany. For six days the ship remained here while small boats were sent out to see how much farther the stream was navigable. News of the strangers' coming undoubtedly preceded them, and the great canoe with white wings, full of men with unearthly complexions, provided a tourist attraction of surpassing interest. The natives swarmed about the ship during its entire stay, and garbled accounts of the white man's first arrival survived for generations in Indian legend.[2]

Trade proceeded briskly, and the Indians gave not only foodstuffs, but beaver and otter skins as well, for the trinkets every crewman had close at hand. Apart from the shiny knives of utilitarian value and the beads, ribbons, bells, or other items which passed for costume jewelry on the farther side of the frontier, the Indians were due for another treat, far more potent. Juet reports that Hudson and he "determined to trie some of the chiefe men of the Countrey," to see "whether they had any treacherie in them." The ship's officers accordingly took some of the leaders below decks and plied them with "so much Wine and *Aqua vitae*, that they were all merrie." At least one of the natives passed out, and when the rest went ashore at night, he was left aboard to sleep off the effects of his European tonic. The next day his friends were relieved to find him alive and well. That afternoon the Indians "made an Oration" to Hudson and, undoubtedly at his request, described "all the Countrey round about."

By September 23 Hudson heard from his reconnaissance parties that navigation was possible for only a few more miles. This intelligence, plus that gleaned from the natives, led him to abandon any hope of a western passage here, and he therefore commenced the downward

---

[1] *NNN,* 18–20.

[2] *Ibid.,* 21–23; *NYCD,* III, 775; John Heckewelder, "Indian Tradition of the First Arrival of the Dutch at Manhattan Island, now New York," in New York Historical Society, *Collections,* 2d ser., I (1841), 68–74.

journey. The Indians downstream continued to be friendly, and trading occurred whenever circumstances allowed. Only after the *Half Moon* had passed Stony Point was there a recurrence of the earlier hostility. A single Indian paddled his canoe to a point beneath the ship's stern. Climbing up by the rudder to a cabin window, he seized the mate's pillow and some clothing. Juet, perceiving the theft, shot and killed the culprit while his souvenirs fell into the water. The other Indians, hovering about in canoes, were terrified at first, and some of them jumped overboard in their haste to escape the thunderbolts hurled by these testy visitors. Crewmen retrieved the stolen articles only after chopping off the hand of a swimming Indian who tried to upset their boat. On the next day, as the *Half Moon* neared the upper end of Manhattan Island, Hudson refused to allow on board some Indians whom he recognized from the upward voyage. Following this rebuff, Juet reports, "two Canoes full of men, with their Bowes and Arrowes shot at us after our sterne: in recompence whereof we discharged six Muskets, and killed two or three of them." Then more than a hundred natives gathered on a promontory overlooking the river in order to shoot at the boat as it passed by. Juet fired a small cannon in reply, killing two more men, and the rest fled into the woods. Nine or ten Indians, nothing daunted by the white man's superior firepower, set out in pursuit in another canoe. The cannon was then trained on them, and, together with the fire of several muskets, it dispatched at least half the party. By now the Indians had had enough, and the *Half Moon* continued on its course without further disturbance. On October 4, just a month after the first Indian visit near Sandy Hook, the ship passed the Narrows and stood out to sea on its way to Europe.[3]

Although it brought the Netherlands no closer to the Orient, Henry Hudson's voyage was immediately and permanently significant. His visit made a lasting impression on the Indians. Before the *Half Moon* sailed out of New York Bay "a number of red men had taken three steps toward civilization. They had seen the effect of firearms, they had got drunk and they had learned to want European goods."[4] In the space of a single month they were introduced to a new way of life, a culture entirely different from anything they had ever heard of. Some of the

[3] *NNN*, 22–27.

[4] Mrs. Schuyler Van Rensselaer, *History of the City of New York in the Seventeenth Century* (New York, 1909), I, 60.

material evidences of this culture—guns, liquor, and clothing—they came to want so badly that no price seemed too high to pay for them. From this desire it was but another step to partial and then complete dependence on Europe and its works. Finally, but long after it was too late, the Indian realized that the material effects he had welcomed with open arms were inevitably accompanied by the dissolution of his own civilization, even the parts of it which he treasured most. The white man's guns brought continuing dependence for ammunition, repairs, and replacement. The white man's liquor brought uncontrollable orgies ending all too often in fratricidal strife within the tribe. The white man's trading goods were less harmful in themselves, but in time the Indian found himself neglecting his former activities and forgetting his old skills, all in the rush to trap the furs by which alone he could satisfy his new-found needs. But all of this, and the white man's diseases and land hunger, lay in the future. In 1609 these Indians had had a taste of a different life and they were ready for more whenever it should come.

In Europe merchants saw to it that the Indians need not wait long. The *Half Moon* reached home in July 1610 after a long detention in England, and Hudson's employers were able at last to read of the discoveries they had financed. Although the larger commercial interests in Amsterdam, including the East India Company, were chiefly concerned with the New World as a route to Asia, lesser capitalists conceived that the humbler resources of North America might also repay a small investment. In this same year about a dozen merchants and shipowners, most of them living in Amsterdam, fitted out a ship to see what advantages the new land might offer.[5]

From the beginning these advantages were centered around the fur trade. Hudson brought back only one item that promised to be of any value—the beaver and otter skins that he had traded from the Mahican Indians. But the European demand for this commodity was such that if only a single ship each year returned with a cargo of furs these merchants might expect a comfortable annual profit. There were incidental possibilities, of course, which might further enhance the investment. Gold might be found in Dutch America as it had been

[5] *NNN*, 38; *NYCD*, I, 51; Edward H. Hall, "The New York Commercial Tercentenary, 1614–1914," in American Scenic and Historic Preservation Society, *Annual Report*, XIX (1914), 464–465.

in the Spanish colonies, and fisheries might prove valuable as they had off the Grand Banks. But furs were the primary goal, and it was of more than passing significance that the Indians, who trapped the animals and sold their pelts to the traders, were indispensable in bringing this form of wealth to the European market.

The Dutch title to the Mauritius or North River, as they called it—only the English used the name Hudson—existed as yet solely by right of prior discovery. Although the States-General, or parliament, now claimed exclusive jurisdiction there, the river and its bay were open in fact to any ship which cared to enter. In the next few years both English and French vessels traded along the coast and perhaps penetrated far up the river in ignorance or disregard of Dutch claims. Netherlands shipping too appears to have frequented the region, following up the voyage of 1610.[6] All this indicated that the fur trade was becoming a profitable venture, worthy of more systematic exploitation.

As early as 1611 Dutch merchants had petitioned for certain trading rights in newly discovered regions, presumably meaning America. On March 27, 1614, the States-General complied with these requests by granting to the discoverer of any "Passages, Havens, Countries or Places" the right to make four voyages there without interference or competition.[7] As the first men to take advantage of this offer were those who had sent out the vessel in 1610, they very likely had kept up their interest in this trade ever since. No sooner had the ordinance been passed than they dispatched five ships to explore and trade in the vicinity of the Mauritius River.[8] Their purpose was not primarily to establish a claim to the trade on the river itself, because their previous voyages had probably already assured that. Rather they wanted to explore the regions on either side in order that the expected monopoly might embrace as large an area as possible. Furthermore, as the merchants felt sure of a monopoly on the main river, they wanted to build a trading post there at the first opportunity.

Of the five skippers who went out that spring, Adriaen Block and Cornelis Jacobsen May explored the coast between Manhattan and Cape Cod, and the latter may also have sailed as far south as Delaware Bay. A third captain, Hendrick Christiaensen, occupied himself chiefly

---

[6] Hall, "Commercial Tercentenary," 463–464, 466–468.   [7] *NYCD*, I, 4–6.
[8] *NNN*, 38; Hall, "Commercial Tercentenary," 465, 475–476.

with the Hudson River and constructed a trading post on the site of Albany.[9] In view of the boundaries expressed in the subsequent charter, it seems likely that the remaining captains, or at least one of the five, explored the coast of Maine.

When the news of these voyages reached Holland in the fall, the shipowners hastened to petition for the benefits of the March ordinance. On October 11 the States-General granted them a charter based on the lands their captains had explored. Giving the region a name for the first time, the new proprietors styled themselves the United New Netherland Company. The charter endowed them with exclusive rights to trade in New Netherland for up to four voyages within a period of three years, beginning January 1, 1615. The territory involved took in all the land "situate in America, between New France and Virginia, the Sea coasts whereof lie between forty and forty-five degrees of Latitude." Thus at the beginning New Netherland officially reached from Eastport, Maine, to Barnegat Bay in New Jersey.[10]

While the fur trade was still in its infancy and open to all comers, little regularity or organization was possible. Merchants in Holland individually or collectively dispatched ships across the ocean to look around and pick up a cargo wherever it was to be found. The fur-bearing animals, especially the valuable beaver, and the Indians who trapped them were scattered throughout the region. The common procedure of every captain, therefore, was to sail along the coast, stopping at each harbor on the way and picking up whatever peltry the local natives had to offer. In time, as the seaboard fur supply declined in volume, ships began more and more to sail up the navigable rivers in search of the untapped interior supply. Thus the Hudson, the Connecticut, and the Delaware soon became important trading arteries.

Of these rivers the Hudson was exploited first, and it yielded the greatest profit. Deep and wide enough for most ocean-going vessels, it formed an easily accessible roadway as far into the interior as the site of Albany. A second reason for its pre-eminence lay in the nature and distribution of the Indian tribes at its head. Although the Mohawk had little if any direct contact with the early traders, the then powerful Mahican were a valuable source of furs from the start. Their own lands were well stocked with beaver, otter, and deer, and they had

[9] *NYCD*, I, 11; *NNN*, 39–52.   [10] *NYCD*, I, 11–12.

connections of blood and sympathy with Algonquian tribes to the north and east. Much of the peltry throughout this region must have gravitated toward the Hudson traders. While some captains continued to trade along the coast and up the lesser streams, others therefore found cargoes at a single spot far from the coast.

As soon as the New Netherland Company could look forward to the enjoyment of a monopoly, it sought a more businesslike method of exploitation than had served heretofore. On the upper Hudson the general rule had been for ships to arrive in the spring, when the hunting season was about over, and to wait there until the natives had drifted in with enough peltry to make up a cargo. An obvious improvement would be to establish a trading post there with warehouse facilities and a group of traders constantly in attendance to buy the furs as the Indians brought them in. Such a plan had the merit of avoiding costly delays by ships which might be gainfully employed elsewhere, and it might bring in a greater volume of furs by assuring the Indians of a constant market for the products of their hunt.

It was probably for these reasons that Christiaensen was sent on his special mission in 1614 to establish such a post on the upper Hudson. The location he chose was Castle Island, which today has lost its insular character and lies within the Albany city limits on the west bank. An island was probably chosen for defensive reasons—it provided easier control of the river and helped insulate the traders from any surprise attack by the Indians. Although the surrounding Mahican were friendly, they were engaged in nearly constant warfare with the not-too-distant Mohawk. There was no telling what explosive situation might arise, and a handful of traders surrounded by savages, with the nearest European settlements at Jamestown and Quebec, might understandably have felt solicitous for their own safety. The post, which they christened Fort Nassau, measured thirty-six by twenty-six feet and was enclosed by a stockade and a moat. Armed with two cannon and eleven smaller guns, it was garrisoned by ten or twelve traders.[11]

Over-all command of the New Netherland trade probably belonged to Captain Christiaensen. He seems to have spent most of his time trading along the coast and carrying cargoes across the Atlantic. Fort

[11] *NNN*, 47, 67; Hall, "Commercial Tercentenary," 484–486; S. G. Nissenson, *The Patroon's Domain* (New York, 1937), 6.

Nassau and the trade thereabouts were under the direction of Jacob Elkens, a former clerk in an Amsterdam countinghouse. Elkens remained at Fort Nassau as long as the post was maintained, learning the Indian language and conducting a prosperous trade.[12] The charter of October 1614 granted the New Netherland Company only a limited trading monopoly. No political powers were granted, and the question of colonization had not yet arisen. The "few men in garrison at Castle Island were rather armed traders, holding formal possession of an unoccupied territory, than emigrants to subdue a wilderness." Trade was their business, and harmonious Indian relations were a necessary ingredient. So far as is known, this policy was faithfully adhered to by most of the Dutch traders wherever they pursued their calling. Peaceful relations were not only a guarantee of uninterrupted trade—they were often insurance of life itself.

The peltry supply at Fort Nassau was furnished entirely by the surrounding Indians, who carried them to the post and exchanged them for trading goods from Holland. Neither at this time nor later did Dutchmen as a rule attempt either to trap the animals themselves or to penetrate the interior for the purpose of acquiring peltry at the Indian villages. On the other hand, there is evidence to suggest that from the earliest years expeditions were sent out to discover the lay of the land and its inhabitants and to engage in sales promotion. In the summer of 1615 or thereabouts one Kleynties and two companions set out from Fort Nassau toward the west. Reaching the headwaters of the Delaware, it is supposed, they headed southward, carefully noting the Indian tribes they encountered. Eventually falling into the hands of the warlike Susquehanna, they were taken to the mouth of the Schuylkill. Here, in the summer of 1616, they were ransomed by Captain Cornelis Hendricksen, who was currently exploring and trading along the Delaware and its tributaries.[13]

[12] *NNN*, 47, 81; John R. Brodhead, *History of the State of New York* (New York, 1853–1871), I, 55, 66–67.

[13] *NYCD*, I, 14 and map facing 11; Flick, *History of New York*, I, 167; Brodhead, *History of New York*, I, 78–79. In 1615 a group of Susquehanna Indians told Samuel de Champlain that in the previous year they had captured three Dutchmen who were aiding the Iroquois against them. The Susquehanna returned the captives unharmed, they said, under the impression that they were Frenchmen. See Samuel de Champlain, *Works*, ed. by H. P. Biggar (Toronto, 1922–1933), III, 54–55. Although there are several inconsistencies between the two stories, they may refer to the same occurrence. Such is the opinion of Jean E.

The location of Fort Nassau turned out to be less than ideal. Freshets caused by melting ice upstream subjected Castle Island to almost annual floods, and in the spring of 1617 the post had to be abandoned.[14] Tradition has it that Elkens constructed a new post about two miles south, on the banks of the "Tawasentha" or Norman's Kill.[15] If this account be true, there is no confirmation of it in the contemporary sources. Tradition further states that here, in 1618, was concluded the first formal agreement between the Dutch and the Iroquois. There is no foundation for this story either, and a number of factors mitigate against it. In the first place, it divides the Iroquois into their constituent nations and gives more information concerning them than the Dutch were to have for many years. In 1659 the Mohawk themselves stated that their "first treaty of friendship and brotherhood" with the Dutch had occurred only sixteen years previously. Furthermore, the Mahican tribe loomed larger on the Dutch horizon in these years than did the Mohawk, to say nothing of the remoter western members of the confederacy. The Mohawk-Mahican hostility of this period would make such a treaty unlikely even if the Mahican and Delaware were not alleged to have been present as witnesses.[16] The New Netherland Company's monopoly expired at the beginning of 1618, and following the abandonment of Fort Nassau trade conditions probably reverted to the informality of earlier years.

At home a number of men had been working zealously for the incorporation of a West India Company to exploit trade possibilities on a much larger scale in Africa and America. Many of its backers, moreover, looked to such a company as a vehicle for privateering raids on the Spanish Main, since a twelve years' truce with Spain was about to expire. Whatever the relative weight of their arguments, the promoters succeeded on June 3, 1621—just three months after the truce had

Murray, "The Early Fur Trade in New France and New Netherland," *Canadian Historical Review*, XIX (1938), 367n.

[14] *NNN*, 47–48; Brodhead, *History of New York*, I, 80–81; cf. *NNN*, 67.

[15] John V. N. Yates and Joseph W. Moulton, *History of the State of New York*, I, pts. i and ii (New York, 1824–1826), 346; Edmund B. O'Callaghan, *History of New Netherland* (2d ed.; New York, 1855), I, 78; Brodhead, *History of New York*, I, 81.

[16] *NYCD*, XIII, 112–113. See the more extended discussion, with references, in Hunt, *Wars of the Iroquois*, 26–27. Hunt also (pp. 25–31) disposes effectively of two other attempts at establishing a Dutch-Iroquois treaty before that of the French in 1624.

ended—in procuring a charter from the States-General. By this grant the African coast from the Tropic of Cancer southward and the American coasts from Newfoundland to the Straits of Magellan were forbidden to all Dutch shipping save that of the new West India Company. Together with this trade monopoly the company was granted political jurisdiction over the territories that it acquired, subject only to supervision by the States-General. Government of the company itself was vested in five chambers located in as many Dutch cities, with that of Amsterdam having the largest voice. The executive power was vested in an "Assembly of the Nineteen," representing the five chambers and the States-General.[17]

Although New Netherland was not specifically mentioned in the charter, it certainly fell within its scope. This province, however, was never the only interest of the West India Company, nor was it even the most important. For financial reasons chiefly the company was unable to begin operations until 1623. In the meantime trade with New Netherland continued on the same basis as before, with an apparent requirement that all ships sailing for that destination first obtain a license to do so from the States-General.[18]

Early in 1624 the West India Company was finally in condition to attempt the settlement and formal exploitation of New Netherland. The first shipload of colonists, consisting of thirty families and some traders, arrived at Manhattan in the month of May. The captain of this vessel and first governor of the province was Cornelis Jacobsen May, who had been sailing in New Netherland waters since 1614. Part of his colonists were sent up the Hudson, and he seems also to have established a commercial station on Governors Island, off the tip of Manhattan. The former group built a new trading house and stronghold on the west bank of the river, nearly opposite Castle Island, naming it Fort Orange. Meanwhile Captain May took the remainder of his colonists to the Delaware, where he erected another Fort Nassau.[19] With the planting of these settlements the province of New Netherland was fairly begun. During its first two years—something of an experi-

[17] *VRBM*, 86–115.
[18] *NYCD*, I, 21–22; O'Callaghan, *History of New Netherland*, I, 81, 93–95; Brodhead, *History of New York*, I, 90, 137–138; Flick, *History of New York*, I, 222.
[19] *NNN*, 75, 271; *NYCD*, I, 149; A. J. F. Van Laer, ed., *Documents Relating to New Netherland, 1624–1626, in the Henry E. Huntington Library* (San Marino, Calif., 1924), xiv ff.

mental period—the Delaware was given equal consideration with the Hudson as the place for concentrated settlement. Captain May, who served for a year as governor, appears to have made his residence on the Delaware, as did his successor, Willem Verhulst.

The year 1626 was of considerable importance in New Netherland's early history. It marked the installation of Peter Minuit in what proved to be a six-year term of office as director general or governor, and, more important, it marked the founding of New Amsterdam as the colonial metropolis. By now the authorities at home recognized that the central location and easy access of New York Bay afforded the best prospects for the main settlement. Assuming office in the summer, Minuit settled the most recent emigrants at the lower end of Manhattan Island and began constructing a fort at what is now the Battery. For reasons of safety the eight families at Fort Orange and those on the Delaware were resettled here too. Fort Orange was left with a garrison of about twenty-five traders, and the posts on the Delaware and on Governors Island were abandoned altogether.[20]

It is well established in American mythology that Peter Minuit during the course of this summer bought Manhattan Island from the Indians for twenty-four dollars. Actually the price was sixty guilders, and in view of the silver content of the guilder at that time and the price of silver today, the equivalent is nearer thirty-nine dollars.[21] Estimated at about 360 acres per dollar, this has been regarded as one of the greatest real-estate bargains in all time. However, value is always relative to the time and place involved, and sixty guilders in trading goods was a considerable prize in 1626 to the Canarsee Indians, who had other lands equally useful for their own purposes. As Indians made later sales in this locality, prices went up.[22] This tendency reflected a rise in real-estate values owing to the expansion of settlement and the steady decrease in the amount of land left for Indian habitation. But in 1626 the process had barely begun.

Under the conditions of early settlement Indian relations were a mat-

[20] *NNN*, 83–84, 86, 88; Victor H. Paltsits, "Founding of New Amsterdam in 1626," in American Antiquarian Society, *Proceedings*, XXXIV (1924), 39–65.

[21] *NYCD*, I, 37–38; Henry H. Kessler and Eugene Rachlis, *Peter Stuyvesant and His New York* (New York, 1959), 40, 282.

[22] See the table of land prices paid in the Newark area between 1626 and 1702 in E. S. Rankin, "The Purchase of Newark from the Indians," in New Jersey Historical Society, *Proceedings*, n.s. XII (1927), 444.

ter of primary importance. The initial Indian policies promulgated for New Netherland have survived in a series of four documents issued by the West India Company for the guidance of its new colonists and officials. The first of these documents, a set of provisional regulations for the colonists, was adopted in March 1624, just prior to their departure. The others, dating from January and April 1625, were instructions for Director Verhulst and his councilors.[23]

From the beginning the director and other officers were empowered to deal with the Indians and to make treaties or alliances with them "upon such conditions as shall be deemed most advantageous to the service of the Company, without paying heed in such treaties to any one's private interests." Colonists were enjoined to observe such agreements, even if "by so doing they should be involved in war . . . and even be obliged to take the field." However, as peaceful relations were important to everyone, colonists were "faithfully to fulfill their promises to the Indians . . . and not to give them any offense without cause as regards their persons, wives, or property," on pain of rigorous punishment. Verhulst was further instructed to see that in all transactions with the natives they were shown "honesty, faithfulness, and sincerity," so that no cause for hostility might arise.[24]

With an eye to expanding the company's returns from New Netherland the directors instructed that Verhulst should "by small presents seek to draw the Indians into our service, in order to learn from them the secrets of that region and the condition of the interior"; but he was not to "feed them in idleness or give in too much to their wanton demands." In the absence of an adequate labor force, Indians were to be hired to work on the fortifications or other projects should they prove willing. Their wage, however, was set at half that paid to Dutchmen for the same work.[25]

If in spite of all precautions an Indian wronged a Dutchman and his tribe failed to punish him, the Dutch officials were authorized to seek out the culprit and administer justice themselves. As an equally important corollary, the officials were warned to provide speedy and effective justice for any Dutchman who wronged an Indian, on pain of receiving corporal punishment themselves.[26]

The Amsterdam directors had heard that the Indians were "very quar-

---

[23] Van Laer, *New Netherland Documents, 1624–1626*, docs. A, C, D, and E.
[24] *Ibid.*, 5, 17, 39.   [25] *Ibid.*, 55, 140.   [26] *Ibid.*, 110–113.

relsome amongst themselves," because of their "suspicious and vindic-tive" nature. Although Verhulst was empowered to make treaties and alliances at his own discretion, he was enjoined to maintain a strict neutrality in Indian disputes, always attempting to arrange a peaceful solution between the contending parties. Warlike steps should be taken only if some tribe were fighting on the Dutch account and pacific measures proved unavailing. Above all, Verhulst and his council were advised to make no "efforts the success of which they have reason to regard as doubtful." [27] The intent of the West India Company could hardly be clearer. Good understanding was required, not out of love or respect for the Indian—there was very little of that—but out of common prudence.

Precautions were necessary lest friction occur despite these good intentions. No colonist was permitted to let Indians ride the horses brought over by the company, "much less to teach them to ride or to raise" these animals. Offenders must forfeit their property and wages and, together with the Indian pupil, suffer expulsion from the colony. Fortifications, moreover, were the first order of business, and detailed instructions were sent over for their construction.[28]

The problem of saving Indian souls was never as pressing among the Dutch as it was in either New France or New England. In the regulations of 1624 and 1625 colonists and officials alike were en-couraged to work for the Indians' conversion through education and provision of a good example in Christian conduct.[29] Johan de Laet, an informed Dutch observer of things in America, wrote in 1624 of the Indians' fidelity in performing services for their new neighbors. It is possible, he held, that "with mild and proper treatment, and espe-cially by intercourse with Christians," the Indians "might be civilized and brought under better regulation; particularly if a sober and dis-creet population were brought over and good order preserved." It is typical of the Dutch approach that De Laet should have considered civilization and regulation before the less secular question of eternal salvation. Only in the later editions of his book did "worship of the true God" creep into the text as a desirable outcome of the Indians' "intercourse with Christians." [30]

The established church in the Netherlands was the Dutch Reformed.

[27] *Ibid.*, 52–55, 109.   [28] *Ibid.*, 93–94, 132 ff.
[29] *Ibid.*, 2, 36.   [30] *NNN*, 50.

Its first clerical representative in North America was Domine Jonas Michaëlius, who arrived in 1628. Doubtless among the instructions which Michaëlius, like every public functionary, was required to bring with him for guidance there was some mention of Indian conversion. Certainly the problem occurred to him. But Michaëlius was repelled by the Indians at first contact, as were most Europeans, and dismayed at the prospect of making them Christians. "I find them entirely savage and wild," he wrote back some months after arriving at Manhattan, "strangers to all decency, yea, uncivil and stupid as garden poles, proficient in all wickedness and godlessness; devilish men, who serve nobody but the Devil. . . . They are as thievish and treacherous as they are tall; and in cruelty they are altogether inhuman, more than barbarous, far exceeding the Africans" with whom he had earlier served.[31] Expressing a wholly natural surprise at the rumors that had gained currency in the Fatherland of docility and primordial religious instincts among these people, Michaëlius enlarged upon the obstacles attending their conversion. In the first place, some knowledge of the native tongue was required, but that "made-up, childish language" was virtually impossible to master. Traders who knew enough of it to carry on their business were totally at a loss to understand an ordinary conversation. The only hope of success lay in abandoning the adults and getting control of their children, but the parents invariably opposed any such program.[32] So as not to appear completely pessimistic about this branch of the Lord's work, he tried to end on a positive note:

Nevertheless, although it would be attended with some expense, we ought, by means of presents and promises, to obtain the children, with the gratitude and consent of the parents, in order to place them under the instruction of some experienced and godly schoolmaster, where they may be instructed not only to speak, read, and write in our language, but also especially in the fundamentals of our Christian religion; and where, besides, they will see nothing but good examples of virtuous living.

Praying for their eventual salvation somehow, Michaëlius promised to "keep a watchful eye over these people," to learn what he could of their language, and to seek some means for their instruction.[33] Needless to say, he had accomplished little or nothing when he returned home a few years later. Orderly, pious colonists—the type who could

[31] *Ibid.,* 126–127. [32] *Ibid.,* 127–129. [33] *Ibid.,* 129.

serve as examples of Christian conduct—were notably lacking in early New Netherland and especially so on the Indian frontier. In truth the domine's points were well taken, and the problem got little further attention for a number of years.

The touchiest question in Indian relations was how best to take his land. The West India Company charter envisaged commerce rather than colonization as the major corporate aim. Therefore it gave the company no original land title. Ownership remained in the native occupants, and the charter grant, as well as the patents issued under it by the company, conferred only the ultimate right of ownership once Indian titles were extinguished.[34] The instructions to Verhulst specified that he first pay the Indians for lands which he intended to colonize. Land cessions were, moreover, to be voluntary, not obtained "by craft or fraud, lest we call down the wrath of God upon our unrighteous beginnings."[35] This sentiment continued to reflect official policy down to the end of Dutch control.

The setting of a policy does not guarantee its observance. Since most of the documents of this period are lost, it is difficult to establish a pattern of conduct prior to the 1630's. There is positive evidence, however, to indicate that the first land purchase of any importance was that of Manhattan Island in 1626. Four years later the Mahican tribe sold the land around Fort Orange (including that on which the fort itself stood) to Kiliaen van Rensselaer, who said afterward that they had refused to sell land to the company in 1625.[36] On the Delaware too the first land purchase seems to have occurred a generation after the construction there of Fort Nassau, and Governors Island was formally acquired in 1637.[37] Although Indians were known to sell the same tract over again, there is no indication that this was done here. The evidence implies that the company made little real effort to buy the lands on which trading posts stood, even when these posts were surrounded by the homes of a few colonists. Strict adherence to official policy began only with attempts at more concentrated settlement. In any event, Indian relations in each of these areas were apparently

[34] C. W. Rife, "Land Tenure in New Netherland," in *Essays in Colonial History Presented to Charles McLean Andrews* (New Haven, 1931), 48–49; Nissenson, *Patroon's Domain*, 9–10.

[35] Van Laer, *New Netherland Documents, 1624–1626*, 51–52, 106.

[36] *VRBM*, 166–169, 306.

[37] *NYCD*, XII, 48–49; XIV, 4; Brodhead, *History of New York*, I, 510–511.

harmonious. Trading posts took little space, and the Indians were more than willing to see them established in view of the benefits they brought. Very likely the question of a land problem never occurred to them.

In 1624 the first colonists were ordered to establish commercial relations with the Indians as soon as they had gotten settled, and Verhulst's instructions the next year attempted to spell out a trade policy in more detail. The governor was first to increase the volume of trade as much as possible, both in furs and in other items that the natives might have to sell. A warehouse was to be built, probably at Fort Orange, which was the greatest source of supply, and at least one sloop should be sent there regularly in order to replenish the stock of trading goods and carry off the peltry. The sloops went only as far as the post at Governors Island (later Manhattan), whence their cargoes were transshipped to Holland. These cargoes, the directions continued, must be sent across at every opportunity together with an accounting of the trade and advice as to what merchandise was most in demand among the Indians.[38]

The company adopted a highly restrictive policy in determining who could participate in the fur trade. Strangers—meaning those not under the company's jurisdiction—were forbidden to trade altogether, and measures were prescribed to discourage their competition.[39] At first the colonists were allowed to share in the Indian trade "on the express condition that they shall sell the goods they have purchased or collected to no one but the Company's agents." [40] Within a year, however, the directors at home became dissatisfied with this arrangement. One of them later explained "that if this trade should be free to all without restriction, the fur-bearing animals would be too much hunted and the furs would be sold here below their value," to the company's loss. But if the company ever consciously restricted the volume of traffic in order to preserve the supply or to sustain the market price, no evidence of it has come to light. It is more likely that the directors feared the effects of competition on the price they had to pay for furs, both to private traders and to the Indians.[41]

[38] Van Laer, *New Netherland Documents, 1624–1626,* 6, 64–67.
[39] *Ibid.,* 14, 56.   [40] *Ibid.,* 10.
[41] *VRBM,* 235. The explanation quoted above was made by Kiliaen van Rensselaer at a time when he was trying to win a share of the trade for himself. It is unlikely, therefore, that he would dwell overlong on the real effects of private

This fear led in 1625 to the adoption of stricter measures. Colonists were still permitted "to trade in the interior and to catch the animals with the skins, but they must deliver up the said skins . . . to the Company at the price for which we obtain them at the trading-place from the Indians." Private traders again were not to sell their peltry to other persons, thereby forcing the company eventually to pay a higher price for them. In order to complete the circle, colonists were forbidden to send to Europe for trading goods on their own account. Instead they must purchase these commodities "from the Company at the price they are traded for with the Indians."[42] Thus private traders were theoretically forbidden to make a profit.

The fur trade in all its branches was a virtual company monopoly after 1625, although it apparently made no direct or specific enactment to that effect for some time.[43] This ambiguity perhaps arose from the fact that private traders, operating in localities where the company maintained no agents of its own, could swell the total peltry returns without really competing with the company. The directors probably tolerated this activity, but elsewhere they hoped to suppress competition altogether. In January 1625 they asked Verhulst to consider the advisability in certain regions of agreeing with the Indians to buy all their peltry at a stipulated price in return for the latter's promise to sell only to company agents. This may have been done with the Mattabesec or Sequin Indians on the Connecticut, but there is no record of any other such agreements.[44] Wherever private traders operated, they necessarily did so either by violating the law or by exploiting loopholes in it, and both practices were common. Company servants traded on their own account, and private individuals smuggled in trading goods on company ships.[45] In other cases they evaded the directors' intent by using locally obtainable wampum in trading instead of European merchandise. By 1626 this practice was so widespread that company officials regularly bought wampum from those colonists who had acquired it, in order to keep them from using it to purchase skins.[46]

---

competition. Fear of this competition is further reflected in the restrictions enacted in 1625 and 1638.

[42] Van Laer, *New Netherland Documents, 1624–1626*, 67–68.

[43] Cf. Nissenson, *Patroon's Domain*, 15–16; *LONN*, 13–15.

[44] Van Laer, *New Netherland Documents, 1624–1626*, 52; *NNN*, 86.

[45] *LONN*, 10, 13–14.

[46] Van Laer, *New Netherland Documents, 1624–1626*, 251.

Beginnings of New Netherland

Meanwhile both the volume and value of the fur trade were increasing steadily. In 1624 a total of 4,700 beaver and otter skins reached Holland, bringing a sum of 27,125 guilders when sold on the market. By 1628 the number of skins had risen to 7,685, worth 61,075 guilders, and by 1635 to 16,304 skins, bringing 134,925 guilders. The price per skin, moreover, had risen from 5.77 to 8.21 guilders during the same period. It was clearly a growing business, and no one knew what heights it might attain in the future.[47]

Under these circumstances a number of West India Company directors and shareholders in 1628 procured from the Assembly of the Nineteen a charter of "Freedoms and Exemptions" for those who would establish agricultural colonies in New Netherland. On the surface this charter reflected a desire to populate with farmers what had hitherto been almost exclusively a trading preserve. Actually its promoters were looking to a greater share in the fur trade, which would more than compensate for the expense of sending over colonists. The charter of 1628 kept a close grip on the company's fur monopoly, however, and no one stepped forward to accept the proffered conditions. By dint of continued efforts these merchants managed to secure a more favorable charter on June 7, 1629.[48] This document marks a turning point in New Netherland history. Although it was devised primarily as a means of sharing in the trade, it nevertheless introduced a second dimension into the purpose and character of the colony.

The Freedoms and Exemptions of 1629 established as a "Patroon of New Netherland" anyone among the company's directorate who should undertake to plant a colony there of at least fifty persons above the age of fifteen. The charter made liberal provision for the choosing of lands, exempting only Manhattan Island from the available locations, and the permissible size of each patroonship was such as to make an Old World feudatory look on with envy. The whole system, in fact, was feudal, each patroon possessing full jurisdiction over his colonists, who held their lands on a tenancy basis. Adhering to previous policy, the company required that every patroon "must satisfy the Indians" before taking up any land. The fur trade was again reserved, but this time with a modification. "Permission for even this trade is granted at places where the Company has no agent, on the condition that such traders must bring all the peltry they may be able to secure" to Man-

[47] Ebenezer Hazard, *Historical Collections* (Philadelphia, 1792–1794), I, 397.
[48] Nissenson, *Patroon's Domain,* 21.

43

hattan Island. Here at New Amsterdam the company was to collect a duty of one guilder for each salable skin exported.[49] With the granting of this concession at least six patroonships were registered for lands in New Netherland, although no more than half of these were actually established and only one of them outlasted the original impulse.

No sooner had the patroons wrung this concession from the reluctant company than they began to lobby for unrestricted trading privileges. The less fortunate (or less adventurous) directors were not far behind in their efforts to preserve the monopoly. Their hostility to the patroons inspired the issuance of a company ordinance in June 1632 forbidding all "private persons" to deal in "peltries, maize, and wampum." A new director general, Wouter van Twiller, was dispatched in 1633 with instructions to enforce this ordinance. Van Twiller carried out his orders, and a widening gulf between the two factions began to threaten the company's very existence. In the summer of 1634 the States-General attempted to restore harmony, but after hearing both sides it refused to make a decision and handed the dispute back to the company.[50] For four more years the majority directors clung to the trade monopoly, ordering a renewal of the previous regulations and acting to prevent private competition by the company's own employees.[51] Only a threat of more drastic intervention by the States-General brought a solution in 1638 or 1639 to the problem of who should trade with the Indians.

Meanwhile colonization and settlement advanced farthest in the vicinity of New Amsterdam. Here the traffic in furs had already declined to relatively small proportions, and the Indian trade was largely comprehended in the purchase of foodstuffs which the settlers were not yet able to produce in sufficient quantity for themselves. This trade too was bound to decline within a few years as new farms were established.

A necessary prerequisite of settlement was acquisition of the land. Beginning in 1630 there is a succession of Indian deeds which extends throughout the rest of the province's history. These documents are incomplete, but nevertheless they suggest the practices followed. The first purchases were for patroonships on the upper Hudson, the lower Delaware, and opposite Manhattan Island. In the wake of these there

[49] *VRBM*, 137 ff. The provisions respecting the fur trade and land purchase are in Articles XV and XXVI respectively.
[50] *NYCD*, I, 83–91; O'Callaghan, *History of New Netherland*, I, 137; Brodhead, *History of New York*, I, 247–248.
[51] *LONN*, 10–11, 13–15.

were smaller purchases on behalf of individual colonists who came over at their own expense or as servants of the company.[52] The deeds indicate that the common practice at this time was for each colonist or patroon's agent to seek out for himself whatever lands appealed to him. He made his own agreement with the natives regarding boundaries and purchase price and gave at least a partial payment as soon as the terms were agreed upon. Finally, both parties appeared before the director general and council, who formalized the transaction by issuing a deed to the new owner. This certification provided a wholesome check by limiting to the company's discretion both the quantity of land purchased and the methods by which it was acquired. It is impossible today to know how fully the regulations were observed, but Van Twiller remarked in 1633 that the Dutch hitherto had purchased beforehand all the lands they had taken up.[53] Except for the failure to do so around the early trading posts, his boast was probably accurate.

Few settlements were made on Long Island before the 1640's, and the earliest colonists there clustered around the spots most accessible to New Amsterdam. The first recorded land purchases occurred in 1636 around modern Brooklyn. One of the chief buyers was Director Van Twiller himself, who in the next year acquired for his own benefit Governors Island (therefore its present name) and two more small islands in the East River. These and other scattered holdings made Van Twiller one of the greatest landowners in New Netherland by the time his employers retired him in 1638.[54] Michael Pauw, one of the company directors in Holland, established himself as a patroon in 1630 by purchasing and colonizing Staten Island and the Bayonne–Jersey City region opposite Manhattan. This domain, which he called Pavonia, sat astride the terminus of an Indian trail by which the natives brought their peltry and other goods to New Amsterdam. Despite this promising location, which aroused considerable suspicion among his fellow directors, the patroon encountered financial difficulties and Indian frictions which induced him to sell out to the company by 1635.[55]

The cause of these Indian troubles is now obscure. In 1633 the

---

[52] *NYCD*, I, 43–44; XII, 16–18; XIII, 1–3 and *passim;* XIV, 1–5 and *passim.*
[53] *Ibid.*, III, 19.   [54] *Ibid.*, XIV, 2–5; Brodhead, *History of New York*, I, 267.
[55] *NYCD*, XIII, 1–3; *NNN*, 210; *VRBM*, 314, 316; Brodhead, *History of New York*, I, 202–203, 268.

Raritan attacked several of the company's traders, and other hostilities followed. Nothing more is known except that Van Twiller concluded an advantageous peace the next year.[56] In all other respects Indian relations around New Amsterdam were relatively placid.

The original command at Fort Orange had been entrusted to one Adriaen Jorissen Thienpont, but by 1626 the commissary there was Daniel van Krieckenbeeck. The commissary here and elsewhere was both a commercial agent for the company and its chief political officer on the spot. He not only commanded the fort and its garrison of traders, but also any colonists who lived in the vicinity. Most important, he supervised Indian relations and the conduct of the fur trade. It was his responsibility to entertain Indians who dropped in for purposes of trade, conversation, or curiosity, and he had to keep abreast of the latest developments among the tribes as well as their relations with both the French and the English. Especially because of the isolated and relatively defenseless position of Fort Orange, the commissary there occupied a position of high responsibility requiring coolness and clearness of judgment, a sound knowledge of Indian character, and all the arts of forest diplomacy.[57]

During the first years of Fort Orange the neighboring Mahican and Mohawk tribes continued the intermittent hostilities which had marked their relationship for a generation or more. As yet no decisive advantage had been won by either party, and the Mohawk were still unable to reach the Hudson in any strength. Therefore the Dutch traders carried on their commerce largely with the surrounding Mahican and the related or allied tribes to the north and east. The Mohawk appear in the earliest Dutch annals largely as obstacles to the conduct of peaceful and profitable trade relations—troublesome interlopers who occasionally erupted in foraging raids on the commercial artery along Lake Champlain and who prevented the more co-operative tribes from attending to their hunting.[58] It was under these conditions that a group of Mahican in 1626 solicited the aid of Commissary Van Krieckenbeeck against a marauding Mohawk war

[56] *NYCD*, XIII, 7; O'Callaghan, *History of New Netherland*, I, 157, 167; Brodhead, *History of New York*, I, 244–245.

[57] Nissenson, *Patroon's Domain*, 17–18.

[58] Hunt, *Wars of the Iroquois*, 25–31; Léo Paul Desrosiers, *Iroquoisie* (Montreal, 1947), 89, 94; Murray, "Early Fur Trade," 368.

IV. Redraft of the Castello plan of New Amsterdam in 1660. (Original owned by the Italian Government; facsimile in Museum of the City of New York.)

party. The Indians held European firearms in great respect, and the Mahican warriors were probably confident that a volley or two would make the formidable Mohawk take to their heels in consternation. Dutch policy, as already indicated, called for strict neutrality in Indian disputes and permitted hostilities only when they were unavoidable or were assured of success. Van Krieckenbeeck was probably satisfied on the last score; Champlain in 1609 had easily routed the Mohawk with a few rounds of musket fire. This tribe's disruptiveness led the commissary to abandon caution and accede to the wishes of the hard-pressed, friendly, and profitable Mahican. Van Krieckenbeeck and six of his men thus set out with a Mahican war party in search of the Mohawk and had advanced to within a league or so of the latters' fort when they walked into an ambush. The Mohawk "fell so boldly upon them with a discharge of arrows, that they were forced to fly, and many were killed, among whom were the commander and three of his men." One of the Dutch victims was roasted and devoured, and two others were consigned to flames, except for a leg and an arm which the Mohawk braves carried back to their families as a trophy of their victory. The other three soldiers escaped, although one of them received an arrow in the back while swimming to safety. Some days later Pieter Barentsen, an itinerant company trader, paid a regular visit to Fort Orange. Seeking to avert the consequences of Van Krieckenbeeck's action he visited the Mohawk, who expressed sorrow for the act and surprise at the white man's interference when they had never done him any harm. Barentsen patched things up successfully, since no harm had been done the Indians and they had little to gain by keeping a grudge.[59]

Van Krieckenbeeck's expedition was a direct outgrowth of trading conditions in 1626. As late as September of that year Isaack de Rasiere, the provincial secretary of New Netherland, had eyes only for the northern trade with Indians along the St. Lawrence. He even requested permission to lead a stronger force against the Mohawk if the latter would not agree peaceably to allow the Canadian tribes a perpetual right of way through their country. The Amsterdam directors refused to endanger what they already had in order to grasp at more, but meanwhile trade fell off badly at the fort because of the inter-

[59] *NNN,* 84–85; *VRBM,* 306.

tribal hostilities.[60] At this time Director Minuit consolidated the province's settlers at New Amsterdam. Although this plan had already been formulated, the occurrences at Fort Orange must have emphasized its importance. In 1628 or 1629 the Mohawk dealt a stunning defeat to the Mahican and began the long process of subjugating them completely. For the moment only a part of the vanquished tribe was compelled to give up its home on the west bank of the Hudson and move eastward. The Mahican remained in force around the post, but hereafter the Mohawk as well were seen there more frequently.[61]

The volume of trade at Fort Orange may temporarily have declined, but the Dutch possessed one commodity which ensured the frequency of Indian visits. The center of the wampum industry was Long Island and the nearby mainland, where the local tribesmen gathered seashells and transformed them into the currency of primitive America. Wampum was in constant demand among the Algonquian tribes, and later the Iroquois as well, and a heavy trade had developed in it long before the white man appeared. Control of its manufactories provided the Dutch with a commercial advantage which Pilgrim traders from the new Plymouth Colony were continually trying to share. De Rasiere stated in 1626 that the "French Indians" came from Canada to trade with the Dutch for no other purpose than to secure the wampum unobtainable from the French.[62]

However important, wampum was not the only stock in the growing Indian trade. Newer and stranger items became increasingly important in the Indians' list of wants. Copper kettles, iron hatchets, and hoes were incomparably more useful than the stone and clay implements presently in use. Coral beads, already colored, immeasurably improved one's personal appearance at little cost in labor or time. Above all, the Indian took to substituting, or at least supplementing, his skin raiment with the coarse woolen cloth known as duffels. Most skins could be more profitably sold than worn, and in time duffels be-

---

[60] Van Laer, *New Netherland Documents, 1624–1626*, 212–215. De Rasiere uses the name Minqua (Susquehanna) here instead of Maqua (Mohawk). The passage is unintelligible unless this is a slip of the pen—an assumption rendered the more likely since he was writing of the Susquehanna in the previous paragraph. See *ibid.*, 52–55, 109; Murray, "Early Fur Trade," 370.

[61] *NNN*, 89; *VRBM*, 306; Murray, "Early Fur Trade," 368–369.

[62] Van Laer, *New Netherland Documents, 1624–1626*, 223–224; Murray, "Early Fur Trade," 368–369.

came the prime article in the trade, at least rivaling rum and far outstripping firearms in the quantity and value of sales. A certain amount of experimentation was necessary before European manufacturers and shippers accustomed themselves to Indian taste, and in 1626 De Rasiere advised the sending of darker colors, like blue or gray, as brighter shades made the native wearer too conspicuous to the animals he hunted.[63]

In 1630 Fort Orange and vicinity began to undergo a change. Still primarily a trading post, it also became the center of a growing agricultural community. This development resulted from the enactment of the Freedoms and Exemptions of 1629. Kiliaen van Rensselaer, an Amsterdam diamond merchant and one of the most influential directors of the West India Company, made plans as early as January 1629 to establish himself as a patroon of New Netherland. These plans came to fruition the next year, when his agents bought a vast tract of land in the neighborhood of Fort Orange and sent out a shipload of colonists to populate it. His original purchase from the Mahican Indians, already mentioned, together with others in following years, made Van Rensselaer not only the master of lands on both banks of the river surrounding Fort Orange, but the owner as well of the very land on which the company's post stood. In every case he was meticulous in extinguishing the Indian title before his agents took up the land. The first patroon never himself visited America, but he kept in as constant touch with its affairs as the state of communication in that day permitted. Although times were often hard, Rensselaerswyck, as he called it, remained in the family for generations—the only survivor of the patroonship system.[64]

Whatever his earliest intentions, there is no doubt that Van Rensselaer looked to the fur trade as the only means of recouping his unexpectedly heavy expenses in getting the domain established. For nearly a decade the patroon devoted his best efforts to wresting from the company of which he was a director a personal share in the fur trade that it had monopolized partly through his own efforts. Most of these attempts, undertaken in collaboration with other actual or would-be patroons, occurred in Europe. But Van Rensselaer did not restrict himself to lobbying at home, particularly when success there

[63] Van Laer, *New Netherland Documents, 1624–1626*, 223–232.
[64] *VRBM*, 154, 157–158, 166–169, 181–183, and *passim*.

was not forthcoming. He began to look about for extralegal, if not illegal, means of obtaining peltry on the spot. Although he insisted in 1632, in deference to company policy, that none of his tenants should engage in the fur trade and although such a stipulation was inserted in all his tenants' contracts, he was ready in 1636 to allow them to retain a few furs for their own profit if they would sell him their surplus crops at a reasonable rate. How the tenants obtained these skins in the first place was not mentioned. The truth of the matter was that every farmer, seeing all this wealth about him, began surreptitiously almost from the start to supplement his income by purchasing a few skins from the surrounding Indians, who were not at all concerned about the identity of the buyer providing they got an acceptable price. Peltry thus acquired was then resold, either to the patroon or to some company employee who found it worth his while to encourage rather than repress this illicit activity. The patroon too found it inconvenient to enforce regulations that ran counter to his interests, and the farmer came off with a profit which was small but worth trying for again.

Van Rensselaer's own activities were necessarily more circumscribed. He aimed rather at securing peltry from his tenants and the company itself than at competing with it in direct trade. In this process he was aided immeasurably by the fact that Director General Wouter van Twiller was his nephew, appointed to office largely through the patroon's efforts. Van Twiller, raised from the job of bookkeeper in the company's countinghouse, was probably more able and conscientious than Washington Irving and others have led us to believe. He published placards against illegal trading and seemingly tried to enforce them. Nevertheless he gave in to his uncle's demands and agreed on behalf of the company to pay in peltry for the foodstuffs that he needed from Rensselaerswyck. In the absence of ready wealth in other forms he may have had little choice in the matter. Thus Van Rensselaer, by buying up cheaply his tenants' surplus crops and then reselling them to the company for furs, managed to secure a respectable quantity of peltry for his own account. Officials sometimes protested at this leakage of the company's lifeblood, but the quantity was not large when measured alongside the total product of the colony, and the patroon was always careful to pay duties on the peltry that he shipped home.[65]

[65] Nissenson, *Patroon's Domain*, 81–82 and references.

The Freedoms and Exemptions conferred on patroons the right to trade for furs wherever the company maintained no agents. Aside from Van Rensselaer's minority interest in other patroonships, there is little or no record of his attempting to tap the trade at other points. Certainly it entered his mind, for in 1634 he wrote that if he "had a supply of brandy and were provided with a sloop" he knew of a skipper who would cruise along the coast, selling the liquor to Indians and Christians alike in return for peltry.[66] The most significant part of this statement, however, is its intimation that liquor was becoming a staple of the Indian trade. How far this traffic extended by 1634 is unknown, but in view of the experimentation of Hudson and his contemporaries it is surprising that the first mention of its progress in New Netherland came so late.

In 1633 Hans Jorissen Hontom was appointed commissary of Fort Orange, presumably on account of his long trading experience in the vicinity. His record might have been scrutinized more carefully, for it appeared that he had once kidnaped a Mohawk sachem and, after the ransom had been paid, murdered his victim by emasculation. The Mohawk took an understandable dislike to the man, and when one of their chieftains saw him at the fort again, this time as commissary, he packed up his furs and left. Soon afterward the tribesmen set fire to the company's yacht, threatened the commissary's life, and proceeded to slaughter most of the cattle at Rensselaerswyck. Further consequences were averted when Hontom perished in a brawl some months afterward, but as late as October 1636 Kiliaen van Rensselaer was still asking an indemnity from the Mohawk for the death of his tenants' cattle. It was a measure of the tribe's new importance that he insisted the indemnity must be requested by the governor in New Amsterdam, "in order that the Maquaas [Mohawk] may have less feeling against the people of Fort Orange and also against my people." [67]

Geographical proximity and similar commercial interests made it inevitable that the Dutch at Fort Orange and the French along the St. Lawrence should soon become rivals for the interior peltry supply. This competition grew stronger as the hunting lands close to the respective settlements became depleted. By 1615 Samuel de Champlain had explored the interior as far south as the lake bearing his name and as far

[66] VRBM, 283.   [67] Ibid., 302–304, 330.

west as Lake Huron. In the process he established the foundations of a prosperous Indian trade and secured the friendship of numerous Canadian tribes, including the powerful Huron. The Iroquois were first regarded by Champlain and his associates in much the same light as they were at Fort Orange. Hostile to all tribes about them, the Iroquois made ceaseless trouble for the friendly natives who brought in furs to the storehouses at Quebec. In 1609 Champlain fired European guns at the Mohawk for the first time, with better fortune than Van Krieckenbeeck experienced later. In 1615 he besieged the Onondaga castle, and desultory warfare continued for many years, although a short-lived peace was arranged in 1624. It is paradoxical that the first European treaty concluded by the Iroquois was made not with the Dutch, later to be their traditional friends, but with the French, their consistent foes. Iroquois war parties soon found their way back to the lakes and the Ottawa River, pillaging the Huron tribesmen and carrying their peltry to Fort Orange.

On the surface Dutch-French relations were placid, and the two nationalities themselves rarely came into direct contact. But by 1635 the French were convinced that their southern neighbors, in order to share in the northern fur trade, were using the Mohawk to disrupt the system of Indian alliances they had built up. Nothing would have been more welcome at Fort Orange than deputations of fur-laden Huron, but actually the Mohawk were playing their own game and had no intention of bringing the Canadian Indians to Fort Orange.[68]

In the complicated game of tripartite power politics Dutch and French policies are relatively easy to fathom. French interest naturally lay in preserving a strong system of alliances with and between the western tribes, whereby their fur supplies could find their way unimpeded to the St. Lawrence. Inclusion of the Iroquois in this network was earnestly desired, as it would not only help to ensure the safety of the western trade, but also lead to a commerce with the Five Nations themselves. Only when the warlike Iroquois proved incorrigible did the French sanction punitive measures, first to intimidate and later to destroy them.[69]

Dutch policy was similarly inclined to peace in the first resort. Only by harmonious relationships between the Iroquois—at first they were

[68] Thwaites, *Jesuit Relations*, VIII, 59–61; Murray, "Early Fur Trade," 370–371.
[69] Cf. Hunt, *Wars of the Iroquois*, 69–70.

aware only of the Mohawk—and the Mahican, Huron, and other tribes could the furs of all be channeled to Fort Orange. In such an event they and the French would be left to fight it out on a purely commercial basis. But from their viewpoint too the Iroquois proved intractable; Van Krieckenbeeck's consequent attempt in 1626 at intimidation and De Rasiere's hope for a stronger punitive expedition have already been mentioned. In 1633 Kiliaen van Rensselaer again charged the Mohawk with wantonly obstructing the flow of trade, but neither the patroon nor anyone else in authority urged recourse to war as the solution, at least in the present weakness of the province.[70] If peaceful relations among the Indians themselves were not forthcoming and intimidation—to say nothing of destruction—of the Iroquois was out of the question, the Dutch were willing to compromise. In the absence of a better arrangement they probably favored whatever Iroquois depredations helped to enlarge the volume of their own trade. They did not go so far, however, as to plot the disruption of the French alliances, because without positive Iroquois co-operation they were powerless to effect it.

The problem of Iroquois motivation is far more difficult. For the most part they left no records of their deeds or aspirations, nor did they necessarily have the same objectives that the white man would have had under similar conditions. Although economic motivations are just as attributable to "savage" people as to those in later stages of development, they are not the basis for all human activity. Indian civilization, including that of the Iroquois, was a composite of more ingredients than the search for wealth. Indian wars were fought for the sake of tribal prestige and personal glory, for revenge and self-preservation, at least as often as they were fought for economic gain, including direct plunder. Iroquois hostility toward surrounding tribes antedated the coming of the white man and had its roots in a myriad of causes, of which the economic was only one. With the white man's arrival, on the other hand, economic considerations of a new kind, involving the fur trade, came to the fore.[71] After 1609 furs represented wealth on both sides of the frontier, and it took no particular insight for the Iroquois to realize that skins plundered from the Huron could

[70] *VRBM*, 248.

[71] For the best analysis of the motives in Iroquois warfare, see Snyderman, "Behind the Tree of Peace," 30–37.

be sold at Fort Orange with profit to themselves. The hope of profitable robbery added zest to the pursuit of a war which had already become something of a social custom. The Iroquois prevented their northern enemies from passing through their territory because in the first place they *were* enemies and in the second place such accommodation would have brought little benefit to them compared with the existing arrangement.

Except for the factor of comparative prices the Iroquois cared little in this period whether they traded with the Dutch or the French. In 1634 the Dutch heard reports that the Mohawk had concluded a truce with the Canadian tribes in order to trade with the French.[72] The latter, hoping to kill two birds with one stone, may well have made such a truce the prerequisite to normal trading relations with the Iroquois. This news of a change in tactics naturally alarmed the Dutch authorities, who sent a delegation of three men into the Iroquois country in December 1634 to investigate the situation and boost the advantages of trading on the Hudson. The journal of this expedition was probably kept by Harmen Meyndertsen van den Bogaert, the surgeon at Fort Orange. It came to light only in 1895 and provides a first-rate account not only of Dutch commercial relations but also of Iroquois ethnology. After traversing the Mohawk country the party penetrated as far as the Oneida castle, midway between modern Utica and Syracuse, before it turned back with the information it sought.

The Indians' major grievance was that the Dutch charged more than the French for trading goods. The Oneida insisted that Bogaert promise them four hands of wampum or four handbreadths of cloth for every large beaver skin they should bring to Fort Orange. When the surgeon replied that he had no authority to make such commitments, but would check with the director general and send them an answer in the spring, the Indians reluctantly dropped the subject. The immediate results of this journey are unclear, but every complaint that the Indians made was repeated over and over for years to come.

The Connecticut, or, as the Dutch termed it, the Fresh River, was one of the early trading regions of New Netherland, but until 1633 it was subject only to periodic visits, and no attempt was made at settlement. As early as 1622 the Dutch ran into trouble there after an

[72] *NNN*, 139.

itinerant trader seized and held for ransom a sachem of the local Mattabesec tribe. The Indians recovered their chief after paying the desired tribute and remained distinctly unfriendly toward the Dutch for several years. When the news reached home, the West India Company indignantly expelled the offender, replacing him with the same Pieter Barentsen who was soon to repair the damage created by Van Krieckenbeeck at Fort Orange. By that time Barentsen had managed to win back the confidence of the Mattabesec chief to the extent of receiving a promise that the latter would trade with no one else.[73]

The Dutch position on the Connecticut grew more and more precarious as English settlements began multiplying to the eastward. For this reason the West India Company thought it expedient in 1632 to reinforce its previous rights conferred by discovery and constant visitation with purchase of the surrounding lands from the Indians. In that year and the next, Dutch agents bought territory on either side of the river and, near the site of Hartford, built a trading post which they named the House of Good Hope. This spot marked the head of navigation, and, like Fort Orange, it represented the nearest convenient approach to the interior fur supply. Despite all this activity the Dutch position was undermined within a year when traders from the Plymouth Colony seated themselves at Windsor, a few miles upstream. The Dutch protested loudly at this intrusion and even sent an expedition of seventy men against them, but when the Pilgrims offered resistance, they withdrew without firing a shot.[74] Wouter van Twiller was well acquainted with the States-General's maxim of 1625 and refused to begin a war that he could not finish. Thus the Plymouth men were suffered to skim the cream of the Connecticut trade from Indians bringing their peltry downstream.

The unintentionally ironic title of the Dutch post was rendered doubly so by the events which followed. In 1634 the neighboring Pequot tribe violated an earlier agreement by killing some Indians who had come to trade. As a result of this action the Dutch became embroiled in desultory warfare with the Pequot that lasted for several years and must have disrupted the trading activity for which the post

---

[73] Brodhead, *History of New York*, I, 145–146; *NNN*, 86, 187–188.

[74] *NNN*, 309; *NYCD*, II, 139–140; Brodhead, *History of New York*, I, 235, 240–242.

was created. Meanwhile the Pequot negotiated a treaty with Massachusetts by which they ceded the surrounding region to the English.[75] This pact led in 1635 to the founding of Hartford, right under the noses of the Dutch garrison, and of Wethersfield, a few miles downstream. In the long run these developments were more disastrous for the Pequot than for the Dutch. The English in 1637 fought a much more thorough Pequot War which ended in the virtual extermination of that tribe and redoubled the flow of English settlers into Connecticut. The Dutch now received their first forcible reminder that the key to control in America lay in colonization rather than in trade alone. They retained Fort Good Hope for a generation longer, but from the beginning it was an empty possession.

Unlike the Connecticut, the Delaware River was colonized by the Dutch at the outset, but their settlements there were never stable or permanent. The Delaware Indians were in a position analogous to the Mahican around Fort Orange, and in the early years a trade was driven with them on the river and along the New Jersey coast. As early as 1616 Captain Cornelis Hendricksen had discovered their enemies the Susquehanna, who lived farther west and whose trade potential was much greater. Fort Nassau was erected in 1624, not at the head of navigation, but opposite the mouth of the Schuylkill River, which formed the easiest route to the Susquehanna country. Director Verhulst apparently complied with his superiors' wishes in establishing a trading post farther upstream near Trenton.[76] The trade possibilities here were less promising than those below, but the upper post provided a convenient outlet for the Minisink and other northern Delaware bands, who must otherwise have carried their furs across the mountains to the Hudson. As the Delaware and Susquehanna bands were chronically at odds in this period, whatever expectation the Dutch had of opening a profitable western trade in this region were temporarily frustrated. The Susquehanna were either unable or unwilling for the present to establish more than the most fleeting relationships with their willing Dutch customers.[77] In 1626, when Peter Minuit effected his consolidation policy, the Delaware trade had proved disappointing, and the

[75] John Winthrop, *Winthrop's Journal, 1630–1649,* ed. by James K. Hosmer (New York, 1908), I, 138–140, 219; *Winthrop Papers* (Boston, 1929–1947), III, 177.

[76] *NYDH,* III, 50.

[77] Van Laer, *New Netherland Documents, 1624–1626,* 211.

post at Trenton as well as Fort Nassau itself were abandoned. From this time forward the company concentrated its efforts on the Hudson, and the Delaware trade was for several years entrusted to a single yacht making regular visits up the river.[78]

The third major patroonship of New Netherland (after Pavonia and Rensselaerswyck) was commenced on Delaware Bay under the aegis of Samuel Godyn, another company director, and several associates. Lands were bought from the Indians in the summer of 1629, even before the issuance of the revised Freedoms and Exemptions. An expedition arrived at Cape Henlopen in April 1631, and here, near the present town of Lewes, Delaware, a settlement of about thirty persons was established and given the name Swanendael—Vale of Swans.[79] The major occupation of the colonists was farming, but they profited, in the absence of a company agent, by entering into the fur trade on behalf of the patroon. This commerce, later based on shipboard visits, persisted for two years until the exasperated company officials sent a commissary to break it up. Commenting on a similar episode shortly afterward, Van Rensselaer remarked with probable truth that the company had procured the same number of skins along the Delaware that it was accustomed to getting, while the patroon had opened a new field which he and the company could have shared through the payment of the normal duty. By breaking up this trade without substituting facilities of its own, he said, both parties were losers.[80]

The company's action provided the final but not the most serious blow to Godyn's hopes. Less than a year after its founding the Swanendael colony was wiped out to the last man by Indians. In December 1632 David Pietersen de Vries, one of the patroon's associates, came to survey the ruins. Cautiously looking up the neighboring tribesmen, he heard their version of the massacre—necessarily the only one extant. The colonists apparently had protested the thoughtless action of an Indian in making off with a piece of tin bearing the arms of Holland. Seeing them displeased, the other Indians slew the offender, bringing back a token of their speedy justice. The commissary explained that only a reprimand had been called for, and the friends of the deceased, who held the Dutch accountable, demanded revenge. It was they,

[78] *NNN*, 84, 86, 88.
[79] *NYCD*, I, 43; XII, 16–18; Brodhead, *History of New York*, I, 206.
[80] *VRBM*, 241–242, 246.

according to De Vries and his informants, who perpetrated the massacre while the settlers were dispersed in their fields. De Vries knew that he was powerless to avenge the massacre, and with great aplomb he looked instead to the restitution of trade relations as soon as possible. No attempt was made to recolonize Swanendael, and in 1635 Godyn's heirs sold their rights back to the company.[81]

With the coming of Director Van Twiller in 1633 a policy of expansion was begun which brought not only the establishment of Fort Good Hope but the renewal of activity on the Delaware. The Susquehanna by this time had gained a definite ascendancy over the nearby Delaware bands, much as the Mohawk were gradually triumphing over their Mahican adversaries farther north. Furthermore, they had sent envoys all the way to New Amsterdam immediately after Fort Nassau's abandonment, expressing their friendship and willingness to trade.[82] Under these conditions Van Twiller in 1633 sent a new commissary to the Delaware who bought land from the natives and erected a trading house on the site of Philadelphia.[83] This post too was soon abandoned, but two or three years later, after the Dutch had forcibly expelled a group of interlopers from Virginia, they reoccupied Fort Nassau and once again controlled the river.[84]

When Wouter van Twiller gave way to Willem Kieft in 1638, New Netherland was a province almost devoid of people. The total population, estimated at 270 in 1628, had probably failed to reach a thousand in the course of the next decade. The province boasted but a single town—New Amsterdam—which with its "metropolitan district" must have accounted for well over half the population. The entire Delaware valley was in the hands of a few traders at Fort Nassau. Fort Orange and Rensselaerswyck were occupied by perhaps a hundred traders, farmers, and their families. To the east the handful of men in garrison at Fort Good Hope were little more than nonvoting resi-

[81] Albert C. Myers, ed., *Narratives of Early Pennsylvania, West New Jersey, and Delaware, 1630–1707* (New York, 1912), 9, 15–18; Brodhead, *History of New York*, I, 249.

[82] Myers, *Narratives of Early Pennsylvania*, 23–24, 38 ff.; Van Laer, *New Netherland Documents, 1624–1626*, 211.

[83] *NYCD*, I, 588, 593; XII, 37; Brodhead, *History of New York*, I, 232; Amandus Johnson, *The Swedish Settlements on the Delaware* (Philadelphia, 1911), I, 178–179.

[84] Myers, *Narratives of Early Pennsylvania*, 37 ff.; *NNN*, 195; Brodhead, *History of New York*, I, 254–255, 279; Johnson, *Swedish Settlements*, I, 179–181.

dents of Hartford, Connecticut. An exclusive trade policy and a feudal plan of colonization, superimposed on thriving economic conditions and religious toleration at home, discouraged settlement of the province and made it a losing venture to the trading company which had founded it.

III

Governor Kieft's War

THE YEAR 1638 opened a new chapter in New Netherland history. Not only did Willem Kieft arrive to replace Van Twiller in the governorship—a post he was to hold for nine years—but colonization began to increase, perhaps doubling the total population within five years. In this year too the continuing quarrel between the company and patroons over sharing in the fur trade came to a head.

All parties agreed that the imperative need in New Netherland was large-scale colonization, but they were not agreed on the means of accomplishing it. The company and patroons, moreover, looked upon the fur trade, hitherto the colony's major source of income, as the key to its future development as well. It was clear by now that the company's trade monopoly existed only on paper and that its enforcement was next to impossible. The States-General at the same time was demanding that unless something were done to develop New Netherland it would confiscate the province itself. Although New Netherland had been a losing proposition, the company directors were always hopeful that the colony by some new management could be made to repay the original investment with interest. In August 1638, therefore, they proposed a colonization scheme which at least by implication would have thrown open the trade to all but the company's own servants. By allowing private colonists to compete in the traffic they hoped to stimulate further immigration. This proposal was no more agreeable to the patroons than the existing monopoly, and their plan was to extend the trading privilege only enough to include themselves.[1]

---

[1] *NYCD*, I, 98, 107, 112–114; *VRBM*, 79–80, 425; O'Callaghan, *History of New Netherland*, I, 198; Nissenson, *Patroon's Domain*, 212.

Both projects, as it turned out, were unacceptable to the States-General, but the fur trade was nevertheless opened late this year or in 1639. Henceforth all persons were permitted to ship goods to New Netherland, to trade directly with the Indians, and to export peltry to Europe on their own accounts. The only limitation on the trading privilege was an obligation to pay a duty on all goods taken in or out of the province.[2] In the summer of 1640 a new charter of Freedoms and Exemptions was issued in order further to stimulate immigration. It reduced the size of future patroonships, created the rank of "master or colonist" for persons who settled five adults in New Netherland, and confirmed the freedom to trade for peltry, subject to a duty of 10 per cent on all skins shipped out of the province.[3] Thus after 1639 the West India Company hoped by customs duties and its own trading operations, together with increased population, to make up the perennial deficit which it had previously incurred in the province.

However it influenced immigration, one of the immediate effects of open trade was to encourage an influx of transients who returned home once a profit had been made and thus benefited the province very little. These traders were cordially disliked by the company and colonists alike, in the one case because they frequently evaded customs duties and in the other because they entered the province only to compete with its inhabitants. More than once it was proposed to restrict the fur trade to residents, but no such limitation was enacted until March 1648. The ordinance issued at that time forbade anyone to sail or trade on the Delaware, the Hudson, "or in any Bays, Kills and Creeks situate up and between them" except residents of New Amsterdam and Rensselaerswyck.[4] The Holland directors found this too restrictive, however. Sympathizing with the desire "to prevent all the trade of these private hucksters," they nevertheless required the governor to "temporize in all these matters," as the company needed the duties they paid. In terms of who could and who could not trade

---

[2] *VRBM*, 79–81, 440–441; Nissenson, *Patroon's Domain*, 178; Ruth L. Higgins, *Expansion in New York with Especial Reference to the Eighteenth Century* (Columbus, Ohio, 1931), 6–7. Cf. O'Callaghan, *History of New Netherland*, I, 201–203; Brodhead, *History of New York*, I, 288. There is some basis for arguing that the trade *to* New Netherland was still limited somewhat, but this did not affect the fur trade *within* the province. See *NYCD*, I, 162; *VRBM*, 81.

[3] *NYCD*, I, 119–121.

[4] *Ibid.*, 135–136, 154, 162; *LONN*, 86–92; Brodhead, *History of New York*, I, 488–490.

with the Indians, therefore, the law had little effect and persons continued to enter the province freely for that purpose.[5]

Although population increased in the first few years after the trade was thrown open, the lifting of other restrictions at the same time was probably more responsible for the influx of colonists.[6] Rensselaerswyck and Fort Orange received a share of the new immigrants, but by far the greater number settled in and around New Amsterdam, where the fur trade was fast disappearing. The prevailing economic pattern in New Netherland, which these immigrants helped to establish, was basically agricultural, with the Indian trade in most areas a common but relatively minor side line. The actual number of immigrants was disappointingly small, despite an impressive proportional increase. To double a population of eight hundred persons, after all, requires only eight hundred more. Moreover, the national origins of these new colonists must have been almost as disturbing as their small numbers. A majority were probably Dutch, but there was a sprinkling of Walloons and French Huguenots, Germans, and especially Englishmen. These last were mostly New Englanders who began in this period to colonize Long Island. Most of them settled near its eastern tip and retained an affiliation with the colonies of Connecticut and New Haven, but others moved farther west and submitted to Dutch authority. This diversity of population helped to create the cosmopolitan character which has always marked New Amsterdam and New York, but the authorities were to find that the Englishmen in particular made poor components of a Dutch empire.

In order to accommodate the new settlers with land Director Kieft bought several large tracts from the natives shortly after his arrival. In 1639 the Rockaway Indians sold a large area on Long Island extending from shore to shore and including most of modern Queens. The next year Kieft completed Dutch holdings in the Brooklyn area so that the Indian title was now theoretically extinguished in all of Kings and Queens Counties.[7]

The Indians remained very much in evidence, however. Penhawitz, the Canarsee sachem, had reportedly sold all the Canarsee lands on

[5] *NYCD*, I, 500; XIV, 105.

[6] Cf. *ibid.*, I, 150; O'Callaghan, *History of New Netherland*, I, 222–223; Brodhead, *History of New York*, I, 288–290.

[7] *NYCD*, XIV, 15; Brodhead, *History of New York*, I, 290, 297; O'Callaghan, *History of New Netherland*, I, 215.

Long Island, but he and his people remained there and played a significant role in future developments. At least one of the purchase deeds —that for the Rockaway land—stipulated that the Indians be allowed to remain and "plant corn, fish, hunt and make a living there as well as they can," under Dutch protection.[8] Furthermore, the Indians did not look upon these transactions with the same finality as the Europeans, and in 1643 the Massapequa and Merric bands joined the Rockaway in selling to the new town of Hempstead certain lands that the Rockaway had apparently already sold in 1639.[9] In succeeding years the same thing happened elsewhere. The mainland shore of Long Island Sound from Norwalk Bay to Hell Gate, purchased all at once by the Dutch in 1640, was later resold piecemeal to English colonists moving in from the opposite direction.[10] Staten Island was purchased in 1630, and, as there was no immediate push of settlers to displace them, the Indians remained there for many years. Later, as the white population increased, the Indians began getting in the way, and farmers grumbled about "Indian givers." Eventually the island had to be purchased two more times before the native occupants departed.[11] Whether the deeds specifically provided for it or not, such wholesale land purchases failed to terminate native occupancy and consequently bred hard feelings between the Indians and the new colonists who moved in beside them, each people feeling that its own position was the legally correct one.

The Indian's land, like his peltry and other commodities, was bought with liquor, trading goods, and wampum. If a study made of Westchester County may be given broader application, there was little relation between the quantity of goods given and the extent of lands received. Rather the amount of goods seemed to reflect the number of Indians involved in the transaction. There were about twenty-five separate conveyances covering the county, the earliest being in 1639. The articles paid for these 299 square miles included: more than 300 knives; 185 hatchets, axes, and adzes; 141 hoes; 67 guns; 227 pounds

[8] *NYCD*, XIV, 15.

[9] Henry Onderdonk, Jr., *Queen's County in Olden Times* (Jamaica, N.Y., 1865), 3; Bernice Schultz, *Colonial Hempstead* (Lynbrook, N.Y., 1937), 10–11. As the Rockaway by no means controlled all of Queens, they had no right unilaterally to sell it in 1639, if that was their intention.

[10] Bolton, "New York City in Indian Possession," 232.

[11] *Ibid.*, 232–233. The three deeds for Staten Island appear in *NYCD*, XIII, 2, 455–457, and XIV, 393–394. For similar examples on Long Island see Chapter VI below.

of gunpowder; 130 bars of lead; 3 melting ladles; 5 bullet molds; 182 coats; more than 300 yards of trade cloths; 113 shirts; 92 pairs of stockings; 87 blankets; 10 "corals or beads"; 117 iron or brass kettles; 76 earthenware or stone jugs; 12 firesteels; 20 spoons; 1,000 fishhooks; 220 needles; 120 awls for drilling holes in wampum; 130 clay pipes; 10 bells; 10 jew's-harps; a few rolls of tobacco, with 32 tobacco boxes; 25 half-vats of strong beer; 16 ankers (162 gallons) of rum; and 1,800 yards of wampum. The money value of all these goods, which were paid over a long period of time, is estimated at $4,750 (not counting the wampum, which fluctuated widely in value) or about ten dollars and four yards of wampum per square mile. This figure is comparable with those estimated for purchases in northern New Jersey over a similar time span.[12]

As settlement advanced, Indian relations deteriorated proportionately. Apart from disputes over landownership, day-to-day quarrels arose from a multiplicity of causes. On Long Island the Indians' dogs —or, more accurately, half-tamed wolves—were a constant source of harassment to settlers' livestock and poultry. On the other hand, the same livestock wandered unattended into the Indians' unfenced fields of corn which they ate and trampled. The Indians complained, but often no redress was made, and they frequently retaliated by killing the offending animals.[13] In 1640 Director Kieft enacted an ordinance to combat this grievance, and its preamble, like that of other seventeenth-century laws, is even more revealing than the enactment itself. It deprecates the trampling down of Indians' corn because "the Maize will be dear at the time of the Harvest and our good people [will] suffer want." Furthermore, the Indians might be antagonized to the point of combining against the Dutch. The remainder of the law, fining colonists for letting their livestock stray, was enacted for their own protection, not for that of the Indians.[14] There is little that can be known today about individual relationships with the Indian, but fragmentary court records indicate that he retained some legal protection beyond the backhanded assistance of statutes like that quoted above. In 1638 the provincial council, sitting as a court, fined a man and made him return certain goods he had acquired through assault

[12] Bolton, "New York City in Indian Possession," 298–301; Rankin, "Purchase of Newark from the Indians," 444.
[13] *NNN*, 273; *NYCD*, I, 150.   [14] *LONN*, 22.

and robbery of Indians. A year later another man was ordered to restore wampum that he had taken from them illegally.[15] The Indians
were protected, but largely to avoid the consequences of their anger.
Although they profited by the system, this result was subsidiary, and
the distinction is important.

The ordinary frictions engendered by living in the same neighborhood were potentially dangerous enough, but Director Kieft managed
to hasten a conflict through a series of ill-advised governmental measures. The company was usually hard-pressed financially, and Kieft
determined to help recover the cost of fortification and maintenance of
soldiers by taxing the Indians who in part made the expenditure necessary. Accordingly the council (which consisted of Kieft with two votes
and Dr. Johannes la Montagne with one) resolved in September 1639
to levy a contribution "in peltries, maize or wampum" on the Indians
around Manhattan. The excuse given, that the Dutch had hitherto
protected these tribes against their enemies, was completely specious
since that service was neither asked for nor rendered. Compulsion was
looked to in the event any tribe "will not willingly consent to contribute." Although Kieft claimed later that the Amsterdam directors
had authorized this step, they positively denied it and even claimed
ignorance of its having been made.[16]

The extent to which Kieft tried to enforce his ordinance is unknown. The winter passed quietly, but in May 1640 he felt obliged to
order that each inhabitant provide himself with a gun and keep it in
constant repair. Every man was placed under a corporal, and warning
signals were arranged in case of sudden alarm.[17] Presently the Raritan
Indians brought matters to a head by attempting to capture the sloop
that was sent to trade with them every spring. The three-man crew
drove them off, but the damage was done. Shortly afterward the Raritan were blamed, perhaps unfairly, for killing some pigs on Staten
Island. When the Indians refused a summons to come in and make
reparation, Kieft sent an expedition to attack them and take prisoners
unless they submitted. This force, composed of about eighty soldiers
and sailors, was commanded by Cornelis van Tienhoven, secretary of

[15] Edmund B. O'Callaghan, ed., *Calendar of Historical Manuscripts in the Office
of the Secretary of State* (Albany, 1865–1866), I, 65, 70.

[16] *NYCD*, I, 332, 338; XIII, 6; *NNN*, 322, 334; Brodhead, *History of New York*,
I, 309.

[17] *LONN*, 23.

the province. When it reached the Raritan village, Van Tienhoven demanded payment according to his instruction; but the men wanted to punish the Indians without further ado while they were within reach. Van Tienhoven—hardly a friend of the red man himself—gave in after a token resistance and left the field to his unruly subordinates. Before he had gone a mile, they put several Indians to death and captured and tortured the sachem's brother.[18] The Raritan nursed their wounds and waited for a time to retaliate.

In October 1640, a year after the enactment of Kieft's Indian tax, a sloop visited the Tappan band for the purpose of exacting a tribute in corn. David P. de Vries, who now owned a plantation on Staten Island, had sailed up the river to trade cloth for the Indians' corn. The natives warned him away until the company boat had gone, declaring that "the Sachem [Kieft], who was now at the Fort . . . must be a very mean fellow to come to live in this country without being invited by them, and now wish to compel them to give him their corn for nothing." [19]

Again the winter passed quietly, but in June 1641 the Raritan attacked De Vries' bowery on Staten Island, killing four of his tenant farmers and burning the house and barn.[20] Instead of sending another military force to punish them Kieft this time offered to reward other Indians for taking up arms against the Raritan. Ten fathom of wampum were promised for each head brought in, and twenty fathom for the head of each participant in the Staten Island murders. In September he ordered a small redoubt to be built to protect the people who still cared to live on that troubled island.[21] It was not long before the governor's stratagem for securing retribution bore fruit. Pacham, the sachem of the Tankiteke band in upper Westchester and Fairfield Counties, entered New Amsterdam in November "in great triumph, bringing a dead hand hanging on a stick," and said that it belonged to the chief who had killed the settlers on Staten Island. He had taken revenge, he declared, "because he loved the Swannekens (as they call the Dutch), who were his best friends." Apparently some Long Island

[18] *NYCD*, I, 150; XIII, 7; *NNN*, 208, 211. [19] *NNN*, 209.

[20] *LONN*, 28; *NNN*, 211. De Vries, writing years after the event, erroneously places it on September 1. Cf. O'Callaghan, *History of New Netherland*, I, 239–240, and Brodhead, *History of New York*, I, 313–315.

[21] *LONN*, 28–29; *NYCD*, XIII, 9.

Indians too were induced by the reward to hunt the Raritan, and that band was soon forced to seek its peace.[22]

This event had not yet taken place, however, before trouble developed with the Wecquaesgeek Indians in Westchester. One of that band, coming to trade at the isolated home of an old man on Manhattan Island, had murdered him with an axe and stolen his trading goods. News of this murder caused a wave of excitement in New Amsterdam. The circumstances were bloodcurdling to begin with, and it was committed just outside town—too close for comfort. Kieft promptly sent to the Wecquaesgeek sachem demanding satisfaction, but the sachem answered that he was sorry twenty Christians had not received the same treatment. The killer, he said, was merely avenging in Indian fashion the death of an uncle who had been murdered by the Swannekens fifteen years earlier.[23]

This defiance raised a serious problem for the director and those around him. Dutch authority had been directly challenged by a tribe of savages, and if they went unpunished, it would create a dangerous precedent. The Indians, who themselves were believers in speedy atonement, could interpret inaction now as a sign of cowardice or weakness, sufficient perhaps to justify more ambitious ventures against the Swannekens. On the other hand, the use of force against the Wecquaesgeek would bring war and destruction, just as it had when it was employed against the Raritan. Men like De Vries, who lived virtually in the midst of the Indians, tended under the circumstances to be more conciliatory than Secretary Van Tienhoven or Kieft, safe within the walls of Fort Amsterdam. The director's subsequent course indicates that he strongly favored a punitive expedition; but before undertaking a second war he wanted some expression of public support. To secure this he had recourse to a political tactic which was unprecedented in New Netherland—he called a meeting of all the heads of families living in or near New Amsterdam.

These men were called together on August 28 and considered three propositions put to them by the governor. To the first question, whether it was not right and proper to punish the old man's murderer and, in

---

[22] *NNN*, 211, 277; *NYCD*, I, 199, 410; O'Callaghan, *History of New Netherland*, I, 240.

[23] *NNN*, 213, 274–275; *NYCD*, I, 150.

case he was not surrendered, to destroy the whole village to which he belonged, the commonalty answered with a general affirmative. To the second and third questions—in what manner, when, and by whom an attack should be made in the likely event that the murderer was refused—they replied at greater length. They urged that friendly relations be continued "until the maize trade be over" and that no one commit any hostility against the Indians, the murderer alone excepted, until winter, when the Indians were hunting. Then, it was hoped, a surprise attack launched simultaneously from the east and west would properly chasten the Wecquaesgeek for many years to come. The citizens struck out obliquely at Kieft, who had scarcely left the fort since assuming the government, by demanding that he lead them personally to ensure popular backing. Finally they recommended that, "for the purpose of lulling the suspicions of the Indians without using any threats," Kieft should send as often as three times to demand surrender of the murderer in a peaceable manner. Before adjourning, the commonalty elected a standing committee of twelve, headed by the omnipresent David Pietersen de Vries, empowered on their behalf "to resolve on everything with the Director and Council."[24]

To the opinion of the public, thus formally expressed, De Vries added his own in a private conversation. "I told Commander Kieft that no profit was to be derived from a war with the savages; that he was the means of my people being murdered . . . on Staten Island in the year forty"; and, furthermore, that Kieft's superiors would oppose an Indian war.[25] At least this is what, years after the governor's death, De Vries says that he told him. If all the testimony is taken at face value, De Vries was farther from the commonalty's position than was Kieft. As the commonalty and their representatives were frequently willing to oppose Kieft whenever they disagreed with him, the opinions that they expressed here were probably genuinely held. They differed with him chiefly over the immediacy of a punitive expedition. The commonalty agreed that such a blow was probably required to maintain Dutch prestige and to prevent further incidents, but they were anxious first to exhaust peaceful means of obtaining satisfaction. Secondly, they were stalling in order to prepare for the expedition more carefully should it prove necessary. They wanted the attack to be so

[24] *NYCD*, I, 414–415; *NNN*, 214.   [25] *NNN*, 214.

thorough as to discourage retaliatory efforts either by the Wecquaes-geek or by their possible allies and to provide a weighty example for other bands.

With winter the hunting season came, and Kieft impatiently asked the Twelve Men on November 1 to agree to an immediate attack. A majority counseled further patience on the ground that the savages were not yet sufficiently lulled.[26] This advice prolonged the peace for several more months, but still there was no indication that the Indians would ever deliver up the culprit for punishment. In January 1642 Kieft recalled the Twelve Men and put the question once more. On this third attempt he got agreement that "the most favorable time and opportunity for our nation now offer." They requested the governor to make preparations and promised on behalf of the people to follow wherever he led. The last point they reiterated by stipulating again that "he himself accompany us to prevent all disorder." [27] After providing for supplies and care of the wounded, the Twelve Men turned to matters of political reform. In this sphere they and the director fell out completely, and on February 18 he dissolved them with an admonition never to meet again without his permission.

Having disposed of his troublesome parliament, Kieft proceeded with his long-cherished plan to subdue the Wecquaesgeek, assured now of at least formal public consent. An expedition was organized early in March which Kieft refused to accompany, much less command, despite the tongue-in-cheek solicitation of the commonalty. Instead, Ensign Hendrick van Dyck led the party of eighty men across the Harlem River and into the wooded hills of Westchester. As darkness set in, the guides lost their way, and an hour was wasted in spite of the need to strike quickly before the Indians learned of their presence. In the confusion Van Dyck lost his temper and ordered a retreat, and the avenging army returned to Fort Amsterdam in humiliation. Yet the expedition was not a complete loss, for the Indians soon discovered the fate that they had narrowly escaped. Fearing a more successful attempt later, they sued for peace, and a treaty was concluded that spring. This document called on the Indians either to sur-

[26] O'Callaghan, *History of New Netherland*, I, 243; Brodhead, *History of New York*, I, 318–319.
[27] *NYCD*, I, 415–416.

render the murderer or to punish him themselves, but neither provision was ever carried out.[28]

In 1642 trouble arose for the first time with the Hackensack Indians. A plantation had been established the year before on Newark Bay, close to the main Hackensack village. It was done against the Indians' will, although the land had been purchased long before, and over Kieft's objection as well. The farmers' cattle frequently trespassed on native cornlands, and the settlers sold brandy to the Indians. To make matters worse, if De Vries may be believed, they cheated the Indians by adulterating the brandy with water. The tension engendered by these grievances presently resulted in two murders.

Immediately after the second crime some Hackensack and other nearby chiefs offered to pay the victim's widow a wampum atonement that would suffice in Indian jurisprudence to "wipe away her tears." But when Kieft, following Dutch jurisprudence, asked for the murderer's surrender, the chiefs claimed that he had fled beyond their jurisdiction. Offering once more to pay for the crime according to their own custom, they blamed the incident on the Dutchmen who sold liquor to the young braves and asked that this dangerous traffic be prohibited. The chiefs finally promised Kieft to do all that they could to get the murderer, but they explained privately to De Vries that he was a sachem's son and could never be handed over. The matter stood as they reported, and the culprit never appeared.[29]

In February 1643 God took vengeance, as the Dutch saw it, on the Indians of Wecquaesgeek. Unknown to the colonists a party of eighty to ninety hostile warriors from the vicinity of Fort Orange, "each with a gun on his shoulder," descended upon the Wecquaesgeek and adjacent bands in order to enforce a payment of tribute. These Indians, armed with nothing more than bows and arrows, were filled with con-

---

[28] *NNN*, 213, 275; *NYCD*, I, 199, 410; Brodhead, *History of New York*, I, 330. During this same spring Miantonomo, the chief sachem of the Narraganset, visited parts of southern New England and eastern Long Island in an effort to form a general Indian alliance against the English. His plot does not seem to have been aimed at the Dutch, but it may have added to the feeling of alarm pervading New Netherland at the time. See Nathaniel B. Shurtleff and David Pulsifer, eds., *Records of the Colony of New Plymouth in New England* (Boston, 1855–1861), IX, 50; *NNN*, 276; David Gardiner, *Chronicles of the Town of Easthampton* (New York, 1871), 14–15; James Truslow Adams, *History of the Town of Southampton* (Bridgehampton, N.Y., 1918), 69–70.

[29] *NNN*, 215–216, 276; *NYCD*, I, 150; XIII, 11.

sternation as the invaders killed at least seventeen of their number and carried off many women and children as prisoners. The remainder, numbering several hundred, fled in abject terror to the Dutch settlements, begging protection. The colonists received them with hospitality and supported them for two weeks, Director Kieft himself ordering corn to be sent them. Shortly afterward, probably having returned to their homes, the Indians experienced another scare and fled once more to the Dutch. On this occasion they gathered at two places: Corlaer's Hook on Manhattan Island, northeast of New Amsterdam, and across the river at Pavonia in the territory of the Hackensack band.[30]

While the Indians were a second time at their mercy, it occurred to some of the colonists that this was the perfect opportunity to avenge the unpunished frontier incidents of the last few years. On February 22 three of the Twelve Men handed in a petition to Kieft, allegedly on behalf of "the whole of the freemen," asking for permission "to attack the Indians as enemies, whilst God hathfully [sic] delivered them into our hands." Should the soldiers attack one of the Indian parties, these freemen promised to take care of the other.[31]

Public opinion was sharply divided concerning the best policy to adopt toward the Indians, but the public was probably unaware of the petition itself and of its aftermath until it was too late. That a portion of the commonalty favored violence was indicated by their subsequent participation in it, although this group may not have been large. One of the foremost counselors of direct action was Cornelis van Tienhoven, who appears to have been charged by Kieft with the conduct of Indian affairs from the beginning of his administration. He was later accused of writing the petition himself at the request of the signatories. Whether or not Kieft, too, had actively encouraged these men to submit their petition, as his enemies alleged, he undoubtedly favored their program and could have vetoed it had he so desired. Although he later used the petition to cast blame on the commonalty

[30] *NNN*, 225–226, 276–277; *NYCD*, I, 151, 200, 412. O'Callaghan (*History of New Netherland*, I, 264) and Brodhead (*History of New York*, I, 349) refer to the northern attackers as Mohawk, but they are identified as Mahican by the sources. On the other hand, the Mohawk are referred to elsewhere as enemies of these Algonquian bands at this time. See *NYDH*, IV, 104. Cf. Ruttenber, *Indian Tribes of Hudson's River*, 105n.
[31] *NYCD*, I, 193.

for what ensued, Kieft was in the forefront of the movement. His own contemporaries and later historians alike have been virtually unanimous in placing the direct, personal responsibility for what followed on his shoulders.[32]

The plot was carefully planned over a period of at least three days. On February 24 Kieft sent Van Tienhoven over to Pavonia with Corporal Hans Steen to scout the Indians' position and weigh the prospects of a successful attack. They must have reported favorably, for the next day Kieft sanctioned the burghers' proposal. Maryn Adriaensen, who had signed the petition first, was empowered "at his request to make with his men an expedition against the party of savages encamped behind Curler's Hook . . . and to act towards them, as they shall deem proper according to the circumstances." At the same time Sergeant Rodolff was ordered to take a troop of soldiers that night to Pavonia, "there to destroy all the Indians encamped behind Jan Evertsen's, but to spare the women and children as much as possible, endeavoring to capture the same." In order to show the way, Corporal Steen was ordered to accompany him.[33]

On the night of February 25 the soldiers, about eighty strong, crossed the river, reaching their destination about midnight. The details of the massacre which followed survive in only one highly colored narrative:

Young children, some of them snatched from their mothers, were cut in pieces before the eyes of their parents, and the pieces were thrown into the fire or into the water; other babes were bound on planks and then cut through, stabbed and miserably massacred, so that it would break a heart of stone; some were thrown into the river and when the fathers and mothers sought to save them, the soldiers would not suffer them to come ashore but caused both old and young to be drowned. Some children of from 5 to 6 years of age, as also some old infirm persons, who had managed to hide themselves in the bushes and reeds, came out in the morning to beg for a piece of bread and for permission to warm themselves, but were all murdered in cold blood and thrown into the fire or the water. A few escaped to our settlers, some with the loss of a hand, others of a leg, others again holding in their bowels with their hands, and all so cut, hacked and maimed, that worse could not be imagined; they were indeed in such a state that our people supposed

[32] *Ibid.*, 194–195; XIII, 10–11; *NYDH*, IV, 102; *NNN*, 277, 341.

[33] *NYDH*, IV, 103; *NYCD*, I, 199, 345, 411; XIII, 10–11; cf. *ibid.*, I, 194, 416.

they had been surprised by their enemies, the tribe of the Maquaes [Mohawk].[34]

What actually occurred at Pavonia that night was grisly enough even if it failed to live up to this account. A similar attack took place on a smaller scale at Corlaer's Hook, where the Indians were surprised in their sleep by citizens of New Amsterdam under Maryn Adriaensen. The number of Indian dead in both places was between 80 and 120, and 30 more were said to have been taken prisoner. According to the version quoted above, Kieft personally thanked the soldiers on their return the next day.[35]

No sooner had the parties returned than the smell of blood attracted other colonists of similar bent. On February 27 five residents of Long Island petitioned for authority "to ruin and conquer" the Canarsee Indians "from time to time" until "the previous and much wished for peace of this place, may be and remain permanent." The recent night's work appears to have chastened the director general and his advisers, however. In answer they correctly pointed out that since these Indians had given no provocation such action at this time "would draw down an unrighteous war on our heads, especially as we are assured that they would be on their guard and hard to beat." But if they showed signs of hostility, the council added, "every man must do his best to defend himself." [36] Notwithstanding this official damper, a group of settlers killed three Indians in an effort to seize corn from the Canarsee wigwams.[37]

In the meantime, border warfare lit up the frontier around New Amsterdam after the massacres of the night of February 25–26. The Indians began burning, looting, and murdering throughout the countryside, and the toll of lives and property mounted. The scattered farmers had not been warned of what was afoot at New Amsterdam, apparently in the belief that the massacre, like previous expeditions, would demoralize the Indians whom it did not dispose of altogether. Kieft and his advisers gravely miscalculated and thus brought down on their heads a stream of abuse which hounded most of them to their graves.

[34] *NYDH,* IV, 103–104. De Vries copied this in giving his own account of the massacre. See *NNN,* 228.

[35] *NNN,* 227–229, 277; *NYDH,* IV, 103–104; *NYCD,* I, 151.

[36] *NYCD,* I, 416–417. The petition failed to specify which Indians were intended, but the reply named the "Indians at Mareckkawich," a Canarsee village in Brooklyn.

[37] *NNN,* 277–278.

De Vries again lost property at the hands of Indians whom he had never personally offended. His servants found safety in the main house while the rest of the farm, including its crops and buildings, went up in smoke.[38]

Eleven bands of Indians are said to have taken to the warpath, and on February 27 Kieft conscripted all the planters in the vicinity for "one or two months" to meet the emergency. He took this measure in the first place because many colonists were on the point of moving to Fort Orange, where they could farm the land in peace, and secondly because the number of soldiers on hand was far too small to protect the scattered settlements. The optimism reflected in Kieft's two-month call was not long in evaporating. Roger Williams, desiring to take a boat for Europe and forbidden to do so at Boston, had just come to New Amsterdam for that purpose. Here, as he later reported, "mine Eyes did see yt first breaking forth of ye Indian War," which the Dutch "questioned not to finish . . . in a few dayes . . . But before we waighed Anchor their Bowries were in Flames[.] Dutch & Eng[lish] were slaine[;] mine Eyes saw . . . flames at their Townes . . . & ye Flights & Hurries of Men, Women & Children, the present Remoovall of all yt Could for Holland." [39]

In the wake of destruction came recrimination. The owner of one of the burned houses upbraided Maryn Adriaensen as the cause of the present troubles. Kieft now shifted all the responsibility on the commonalty, saying that they had forced his hand. Adriaensen had just undertaken two bootless forays against the enemy, and, maddened with rage and disappointment at the turn of events, he conceived that Kieft was singling him out as the culprit. On the afternoon of March 21 he tried to assassinate the governor and was thrown into prison. About an hour later one of his servants made a second attempt, which almost succeeded, but he was shot down by a sentry. As a number of Adriaensen's partisans began agitating on his behalf, Kieft was afraid to proceed with a trial himself and finally sent the culprit to Holland. Whatever the outcome there, he was back in New Netherland and accepting a land grant from Kieft in 1647.[40]

In the spring the Indians were accustomed to plant corn and settle

---

[38] *Ibid.*, 227, 229; NYDH, IV, 103–105; Brodhead, *History of New York*, I, 354.
[39] NYCD, I, 151; XIII, 11–12; quotation in *Plymouth Colony Records*, X, 440.
[40] NYCD, I, 194–195; XIII, 11–13; NNN, 278; O'Callaghan, *History of New Netherland*, I, 274n.

down to a more sedentary life than in the winter hunting season. Under these conditions warfare was hazardous; if an enemy should destroy the cornfields before harvest time, starvation might follow in the months ahead. Toward the end of March, therefore, the Rockaway Indians approached the Dutch with an offer of peace, apparently on behalf of all the Long Island bands. Their proposal was accepted, and a treaty was concluded without delay.[41] Now that hostilities were ended on Long Island, where Dutch-Indian differences had not been as serious, Kieft tried to arrange a peace with the bands to the north and west, using the Long Island sachems as intermediaries. On April 22 Oratamin, the Hackensack sachem, appeared at the fort and made peace for his own and several neighboring communities. By the terms of this treaty all injuries were mutually forgotten and forgiven, either party promising to conduct itself peacefully toward the other. The Indians promised to warn the Christians about meditated hostilities on the part of bands not included in the compact and to refuse admittance of such Indians within their own tribal limits. Presents were exchanged in ratification of the treaty, but according to De Vries the Indians went away grumbling that the gifts they received were too few to wipe away all memory of the past. Kieft, they said, "could have made it, by his presents, that as long as he lived the massacre would never again be spoken of; but now it might fall out that the infant upon the small board would remember it." [42]

Many presents indeed were required to erase the memory of what had happened at the hands of the Swannekens just two months before. As someone remarked later, peace was concluded more through "the importunity of some than because it was generally expected that it would be durable." [43] The mainland bands had the same immediate need for peace as those on Long Island, but they and the Dutch both realized full well that the peace was in reality a truce. In July one of the New Jersey chiefs told De Vries that the younger braves were champing at the bit to commence hostilities again despite the peaceful inclinations of older men like himself. The chiefs, though he did not say so, were possibly restraining themselves only until after the harvest. At De Vries' request he crossed the river and repeated these things to Kieft. The director with his usual lack of finesse advised the sachem

---

[41] *NNN*, 229–232; *NYCD*, XIV, 44–45. De Vries mistakenly dates this episode twenty days earlier.

[42] *NNN*, 232; *NYCD*, XIII, 14.   [43] *NNN*, 278–279.

to "kill these young madcaps . . . and he would give him two hundred fathoms of *zeewan* [wampum]." The sachem was not interested, but he hinted broadly (and vainly) that a larger present might induce the warriors to calm themselves.[44]

When trouble did break out again, it was on a new front. Pacham, the Tankiteke sachem, had been going from village to village in the Westchester area and beyond, inciting the Wappinger bands to a general massacre. On August 7 the Wappinger proper near Poughkeepsie, who had never quarreled with the Dutch before, erupted with a series of attacks on the boats which plied regularly between Fort Orange and New Amsterdam. In all, the Dutch lost twelve persons killed or captured in these raids. Elsewhere, once the corn had ripened, other bands resumed hostilities and committed isolated murders. Four more boweries went up in flames across the river from New Amsterdam, and a report reached Boston that fifteen Dutchmen had lost their lives.[45]

To meet the new crisis Kieft was again forced reluctantly to call on the people for advice. This time, at their suggestion, he chose a panel of eight, who were subject to a popular veto. The Eight Men first met on September 15 and resolved to exclude from their number Jan Jansen Damen, another signer of the February 22 petition. Damen protested, as much against Kieft for allegedly procuring his signature by deceit as against his colleagues for expelling him, but in vain.[46] Once organized, the Eight Men resolved to wage war against all hostile Indians. The Long Island bands were to be left alone, except as the Dutch might enlist them against their brethren. The delegates voted to recruit as many men as possible, and Kieft lost no time in making necessary preparations. Colonists and company employees were armed and trained, and fifty English settlers, who were threatening to leave the province, were also enlisted. Command of this force was entrusted to Captain John Underhill, an ex-New Englander and a hero of the Pequot War of 1637.[47]

[44] *Ibid.*, 232–233.
[45] *Ibid.*, 279; *Winthrop's Journal*, II, 134; O'Callaghan, *History of New Netherland*, I, 282–283; Brodhead, *History of New York*, I, 346.
[46] *NYCD*, I, 193; XIII, 16; O'Callaghan, *History of New Netherland*, I, 282–285; Brodhead, *History of New York*, I, 364–365.
[47] *NNN*, 280; *NYCD*, I, 151; XIII, 16; O'Callaghan, *History of New Netherland*, I, 286, 420; Brodhead, *History of New York*, I, 365–366.

These preparations were made none too soon, for the war continued to spread. The Wecquaesgeek took up the hatchet again and attacked several families who had settled near the present New Rochelle. Aside from the devastation of property, eighteen persons lost their lives, including the exiled Anne Hutchinson and nearly all her family. Another New England refugee, Lady Deborah Moody, had scarcely settled with a group of Baptist followers at Gravesend, in Brooklyn, when Indians descended upon her house. Forty colonists had gathered here to defend themselves, and they managed to repel each attack. A third New England settlement, at Mespath or Newtown, was almost entirely destroyed. In New Jersey the Hackensack resumed hostilities on September 17 with an attack on the bowery at Newark Bay. A small garrison of six men and five boys, detailed to defend the place, barely escaped with their lives, and this settlement too was totally destroyed.[48]

No place outside New Amsterdam was safe, and even there a sentry was wounded at one of the outposts. Staten Island had not yet been attacked, but the colonists who remained there must have looked to the future with apprehension. Pavonia and Westchester—the surrounding mainland—were abandoned, and only a few spots were precariously occupied on Long Island. Even on Manhattan most of the farms were abandoned by their tenants, who felt safer under the very walls of the fort.[49] Many of the dispossessed colonists, including our informant De Vries, gave up altogether and returned to Holland. At least seven bands of Indians, which the colonists estimated at 1,500 warriors, were on the warpath. This figure was probably exaggerated, but opposite them the Dutch could muster only fifty or sixty soldiers and about 250 colonists with a very limited supply of ammunition. Conditions were truly deplorable, and the Eight Men on October 24 penned a letter to the Assembly of the Nineteen in Holland pouring

[48] *Winthrop's Journal*, II, 137–138, 276–277; *NNN*, 233–234, 334–335; *NYCD*, XIII, 16–17; Brodhead, *History of New York*, I, 366–368.

[49] If the seriousness of the situation as painted by contemporaries is accepted, a surprising event was the settlement of Hempstead, Long Island, in the midst of these hostilities. On December 13, 1643, the Rev. Robert Fordham and John Carman purchased land there from the Massapequa, Merric, and Rockaway Indians. The new town was attacked, however, the following spring. See Schultz, *Colonial Hempstead*, 10–11; John H. Morice, "Hempstead Indian Deeds," *Long Island Forum*, XII (1949), 203.

out their woes to a company which, it developed, was too poor to render any assistance.[50]

The Eight Men suggested applying to New England for 150 men and a loan of money. To such an extremity was New Netherland reduced that they were willing to mortgage the province to the English as security for the repayment of this sum. The plan was apparently shelved, but when the New Haven Colony alone was asked for one hundred men in October, it refused on the ground that it doubted the war's justification and that it could hardly make such a move without the concurrence of the other New England colonies. New Haven did promise, however, to supply the Dutch with corn and fodder to replace whatever the Indians might have destroyed.[51]

For the time being the Dutch military record was no more encouraging. On October 17 a council of leading military and political figures resolved to attack the Wecquaesgeek band, but nothing apparently happened. In December a party of soldiers and colonists crossed over to Staten Island and spent a night marching over it, only to find that the local Indians had anticipated their visit and fled. The men took some four hundred bushels of corn, burned the remainder, and then departed. A few days before the new year Kieft received word from the English settlers at Greenwich, who had submitted to New Netherland in 1642, that the Indians there had attacked a party of Christians. One condition of the town's allegiance was that the Dutch should give it protection. Kieft felt obliged, therefore, to answer its call and sent a force of 120 men. They arrived after an all-day boat trip from Manhattan and spent the whole night marching about in the surrounding hills, looking in vain for the enemy. Turning back toward the boats, the men passed through Stamford, where they were directed to a small party of Indians. In a surprise attack the Dutch killed or captured about twenty of them and then returned to New Amsterdam.[52]

Soon afterward a party of sixty-five men was sent out on a second expedition against the Wecquaesgeek, who reportedly possessed three

[50] *NYCD*, I, 141–142, 190–191; *Winthrop's Journal*, II, 138; Brodhead, *History of New York*, I, 369.

[51] *NNN*, 280; Charles J. Hoadly, ed., *Records of the Colony . . . of New Haven* (Hartford, 1857–1858), I, 116–117.

[52] *NNN*, 280–281; O'Callaghan, *Calendar of Historical MSS*, I, 87; Brodhead, *History of New York*, I, 386–387.

V. Governor Peter Stuyvesant. (Courtesy of The New-York Historical Society, New York City.)

VI. Governor Edmund Andros. (From *The Andros Tracts*, 1868.)

VII. Robert Livingston, secretary for Indian affairs. (Courtesy of Henry H. Livingston, Hudson, N.Y.)

VIII. Colonel Peter Schuyler, first mayor of Albany. (Courtesy of J. A. Glenn, Albany, N.Y.)

fortified villages. They managed this time to reach their destination, but the Indians were still elusive. Although the towns were more than strong enough to have withstood the present attacking force, the soldiers found them deserted. They burned two, reserving the third as a stronghold for themselves in case of retreat. Marching about thirty miles farther, the soldiers attacked a few Indian huts and then returned, having killed or captured only a handful of the enemy. More important, however, they burned a good deal of the natives' winter corn supply.[53]

The Dutch were aware that Penhawitz and his Canarsee band were behind at least part of the killing and burning on Long Island. At this time—about February 1644—it was therefore resolved to carry the war to the western Long Island bands. Under the command of La Montagne a party of 120 men landed at the head of Manhasset Bay and marched south toward the new village of Hempstead. The men split into two groups, with Underhill leading a small detachment of Englishmen against a minor Indian village and the rest proceeding toward a larger enemy concentration. Nothing is known of the ensuing battles except that the Dutch and English reportedly lost only one man killed and three wounded, whereas the Indians are said to have suffered about 120 deaths. As the Canarsee probably boasted less than 120 warriors to begin with, the vanquished enemy were very likely a combination of several bands.[54]

As soon as this expedition had returned, Captain Underhill was sent to Stamford to inquire further about the Indians in that quarter. The information he got was sufficient to warrant a second foray against them, and in March he sailed from New Amsterdam with a contingent of 130 men. Disembarking at Greenwich, they marched northwestward

[53] *NNN*, 281–282.

[54] *Ibid.*, 282; *NYCD*, XIV, 56; *Winthrop's Journal*, II, 161; cf. O'Callaghan, *History of New Netherland*, I, 299–300, and Brodhead, *History of New York*, I, 388–389. If the Indian village of "Matsepe," stated as the larger of the two goals, really meant the Canarsee village of Mespath as O'Callaghan and Brodhead affirm, it is strange that a Dutch force coming from New Amsterdam, directly across the East River, should travel all the way to Hempstead to reach it. For a discussion of this point and the alleged battle of Fort Neck, see Schultz, *Colonial Hempstead*, 39–41. O'Callaghan and Brodhead also bring in at this juncture a thoroughly suspicious tale, printed in *NYDH*, IV, 105–106, according to which Kieft, Van Tienhoven, and La Montagne revel in the atrocious butchery of some Indian captives. Whatever grain of truth lurks in this story is probably hidden there forever.

for a full day over snow-covered hills which in some places were so slippery as to require moving on all fours. In the evening they approached their destination, an Indian castle in what is now the town of Poundridge, Westchester County. It was composed of three rows of wigwams and nestled in a low pocket between the surrounding hills. There was a full moon which, in the words of a contemporary account, "threw a strong light against the hills so that many winter days were not brighter than it then was." When the soldiers drew close, they found the Indians already on guard, and it was decided to encircle and attack them without further ado. The Indians "demeaned themselves as soldiers and deployed in small bands," but they were hemmed in by the surrounding ring of musket fire. "In a brief space of time there were counted one hundred and eighty dead outside the houses. Presently none durst come forth, keeping within the houses, [and] discharging arrows through the holes." Then, following tactics which Underhill had adopted successfully against the Pequot, his men set fire to the bark wigwams. "The Indians tried every means to escape, not succeeding in which they returned back to the flames preferring to perish by the fire than to die by our hands." According to the Indians' own estimate more than five hundred of their number perished in this attack, and only eight men escaped, three of them seriously wounded. The victims were probably Tankiteke or Siwanoy, but a group of twenty-five Wappinger was also present for the purpose of celebrating a festival. The Dutch and English lost only one dead, although Underhill himself and several others were wounded.[55]

As late as the end of March the Indians continued to menace cattle on Manhattan, but the last two expeditions permanently weakened the bands that they had attacked. Soon after the Poundridge battle the sachems of four nearby bands arrived at Stamford to ask for peace, which Kieft granted on April 6. Nine days later the Matinecoc sachem made peace for some of the western Long Island bands, promising to remain aloof from the Canarsee and Rockaway, who were still hostile.[56] The recent Dutch *tours de force* were probably influential in bringing about these treaties, but the spring planting season very likely was just as responsible; none of the Indians hardest hit by the war were among those who sued for peace.

[55] *NNN*, 282–284; Bolton, "New York City in Indian Possession," 249, 311.
[56] *LONN*, 37; *NYCD*, XIII, 17–18; XIV, 56.

These successes, moveover, did little to improve conditions in New Amsterdam. Many bands were still on the warpath, and the officials were still out of money. Recourse to the Fatherland was limited because the West India Company faced insolvency after recent military reverses in South America. A bill of exchange drawn on the Holland directors for only 2,622 guilders was protested, and special duties had to be levied in June to raise money for the soldiers' wages. A bit of welcome aid came in July with the arrival of 130 company soldiers whom the Portuguese had expelled from Brazil. No use was made of them, however, and most of the year was spent in factional turmoil between Director Kieft and the Eight Men. The latter expected the company to pay for defending the colony as it had originally promised to do, whereas Kieft, seeing no support coming from Europe, endeavored to raise more money through arbitrary taxes.

On October 28 the Eight Men wrote a long letter to the Amsterdam chamber detailing the follies of Kieft's administration and explaining the situation around New Amsterdam as they saw it. In one breath they arraigned the governor for starting the war, and in the next they upbraided him for failing to prosecute it. While three to four hundred men rested in New Amsterdam, they complained, the Indians were suffered to store their fish and corn virtually unmolested. The enemy "continually rove around in parties, night and day, on the Island of Manhattans, killing our people not a thousand paces from the Fort; and things have now arrived at such a pass, that no one dare move a foot to fetch a stick of fire wood without an escort." Captured Indians who might have served as guides were given to the soldiers or sent as presents to the English governor of Bermuda. The most experienced soldiers, moreover, had been sent back to Holland. The delegates closed with an appeal for a new governor who could bring peace and for more colonists who would settle in organized villages under representative political institutions, "so that the entire country may not be hereafter, at the whim of one man, again reduced to similar danger." [57]

Meanwhile the States-General, after receiving an earlier memorial from the Eight Men, had ordered the company to do something about New Netherland. The directors replied with an expression of sympathy for the "miserable and desolate" colonists, but could think of no other expedient than a governmental donation of a million guilders. New

[57] *NYCD,* I, 209–213.

Netherland affairs were under discussion throughout 1644, and in December it was decided to recall Director Kieft and require him to justify his administration. Shortly afterward a company investigating committee submitted a full report on the province's condition with an urgent recommendation that it "be again reduced to peace and quietness." The advice which they attributed to Kieft, of utterly exterminating the enemy Indians, should by no means be adopted, the committee said, "not only because it is impossible and unchristianlike so to do, but it would not be advantageous to the Company to incur so great an expense as it requires on so uncertain a result and so small an appearance of profit." Therefore they urged adoption of the commonalty's recommendations: "to endeavor, by all possible means, to conciliate and to satisfy the Indians by recalling the Director and Council, who are responsible for that bloody proceeding of the 28th [*sic*] February, 1643." The new governor should be "endowed with sufficient qualities to promote, on the one side, the interests of the Company and the welfare of the Commonalty, and to maintain, on the other, good correspondence with the neighboring people, and especially with the Indians." Accordingly in the spring of 1645 Peter Stuyvesant, recently governor of Curaçao, was chosen to replace Kieft. Almost two years were permitted to elapse, however, before the company's new plans were implemented. The delay was owing to financial disagreements within the company itself, as well as more encouraging news from New Netherland.[58]

With the coming of warmer weather in 1645 some of the Indians again considered the expediency of making peace. Representatives of several unnamed bands appeared at New Amsterdam on April 22 and buried the hatchet amid great fanfare and firing of cannon. Many Indians were still hostile, however, and a specially assembled council resolved once more to enlist friendly natives against them. Toward the end of May a Matinecoc chief with forty-seven followers was sent out on this service, with comparatively minor results.[59]

Nothing accomplished so far had significantly diminished the scope of the war. Nevertheless Kieft was now encouraged enough to leave Manhattan Island, for the first time since he had assumed office in

---

[58] *Ibid.*, 141–142, 153; Brodhead, *History of New York*, I, 403–406, 413–416.
[59] O'Callaghan, *History of New Netherland*, I, 354–355; Brodhead, *History of New York*, I, 407–408; *NYCD*, XIV, 60.

1638, in order to negotiate a treaty with the Mohawk and Mahican at Fort Orange. He accomplished this in July, and on his return to New Amsterdam, safe and sound, the local bands began at long last to indicate a general desire for peace. On August 29 the terms of a proposed treaty were publicly read and approved, and on the next day an unprecedented assembly of Indian notables gathered at the fort "under the blue canopy of heaven in [the] presence of the Council of New Netherland and the whole community." Also in attendance, and adding significance to the recent negotiations at Fort Orange, were Mohawk ambassadors who had asked to attend as mediators and a Mahican sachem who had come on behalf of four Wappinger bands. The treaty was concluded with at least ten bands of Indians, from the Hackensack and Tappan west of the Hudson and the Canarsee on Long Island to the Wappinger in Dutchess County. The terms were simple. Both sides agreed to keep the peace and to resolve all grievances by negotiation between the governor and the respective sachems. Prompt justice should be accorded in case of murders involving both parties. The Indians promised never to approach the houses on Manhattan Island while armed, and the Dutch pledged themselves not to go, under arms, near any Indian dwellings without giving warning. The next day, August 31, 1645, a general day of Thanksgiving was proclaimed in New Amsterdam to celebrate the advent of a secure peace for the first time in five years.[60]

Close to a thousand Indians had probably lost their lives since 1640, and, during the war years at least, the white population of New Netherland had also declined, although this was owing more to emigration than to wartime casualties. For the Indians these losses could never be recovered, whereas among the Dutch the population and property losses were more than made up in the years immediately ahead. This statement tells only half the story, however. Kieft's policy of intimidation had been a failure, from whatever point of view it was regarded. The Indians were neither eradicated nor permanently cowed into submission, and despite their losses they were at least a potential threat to outlying colonists for more than a decade to come. Thus the policy and the war that it spawned failed to accomplish their objective. Whatever the surface appearances, moreover, the real danger to New

---

[60] *NYCD*, XIII, 18–19; O'Callaghan, *History of New Netherland*, I, 356–357; Brodhead, *History of New York*, I, 408–409.

Netherland was the rival imperialism of England and her neighboring colonies in America. Against this menace the only possible defense was a rapidly expanding population and a military establishment strong enough to sustain it. It is highly unlikely that Kieft or any other governor could have attained this end, but in any case the effect of his policy was just the opposite. Not only did the war discourage immigration, but it actually caused more people to leave the province than to enter it. Statistically, it is true, these losses were soon made up, but in another and more realistic sense they could never be recovered.

IV

The Perils of Coexistence

PETER STUYVESANT, who arrived at New Amsterdam in May 1647, was a much different man from his predecessor. Despite his wooden leg, acquired after a West Indian military engagement, Stuyvesant was constantly on the move, visiting places throughout the colony and as far afield as the West Indies, which also fell within his jurisdiction. Even more than Kieft, and in conformity with the company's wishes, Stuyvesant was a complete autocrat brooking no opposition within the province. Several of Kieft's subordinates, Van Tienhoven and La Montagne, for instance, were retained in office by the company, but there was no longer any question as to who called the tune. Stuyvesant's irascible temper and his stubbornness, particularly in 1664 at the time of the English conquest, come to mind almost as readily as the peg leg embroidered with silver bands; but, what is less well known, he was an able executive who could be flexible in the face of powers beyond his control. Riding roughshod over domestic opponents, he could assume the air of a holy martyr in dealings with the stiff-necked officialdom of New England. In view of the company's wish for a more or less benevolent despotism in New Netherland, Stuyvesant was probably the ablest governor it could have obtained. That the Amsterdam directors were of this opinion is indicated by his retention in office for seventeen years—and his eventual deposition was beyond their control.

The last years of Kieft's administration had been anticlimactic, and in 1647 affairs were still at low ebb after the Indian war. The entire province, Stuyvesant reported, could muster only 250 to 300 armed men, indicating a population of perhaps 1,200 souls. In less than a decade immigration probably tripled this figure, causing the older towns to grow and new ones to rise around them. Most of the newcomers settled on western Long Island, where villages had started in Kieft's time. By 1654 there were four towns, including Breukelen, on the site of modern Brooklyn, and half a dozen more were founded as far east as Oyster Bay. Beyond that point the Dutch made little effort to extend their jurisdiction, and the towns of East Hampton, Southampton, and Southold at the far end of the island continued in their affiliation with New England. Midway up the Hudson a village was established in 1652 at the Esopus, or modern Kingston. Staten Island and Pavonia were gradually returned to cultivation, but colonists were understandably reluctant to settle there in numbers. A group of Englishmen under Thomas Pell established themselves in 1654 at Pelham, near Anne Hutchinson's former home on Long Island Sound.

A period of uneasy calm had set in around New Amsterdam after the treaty of 1645, while Indians and colonists alike recuperated from the protracted dislocations of the war. The conflict itself had solved none of the old problems of coexistence, and loss of their lands threatened the natives more urgently than ever before. For either party to live with the other was an unpleasant assignment. This was particularly the case in the town of Hempstead, which complained in August 1647 that the neighboring Indians had combined with those on eastern Long Island in a plot to destroy them. The council sent Cornelis van Tienhoven to the far end of the island to investigate, but the alarm proved to be exaggerated if not altogether fanciful. At the same time there were rumblings from the Raritan band in New Jersey and the Matinecoc on Long Island concerning presents which were promised them at the end of the war and which remained unpaid.[1]

Despite mutual provocations no serious incident occurred until March 1649, when an unknown Indian murdered a colonist at Pavonia. The neighboring tribesmen took flight, apprehending another punitive expedition, but no such move was attempted. Instructions from home as well as bitter experience forbade Stuyvesant to embark upon a course of revenge like that of his predecessor. When the Indians found

[1] *NYCD*, XIV, 79; O'Callaghan, *Calendar of Historical MSS*, I, 112, and *History of New Netherland*, II, 36, 45.

a readiness on the part of the Dutch to negotiate, they willingly complied. Through the mediation of the Susquehanna, representatives of several local bands appeared in New Amsterdam in July to renew the peace and exchange tokens of their good intentions.[2]

Such treaties, laudable as they may have been, were only temporary expedients; they could not solve the basic points of contention between Indian and colonist. Most of the Long Island bands, moreover, were not included in the July pact, and Indian depredations continued there in both Dutch and English jurisdictions, with a resultant epidemic of "Indian nerves" among the settlers.[3] In the face of these alarms, partly real and partly imaginary, the colonists were thrown largely on their own resources. Stuyvesant was lax in providing them with arms and ammunition, in holding militia musters, and in taking other security precautions. The province's financial condition and an unwillingness to alarm the Indians probably go far to explain his inactivity. In their existing state of mind, he also mistrusted the citizens' intentions and may deliberately have withheld from them the means of taking direct action against Indian marauders. Some towns, like Gravesend, required their inhabitants to settle more closely together and keep well armed,[4] but the failure of provincial authorities to take more responsibility for defense became a constant popular grievance.

Stuyvesant himself had created a sounding board for such discontents in 1647. Finding himself in dire financial straits, he turned to the commonalty as Kieft had done twice before and chose a panel of nine men to act as a permanent advisory body. He had intended that the Nine Men should speak only when spoken to, but they soon disabused him of that notion and raised their voices on behalf of a thoroughgoing political reformation of the province. In July 1649 they drew up a remonstrance and sent it off with lengthy supporting documents to the States-General, hoping thereby to rid themselves of company proprietorship as well as arbitrary government. In the broadest sense the company itself was the target of this appeal, but Directors Kieft and Stuyvesant received their full measure of personal attention. Kieft had been lost in a shipwreck in 1647 while traveling home to face an

[2] *NYCD*, XIII, 25; O'Callaghan, *History of New Netherland*, II, 94–96.
[3] *Plymouth Colony Records*, IX, 209; John Lyon Gardiner, "Notes and Observations on the Town of East Hampton" (1798), *NYHSC, 1869*, 236; Adams, *History of Southampton*, 78–79.
[4] *NYCD*, XIV, 128–130.

angry directorate. But the memory of his war lived after him, and most of the citizens were determined that history should not repeat itself. The reluctance to provide for civil defense and a questionable involvement in the firearms traffic were only two of many counts in the popular indictment of Stuyvesant. These charges and the governor's replies to them were referred to an investigating committee of the States-General.[5] After months of sifting the evidence the committee submitted a report in April 1650 that called for a number of political reforms, including Stuyvesant's recall, but recommended the retention of the company proprietorship.

Indian affairs received the highest billing in the committee report, which explicitly condemned the forced contribution of 1639 and the events leading to the massacre in 1643. Jan Jansen Damen and Abraham Planck, two signers of the famous petition, were to be summoned to Holland to justify their action. Apparently Maryn Adriaensen had already purged himself during his trial several years before for attempting to murder Kieft. More important, the committee recommended that "the Director and Council shall in future be careful that [no war] be undertaken against the Aborigines of the country or neighbors of New Netherland" without the States-General's knowledge. In case misunderstandings arose, the authorities should use all peaceful means to remove them, keeping that body advised of the measures taken. The committee also noticed that "the people of New Netherland either are not obliged, or have themselves forgotten to possess and make use of arms necessary for their own defence." It recommended, therefore, that each man should be enrolled in a militia company and be required to possess the necessary weapons, which were to be stamped to prevent their sale. (This last precaution, already in practice, was necessary because of the arms traffic with the Indians.) Forts and magazines were to be kept in good repair—which was not presently the case—and settlements were to be formed compactly to aid in defense.[6]

[5] For the Petition of the Commonalty and supporting documents, including the Remonstrance or Representation of New Netherland, see *NYCD*, I, 259 ff. The best edition of the Remonstrance is in *NNN*, 293 ff. Van Tienhoven was sent over by Stuyvesant to argue for the defense. His answer to the Remonstrance is in *NYCD*, I, 422–432, and *NNN*, 359–377. For a narrative account of the controversy, see Brodhead, *History of New York*, I, ch. xv.

[6] *NYCD*, I, 388–391.

Perils of Coexistence

The Amsterdam directors resented the aspersions cast on their management and opposed most of the political changes as a matter of course. But as the other company chambers and the States-General appeared to favor these or similar reforms, the directors took refuge in procrastination. They granted a few of the most pressing demands, such as municipal government for New Amsterdam, but Stuyvesant continued to govern the province much as he had before.

Even before the report was issued, the States-General ordered Stuyvesant to furnish the inhabitants with guns for self-defense and permitted representatives of the Nine Men to purchase muskets in Holland for that purpose. Jacob van Couwenhoven, one of the delegates, accordingly bought a hundred guns, with ammunition in proportion, which he was authorized to distribute among the colonists. But when Van Couwenhoven returned home in June, Stuyvesant seized the weapons and allegedly sold some of them to the Indians, retaining the rest in his own possession.[7] At best this highhanded flouting of the States-General indicates how far Stuyvesant was willing to go in order to prevent another war. At worst his insubordination and reputed (but unproved) willingness to trust Indians with the guns ahead of his own colonists amount to near treason. Knowing that he had the backing of the Amsterdam chamber, Stuyvesant was prepared to follow his own course with little regard for either the commonalty or the States-General. This was a dangerous course, and in 1652 the States-General ordered his recall; but under the threat of a war with England, in which Stuyvesant's experience and military abilities were at a premium, they withdrew the order. Meanwhile the director continued his policy of unpreparedness. In November 1650 the Nine Men complained that it had been more than two years since the citizens were last under arms. Predicting as long a delay in the future if Stuyvesant were not compelled to act, they feared "that for divers reasons and from daily experience, the Indians will anticipate the Director and exact from us a woful inspection of our guns." The Holland directors promised in 1652 to send over limited quantities of arms and ammunition for defensive purposes, but there is no record of their being distributed.[8]

Meanwhile Indian incursions continued to multiply. In September 1651 the magistrates of Gravesend and Hempstead separately com-

[7] *Ibid.*, 382–383, 397, 438, 451, 455, 501.
[8] *Ibid.*, 451; cf. 455; XIV, 176.

plained to the Holland directors that Long Island or other Indians were continuing to slaughter their cattle and even were selling the meat in New Amsterdam as venison. They also complained of murders, robberies, and other outrages, which were not limited to Long Island. The year 1652 saw no less than four murders on Manhattan, and three occurred on Staten Island the next year. Stuyvesant demanded the murderers, but they were not forthcoming, and he seems to have taken no further action.[9]

Again the populace rose in wrath, but although they demanded positive action to prevent further incidents, there was no public call for measures of the Kieft variety. By the end of 1653 the Long Islanders, particularly those of English nationality, threatened to form an autonomous league in order to stem the loss of life and property. Lacking the power to control such a movement, Stuyvesant reluctantly called a convention of representatives from New Amsterdam and the seven New Netherland towns on Long Island. Meeting at New Amsterdam in December, the delegates once more protested at arbitrary government; but the immediate problem was that of Indian incursions. Confessing ignorance of the marauders' identity, they charged nevertheless that Stuyvesant heartlessly disregarded their plight by ascribing the acts to "Indians living at a great distance," who therefore were beyond his power to punish. Whatever the justice of this complaint, the colonists' appeals had a familiar ring which their frequent disavowals of Kieft's avenging policy did not obscure. Rightly or wrongly Stuyvesant may have preferred to incur the charge of neglect rather than furnish the inhabitants with the means of starting a new war. Such a course threatened far more damage to them, to the company, and to himself than the isolated incidents which had happened to date. Having heard the accusations against him, the governor now issued an angry counterblast and summarily dissolved the convention.[10]

From the Indian standpoint the incidents which had provoked this furor were unpremeditated. Each of them was undoubtedly the work of small groups or of single Indians motivated by a desire to rob or to avenge some real or pretended wrong. There is no indication that the tribesmen wanted war, which under the circumstances might have been disastrous for both parties. Moreover, the crisis now began to

[9] *Ibid.*, I, 497; II, 155–158; XIII, 30, 49.
[10] *Ibid.*, I, 551–552, 554; XIV, 234; Brodhead, *History of New York*, I, 570–575.

subside, almost as if the Indians recognized its gravity. In 1654 a single murder was reported, and for more than a year afterward peace reigned throughout this part of the colony.[11] Indeed, affairs were so quiet that Stuyvesant embarked in December 1654 on an official trip to the West Indies. He returned the following July and a few weeks later departed again, this time for the Delaware.

Land disputes had undoubtedly given rise to many of the earlier depredations. Since Kieft's administration the official practice had usually been for the company to purchase Indian lands before granting them to settlers. The English colonists on Long Island, however, generally came to the province, bought their land, and established towns on their own responsibility. Only after this process was complete did the Dutch authorities issue patents and assume jurisdiction over them.[12] As most of the Dutch on Long Island settled in what is now Brooklyn, where the Indian title had theoretically been purchased by Kieft, his successor had little occasion to buy lands there. But misunderstandings continued to arise with the Indians on this point. By the 1650's there was little room left in Brooklyn and Queens for the Indians to live the life of their ancestors; their continuing right of occupancy had become meaningless as European farmhouses and fields gradually hemmed them in. If the truth had been obscure before, they recognized now the awful consequences of the white invasion. As if to make their position more galling, these tribesmen began hearing from indiscreet settlers what the land now sold for in transactions between white men. Having received a mere pittance in comparison, they demanded additional payment, fully convinced that they had been victims of foul play. From the European standpoint most of these claims were baseless. The lands were bought in good faith, and in most cases the stipulated purchase price had long since been paid. But reference to written documents and talk of the sanctity of contract made little impression on the disillusioned tribesmen. In 1652 the Canarsee demanded payment for some lands at Flatbush which were under settlement and supposedly purchased long since. Stuyvesant bent over backward to be fair. Giving them the benefit of the doubt, he admitted that part of the tract might not have been included in the earlier deeds and ordered that it be purchased again.

[11] *NYCD*, XIII, 49; Brodhead, *History of New York*, I, 587–588.
[12] Thompson, *History of Long Island*, I, 142–143.

The directors in Holland, however, criticized this action, or at least the proposed purchase price, and objected to payment. As a result the nearby settlers were continually plagued with Indian unrest.[13]

Disputes of this nature fanned the flames of Indian discontent, particularly on Long Island. The colonists, looking about for someone to blame for their misfortunes, found no better target than Stuyvesant, whom they accused of stealing the lands from the Indians in the first place. The governor, not to be outdone, threw the same charge back at them, but his real point was that some of the colonists, by showing too much fear of the Indians, by cheating them, and by telling them the present values of real estate, had brought these troubles upon themselves.[14] These accusations shed more heat than light on the real sources of difficulty, but they tended to decline in frequency and vehemence as the number of Indian depredations fell off.

Land speculation was no less a factor on the New Netherland frontier than it was in other colonies. As early as the 1630's Wouter van Twiller had engrossed more property than he could hope to farm himself, and other persons followed his example, buying up vast tracts from the Indians around the perimeter of settlement. These purchases aroused no Indian antagonism at the time because the buyers had no more immediate intention of settling the lands than the natives had of vacating them. The company, however, viewed such transactions as a menace to the future development of the province. Most of them were not properly registered with the authorities, and they threatened to cut down appreciably the amount of land available for future settlement except on the speculators' terms. Furthermore, the speculators had bid up the price of land so much that the company was forced to pay more than had been customary in its own transactions with the Indians. After the Holland directors called for remedial action, a law was passed in July 1652 forbidding anyone to buy lands from the Indians except with the previous consent of either the Amsterdam chamber or the governor and council in New Netherland. The ordi-

[13] *NYCD*, XIV, 183; O'Callaghan, *History of New Netherland*, II, 194–195. For Indian complaints about the taking of their land, see *LONN*, 131, and the references in this and the following footnote. For further references to repeated purchase of the same land, see Brodhead, *History of New York*, I, 297, 410, 536–537, and Jasper Danckaerts, *Journal, 1679–1680*, ed. by Bartlett B. James and J. Franklin Jameson (New York, 1913), 57.

[14] *NYCD*, I, 497, 551–552, 554; XIV, 234.

nance also vacated a number of specific purchases, including some on Long Island which Van Twiller had granted to himself and his friends in 1636. Except for Van Twiller's grants none of them had been registered with the provincial secretary as the law required. In passing this ordinance, it should be emphasized, the authorities were motivated by no desire to preserve Indian rights. Their purpose, in fact, was to speed up settlement by offering the lands gratis to incoming farmers. From the standpoint of colonial administration it was an enlightened measure, but it ran directly counter to the interests of the native inhabitants.[15]

One of the greatest sources of mischief in Indian relations has been the native's weakness for alcohol. The Indian was as unprepared to resist this temptation in the first place as he was to withstand its effects once the temptation was satisfied. Indian drunkenness was a constant source of annoyance and danger in New Netherland, just as it was on other frontiers. Street brawls and altercations between the races—even a great proportion of the frontier depredations—were probably traceable in large measure to this cause. Moreover, it hastened the disintegration of Indian society itself as native villages became scenes of drunken disorder and mayhem. For this reason the sachems in time became the most outspoken advocates of prohibition in the Indian country.

The liquor traffic in New Netherland, which began with Henry Hudson, was probably a constant feature of interracial relations from that time on. But in the absence of the earliest laws the first mention of its regulation occurs during the troubled year of 1643, when the director and council forbade it and prescribed a schedule of fines for violators. The law was unsuccessful, and there is little or no evidence of its enforcement. In November 1646 the prohibition was renewed, with penalties ranging from five hundred guilders for the first offense to a double fine, arbitrary punishment, banishment, and responsibility for all damage caused by the sale for the second offense. Drunken Indians nevertheless were an everyday sight, even on Manhattan Island, and three more renewals followed in 1647 and 1648.[16]

The offenders were to be found in nearly all walks of life: Indian traders who carried brandy, wine, and beer as part of their stock in trade, dispensing it at their homes or in the Indian country; tavern-

---

[15] *Ibid.,* XIII. 33; *LONN,* 130–133.   [16] *LONN,* 34, 52, 64, 95, 100.

keepers who served both races with little discrimination; and ordinary farmers or townsmen who took this way of supplementing their normal incomes. The stuff that they meted out to the Indians was usually of the lowest quality in the first place and was frequently watered down as well—particularly if it was not to be consumed on the premises where the fraud could immediately be detected. Whatever the quality of the liquor served, the Indians' weakness for it was a constant temptation to those who were willing to turn a dishonest guilder by accommodating them.

The chief wonder lies less in the universal prevalence of the traffic than in the repeated passage of ordinances to prevent it, while at the same time almost nothing was done to enforce them. Part of the answer lay in the difficulty of proving guilt when many people were implicated and Indian testimony was invalid in court. There is no record of a conviction in this part of the province before 1654, when complaints of the excesses committed by drunken natives led to another renewal. Such Indians were now to be arrested and imprisoned until they divulged their source of supply. Although the testimony that they gave was legally sufficient to convict the violators, only one conviction is recorded—on the day the law was enacted.[17] A thorough enforcement of this prohibition, like that of a later day, would have implicated nearly half the populace; the officials had neither time, money, nor inclination to pursue it that far.

Even more serious than the liquor traffic from the standpoint of the white man was that in guns and ammunition. Every European power with territories in America seriously deplored the sale of firearms to the Indians. The possible result of such action—use of the guns against the very persons who had furnished them—was sufficiently obvious to everyone, and all colonies took steps in the early years to check if not to abolish this trade. They failed in the first place because of the same spirit of greed and lawlessness which made a mockery of the liquor regulations. Just as important in the long run was international rivalry, involving most of these colonies in a competition which none of them individually was able to control. The Indians developed such a craving for firearms that profiteers who catered to it were to be found in every colony, totally oblivious to considerations of national policy or public welfare. The colony or individual who uprightly refused to engage in the arms traffic therefore only drove away

---

[17] *Ibid.*, 182–183; O'Callaghan, *Calendar of Historical MSS*, I, 140.

trade to those who were less conscientious. In areas such as the lower Hudson, where Indians acquired guns relatively late, there was little international competition, trade itself was comparatively unimportant, and the enforcement of prohibitions was somewhat easier. On the other hand, the Mohawk and Mahican as well as the Susquehanna farther south profited by a three-way competition between English, Dutch, and French or Swedish traders. Despite the repeated charges and countercharges, firearms found their way into native hands in the colonies of all four powers.[18]

In 1624 it was said of the New Netherland Indians that "whole troops run before five or six muskets," although they had lost much of their original shock at seeing them fired. There were no guns in evidence among the Mohawk and Mahican at the time of Van Krieckenbeeck's misadventure in 1626, nor is there anything but curiosity about them when Bogaert made his visit in 1634–1635.[19] By 1639, however, a change seems to have occurred, and after that date there are many references to Iroquois armament. Probably the Mahican were similarly favored. Concerning the Algonquian bands farther south, the Eight Men reported in 1643 that they too were "well provided with guns, powder and lead," which they bought from private traders or took from their murdered victims. An ordinance of 1645 essentially repeats the statement, attributing the supply by implication to the Indians at Fort Orange. Both assertions are questionable, for all the specific references to Indian armament during the war mention nothing more volatile than bows and arrows. The great differences in battle casualties, even if exaggerated, between the white and Indian contenders and the difficulties of supply and repair indicate that it was practically impossible for these tribesmen to have been effectively armed with guns. One of the most commonly assigned reasons for the outbreak of this war, furthermore, was the alleged resentment of the coastal bands at being denied a share of the firearms which then were being sold to the Mohawk and Mahican.[20] Fortunately for the Dutch colonists, the coastal Indians acquired guns in quantity only after the war had drawn to a close in 1645.

Because of their position relative to the Iroquois and the Iroquois

[18] See Hunt, *Wars of the Iroquois*, 165 ff.
[19] *NNN*, 73, 84–85, 139 ff.; Hunt, *Wars of the Iroquois*, 166–167.
[20] *NYCD*, I, 140, 190; *LONN*, 47; Ruttenber, *Indian Tribes of Hudson's River*, 100n.; *NNN*, 274; O'Callaghan, *History of New Netherland*, I, 224; Brodhead, *History of New York*, I, 308.

position relative to the main fur supply, the Dutch unquestionably led in the northern arms trade. Whether they began the traffic is unknown, although an authority friendly to Kieft accused Rensselaerswyck traders of carrying it on after the Mohawk had bought and acquired a taste for guns in New England. Estimates have gone much higher, but the Iroquois probably possessed no more than four hundred guns by the mid-1640's, nearly all of them in the hands of the Mohawk, and these were subject to almost immediate damage in the hands of their unaccustomed owners. Virtually all of these weapons were furnished by the Dutch. The English provided effective competition only when conditions from the Indian point of view were particularly bad at Fort Orange, and the Dutch were careful to hold such times to a minimum. The French seldom sold firearms to the Iroquois because the two were usually at odds, but they did supply them to the Huron and other Iroquois enemies.[21]

Attempts at regulating the arms traffic in New Netherland were many, but for reasons already suggested they were uniformly unsuccessful. The first indication that such a trade existed appears in an ordinance of 1639 forbidding it. It may be coincidental that the fur trade was thrown open at this time, but the reason given for the enactment was that company servants and private colonists alike had presumed to sell guns, powder, and lead to the Indians contrary to previous commands of the States-General and the company. Such sales were now prohibited unequivocally on penalty of death. There was little attempt to enforce the law, and to do so would probably have ruined the trade at Fort Orange and alienated the Indians. The severity of the penalty may also have defeated itself by discouraging enforcement. In 1641 the authorities at Rensselaerswyck, where most of the violations took place according to company sources, forbade the traffic within the domain, but lowered the penalty to a fine of one hundred guilders and deportation to Holland. Only one man apparently was convicted under this law. The prosecutor held that he had forfeited his life under the general ordinance of 1639, but the local court eventually let him off with an accumulation of fines for several offenses.[22]

[21] *NNN*, 274. The best discussion of Iroquois armament and arms supply is in Hunt, *Wars of the Iroquois*, 9–10, 166 ff.

[22] *LONN*, 18–19; *VRBM*, 565–566; *RCM*, 34–39, 44, 77, 96, 124, 169–170; Nissenson, *Patroon's Domain*, 203 ff.; cf. Hunt, *Wars of the Iroquois*, 167–168.

The failure of traders to heed these injunctions and of the officials to enforce them led to international complications. In September 1644 the commissioners of the New England confederation forbade the sale of arms and ammunition to Indians in any of the member colonies and recommended, further, that each colony prohibit the sale of these commodities to the Dutch, French, "or to any other that do commonly trade the same w[i]th Indians." At least one colony, Connecticut, passed such a ban the next month. Similarly a protest from the king of France at contraband trade on the upper Hudson was partly responsible for a re-enactment in February 1645 of the earlier Dutch ban.[23] Two years later, when the New England commissioners wrote to congratulate Stuyvesant on his arrival, they took the opportunity also to point out the "dangerous liberty" taken by many Dutchmen in selling arms and ammunition to the Indians. This occurred not only at Fort Orange, they said, but on eastern Long Island, the Connecticut River, Narragansett Bay, and other places within the English jurisdiction. The Dutch might have laws to prevent this traffic, the commissioners remarked; they themselves, however, had found that it could only be eradicated with "constant care and severe execution."[24]

On May 28, 1648, Stuyvesant suddenly broke with precedent and began to enforce the prohibitions which had been on the books for nearly a decade. On this date he arrested the armorer at Fort Amsterdam for selling company guns to private traders. The frightened prisoner then accused Joost Teunisen and Jacob Reynsen of repeatedly bribing him to sell them arms. The arrest of these two led to evidence against Jacob Jansen Schermerhorn and his brother, traders at Fort Orange, who were soon brought down the river to face similar charges. Reynsen, it appeared, had been a middleman, procuring guns at New Amsterdam and selling them up the river to the Schermerhorns, who in turn sold them to the Indians. When the men were put on trial, Jacob Schermerhorn and Reynsen were convicted of violating the ordinance of 1645 and according to its provisions were sentenced to death. The commonalty were shocked at this unwonted vigor in enforcing the law, and some of them succeeded in having the sentence commuted to banishment for five years and confiscation of their

---

[23] *Plymouth Colony Records,* IX, 21–22; James H. Trumbull and Charles J. Hoadly, eds., *Public Records of the Colony of Connecticut (1636–1776)* (Hartford, 1850–1890), I, 113–114; *LONN,* 47.

[24] *Plymouth Colony Records,* IX, 107.

property. Even this was too severe for some private traders and "respectable Burghers" of New Amsterdam, and at their insistence Stuyvesant again relented by lifting the requirement of banishment. The two men lost their property, however, which in the case of Reynsen amounted to more than $15,000. The armorer for his part was sentenced to a year's work in the company forge, and Stuyvesant arbitrarily detained Teunisen in prison despite insufficient evidence to prosecute him.[25]

Meanwhile the director heard reports that Dutch traders, specifically including Govert Loockermans, one of the Nine Men, were selling arms and ammunition to the Indians of eastern Long Island and were inciting them against the English. On the same May 28 he requested Governor Theophilus Eaton of New Haven to check the truth of these charges, promising to punish the offenders if their guilt were established. Stuyvesant also wrote this day to Commissary Andries Hudde on the Delaware, where Loockermans had also gone to trade. Noting that Governor Printz of New Sweden had complained against Loockermans for selling contraband goods in that region too, Stuyvesant asked Hudde to arrest the trader if he uncovered positive evidence of his guilt. Soon afterward the authorities seized a cargo belonging to Loockermans on suspicion that it contained contraband and held a lengthy investigation into his widespread activities. At the trader's request three men swore that they had sailed along the Long Island and Connecticut coasts with him in the fall of 1647, on which voyage the only contraband transactions were three sales or gifts of powder. For one reason or another Loockermans seems to have escaped trial in New Netherland. He was less fortunate at Hartford, however, where he was apprehended on a similar charge and forfeited a bond of £200 by failing to appear in court.[26]

The two cases above were merely the most prominent, and during the summer of 1648 Stuyvesant pushed his enforcement campaign to the hilt. Arrests were made, inquiries were initiated into suspicious activities and personalities, and contraband goods were seized. In

[25] *NNN*, 345–346, 369–370; *NYCD*, I, 326–328, 335, 337, 342, 345, 501; XIV, 88–89; O'Callaghan, *Calendar of Historical MSS*, I, 117–118; *History of New Netherland*, II, 62–64.

[26] *New Haven Colony Records*, I, 522–523; *NYCD*, XII, 59; XIV, 94; O'Callaghan, *Calendar of Historical MSS*, I, 117–118; *History of New Netherland*, II, 63; *Plymouth Colony Records*, IX, 143, 173, 176–178, 180, 183.

August the ordinance of 1645 was renewed. Seemingly the director was determined to reverse the trend of Dutch officialdom and to exterminate a trade which was putting his nation in bad odor with its neighbors. Despite his efforts the trade went on, apparently as usual.[27] Thorough enforcement proved impossible, and, to make matters worse, Stuyvesant was forced by his superiors and by the necessities of the fur trade to play a double game.

When the Amsterdam directors were apprised of the persistence with which the Indians demanded guns and ammunition, they feared that a complete refusal might stir up another war. As this was unthinkable, they advised the governor in April 1648 "to supply the tribes very sparingly" with these commodities and through company officials rather than private traders.[28] Stuyvesant received this message during the summer, in the midst of his enforcement campaign. At about the same time a petition arrived from the traders at Rensselaerswyck asking for such permission before the Indians murdered them in retaliation for withholding arms. Under this pressure Stuyvesant relented, and in August he secretly ordered a case of guns from Europe. When these reached New Amsterdam in April 1649, they were landed and delivered to the company commissary without the necessary formalities, but in open view so that the action became common knowledge. Immediately a storm of criticism broke out, and Stuyvesant was accused of participating in the forbidden trade himself at the very time he was prosecuting others for that offense. The charge was probably untrue, but appearances favored it. He may have procured the guns for the Indians at Fort Orange according to instructions, but both he and the company directors steadfastly denied it, even to each other. When the charge of personal trading was aired, Stuyvesant displayed his instructions and attempted to explain away the shipment by saying that, as he was unable to secure enough guns to satisfy the Indians, he was importing muskets for the colonists instead. The director at home were unaware of this shipment, but when they did hear of it, they jumped to the same conclusion as the commonalty and reprimanded the governor for letting personal greed ensnare him in a public

---

[27] O'Callaghan, *Calendar of Historical MSS*, I, 118–120; *NYCD*, XIV, 88; *New Haven Colony Records*, I, 528; *LONN*, 101; *Plymouth Colony Records*, IX, 113.

[28] *NYCD*, XIV, 83.

scandal.[29] Whatever Stuyvesant's intention, his career as a contraband buster was plainly compromised, and he gave up the task of enforcing the troublesome law. In July 1649 he authorized the payment of a gun, powder, and lead to the Wecquaesgeek Indians in a land transaction and five days later gave a gun to Oratamin, the Hackensack sachem, in confirmation of the newly concluded Indian treaty.[30]

The investigating committee of the States-General which reported on New Netherland affairs in April 1650 recommended the punishment of all persons who had illegally sold arms and ammunition to the Indians. On the other hand, it agreed that "this evil" had now reached such a stage that it could not be forbidden without danger of war. For the future, therefore, the provincial government should see that no contraband was sold except by its order, "the guns to be charged at 6 guilders, the pistols at 4 guilders, the pound of powder at six stivers." In time, the committee hoped, the trade might be cut off altogether, although it gave no convincing ground for this optimism. In their reply to the committee's report the company directors opposed giving private persons "so much latitude" for the present. They suggested instead, as they had to Stuyvesant two years before, that the Indians be supplied "with a sparing hand . . . by the Director and Council, with knowledge of circumstances and only when necessary." They were also dubious about the committee's price schedule, "inasmuch as the Indians will readily purchase guns in the spring, @ 120 guilders, and a pound of powder, @ 10 or 12 guilders."[31] This exchange, incidentally, suggests the tremendous profits which induced traders to defy the law so consistently.

The committee report had little effect on the company's subsequent arms policy. Political and military expediency continued to guide its decisions, and administration in New Netherland was tempered by economic considerations as well. The charge that Stuyvesant sold to the Indians some of the guns ordered by the States-General for the colonists' defense is strengthened by other complaints, all of them indicating that the arms traffic had become another facet of his appeasement policy toward the Indians. The English settlers at Grave-

---

[29] *NNN*, 344–345, 368–370; *NYCD*, I, 335, 337, 342, 345, 373–374, 501; XIV, 119, 124; O'Callaghan, *Calendar of Historical MSS*, I, 122; *History of New Netherland*, II, 64–65, 92–93.

[30] *NYCD*, XIII, 24–25.   [31] *Ibid.*, I, 388–389, 392.

send, among others, gave the Canarsee Indians some stamped guns in payment for land, and when a complaint was lodged with the provincial authorities, they reportedly sanctioned the act and refused to intervene. In September 1651 the English at Southampton, Long Island, reported that Dutch traders had been so active there that the Indians were as well armed as they. In the same month the magistrates of Hempstead and Gravesend ascribed most of the Indian depredations in their respective towns to the arms traffic, by which the natives had become "obstinate and daring enemies." [32]

It was typical that some of these remonstrants, particularly the Gravesend officials, were at the same time supplying the natives with arms themselves. All agreed that the traffic was pernicious, but no one wanted to be the first to stop. In 1652 the company directors replied to colonists' complaints by sending over an ordinance against the sale of arms by private traders. It was not enforced, however, and at Fort Orange if not elsewhere private traders carried on business as usual despite protests from the authorities at Rensselaerswyck. [33]

Taking notice of the latitude with which Stuyvesant carried out their restrictive policy, the directors admonished him in June 1653 to hold this trade to a minimum. He must take care, they cautioned, "that by such connivance not a larger quantity of ammunition is sold to the savages, than each requires for provisioning his household and for gaining his livelihood, that this savage and barbarous people may not at some future day take up and turn these weapons against us, with more than too many of which, as we regret to learn, they have already been supplied by smugglers and evil minded persons." Incoming ships must be examined for contraband, and smugglers and illegal dealers prosecuted "strictly in accordance with the . . . placats without mercy." [34] Stuyvesant, however, continued to be more impressed with the positive than the negative results of the traffic, and he was led by Mohawk demands to enact a special ordinance on their behalf in February 1654. These tribesmen "are now our good friends," the ordinance pointed out, and to deny them armaments at Fort Orange would only drive them to the English. If they succeeded in obtaining

---

[32] *Ibid.*, 449; II, 155, 157; *Plymouth Colony Records*, IX, 209.

[33] *NYCD*, I, 501, 524; XIV, 166, 176; *LONN*, 128. For the single prosecution of this period see *RCM*, 48 ff.

[34] *NYCD*, XIV, 206.

them there, the whole fur trade, along with Mohawk friendship, would soon be diverted from New Netherland, "a circumstance which in this dangerous situation would bring more and greater misfortune on this province." It was "proper and highly necessary," therefore, to accommodate the tribe with "a moderate trade in ammunition." This was to be sold them through Rutger Jacobsen, a local magistrate, "but as sparingly and secretly as possible." [35]

Meanwhile the excessive liberties taken by Dutch traders within and without the province embroiled Stuyvesant in constant disputes with neighboring colonies. In the case of New England these quarrels were a matter of particular concern because of the wide disparity in population and power between that region and New Netherland. In 1650 the latter's population had increased to about 1,500, but at the same time New England, which often acted as a unit in external affairs, numbered nearly 30,000. The fact that at least a third of New Netherland's population was English merely heightened the disproportion. At a time when Anglo-Dutch relations were worsening both in Europe and America, the greatest diplomatic ingenuity was called for on the part of the Dutch governor. Stuyvesant could be tractable as well as firm under these conditions, and in fact he was accused of overplaying his hand in attempting to conciliate the next-door colossus.

The course of Indian relations in New England was no more placid than among the Dutch, and the English colonists were in frequent apprehension of Indian outbreaks from the time of their first arrival until the turn of the century. Thus they were particularly sensitive to the Dutch practice of selling firearms to these potential enemies. New England had its own contraband traders, but as the fur trade diminished in importance there, the number of such persons declined and the officials were at liberty to enforce prohibitions more strictly. After the commissioners' gentle admonition to Stuyvesant in 1647 had apparently proved unavailing, they warned him again the next year of the danger to all nationalities of continuing to arm the Mohawk as the Dutch were doing at Fort Orange.[36]

Meanwhile another and more serious charge was leveled by Governor Eaton of New Haven, who in a letter to Stuyvesant in November

---

[35] *Ibid.*, XIII, 35–36. For an example of such a sale see *FOBCM*, I, 175.
[36] *Plymouth Colony Records*, IX, 113.

1647 accused Cornelis van Tienhoven of attempting by "a slanderous report" to provoke trouble between Long Island Indians and his colony. Furthermore, Eaton charged, the Dutch governor himself had tried to incite the stronger northern tribes against the English when he had visited them recently at Fort Orange. Eaton had only Indian testimony to substantiate this charge, as he admitted to John Winthrop of Massachusetts, but pointed out that there was apt to be little else in affairs of this nature. Stuyvesant did not choose for a time to dignify either the accusation or the man who made it by sending a direct reply. Instead he wrote in an injured tone to the deputy governor at New Haven, implying that the charge was groundless,[37] and reserved an explicit denial for a letter to Winthrop the following April. Writing painfully in English, he expressed sorrow that his personal reputation had been wounded and his

reall intentions of mutuall amitie and good will . . . in parte obstructed . . . [by] scandalous reportes . . . of my indeauours to raise the Mohocke Indians against the English . . . it being soe farre from the rules and principles of Christianitie and Charitie . . . to haue a thought thereof, much more to put in practise such a diuilish and wicked deuice; but according to my bownden duty to God and my neighbour, att my being att our fort of Aurania [Orange] I reallie indeauoured to establish a firme peace, not only betwixt the Mohocks and all the Indians there & us here . . . [but also] betwixt them and my brethren the English and Ffrench, w[hi]ch was for present well accepted . . . [by] them.[38]

Governor Eaton's attitude toward his neighbor did not improve, and when Stuyvesant asked him a few months later for evidence concerning contraband traders, Eaton curtly admonished him to enforce his own laws. He was willing, however, to forward additional reports of anti-English activities by Dutchmen among the Indians in his jurisdiction. Both governors had much to gain and nothing to lose by cooperating in these matters, but Eaton's suspicions repeatedly frustrated any joint action, and eventually Stuyvesant gave up asking for it.[39]

This is not to deny the truth of all of Eaton's charges or to claim

[37] *New Haven Colony Records*, I, 515, 518, 521.
[38] *NYCD*, XIII, 23.
[39] *New Haven Colony Records*, I, 523–524, 528–529; Brodhead, *History of New York*, I, 478–479.

that English resentment was groundless. There is no question about the contraband dealings of Dutch traders, and they were probably not above trying to eliminate English competitors and law enforcers by arousing the Indians against them. But these were private individuals who acted without Stuyvesant's backing or knowledge. It would have been suicidal as a matter of official policy to instigate hostilities with New England, and no one was more aware of the fatal disparity of strength between the two regions than he. For this very reason, however, it would have been natural in the face of deteriorating relations to seek assistance from the Indians or anyone else if hostilities should break out. So much smoke indicated a fire, but there is no good evidence that Stuyvesant was doing more than lining up allies in case of attack.

There is concrete evidence, moreover, that the director was trying to form an anti-Indian alliance with the English at the same time. As Indian depredations began to multiply around New Amsterdam, it was arguable that they constituted a greater threat than the English. Short of a full understanding with New England, which was probably too much to expect, nothing could be more wholesome from the Dutch point of view than an alliance with her against the Indians on the one hand and a defensive pact with the Indians on the other in case the first should miscarry. This consideration may conceivably go as far to explain the alternate prohibition and connivance in the arms traffic, both at Fort Orange and around New Amsterdam, as simple appeasement or the possibility of losing the fur trade. Throughout this period Stuyvesant attempted to conciliate all parties—the English, the troublesome Indians around New Amsterdam, and the powerful and profitable Mohawk at Fort Orange—in order to avoid a war which the Dutch were totally unprepared to fight. To this end he proposed to Winthrop in May 1648 an offensive and defensive alliance against Indian enemies and a personal meeting with him and Governor William Bradford of Plymouth in order to foster a good understanding between the two nationalities. Winthrop replied favorably, but Bradford's infirmity and other complications prevented a meeting that year. As any formal agreement with the confederated colonies required approval by the commissioners of that confederation negotiations revolved around them. They found it inconvenient to meet at Hartford during 1648 and 1649, however, and Stuyvesant was unwilling to travel any farther. When he proposed a conference with Governor Eaton at New Haven, his efforts were promptly discouraged.[40]

The commissioners had, meanwhile, complained a second time of the arms traffic. As Stuyvesant apparently did not intend to prohibit it, they said, the English henceforth would seize any contraband items they found on Dutch ships within the New England jurisdiction. Stuyvesant returned an immediate answer, deprecating the arms traffic and protesting with some truth at the time that he had done all in his power to prevent it. He agreed wholeheartedly, moreover, with their intention of searching for contraband.[41] The English had also complained of trade restrictions at New Amsterdam, and when neither grievance was abolished, they imposed restrictions of their own. As early as 1647 Rhode Island, New England's unloved stepdaughter, had forbidden foreign nationals to trade with the Indians in her jurisdiction. In August 1649 the commissioners announced a similar ban for the confederated colonies of Massachusetts, Plymouth, Connecticut, and New Haven. Basing their action on the arms traffic, Connecticut and Massachusetts individually followed suit with laws of their own.[42]

In the midst of these difficulties the commissioners announced a meeting at Hartford in September 1650, and Stuyvesant went there to meet them. After considerable argument the two parties chose arbitrators to negotiate the outstanding issues between them pending a final settlement in Europe. The arbitrators' award, since called the Treaty of Hartford, was issued on September 29. Its principal accomplishment was to fix a boundary between the English and the Dutch. The line bisected Long Island at Oyster Bay, and on the mainland it ran twenty miles northward from Greenwich Bay. The Dutch furthermore were permitted to retain their plot of land around Fort Good Hope at Hartford.[43] Stuyvesant lingered at Hartford, still hoping to

[40] *Winthrop's Journal*, II, 342–343; O'Callaghan, *History of New Netherland*, II, 99–101; Isabel M. Calder, *The New Haven Colony* (New Haven, 1934), 190.
[41] *Plymouth Colony Records*, IX, 113–115; O'Callaghan, *History of New Netherland*, II, 103–104.
[42] John R. Bartlett, ed., *Records of the Colony of Rhode Island and Providence Plantations* (Providence, 1856–1865), I, 153, 243, 279; *Plymouth Colony Records*, IX, 148–149; *Connecticut Colonial Records*, I, 197–198; Nathaniel B. Shurtleff, ed., *Records of the Governor and Company of the Massachusetts Bay* (Boston, 1853–1854), III, 208–209.
[43] *Plymouth Colony Records*, IX, 188–190.

conclude an alliance against the Indians. As the English were far more numerous than the Dutch, he proposed that they should bring twice as many men into the field in case of hostilities. The commissioners would agree to this only if they were permitted a double vote in questions of proclaiming war or peace, but this stipulation would have taken such decisions completely out of Dutch hands. Thus Stuyvesant was unable to accept it on his own authority, and further consideration was deferred until consultation could be had with the respective mother countries. In April 1652 the company directors advised Stuyvesant that in case of emergency he might form a league with New England; but under no circumstances should the English be given a preponderance that would compromise Dutch honor. In Europe, meanwhile, similar political and religious institutons failed to prevent a growing commercial antagonism between the Netherlands and Cromwellian England, the two greatest maritime powers in the world. War broke out in the spring of 1652, and four months after they had sanctioned an Anglo-Dutch alliance against the Indians, the directors advised Stuyvesant to combine with the latter in case of an English attack on New Netherland.[44] The Dutch had no thought of undertaking hostilities themselves in America, and Stuyvesant wrote to New England and Virginia expressing a desire for neutrality.

The war only intensified New England suspicions of Dutch machinations among the Indians. In March 1653 Uncas, the Mohegan sachem in Connecticut and a steadfast English ally, spread reports that his enemies the Narraganset were plotting with the Dutch to attack New England. The commissioners thereupon went into special session to examine the charges. Their meetings, in fact, became a clearing point in the months ahead for multiplying rumors of Dutch duplicity and hideous plots to wipe out the English settlements. The Narraganset sachems were closely interrogated, especially as one of them had recently paid a visit to New Amsterdam. The sachems' denials appear convincing today, but they failed to ease the tension which gripped southern New England, and the commissioners drew up a lengthy indictment of Dutch actions in recent years. That the confederation did not go to war with New Netherland at this point was owing almost entirely to the government of Massachusetts, which approved the commissioners' indictment but recommended that Stuyvesant be allowed to

[44] O'Callaghan, *History of New Netherland*, II, 155; *NYCD*, XIV, 166, 186.

clear himself before hostilities were undertaken. The Bay Colony had had relatively little direct contact with the Dutch, and it was Connecticut and New Haven who favored carrying fire and sword to exterminate New Netherland as soon as possible. Stuyvesant meanwhile had not waited for an invitation to answer the charges brought against him. He immediately and categorically denied the existence of any plot and offered to come to Boston if that were necesary in order to prove it. The commissioners chose instead to follow an alternative suggestion which the desperate governor had thrown out, and appointed three delegates to go to New Amsterdam and investigate the reports for themselves. At the same time they sent him an ultimatum demanding "speedy and Just Satisfaction for all former greivances, and due cecuritie for the future." [45]

The three ambassadors were fully aware of their superior bargaining power. No sooner had they arrived at New Amsterdam on May 22 than they proposed a virtual trial of Stuyvesant and Van Tienhoven, to be held in New England. When the director declined this honor, they suggested holding it at Flushing or Hempstead, where the inhabitants were as English as Bostonians and where Captain John Underhill had already raised the standard of revolt. Stuyvesant was so eager to conciliate that he agreed to this plan, provided three Dutchmen sit with the Englishmen and the proceedings be held in accordance with Dutch law. The New Englanders flatly rejected these conditions and prepared to leave. Stuyvesant offered again to negotiate a general agreement, including an alliance against mutual Indian enemies, but this overture was also rejected and the agents departed, leaving a letter behind which threatened the Dutch with dire consequences should New England suffer any further injury. On the way home they stopped at Flushing, Stamford, and New Haven, gathering testimony against the Dutch from nearly every disaffected Indian or Englishman whom they encountered. The most damning evidence they could produce was the testimony of several persons who had been told by Stuyvesant that "hee had noe hand in any such plott; but confessed that in case any English should come against him then hee would strengthen himselfe

[45] *Plymouth Colony Records,* X, 3–34 (quotation from p. 28), 426–427; Brodhead, *History of New York,* I, 550–552; Dixon Ryan Fox, *Yankees and Yorkers* (New York, 1940), 91–94. For the most extreme statement of English charges see the pamphlet, "The Second Part of the Amboyna Tragedy," in O'Callaghan, *History of New Netherland,* II, 571–572.

with the Indians as much as hee could." [46] Reports of this nature continued to reach the commissioners, and they were probably based on fact, for Stuyvesant's instructions sanctioned such a defensive policy. When the delegates returned to Boston in June, the commissioners of New Haven, Connecticut, and Plymouth called for instant war, but Massachusetts again invoked state's rights to veto the proposal. Although the motion was repeated on later occasions, it met with the same response. Oliver Cromwell sent out a fleet in 1654 to reduce New Netherland, but the news of a peace in Europe brought a sudden end to its mission while it lay in Boston harbor. New Netherland's only war loss was the work of Underhill, who, failing in his attempt to start a rebellion on Long Island, fled to New England and captured instead the ill-fated House of Good Hope.

On several occasions the Dutch came close to losing the Delaware River area in the same way that they lost the Connecticut, through an inability to populate it. In March 1638 two Swedish ships sailed up Delaware Bay and planted about fifty settlers as the nucleus of a new colony. Their leader was the same Peter Minuit who had founded New Amsterdam twelve years before. Not only was the founder of New Sweden a former governor of New Netherland, but half of the capital behind this latest threat to Dutch ambitions in the New World was supplied by Amsterdam merchants, some of whom had been founders of the Dutch West India Company. Minuit settled his colonists on the site of modern Wilmington and built a trading house there which he named Fort Christina in honor of the Swedish queen. One of his first acts was to buy the surrounding lands from the local Delaware Indians. In time, as new colonists arrived and other trading posts were erected, additional purchases were made on both sides of the river from Capes May and Henlopen up to the site of Trenton.[47] As elsewhere, the local tribesmen made no effort to move away, and it was often clear that they were not of the same mind as the Europeans about the nature of these transactions. In several cases, moreover, Dutch and Swedish land purchases duplicated or overlapped each other.

Minuit remained in the colony only briefly and was followed by a

---

[46] *Plymouth Colony Records*, X, 35–51 (quotation from p. 50); Brodhead, *History of New York*, I, 552–555; Fox, *Yankees and Yorkers*, 95–96.

[47] Johnson, *Swedish Settlements*, I, 183–184, 200–202, and see map opposite p. 164.

succession of Swedish governors, the most effective of whom was Johan Printz, who served from 1643 to 1653. Governor Kieft, meanwhile, had lost no time in protesting the Swedish intrusion; but having no forces on hand to make good his objections, he looked on helplessly as the Swedes took over the bulk of the Delaware fur trade and established themselves as the major power on the river. The population of New Sweden probably never exceeded three hundred persons, who received only intermittent support from their homeland. Its supremacy on the Delaware was shaky, therefore, and partially dependent on the restraint of the Dutch authorities and their preoccupation with other matters.

The chief trade was with the inland Susquehanna, who profited by a three-way competition between the Dutch, the Swedes, and the English of Maryland. Although the comparative advantage on the Delaware shifted from time to time, Director Kieft estimated in 1639 that Dutch losses from the Swedish competition so far had amounted to 30,000 guilders.[48] The official policy of both nations was to confine this traffic to their respective posts, where it could be supervised. But unlike the authorities at Fort Orange, whose foreign rivals were at a greater distance, both Dutch and Swedish officials sanctioned at least occasional trading expeditions into the interior.[49] International rivalry perhaps helped to intensify other practices as well which elsewhere were somewhat harder to justify. The arms traffic, for instance, flourished here as it did on the Hudson, and each nation was able to point an accusing finger at the other.[50]

Indian relations in general followed the pattern familiar around New Amsterdam. Except for a few incidents which were quickly overlooked, neither nation had difficulty with the Susquehanna, who lived at a distance and came in primarily to trade. Trouble broke out intermittently with the local Delaware bands, however, owing to land disputes and other grievances accompanying the close proximity of Indian and colonist. Most of this difficulty was experienced by the Swedes, since the Dutch in these years consisted of only a handful of traders. At one point Governor Printz suggested a policy of extermina-

[48] *NYCD,* I, 592.

[49] Myers, *Narratives of Early Pennsylvania,* 124; Johnson, *Swedish Settlements,* I, 335; *LONN,* 63; *NYCD,* XII, 38, 57, 66–67.

[50] Myers, *Narratives of Early Pennsylvania,* 123; *NYCD,* XII, 40, 43, 46–47, 59, 67.

tion like that in which Kieft had become enmeshed at New Amsterdam,[51] but he failed to get the necessary permission or reinforcements from home and actual warfare was avoided.

The real menace to Swedish occupancy on the Delaware lay not in the surrounding Indians but in the greater potential resources of New Netherland. With the conclusion of Kieft's War in 1645 the Dutch could devote more attention to this part of their province, and friction mounted steadily between the rival colonies. In 1651 Stuyvesant visited the region personally. Abandoning Fort Nassau for good, he moved the Dutch traders to a new post which he erected on the site of New Castle, just below the Swedish stronghold of Fort Christina. Three years later a new Swedish governor, Johan Rising, rashly forced the Dutch garrison to capitulate, and for the moment the Swedes reigned supreme on the Delaware. Stuyvesant was furious, of course, and struck back with finality on his return from the West Indies in 1655. When Governor Rising was confronted in September of that year with a Dutch fleet of seven ships and an army of 317 men—massive retaliation, given the time and place—he had no choice but to surrender. Thus ended the Swedish attempt at colonization on the Delaware. Stuyvesant might have imposed harsher terms than he did, had news not arrived at this moment which called for his immediate presence at New Amsterdam.

For nearly a decade after 1655 the Dutch attempted with little success to populate the Delaware region and make it self-sustaining. Indian affairs and the fur trade continued much as they had before. A succession of minor incidents prevented real harmony, but the area never underwent the horrors of Indian warfare.

Indian affairs throughout the province had become relatively dormant during the ten years which followed Kieft's War, as Stuyvesant at least profited by past experience and successfully maintained the peace. The major importance of Indian affairs in this period arose rather from their relation to other matters. The Indians became unwitting sources of controversy between the Dutch and New England, between the Dutch and Swedes on the Delaware, and between Stuyvesant and his opponents within the province and in Holland. By 1655 the governor, with the support of the Amsterdam directors, had beaten down his domestic opponents and put an end to the Swedish menace. At the same time New Netherland had narrowly escaped a similar in-

[51] Myers, *Narratives of Early Pennsylvania*, 103–104.

undation by the English. Except for the Swedish problem none of these questions was really solved, but for the moment Stuyvesant was entitled to a good deal of satisfaction with the way that he had handled them.

V

The Supremacy of Commerce

at Fort Orange

RENSSELAERSWYCK, with Fort Orange, was a much smaller and more peaceful community than New Amsterdam during the 1640's and 1650's. A visitor described the company post in 1643 as "a miserable little fort . . . built of logs," with eight or ten cannon and other ordnance. Around this unimposing establishment was Rensselaerswyck, "composed of about a hundred persons, who reside in some twenty-five or thirty houses built along the river, as each found most convenient. . . . All their houses are merely of boards and thatched, with no mason work except the chimneys. . . . There is little land fit for tillage, being hemmed in by hills. . . . This obliges them to separate, and they already occupy two or three leagues of country." Most of the inhabitants were farmers, but the fur trade was now free to all, and, as De Vries remarked after a visit in 1640, "every boor was a merchant" on the side. The advantage in this situation lay with the Indians, each colonist "outbidding his neighbor, and being satisfied provided he can gain some little profit." [1]

After opening the fur trade in 1639 the West India Company no longer retained Fort Orange as its own exclusive trading post. At first it competed with private traders through its commissary at the fort, but a steadily decreasing exchequer gradually forced the company to

[1] *NNN*, 207, 261–262.

close its trading house there in 1644. Although Fort Orange was still maintained as a company outpost, it was frequented more and more by private traders. In the course of a decade so many of them gathered that a village developed around the fort.[2]

Kiliaen van Rensselaer, who had lobbied persistently to win a share in the fur trade for the patroons, was more than a little chagrined when it was finally thrown open to the general public. Nevertheless he determined to secure as much of the traffic as possible for himself and entered the competition on a large scale, his commissary acquiring peltry directly from the Indians and indirectly through his tenants. He sent shiploads of merchandise at a time to America, and his heirs continued the practice for many years. It would have been highly impolitic, the patroon was aware, to forbid company servants the use of his land for trading, but he denied this privilege altogether to private traders. With his tenants he adopted a more liberal policy, allowing them free trading rights if they sold their furs to him at a price that guaranteed a mutual profit.

In attempting to destroy private competition Van Rensselaer refused to rely on legal prohibitions alone. He tried overbidding the smaller traders, but this expedient boomeranged. They raised the price of beaver so high by their competition with one another and with the company and patroon that the latter felt obliged to issue a joint ordinance in 1642 fixing a ceiling price on furs. When the ceiling was ignored, the patroon resorted to force. In 1643 he ordered the establishment of a fortified post on Barren Island, at his southern boundary, where all but company ships would have to pass inspection before entering or leaving the domain surrounding Fort Orange. Van Rensselaer took this course reluctantly. The ideal solution, he said, would have been for private traders to sell their merchandise to him for furs and wheat. He in turn would exchange these partly with the Indians for skins and partly with his tenants for skins and wheat, "fixing the prices so judiciously that the patroon on his part and the traders on theirs, as well as the inhabitants of the colony, may each get a share in the profits." The only sufferers, he concluded, would be the Indians, who now were profiting at the patroon's expense by reason of the exorbitant prices they received.

Unfortunately for the success of his plans Van Rensselaer died the

[2] Nissenson, *Patroon's Domain,* 16–17.

same year, and supervision of his domain passed during the minority of his children into the hands of less flexible men, including his nephew Wouter van Twiller. His project of forcibly denying the access of private traders to Fort Orange was an open violation of company sovereignty over New Netherland and especially over its own outpost. Although agents of the company were exempt from the order to stop and clear at the domain's border, this requirement denied it the right to turn over its own facilities to third parties. The patroon himself would probably have proceeded cautiously for the sake of avoiding a conflict, but Van Twiller sent out in 1648 as superintendent of the domain Brant van Slichtenhorst, a man of anything but diplomatic temperament. For the first time company and domain officials came into open conflict. In order to achieve Van Rensselaer's goal—monopoly of the northern fur trade—Van Slichtenhorst adopted a course which the patroon had been too wise to follow. He prosecuted traders for a variety of offenses, inducing some of his most valuable tenants to leave the domain in anger. He made life difficult at Fort Orange by encouraging tenants with trading privileges to settle around the post and cut it off from contact with the Indians. He directly antagonized the company by bringing forward the patroon's legal but exceedingly touchy claim to the lands on which the fort stood. Furthermore, he proclaimed for the first time that the company's ordinances had no effect within the domain.

Van Slichtenhorst and Stuyvesant were too much alike to get along peacefully when their interests crossed. The governor had troubles enough to occupy him elsewhere, but he was not ready to sit by and watch this secession go unopposed, particularly when control of the fur trade was at stake. After a series of incidents covering four years he acted decisively to end the threat. On April 8, 1652, during a visit to Fort Orange, Stuyvesant proclaimed that that post and the surrounding village—which he named Beverwyck, or Beaverville in English—henceforth should form a single jurisdiction subject only to the West India Company. He established a local court there and continued to appoint its members throughout his term of office. This action constituted an equal invasion of the patroon's proprietary rights, but as the governor had the power to back it up, the attempts of Rensselaerswyck to monopolize the trade were permanently frustrated.[3]

[3] *Ibid.*, 82–90, 195 ff.; *VRBM*, 685.

Commerce at Fort Orange

Up to this time Indian relations and the fur trade had been the joint responsibility of the Fort Orange and Rensselaerswyck commissaries. The advantages and disadvantages inherent in their frontier location were common to both jurisdictions, and their respective officials, despite occasional disputes, normally co-operated with each other. Domain inhabitants helped pay for presents to the Indians, and the patroon's commissary did his share of official entertaining when the sachems and their retinues came around. After 1652 these matters came largely under the surveillance of the new court of Fort Orange and Beverwyck although domain officials continued to participate by invitation in Indian conferences and diplomatic missions and shared the expenses of such functions.[4] Unlike his predecessor Stuyvesant made it a practice to visit Fort Orange rather regularly and gave his personal attention to matters which Kieft had handled from a distance, if at all. The result of these changes was more unified control of Indian affairs at the local level and more constant supervision from above than had been the case heretofore.

There was little more trust or affection between the Dutch and Indians around Fort Orange than there was at New Amsterdam. Animals were killed, thefts were reported, and mutual suspicion at times ran rampant, yet neither side ever resorted to war. Peace was maintained because both sides had everything to lose and nothing to gain by hostilities. The fur trade was a going concern—not lucrative enough to support the province but sufficient to maintain and enlarge the local community. The two races regarded each other less often as corn thieves, trespassers, or Indian givers than as sources of economic prosperity; what they thought of each other personally was beside the point.

Economic interest, moreover, was united here with a higher level of diplomacy. A chief negotiator for the Dutch and one of the most important yet elusive figures in New Netherland Indian affairs was Arent van Curler, who attained an influence over the Mohawk and other Indians which was rivaled in later years only by Peter Schuyler and William Johnson. A grandnephew of the patroon, Van Curler owed

<hr/>

[4] Peter Wraxall, *An Abridgement of the Indian Affairs . . . in the Colony of New York . . . 1678 to . . . 1751*, ed. by C. H. McIlwain (Cambridge, Mass., 1915), liii–liv (hereafter cited as *Wraxall's Abridgement*); Nissenson, *Patroon's Domain*, 155.

his start to family connections. Van Rensselaer sent him out in 1638
—he was then only eighteen years old—as assistant commissary of the
domain. He became acting commissary the next year, retaining the
post until his temporary return to Holland in 1645. Van Curler's management of the colony left much to be desired. He repeatedly failed
to turn in reports or accounts to the patroon and in other ways gave
evidence of youthful irresponsibility. After his European visit Van
Curler turned to farming, and probably the fur trade, serving occasionally on the local court and on several Indian assignments. As commissary for the patroon he had been chiefly a trading agent and thus
from the beginning was thrown into frequent contact with the Indians. Whether it was due to honesty in these dealings—sufficiently
rare among traders—or some other quality which no longer stands out,
he won their confidence and retained it for the rest of his life. Some
years later, presumably after he had helped found the village of
Schenectady, Van Curler seems to have been given a special responsibility with regard to Mohawk relations. On his death in 1667 the
Mohawk referred to him as a chief who had "long resided . . . and
ruled in this region." They asked the Albany magistrates to "appoint
a good ruler over us" to take his place, but no successor was named,
and there is no record of such an office existing again under either the
Dutch or the English for nearly a century.[5] Later the Iroquois perpetuated his memory by bestowing the name Corlaer on the successive English governors of New York.[6]

Van Curler's first important service among the Mohawk was undertaken in 1642 concerning the hostilities which persisted with the
French and Indians of Canada. Hearing that three Frenchmen were
held prisoners in the Mohawk country, he and two others from Fort
Orange set out early in September in an effort to ransom them. The
captives, who included Father Isaac Jogues, a Jesuit missionary, had
been taken on the St. Lawrence in August while traveling with a party
of Huron. The Dutch emissaries were cordially welcomed in all three
Mohawk castles, and the Indians saluted them with musket fire. Van

[5] A. J. F. Van Laer, ed., "Documents Relating to Arent van Curler's Death,"
in Dutch Settlers Society of Albany, *Yearbook,* III (1927–1928), 30.

[6] A. J. F. Van Laer, "Arent van Curler and His Historic Letter to the Patroon,"
ibid., 11–14. Corlaer was the oral and written form of Van Curler's name in the
dialect of Holland, from which province came most of the Dutch settlers in New
Netherland. Van Curler himself was a native of Gelderland. See *ibid.,* 16.

Curler brought presents along and took the opportunity to renew formally the friendship which had subsisted with the Mohawk for more than a decade. Despite the earlier explorations and business calls of Bogaert and others this agreement seems to have marked the first formal treaty between the Dutch and the Iroquois.[7] This fact undoubtedly contributed to Van Curler's symbolic importance in the eyes of the Mohawk. He failed, however, in the main object of his trip. After offering up to six hundred guilders for the release of the three Frenchmen, the only promise he could extract from the Indians was to return them to Canada rather than torture them to death. As he may have expected, the promise was not kept. A year later Van Curler and others acted with the greatest secrecy in helping Father Jogues, the only survivor, to elude his captors at Fort Orange and escape on a boat bound for New Amsterdam.[8]

Director Kieft made his only trip to Fort Orange for the purpose of negotiating a second Mohawk treaty in the summer of 1645. Although he was reduced to borrowing money for the necessary presents, the governor succeeded with the help of the local officials in reaching an agreement with that tribe as well as other "Indian nations of the neighboring country."[9] Very likely these talks bore fruit in the appearance of Mohawk and Mahican envoys at the subsequent peace conference in New Amsterdam.

At the same time a degree of mistrust persisted between the Dutch and the Mohawk. In September 1650 a Tappan Indian arrived at Rensselaerswyck with a report that the Mohawk had been among his tribe and others to the southward, persuading them to fall upon the Dutch as soon as the river froze over. Most of the colonists came to believe the story, and some favored repelling force with force. A majority called for negotiation, however, and the Rensselaerswyck authorities resolved to send Van Curler and a party of men to the Mohawk country to renew the peace. The commissary at Fort Orange, reflecting the

[7] Van Laer, "Arent van Curler and His Historic Letter," 27–28; Brodhead, *History of New York*, I, 345–346. In 1659 Van Curler told the Mohawk that "sixteen years have now passed, since we made the first treaty of friendship and brotherhood between you and all the Dutch, whom then we joined together with an iron chain" (*NYCD*, XIII, 112–113). Although this would place the treaty in 1643, he almost certainly referred to the agreement of 1642.

[8] Van Laer, "Arent van Curler and His Historic Letter," 28; *NNN*, 244–253, 403.

[9] *NYHSC*, 2d ser., I (1841), 161.

rivalry between company and domain, refused to accompany them, saying that it mattered little to those in the fort whether there was war or peace. The alarm proved to be false, but the expenses of the mission, including presents to the value of 575 guilders, were all borne by the domain officials.[10] Four years later Indian unrest of a more tangible nature was noted at Fort Orange, and the mortality rate among cattle rose sharply at Rensselaerswyck. Their discontent was apparently economic in origin, stemming from the low price of beaver. The Anglo-Dutch war had decreased the amount of merchandise shipped to New Netherland and brought a corresponding rise in the price of trading goods. Many efforts were made on this and similar occasions to explain the law of supply and demand, but the Indians usually assumed that they were being cheated. A special meeting of the Fort Orange court was called in July 1654 to cope with the disturbances, and as additional presents seemed to be needed to mollify the natives, some of "the most favorably disposed of the citizens" were summoned to contribute trading goods for the purpose. This tactic was apparently successful, and further presents were exchanged with the Mohawk and other Iroquois less than a month later.[11]

The Five Nations were now approaching the climax of their military career. Redoubling their efforts against the Huron, they maintained almost constant patrols along the Ottawa River, lying in wait for enemy parties on their way to trade at the new village of Montreal. In the summer of 1644 only one Huron fleet out of four escaped capture. An explanation given for this burst of activity is that the Iroquois' own beaver supply was reaching the point of exhaustion by 1640, forcing them to grasp for a share of the western supply. This theory is substantiated by the fact that trade seems to have fallen off temporarily at Fort Orange at about this time and the price of beaver rose so high (from this cause or from overcompetition) as to call for regulation soon afterward.[12] If the Iroquois were to retain their fur trade, they must somehow tap the sources of supply in the west. Beyond this

[10] *RCM*, 128–130; O'Callaghan, *History of New Netherland*, II, 162–163.

[11] *FOBCM*, I, 170–171, 175.

[12] Hunt, *Wars of the Iroquois*, 34–37, 73 ff.; *VRBM*, 483–484. However, in 1643 Van Curler wrote that, although neither he nor the company had gotten any skins that year, "so great a trade has never been driven, as this year," and it could be profitable if the private traders did not take all the peltry (Van Laer, "Arent van Curler and His Historic Letter," 24).

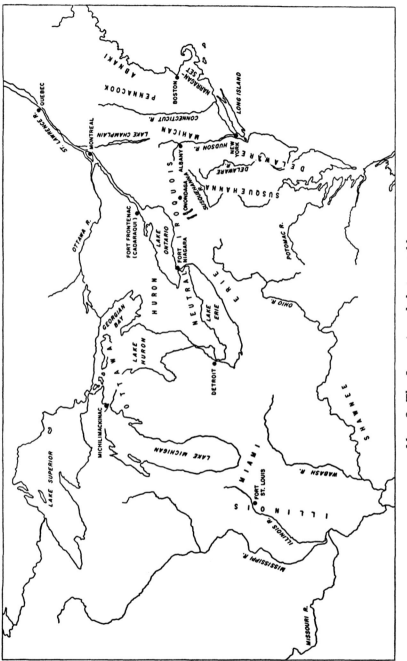

Map 3. The Iroquois and their neighbors

their precise objectives are uncertain. Modern historians have frequently argued that their purpose was to coerce the western tribes into trading with them instead of the French, thus establishing themselves as middlemen between those tribes and the Dutch. This assumption was made by C. H. McIlwain in 1915, and it has since become the standard interpretation. In his book, *The Wars of the Iroquois*, George T. Hunt offered such a quest as the central theme of Iroquois policy during the seventeenth century and explained their power as the result of partial success in achieving a middleman position. The theory has never been proved, however. It rests primarily upon several statements made by Frenchmen, nearly all of them at later dates, and is not sustained in the Dutch and English records, which repeatedly refer to Iroquois hunting activities, along with robbery, as the only significant source of their peltry supply.[13] That the Iroquois would hope to develop peaceful trade relations with the western tribes by waging war with them is on its face improbable. A more reasonable guess, with better substantiation, is that they were reaching out for new hunting lands at the expense of their neighbors and seeking to rob the latter of the peltry they had already gathered. It would be foolish to deny that the Iroquois ever acted or aspired to act as middlemen, but that this was the central feature of their warfare and diplomacy is equally unlikely.

The French, hoping to restore their own badly deteriorated trade, managed to arrange a peace between the hostile tribes in 1645. But whatever the causes of Iroquois hostility, this peace did not remove them, and it proved to be short-lived. The next year Father Jogues, exhibiting unbelievable fortitude, carried the cross a second time into the Mohawk country, this time to suffer martyrdom. His murder signaled the outbreak of another bloody war with the Huron, and in 1649 that tribe was scattered and totally demoralized by the implacable Iroquois. In 1651 they went on to destroy the Neutral Nation living on either side of the Niagara River and thus extended their sway northwestward

---

[13] McIlwain, in *Wraxall's Abridgement*, xlii–xlv; Harold A. Innis, *The Fur Trade in Canada* (New Haven, 1930), 51–53; Arthur H. Buffinton, "The Policy of Albany and English Westward Expansion," *Mississippi Valley Historical Review*, VIII (1922), 333, 343; Hunt, *Wars of the Iroquois*, 100, and *passim*. The earliest Dutch or English allegation that I have seen of an Iroquois middleman position was made by Robert Livingston in 1700 (*NYCD*, IV, 650).

as far as the Ottawa country beyond Georgian Bay. These successes were principally the work of the Seneca, Cayuga, and Onondaga. The Mohawk, however, were no less active at their end of the long house. Besieging Montreal and the whole Canadian frontier, their war parties also struck blows at the Abnaki Indians in Maine, who had allied themselves with the French.

Canada was as sparsely settled as New Netherland, and the French authorities, unable to fend off the enemy alone, turned to New England for aid. In 1650 and again the next year the governor of New France sent envoys to Boston to secure an offensive and defensive alliance against the Mohawk or at least permission to raise volunteers in New England for an expedition against them. He met with refusal, however, as the English had no present quarrel with the Mohawk and did not propose to create one.[14] In these circumstances the French were astounded when delegates from the four western Iroquois nations appeared in Canada early in the summer of 1653 with an offer of peace. Needless to say they accepted the proposition with alacrity. The Mohawk, who had been most enthusiastic in fighting the French, were now fearful of isolation and grudgingly followed suit in August. For the Seneca and their Cayuga satellites especially, this was a peace with a purpose. The Erie tribe, living immediately southwest of the Seneca, had strengthened itself by adopting remnants from past Iroquois conquests and was becoming an increasingly aggressive challenger to the emerging Iroquois empire. Now they too fell victims to that imperialism and by 1656 were no longer a factor in the Indian power struggle.

The peace of 1653 led to an unprecedented harmony between the Five Nations and Canada. For diplomatic reasons primarily the Iroquois began to clamor for "black robes," or Jesuits, to come into their country once more, and the latter were not slow to respond. In returning to the land of Jogues's martyrdom in 1655 they took another step toward the fulfillment of their twofold ambition, salvation of the North American heathen and extension of the power and prestige of France. Within a year priests had been assigned to the Seneca, Cayuga, and Mohawk, and a central headquarters was established at Onondaga consisting of about sixty men—colonists and soldiers as well as mis-

[14] *NYCD,* IX, 5; *Plymouth Colony Records,* IX, 199–203.

sionaries. In general the missionaries were well received, although the Mohawk retained a profound suspicion of Father Simon Le Moyne, who had come to live with them. They were also jealous of the selection of Onondaga as the center of Jesuit operations and made pointed remarks about entering the long house through the chimney instead of the eastern door. Nevertheless the powerful league appeared to be entering the French orbit, and hopes for the future rose to a new high in Canada. Once more they looked forward to the arrival of the great fleets of canoes from the western lakes, bearing the lifeblood of the colony to the storehouses at Montreal.

The Ottawa now replaced the Huron as fur suppliers to New France, and almost inevitably they incurred the same risks in carrying their wares to market. Twelve hundred Iroquois warriors are said to have departed for the northwest in December 1656, and others followed in January, but the watchful Ottawa managed to elude them through flight. Hoping to intercept this trade near the point of delivery, Mohawk and Oneida war parties soon reappeared on the St. Lawrence and Ottawa Rivers. Such visitations led inevitably to another rupture with the French themselves, and the two aggressive tribes persuaded the Onondaga to join them in a plot to destroy the French mission there. Its inhabitants got wind of the plan and began secretly to build bateaux in the garret of the mission house. With incredible difficulty they effected their escape to the north on March 20, 1658, and French hopes of Iroquois submission were disappointed once more. Open hostilities were resumed as Mohawk war parties again besieged the Canadian frontier settlements.[15]

Meanwhile it was business as usual at Fort Orange. The Dutch horizon at this time scarcely extended beyond the Oneida country, but they were fully aware of the Mohawk war in Canada. In 1644 they had ransomed a second Jesuit missionary, Father Joseph Bressani, from the Mohawk. Rescuing fellow Christians from the clutch of savages was part of their Christian duty, but as far as the conflict itself was concerned, they looked upon themselves as entirely neutral. The French, however, despite such occasional kindnesses, had ample reason to be-

[15] Hunt, *Wars of the Iroquois*, 99–104, 131–134, 176; William M. Beauchamp, *A History of the New York Iroquois* (New York State Museum Bulletin no. 78; 1905), 200–210.

122

lieve the contrary, knowing that Fort Orange was in fact the Iroquois arsenal. This kind of neutrality won few friends on the St. Lawrence, and some persons there advocated forcible expulsion of these Dutch neighbors altogether.[16] Moreover, at least once the Dutch protected the Mohawk by forbidding Canadian tribes to pass through Dutch territory in order to attack them. This decision was harder to make than it might appear, for they still hoped to divert the trade of these northern tribes from the French to themselves. The Holland directors suggested in June 1653 that this might be achieved if only the Canadian Indians could reach Fort Orange more easily. Their nearly constant warfare with the Mohawk obliged them to take a circuitous route which redounded to the benefit of the French. In order to avoid this obstacle the directors asked if it might not be a good idea to establish a post fifty or sixty miles north of Fort Orange and make this the staple of the fur trade.[17] Nothing came of the proposal, perhaps because Stuyvesant feared Mohawk resentment, but more likely because of the expense of constructing and maintaining such an establishment.

Although the Dutch did not object to Indian warfare which interrupted the flow of peltry to Montreal, the same war could not help affecting the Iroquois' own fur-gathering activities. Fort Orange was therefore delighted to hear that peace had been made in 1653. On Christmas Day of that year the Mohawk asked the local officials to write Canada requesting French neutrality in case of any further hostilities between the Mohawk and the Canadian Indians. The authorities complied with this request and promised the French, moreover, to do all that they could to keep the Mohawk at peace. But that tribe, as already noted, had no intention of extending to the Canadian tribes the peace that it had so reluctantly made with the French.

Dutch hospitality to Father Le Moyne, who visited Fort Orange in September 1655, created great uneasiness among the Mohawk. Although the Dutch renewed the covenant with them in October, the Mohawk warriors felt obliged to pay another call at Fort Orange soon afterward to make sure that the French had not "poisoned the ears of their Dutch brothers against them." One hundred strong, they announced their intention to attack the Canadian Indians and asked the Dutch to remain neutral. This the magistrates readily assented to, ap-

[16] See Thwaites, *Jesuit Relations*, XXI, 269–271.   [17] *NYCD*, XIV, 171, 208.

parently forgetting their earlier promise to the French to keep the Indians at peace.[18]

Neither Stuyvesant nor the authorities at Fort Orange seem to have regarded the French mission of 1655–1658 among the Iroquois as a serious threat to Dutch interests. Unlike the English at a later date they sought only a commercial relationship with the Iroquois, and at this point a political and military alliance would present incalculable and needless complications. They were probably unaware of the political ramifications of the Jesuit operations or saw no chance of their affecting the fur trade. But the Amsterdam directors were not so confident. They remarked in December 1656 that the French mission "can only be to the disadvantage of our Province and inhabitants" and required Stuyvesant to investigate further. They admitted, however, that it might be "of small consequence only," and as the Jesuits were soon expelled, nothing further came of the matter. By 1661 Mohawk successes had so impressed Stuyvesant that he reported that the French were in danger of expulsion from Canada and by no means posed a threat to New Netherland.[19]

The Dutch in fact were surprisingly unpolitical in their dealings with the Iroquois. When war broke out anew in 1658, the Mohawk came to Fort Orange and requested that a Dutchman accompany them to Canada to facilitate peace talks. The magistrates only reluctantly agreed to co-operate and sent out the town crier to offer a hundred guilders to anyone who should volunteer. Securing an envoy, the Indians set off with a letter from La Montagne, who was now vice-director in charge at Fort Orange. When this mission failed, La Montagne declined a Mohawk request to accompany a second embassy himself and merely sent a soldier instead.[20] All such efforts proved fruitless. The French, with good reason, suspected Mohawk intentions and allowed the war to drag on, relying on their Indian allies to do most of the fighting.

The Dutch commercial attachment with the Mohawk, profitable and even necessary as it was to both sides, was not always entirely happy. Individual Indians continued to kill livestock belonging to the Rens-

[18] *FOBCM*, I, 90–92; Jeremias van Rensselaer, *Correspondence, 1651–1674*, ed. by A. J. F. Van Laer (Albany, 1932), 21; Brodhead, *History of New York*, I, 611–612; O'Callaghan, *History of New Netherland*, II, 306.

[19] *NYCD*, XIII, 205; XIV, 374.

[20] *Ibid.*, XIII, 88–89, 92–93.

selaerswyck colonists, and the domain director reported in June 1656 that these losses amounted to several thousand guilders annually. The Mohawk, on the other hand, complained at various times of the meagerness of Dutch hospitality, of a shortage of gunpowder, of having to pay wampum for repairs to their guns, and of trade practices at Fort Orange.[21] "The Dutch say, we are brothers, and joined together with chains," they complained in September 1659, "but that lasts only as long as we have beavers[;] after that no attention is paid to us." They exhorted the Dutch to "leave off their wickedness" in beating the Indians when they came to the settlement—a reference to the virtually homicidal practices of competitive fur traders. The sale of liquor, they continued, diminished their effectiveness against the French, and they therefore requested the Dutch "not to sell any brandy to our people, but to put the bung in our casks." The Indians were fully aware of their own weakness, however: "When we go away now, we shall take with us a good deal of brandy and after that no more, for we will burn our kegs; but although we propose that now, it will not be carried out. Therefore when the savages come into the country with brandy, we shall come to the chiefs of the Dutch and tell them, who has sold the brandy to them." As a sure sign that the war was not going satisfactorily, they demanded more powder, cheaper and more efficient repairs to their guns, and even fifty or sixty men to help defend them in case of attack. "Look at the French and see what they are doing for their savages, when they are in distress. Do the same for us and help us repairing our castles."[22]

This was a formidable bill of complaints, and when illness prevented Stuyvesant from answering it personally, the local officials sent a special embassy to the Mohawk. Ten men, including Arent van Curler and Jeremias van Rensselaer, volunteered to go, taking with them a present of seventy-five pounds of powder, one hundred pounds of lead, fifteen axes, and some knives. At Caughnawaga, the first Mohawk castle, the envoys made a great point of renewing the covenant which had been in effect, they said, for sixteen years:

Brothers, we now say for once and for all times . . . that you henceforth must have no doubt of our always remaining brothers and whenever some tribe . . . whoever they might be, should come to incite you and say, the

[21] *NYCD*, XIV, 356; O'Callaghan, *History of New Netherland*, II, 306.
[22] *NYCD*, XIII, 109.

Dutch are going to war against you, do not listen to it or believe it, but tell them, they lie, and we shall say the same . . . and shall not believe any prattlers; we are not going to war against you nor leave you in distress, if we are able to help you.

If the Indians did not like the effects of brandy, they should forbid their people to come for it. "Only two days ago we have met 20 to 30 little kegs on the road, all going to obtain brandy . . . if you desire us to take away from your people the brandy and the kegs, then say so now before all these people, but if we do it afterwards, you, brothers, must not be angry." The envoys avoided the subject of military assistance, explained that smiths had to be paid for their work, and closed with an appeal to cease killing livestock belonging to the settlers. The Indians in turn asked "that the brandy kegs . . . be taken from them." Except for their failure to promise the immediate release of eight French prisoners they accepted all the Dutch propositions, and the embassy returned home contented.[23]

Earlier in 1659 war had broken out between the Dutch and the Esopus bands farther south. The Mohawk promised not to assist these Indians and in fact rendered substantial aid to the Dutch. This did not extend, however, to actual involvement in the conflict. As the war progressed and an extra effort seemed necessary to put the Esopus bands in their place, the Amsterdam directors made the natural suggestion that the Mohawk or other friendly tribes be called upon to join the contest. Stuyvesant replied that this had been attempted, but that they were all Indians and hence undependable. The Mohawk were particularly unsafe as allies, he said, "for they are a self-exulting, arrogant and bold tribe, made too haughty through their continuous victories . . . over the French themselves and French Indians in Canada"; if the Dutch were to ask their aid and they were successful, "they would exalt themselves and belittle us so much . . . among the other tribes" that the Dutch would lay themselves open to further attack unless the Indians were continually rewarded.[24] This statement was made in June 1660, just as the war was drawing to a close. Three years later, at the outbreak of a second conflict with the same Indians, Stuyvesant would have been more than happy to receive Mohawk aid.

The Five Nations on their part were not always as firmly united as later observers have assumed. In June 1657, while all the tribes were

[23] *Ibid.*, 110, 112–114.　　　　[24] *Ibid.*, 149–150, 176.

at peace with the French, the Mohawk visited Fort Orange for the purpose of securing Dutch aid in the face of an expected war with the Seneca. The interests and objectives of these two tribes did not always coincide, and they were frequently at odds diplomatically. The cause of the present rupture is unclear, but it perhaps grew out of their respective attitudes toward the French in the north and the Susquehanna tribe to the south. The Seneca were on the verge of a war with the Susquehanna and strongly favored a more conciliatory policy toward Canada than did the Mohawk, who retained friendly relations with the southern tribe. On this occasion the Mohawk solicited the Dutch for three cannon to serve as warning devices and the loan of horses to haul palisades for their castles. They also hoped that the Dutch would shelter their wives and children in case of an attack. The sachems were on their way to the Mahican, presumably to mend diplomatic fences in that quarter, and stopped again for an answer a few days later, on their way home. The magistrates were probably in a quandary, but true to Dutch policy they seem to have made no real attempt to influence tribal action. They promised to protect the Mohawk women and children if necessary and offered to ask private citizens for some horses, but they could not give or loan the cannon without the governor's permission.[25] The immediate crisis between the Mohawk and Seneca seems to have evaporated although harmonious relations between the two tribes were not restored for some time.

Warfare broke out between the Seneca and Susquehanna in 1659 or 1660. The southern tribe was the apparent aggressor, sending warriors far into Iroquoia in order to intercept Seneca trading parties as they carried their peltry toward Fort Orange. The Mohawk were not involved in this conflict, and in fact their relations continued to be more cordial with the Susquehanna than with their brothers of the long house. Mohawk and Susquehanna sachems co-operated in 1660 to make peace between the Dutch and the Esopus Indians, and some months later the Mohawk endeavored unsuccessfully to make a similar arrangement for the Susquehanna and Seneca.[26]

Dutch relations with the Seneca were of recent origin. In July 1660, when Stuyvesant was visiting Fort Orange, they held their first recorded conference, formally renewing a friendship which had first

[25] *Ibid.,* 72–73.
[26] Hunt, *Wars of the Iroquois,* 138–139; *NYCD,* XIII, 179–184, 191–192.

been negotiated only two or three years before at New Amsterdam. The Seneca pointed out the dangers that they incurred in bringing beaver through a gauntlet of enemy fire and asked for more powder and lead to enable them to continue their trade. Like the Mohawk several months earlier, they also complained at great length of the trade practices at Beverwyck and requested better prices for their peltry. Stuyvesant explained that he could do nothing about prices, but he promised to correct the abuses they complained of and said that they should repel illegal traders with force. The director asked them, furthermore, to "make and keep peace with the Macquaas," indicating that this dispute was still smoldering. Presenting the Seneca with a keg of powder, he warned that "they must not use it against our brothers, the Macquaas, [but] only against their distant enemies, where they have to bring the beavers from." [27] Whatever the extent of Mohawk-Seneca animosity, it apparently did not prevent communication between them, for the Mohawk announced in January 1661 that they had visited the Seneca in their efforts to arrange a peace between that tribe and the Susquehanna.[28]

In November 1660 Stuyvesant revisited Fort Orange and met some of the Mohawk, who announced their intention of sending an expedition against the Abnaki Indians in Maine. This was not the first such foray, and the governor of Massachusetts had already written to see if Stuyvesant could not arrange a peace between the Mohawk and New England Indians. The director now advocated this course to the sachems, but his words reached the Mohawk country too late to prevent the warriors' departure. These raids proved so annoying to the English as well as their neighboring Indians that with Dutch permission they sent delegates to Fort Orange in 1661 to make such a peace themselves. They concluded a treaty, but the gifts had hardly been exchanged before the Mohawk violated it with another excursion into Maine. In May 1662 a large war party compelled some English on the

---

[27] *NYCD*, XIII, 184–186. Beauchamp (*History of the New York Iroquois*, 211) holds that the name Macquaas (Mohawk) represents in both cases a clerical error for Minquas (Susquehanna), and Hunt (*Wars of the Iroquois*, 103) cites the governor's statement as additional evidence of a rift within the league. In view of the Susquehanna war and the known Seneca-Mohawk rivalry either explanation is plausible, but it is perhaps safer to assume that the clerk did not make two consecutive errors.

[28] *NYCD*, XIII, 191.

Penobscot to trade with them, professing great friendship all the while, and attacked a group of Indians nearby, taking about eighty prisoners. After killing a few cattle and robbing a house, they built a fort several miles off and stayed two weeks before returning home. When Stuyvesant and another New England deputation reached Fort Orange in August to protest this action, the Mohawk at first were defiant. They had no intention of making peace with the Abnaki, whom they accused of aiding the Canadian tribes against them, and even threatened to attack the settlements in Connecticut if the English did not accept their answer. Finally Stuyvesant obtained a promise to refrain from fighting the eastern Indians until the following spring so that some of the latter could come to make peace. This tenuous arrangement was hardly calculated to satisfy the New Englanders, however, who now took steps to protect themselves in case of further Mohawk invasions.[29]

The Dutch had done everything in their power to promote an understanding between the contending parties. On the one hand, they feared that too much hostility in that direction would so weaken the Mohawk as to diminish their value to New Netherland. On the other, Stuyvesant was still eager to conciliate New England in every way possible. But despite his intercession the peace of 1662 did not last. In the following summer the Sokoki Indians of New Hampshire killed some Mohawk, and the latter again sent warriors to the eastward. When the Dutch warned that they might easily provoke an English attack, the Mohawk replied that their only quarrel was with the Sokoki. They were still willing to make peace with the Abnaki if the Dutch would lend their assistance.[30]

In October 1663 Stuyvesant considered the possibility of arranging a general pacification between the Mohawk, Mahican, and New England Indians, "so that each tribe may go quietly hunting beavers," but other duties kept him at New Amsterdam. The Mahican may also have been involved in the prevailing Algonquian hostility toward the Mohawk at this time. In November, La Montagne wrote that the Mahican had fled and that there was a "strange and unheard of disposition" among the other Indians around Fort Orange. Soon afterward the

---

[29] *Ibid.*, 190–191, 224–227; *Plymouth Colony Records,* X, 282; O'Callaghan, *History of New Netherland,* II, 452–453.

[30] *NYCD,* XIII, 240, 296–299, 308–309, 381.

Mahican apparently returned, but a war party of Mohawk, Oneida, and Onondaga, heading eastward, took their course north of the Mahican village at Cohoes so that neither the Dutch nor the Mahican should get wind of their passage. They stopped at Fort Orange on their return, however, and held a consultation among themselves. They had suffered losses and the Mohawk favored making peace, but at the insistence of the others they went back to the Sokoki territory. The Mohawk proved to have been right, for when they returned a second time, they had lost most of their men. Rumors at Manhattan had it that their casualties totaled two or three hundred.[31]

The Mohawk were now confirmed in their desire for peace with the eastern Indians, and on May 17, 1664, they requested the Dutch to send mediators on their behalf to make the arrangements. The magistrates appointed two men for this purpose, who departed with Mohawk envoys the next day. On May 25 a treaty was concluded with the Sokoki at a point near the upper Connecticut River. But when the Mohawk sent delegates back to ratify the treaty in June, they were fallen upon and massacred by the Abnaki. The Mahican were apparently involved in the plot and immediately began to commit depredations against Mohawk and Dutch alike, threatening if not ending altogether a peace which had lasted for more than thirty years. They overran the country east of the Hudson, killing cattle and murdering three colonists between July 7 and 11.[32] The Mohawk again pressed for peace with the French, but the latter were fully abreast of developments and had no intention of bailing them out of their troubles.[33]

[31] *Ibid.*, 302–304, 355–356.

[32] *Ibid.*, II, 371–372; XIII, 378–382; Van Rensselaer, *Correspondence*, 356, 358. The Mohawk and other Indians claimed that the English had instigated this renewal of hostilities against both the Dutch and the Mohawk. Although Stuyvesant discredited the allegation before all the facts were in, it has a ring of truth. The English were making plans for the conquest of New Netherland, which occurred the next month, and the Indians were being stirred up by Englishmen, with or without official sanction, at Westchester and the Esopus. (See Chapter VI below.) Furthermore, the Indians reported that the English had told them that a fleet was on its way to reduce New Netherland—a statement which was true and which the Indians were not likely to have fabricated themselves. See *NYCD*, XIII, 363–364, 389–390, 392; Van Rensselaer, *Correspondence*, 356.

[33] The Jesuit Relation of 1663–1664 mentions a two-day battle of uncertain date between the two tribes, which ended in a serious Mohawk defeat (Thwaites, *Jesuit Relations*, XLIX, 139–141; O'Callaghan, *History of New Netherland*, II, 519). The French may have confused this battle with the earlier ones fought against the Sokoki, and the fact that no Dutch sources mention it indicates that the account is at least exaggerated.

Commerce at Fort Orange

The colonists around Fort Orange, finding themselves for the first time in the midst of a potential if not an actual war, appealed to Stuyvesant for help. In order to investigate the situation for himself the governor embarked for Fort Orange early in August. Scarcely had he arrived there when an express came from New Amsterdam with news that an English fleet had been sighted off Long Island and that his presence was urgently needed. Hastily returning, Stuyvesant reached Manhattan on August 25, after three precious weeks had been lost on his futile round trip.[34]

Even in these later years New Netherland's chief source of revenue was the fur trade. The number of furs shipped to Europe from all parts of the province is unknown, but the beaver and otter skins moving from Fort Orange to New Amsterdam totaled about 46,000 a year in 1656 and 1657.[35] This is the greatest volume of which there is any reasonably accurate record, in either the Dutch or the English periods. It soon appears to have fallen off as the continual conflicts among the northern Indians impeded their hunting activity. The expenses of three wars with the southern bands cut into company revenues, moreover, and the colony continued to be a losing financial venture for its proprietors. "At Fort Orange almost everybody complains against his neighbor," Stuyvesant wrote in 1659, "wholesale dealers against retailers and vice versa, because of the decline of the trade, which grows worse from year to year." Although beaver was acquired cheaply that summer (and thereby aroused Indian complaints), he said that 100,000 guilders had been expended in Indian presents. In the spring of 1664 he reported that the wars between the Mohawk and the New England and Canada Indians had held the last year's provincial revenues down to 30,000 guilders, whereas expenses had amounted to 80,000.[36]

The opening of the fur trade after 1638 gradually produced a host of unsavory, or at least unorthodox, practices on the part of those competitive souls who entered it. Complaints from the Indians, the vested interests of the company and patroon, and the maintenance of law and order all demanded a growing body of legislation designed to keep the traders within bounds. One of the most consistent objectives of

[34] *NYCD*, II, 372, 495; XIII, 390–391; O'Callaghan, *History of New Netherland*, II, 519–520.

[35] *NYCD*, XIII, 27n.; J. G. Wilson, ed., *Memorial History of the City of New York* (New York, 1892–1893), I, 262; cf. O'Callaghan, *History of New Netherland*, II, 310n.

[36] *NYCD*, XIII, 372–373; XIV, 444 (including quotation).

the authorities was to restrict all trading activity to the settlement itself. Almost from the beginning private traders had endeavored to steal a march on the company, the patroon, and each other by intercepting the Indians before they reached town. The Dutch name for this species of trader was *bosloper* (bushloper); etymologically and in actual fact he was equivalent to the French *coureur de bois*. They differed largely in degree, for while the French Canadian often lived in the wilderness and traded with remote tribes in their own territory, his Dutch counterpart lived at Fort Orange and seldom went as far as Schenectady. The Iroquois probably discouraged long trading voyages through their territory, and the Dutchmen contented themselves for the most part with short-range interception, either buying the furs on the spot or conducting the bewildered natives to their houses. This practice understandably was disconcerting not only to the sedentary traders around the fort, including both commissaries, but to the Indians themselves. Interception in the woods developed in rapid stages from high-pressure salesmanship to outright kidnaping or robbery. The same scenes were also being enacted on the village streets and in outlying farmyards. The Indians thereby lost the advantage of competitive prices and frequently suffered personal injury as well, so keen was the rivalry of their customers. Continuance of peaceful trade therefore required the enactment of certain ground rules.

The joint ordinance of 1642 by which the company and patroon had sought to limit the prices paid to Indians had also outlawed bushloping. It proved ineffective, and a more comprehensive enactment replaced it in 1645. The latter ordinance actually established a whole code of fair-trade practices. The first abuse to receive attention was overbidding, and again the authorities sought to establish a maximum price on beaver. The extent of three years' inflation is indicated by the fact that the limit was now two and a half times as high as before. Continuing, the ordinance forbade anyone "to barter any furs with the Indians during the night or at unseasonable hours outside of his house." Nor was a trader "to meet any savages outside of his house to barter with them, much less to go to the woods," without special permission. Trade and sales promotion alike were henceforth to be indoor activities, and if anyone were "found enticing any savages to him" from the house of either commissary or any private trader he was subject to a fine. The irresponsible element among the traders found it as easy to ignore this statute as the earlier price ceiling. Just how large this group was it is hard to tell, but in the absence of a police force large enough to superintend the activities of every trader the law was repeatedly violated.[37] Its major importance was that it set a precedent for similar regulations (and infractions) in the years to come.

Under Stuyvesant these regulations were amplified somewhat, particularly as they related to bushloping. Although the Amsterdam directors warned him in 1648 not to burden the trade too much with restrictive ordinances of this sort, Stuyvesant cracked down severely on the practice and not only retained the existing restrictions but added new ones as well. The Rensselaerswyck court in 1649 warned three traders against running into the woods to entice Indians to their houses. The men promised to obey, but one of them demanded equal conformity from the traders at the fort, who, he said, were constant offenders. A year later the domain tenants, unwilling to stop the practice while others continued it, banded together and promised over their signatures to abstain if those at the fort would do likewise. If any such agreement was reached, no record of it remains, and in 1655 the magistrates thought that still another ordinance on the subject was called for.[38]

In 1652 the director and council forbade a related practice, that of going into the Mohawk country to trade at the Indian villages. The traders may have been pushed to this extremity by Mohawk preoccupation with military affairs. In any case it had been rare on the upper Hudson and Stuyvesant hoped to keep it so, as its evil effects were being felt on the Delaware. It did not take hold at Fort Orange, and this was the only ordinance regulating it before the English conquest.[39]

As trade fell off in the wake of Indian warfare or depletion of beaver in the Iroquois country, competitive pressures increased still more. The ordinances against bushloping became so unpopular that the Fort Orange court felt obliged in June 1657 to permit the employment of Indian "brokers," or woods runners, for the remainder of the year. By

[37] VRBM, 723. See the Rensselaerswyck commissary's similar statement regarding failure to enforce the provisions enacted in 1642 in Van Laer, "Arent van Curler and His Historic Letter," 24–25.

[38] NYCD, XIII, 39; XIV, 84; RCM, 70–71, 129–130; LONN, 190. For the single conviction which followed, see FOBCM, I, 229–230, 233–234.

[39] LONN, 137; Buffinton, "The Policy of Albany and English Westward Expansion," 329.

limiting this employment to Indians it was probably hoped to divert Iroquois resentment from the Dutch even if the evils of the system were not abolished altogether. For several years the court vacillated between this position, toleration of Dutch as well as Indian brokers, and a flat prohibition on the use of either. Restrictive measures proved to be useless, for the traders ignored them. Although the court occasionally made inquiries and accusations, its consistent failure to follow them up only compounded what was by now a chronic, and partly justifiable, disrespect for the law. The traders fell into two groups on the question of brokers. The wealthier merchants felt that the brokerage fees, amounting, they said, to some 50,000 guilders a year, might better go to Dutchmen than Indians. The smaller traders, on the other hand, less able to pay Dutch than Indian wages, accused their neighbors of attempting to monopolize the trade. The only advocates of a flat prohibition seemingly were members of the court itself. In 1660 they gave up altogether in the face of a petition by eighty small traders. In doing so the officials protested "their innocence of all mischief that may result therefrom, the more so as some of the petitioners have said that they would do it anyway, whether it was permitted or not." [40]

The next step was taken by the Mohawk, who complained to the court of being beaten and forcibly driven into particular traders' houses. If this activity continued, they threatened, the inhabitants here might find the Esopus difficulties repeated on a larger scale, or else the Indians would take their trade elsewhere. Similar grievances the year before had resulted in an ordinance against molesting the Indians, but never before had the case been put so bluntly. The court went into private session and resolved once more to prohibit the use of Dutch brokers. With unaccustomed zeal the magistrates themselves began to scour the countryside looking for offenders. La Montagne made at least eleven accusations after prowling in the woods for several nights with an armed patrol. Prosecutions were instituted and, interestingly enough, several members of the court itself were among those fined. A few days later when the Seneca too complained to Stuyvesant of rough handling by brokers, the governor produced another ordinance. Neither Christians nor Indians were to serve as brokers, nor should anyone take furs or even offer to carry them for Indians. The natives

[40] *NYCD*, XIII, 72, 175; *FOBCM*, II, 189, 191–192, 201–203, 255–256, 261–268 (quotation on p. 268); *LONN*, 378.

were to have complete freedom to move about from house to house selling their peltry wherever they pleased, and the luring of them by promising gifts would incur forfeiture of the gift and a substantial fine besides. For a while offenders were prosecuted more seriously, and the Rensselaerswyck authorities co-operated with an ordinance of their own the following spring. In the summer of 1662 Stuyvesant tried to check renewed violations by having a post driven on the hill behind town, establishing the limit beyond which traders were forbidden to go in search of customers. But hardly had the post been set up when it was necessary to forbid loitering around it. "To the scandal and disgrace of the Christian name and Dutch nation," the exasperated governor declared, "graceless and idle Loafers" hang about the post "entire days from morning until night, even on the Lord's Sabbath and day of rest, in wait for the Indians . . . passing the time in an unprofitable, yea an ungodly, manner, Drinking, Card playing, and other such like disorders." Subsequent renewals of Stuyvesant's ordinance made it clear that infractions were still common as late as the summer of 1664.[41]

In marked contrast with its handling of bushloping and brokerage the Fort Orange court made persistent efforts to enforce the bans on sale of liquor to the Indians. Its record in this connection is superior to that of any other court in the province, and the number of drunken Indians appears to have been less here than elsewhere. Despite these efforts, however, the traffic was never entirely stamped out. The Mohawk proposals in 1659 and the Dutch reply indicated the nature of the problem for both races. When the tavernkeepers themselves were not at fault, the Indians acquired their brandy and beer from someone else. The magistrates even forbade local residents to sail up and down the river without permission since one of the offenders had made that a practice, dispensing brandy to the Indians along the way.[42]

The arms traffic was no longer a subject of regulation or even comment at Fort Orange after Stuyvesant's abortive attempts to stop it in

[41] *FOBCM*, II, 268–270, 278–281, 291–292, 297–298; *NYCD*, XIII, 109, 114, 184–186; *LONN*, 366, 381, 383–384, 394, 425–427 (including quotation), 463–464; O'Callaghan, *History of New Netherland*, II, 421.

[42] *FOBCM*, I, 148; Nissenson, *Patroon's Domain*, 162–163. For court proceedings on this subject see *RCM*, 97; *FOBCM*, I, 69–71, 73–74, 85–86, 94, 148, 179–180, 187, 191–192, 223, 286–291; II, 32–33, 66–68, 71–72, 91–93, 95–96, 135–137, 144–145, 170–171, 236, 281–283.

1648. They had not really affected the sale of armaments to the Iroquois in any case, and most of the official Indian presents contained quantities of powder and lead. By 1664, as the company directors unblushingly pointed out, gunpowder had become the staple commodity of the fur trade, and the merchants "had a well stocked public powder-house to draw on" during the trading season. One trader had a stock of six hundred pounds on hand at the time of the English conquest, and he claimed that others had much larger supplies.[43] Probably no other tribesmen on the continent had such full access to this commodity as the Iroquois who came to trade at Fort Orange.

Owing to several factors—remoteness, the presence of Indians on all sides, and the stifling effects of the patroonship system—the upper Hudson lagged behind other parts of the province in its rate of population growth. Only one significant settlement was made in this period—and that was almost on the eve of the English conquest. When Arent van Curler visited the Mohawk country in 1642 on his mission to rescue Father Jogues, he had noticed an appealing tract of land on the Mohawk River, about fifteen miles northwest of Fort Orange. It was not until 1661, however, that he requested permission on behalf of himself and several others at Rensselaerswyck to buy the land from the Indians and settle on it. This permission having been granted, the Mohawk conveyed the land in July, and fourteen families, led by Van Curler, moved out to found the village of Schenectady.

Even before they had asked permission to buy the land, however, there were rumblings of protest in Beverwyck. That community enjoyed a practical monopoly of the western fur trade and did not relish the prospect of being stopped by a new village closer to the Mohawk. Stuyvesant was little concerned with the vested interests of the Beverwyck traders, but he had long favored restricting the Indian trade to a few places where it could be supervised. Thus when Van Curler in April 1662 requested a survey of the Schenectady tract, the director and council stipulated that the settlers must first agree not to trade with the Indians. A year later the surveyor was sent to do his work, but with orders to lay out no settler's land until he had signed a pledge to that effect. Some of the farmers reportedly were already dispensing liquor and other goods to the natives, and in June 1663, after they had refused to go to Fort Orange to sign the pledge, an ordinance was

[43] *NYCD*, II, 496.

passed to forbid trading in the village or carrying Indian goods there. The survey was eventually made in the spring of 1664, but Beverwyck retained its trade monopoly for many years.[44]

In almost every context the fur trade reigned supreme at Fort Orange. From the company directors down to the lowliest Beverwyck trader the primary object of Indian policy, foreign policy, land policy, and trade policy was to facilitate the flow of peltry toward the Hudson. Dutch policy toward the Iroquois and their neighbors was cautious, unimaginative, and grossly commercial by comparison with that of New France or even that of New York by the 1680's. In these colonies commercialism was leavened by a desire for political and military expansion into the interior. The Dutch, however, had no ambition to dominate North America and had no power to effect it if the dream had existed. Their preoccupation with the fur trade was certainly excessive, in that it helped to discourage other activities which could have contributed greater strength and stability to the province. On the other hand, this orientation kept the Dutch from wasting precious resources in an international contest for continental supremacy. That objective was not only unattainable but unnecessary as long as the Iroquois brought their peltry to Fort Orange. The Five Nations, moreover, needed no protection or assistance that the Dutch could give, beyond a continuance of the existing trade relationship. How the English gradually altered this Dutch policy, and to what effect, will be a subject of later chapters.

[44] *Ibid.*, XIII, 202–204, 215–216, 219, 244, 253–254, 367, 382–383; *LONN*, 442–443; Higgins, *Expansion in New York*, 12–16.

VI

The Subjugation of the Algonquian

WHEN Stuyvesant left New Amsterdam in September 1655 on his expedition to conquer the Swedes, the Indians had been so quiet that he felt justified in taking his entire army. As soon as the soldiers were gone, however, the natives began to take liberties. Before daybreak on September 15 a fleet of sixty-four canoes landed at New Amsterdam, and at least five hundred armed savages began to run riot through the town while most of the inhabitants were still in bed. They beat down doors, ransacked houses, and threatened or manhandled the occupants—all under the pretext of searching for "Northern Indians." After several hours of this the sachems agreed to meet at the fort, where they promised the Dutch to withdraw from the city by sunset and go to Governors Island. But instead of acting on the promise they remained and were joined in the evening by two hundred more Indians.

The council meanwhile called the citizens to arms, and bloodshed followed in short order. Hendrick van Dyck, the ensign under Kieft, was wounded in the chest by an arrow, and another man was threatened with an axe. Cries of murder rang through the streets, and, urged on by Van Tienhoven, the burgher corps hurried in disorder down to the riverbank, where most of the natives had gathered. Shots were exchanged, and both sides lost two or three men. The Indians then crossed the river, where they began a three-day orgy of murder, arson, and robbery. Staten Island and Pavonia were laid waste as completely as a dozen years before. At least fifty colonists were murdered; a

138

hundred more, mostly women and children, were carried off in captivity; and two hundred others lost all their possessions. Twenty-eight boweries and nine to twelve thousand bushels of grain went up in smoke, and five or six hundred head of cattle were slaughtered or stolen. The total damage was estimated at over 200,000 guilders. The province, mourned its rulers soon afterward, "has gone backward so much, that it will not be in the same flourishing state for several years, that it was in six weeks ago." The attackers were variously identified with the lower Hudson bands and with other tribes as far afield as the Mohawk and Mahican, but mention of the last two may safely be ascribed to the swiftness and thoroughness of the onslaught. The Esopus and Wappinger bands were involved, as it later appeared, along with the Hackensack and other New Jersey Indians, but none were present from Long Island.

Thus began the Peach War—so called because it was alleged by the company directors and others to have resulted from Hendrick van Dyck's killing a squaw whom he caught stealing peaches from his orchard.[1] Another explanation for the outbreak was that the Swedes had bribed the Indians to retaliate, or at least create a diversion, while the Dutch were striking at them on the Delaware. The chief sachem of the Susquehanna, a report had it, was on the scene conferring with the attackers.[2] If the Susquehanna were intent on helping the Swedes, however, direct action on the Delaware might have been more to the point. This rumor too was the outgrowth of bewilderment on the part of the Dutch who had been caught so completely off guard. The Indians' own explanation of their visit, that they were looking for other Indians, was lent support by Stuyvesant himself, who later declared his agreement "with the general opinion, that the Indians, upon their first arrival here, had no other intentions, than to fight the Indians on the East end of Long-Island." The bloodshed which followed he attributed to hasty action by "hotheaded individuals" among the populace.[3] Neither the Montauk nor any other Long Island Indians are

---

[1] *NYCD*, XII, 98–99; XIII, 49–50, 55–60, 70; De Sille to [Hans] Bontemantel, Oct. 27, 1655, New Netherland Papers, New York Public Library; O'Callaghan, *History of New Netherland*, II, 290–292; Brodhead, *History of New York*, I, 606–607.

[2] *NYCD*, XII, 99; see also Peter M. Lindestrom, *Geographia Americae*, ed. by Amandus Johnson (Philadelphia, 1925), 235–236.

[3] *NYCD*, XIII, 52, 56.

known to have been hostile toward the Delaware and Wappinger bands heretofore. In fact, they were under attack from a different quarter. In this year the Narraganset tribe launched another commando raid on the Montauk as part of a war which had been in progress since 1653. The Narraganset therefore may have been the "Northern Indians" at "the East end of Long-Island" for whom the attacking tribesmen were searching. It is questionable, of course, how many Narraganset they expected to find at New Amsterdam, but it may be significant that one of the primary objects of search was the house of Isaac Allerton, a merchant who had formerly resided at Plymouth and who kept up his trading connections in New England. If the Indians had designed their whole maneuver as an act of revenge, either for shooting the squaw or for attacking the Swedes, surely they would have begun the massacre right away instead of contenting themselves with a riotous search and then promising to leave. It was the Dutch themselves—with Van Tienhoven again at the fore—who commenced hostilities on the basis of one man threatened and another wounded at eight or nine o'clock in the evening, while most of the Indians were on the strand preparing to embark.[4]

As soon as they had time to take stock of the situation, the council wrote an urgent letter to Stuyvesant reporting what had happened and imploring him to return, arguing that it was better "to protect one's own house, than to gain one at a distance and loose the old property." (The metaphor was appropriate for they had been obliged to hire ten men to go out and protect the director's own bowery on Manhattan.) Apart from New Amsterdam itself, they reported, the whole island was overrun, and nine hundred Indians were encamped on or near its upper end, meditating an attack on the city. Only the dwellers on Long Island remained in their homes; all the rest who had evaded death or captivity crowded into the city.[5] This letter reached Stuyvesant just as he was completing the reduction of New Sweden, and

[4] Three of the contemporary accounts say that the Dutch began the shooting at the riverbank; a fourth reports that the Indians rushed toward them and killed a man first (*NYCD*, XIII, 50, 55–57; cf. XII, 98). Councilor De Sille, who was with Stuyvesant on the Delaware at the time of the attack, reports that the populace generally blamed Van Tienhoven for the outbreak (De Sille to Bontemantel, *loc. cit.*).

[5] *NYCD*, XII, 98–99.

he immediately returned to New Amsterdam, arriving there early in October.

At once the governor moved with his usual vigor to stabilize the situation and reassure the colonists. He sent soldiers to the towns on Long Island and on October 11 laid an embargo on outgoing vessels. About sixty erstwhile passengers were disappointed in their hopes for a speedy exit, as all persons able to bear arms were required to stay in the city. Meanwhile the walls at the upper end of town were heightened in expectation of an assault.[6]

The alarm soon spread to Long Island where Dutch settlers received ominous reports that the Westchester Indians intended to attack them, leaving their English neighbors at peace. When the supposed victims appealed to Stuyvesant for military aid, he asked for his councilors' advice in writing. The governor was obviously determined that posterity and the company directors should have a better idea of what transpired in this emergency than Kieft had provided in 1643 and that the burden of responsibility should not be exclusively his. At the council's advice it was decided at first to withhold troops until a more tangible threat appeared. But a second appeal from the Dutch townsmen a week later, accusing the English settlers of allowing the Indians to come and go at will, led to the assignment of twenty soldiers for their defense. Not far away some Indians captured a party of five men who were on their way to a farm near the Hell Gate. Two of them were sent back to demand ransom, including guns and ammunition, for the return of the others. Stuyvesant ordered stricter defensive measures in this vicinity, and the council resolved not to ransom any persons who were captured after straying into the country against orders. Otherwise, it was felt, the Indians would try to extort equal amounts for the scores of colonists still in captivity after the descent on Pavonia and Staten Island. To avoid further cases of this nature they made their decision public and forbade anyone to go into the interior without official permission.

The authorities were equally concerned to recover the prisoners still held across the river. It soon became clear that their captors had little desire to prolong hostilities. The Indians knew by experience that the most they could hope to achieve in a war with the Dutch was to expel

[6] *Ibid.*, XIII, 43; *LONN*, 196–197.

the outlying settlers, for New Amsterdam itself was too strongly held. The maximum objective, therefore—whether it had been consciously planned or not—was already accomplished, and they now showed a willingness to negotiate. Several times they displayed flags in order to confer about the prisoners, and on October 13 they promised to release them in two days. When this promise was not kept, Stuyvesant sent over a message demanding that the Hackensack chiefs, who appeared to be superintending the operation, state their real intentions. These transriver negotiations were naturally the subject of intense interest to the colonists in New Amsterdam, and crowds gathered at the shore every time a boat was sent across, hoping to receive news of friends and relatives on the other side. Some, in fact, were foolhardy enough to cross the river themselves, out of either curiosity or misdirected philanthropy. On October 18 an ordinance was passed to forbid "crowding and unseemly clamor" at the riverbank, and the Indians were requested, so the ordinance said, to detain those who crossed over without the governor's permission. Stuyvesant's actual message to the Indians, however, merely advised them to disbelieve what they were told by these private negotiators. Meanwhile one of the Hackensack chiefs sent over fourteen prisoners as a token of "his good heart and intention" and asked for some powder and lead in return. The director and council accepted the proposal with alacrity, as it was worded more cordially than anything which had passed so far. They sent over not only a small amount of the requested ammunition but two captive Indians as well and a promise of reward in case the other prisoners were released.

The Indians, as a matter of fact, were finding their charges an encumbrance. Winter was approaching, and there were enough mouths to feed in that season under normal conditions. They had two alternatives, therefore, either to return the prisoners or to put them to death, and they preferred the former if a sizable ransom could be extorted from the anxious Swannekens in town. Thus an arrangement was promptly made for the release of twenty-eight more captives, who were exchanged on October 21 for powder and lead. The Hackensack chief sent word at the same time that if merchandise were not immediately forthcoming for the other prisoners in his possession he would send them into the interior. In answer to a Dutch inquiry he fixed a price of seventy-five pounds of powder and forty bars of lead for the lot. So eager were the Dutch to redeem their brethren that they not only agreed to the price but added twenty-five pounds of powder and ten bars of lead as a good-will present. When these prisoners were released, the total number ransomed so far was sixty or seventy. Approximately thirty more were still in captivity, but in the hands of the Wecquaesgeek, Wappinger, and other tribesmen to the north, who probably had determined to keep them as hostages.

The governor and council now permitted a ship to leave for Europe and penned a long letter describing to the States-General, the burgomasters of Amsterdam, and the company directors the course of Indian relations since 1645. The message culminated in a woeful account of the province's present condition and requested advice as to future action. A war, they stated, would be "impossible to carry on and bring to a desirable result" without considerable outside aid, but at the same time it was virtually the only solution to the constant problem of Indian depredations. It would require three to four thousand soldiers, with supplies and armaments in proportion, who would be willing to settle in the country as a military reserve corps after the war had ended. If the company itself could not provide this help, they concluded, it should try to get it elsewhere.[7]

The question of peace or war became a topic of angry debate throughout the settlements. In order to arrive at an official policy pending word from Holland, Stuyvesant on November 10 proposed a series of questions to the council, to which he again required answers in writing. Is it lawful or justifiable, he queried, to go to war on the basis of the recent occurrences; and if so, when should it be undertaken? If the first question were answered in the affirmative, could a war be fought successfully with the forces now available? And finally, if war is deferred, what should be done in the interim about the losses sustained and the Dutchmen still held in captivity?

Stuyvesant himself blamed the original encounter on Dutch rashness as much as on the Indians, but their subsequent course was inexcusable. The ransom that they had extorted made them eager to repeat the performance, he felt, but an immediate war was not the answer. Instead "their sauciness should be somewhat repressed and curbed . . . by some strict orders, the disobedience to which would

[7] *NYCD*, XIII, 39–52, 59; *LONN*, 198–201; O'Callaghan, *History of New Netherland*, II, 293–294.

make the punishment more lawful and justifiable." The proposition of some, that the Dutch capture a number of Indians as counterhostages, would only endanger the prisoners, who were in the hands of tribes so widely scattered that the Dutch could not hope to take captives from each of them. Besides, he pointed out, the Indians had already shown a reluctance to exchange prisoners, preferring ransom instead. Stuyvesant's Puritanism could be as rigorous as that of his New England neighbors, and the recent visitation, he thought, was a case of divine retribution. Stating that "common sins are the causes of common punishments," he advised stamping out such abominations as drunkenness, profanation of the Sabbath and the Lord's name, and the meeting of sectarians. His more concrete proposals included mandatory consolidation of any settlements to be built or rebuilt in the future and the erection of blockhouses at these places and in the neighborhood of the Hackensack and Wecquaesgeek bands. Furthermore, Indians should be forbidden to stay in colonists' houses overnight, and no armed native should be allowed to approach any settlement. The bans on sale of liquor to the Indians should be strictly enforced, with drunken natives subject to arrest until they revealed the persons who had supplied them. Above all, Stuyvesant said, the prisoners must be regained, even at the cost of ransoming them with more contraband; only when this was done should the above restrictions be enforced. He also urged that all trade and negotiation with the Indians be limited to a single place and that Indian guns be repaired only with his permission.

Councilor Nicasius de Sille agreed in most essentials with Stuyvesant, but the two holdovers of Kieft's administration were more explicit in their denunciation of the savages. La Montagne charged them with malice from the beginning and sought to absolve the citizens who had responded to cries of murder. The Indians had given more than adequate justification for war by their previous murders after the treaty of 1645, he said, but at present the province was unable to execute the judgment that they so richly deserved. "When we shall have received the means, then the time for it will have come"; meanwhile the captives must be ransomed. The colony's other losses, he said, "cannot be recovered either by war or by peace."

Cornelis van Tienhoven agreed that the Indians had given ample cause for war and had violated the treaty of 1645 by initiating hostilities without prior negotiation. Similar tactics, therefore, were fully warranted on the part of the Dutch. He drew upon the experiences of Virginia and New England to show that the colonists could not hope to live in safety until the surrounding Indians were "reduced and brought to submission." The winter months just ahead were the perfect season for such an operation, Van Tienhoven continued, "but to take this step would . . . not be advisable, until we have received special authority . . . from our superiors." Meanwhile the Dutch "must dissemble, though it be unpleasant," and secure a temporary truce in order to redeem the captives and prepare defenses.[8]

As these opinions were being prepared in November, several Indians came in to renew the peace on behalf of Tackapousha, the Massapequa sachem and overlord of the western bands on Long Island. Ever since Kieft's War, they declared, they had been at peace with the Dutch and had nothing to do with the recent outbreak. This was undoubtedly true so far as open hostilities were concerned, but their further claim, that they had not damaged the Dutch "even to the value of a dog," must be taken with diplomatic reserve in view of the depredations of the past few years. On the present occasion, however, Tackapousha promised his undying devotion to the Dutch and offered to assist them against the mainland bands.

The sachem's offer was appreciated and remembered, but there was no rush to accept it. For the present Stuyvesant concentrated on defensive measures and the enlistment of potential allies rather than active preparations for war. On January 18 he submitted further proposals to the council, some of which were designed to implement the recommendations that he had put forward earlier. An ordinance was accordingly drawn calling upon all inhabitants either to gather in more compact settlements by spring or to incur a fine and forfeit all claim to protection. Another proposal would have barred all Indians except a few chiefs from coming to any bowery or plantation. The council agreed to this in principle but voted to delay its enactment. Similar action was taken on proposals to prevent them from lodging with colonists and limiting their trading to a specified place. The council agreed, however, to forbid the mending of Indian guns

[8] *NYCD,* XIII, 51–57.

and voted to make a private inspection of the colonists' armament. On March 3 the burgomasters of New Amsterdam petitioned for and received a number of similar regulations for controlling Indians within the city.[9]

Soon afterward a formal treaty was concluded with Tackapousha, by which the Long Island Indians accepted Stuyvesant as their protector. He promised to make no pact with the enemy without including Tackapousha on his side, and the sachem promised to harbor no such Indians and to make no peace with them without Stuyvesant's consent. Within six months, the governor promised, he would construct a blockhouse at a place to be designated by the Indians on the north shore of the island and would furnish it with trading goods for their convenience. The treaty sought also to improve local Indian relations at Hempstead, where there had been recurrent troubles since the town's establishment. The natives promised to let the inhabitants enjoy their lands in peace, and provision was made for amicable settlement of future injuries. But the basic grounds of dispute were untouched. The natives' very presence, as well as occasional threats from mainland bands, led to a continuing uneasiness among the Long Island colonists.[10]

In March the Holland directors belatedly answered Stuyvesant's communications of the preceding October. The course that they recommended was substantially what he had already adopted. The company's poverty, they said, prevented warfare at this time although it would be the "safest and most necessary" course in the long run. Meanwhile, promising to ask the States-General for aid, they sent over a few soldiers and as much armament as they could spare. The directors, without specifying the means of such an undertaking, urged that Stuyvesant "insist upon restitution of the stolen booty and extorted ransom" which the Indians had amassed since September. Somewhat more practical was their promise to equip all further emigrants to New Netherland with matchlock instead of flintlock muskets. The former were inconvenient to use, but if they fell into Indian hands, as

[9] *Ibid.*, 58–59; O'Callaghan, *Calendar of Historical MSS*, I, 158; *LONN*, 206–208, 228; Berthold Fernow, ed., *The Records of New Amsterdam from 1653 to 1674* (New York, 1897), II, 51–52.

[10] Benjamin D. Hicks, ed., *Records of the Towns of North and South Hempstead, Long Island, New York* (Jamaica, N.Y., 1896–1904), I, 43–45; see also *NYCD*, XIV, 368–369.

many weapons did, it was hoped that the natives would find them doubly difficult.[11]

In a different vein the directors announced that after a series of complaints dating back to 1643 and earlier, ranging from drunkenness and debauchery to financial peculation and the instigation of Indian wars, they were dispensing with the services of Cornelis van Tienhoven and his brother Adriaen, the collector of revenues. When Stuyvesant tried to defend Van Tienhoven some months later, he was promptly rebuked. "Whoever considers only his . . . transaction with the savages" during the incursion on New Amsterdam, the directors replied, "will find, that with clouded brains, filled with liquor, he was a prime cause of this dreadful massacre." Whatever the justice of the charge, there is no doubt that Van Tienhoven's sacking was long overdue. When called upon to render his accounts in November 1656, he staged a sudden exit from recorded history. His hat and cane were found floating in the river, indicating suicide or, just as likely, a ruse to facilitate his escape from the province. His brother Adriaen also absconded, subsequently turning up as a cook on the island of Barbados.[12]

The Peach War turned out to be no war at all in any meaningful sense of the term. In the continuing absence of authorization and support from home the Dutch made no effort to attack the enemy. The Indians too seemed unwilling to reopen hostilities, although at least three colonists were murdered in 1657. Perhaps they knew enough about Dutch policy to realize that any treaty they might conclude would be worth very little if reinforcements arrived from Europe. On the other hand, they were powerless to defeat the Dutch, even without such reinforcements. In any case they did very little either to prosecute the war or to terminate it. In April 1656 the merchants of New Amsterdam were assessed for a contribution of duffels which the natives had demanded for the release of some captive children. There is almost no information as to the return of the last Dutch captives, but the Indians apparently released them a few at a time during 1656 and 1657.[13]

The work of fortifying the settlements continued, and private citizens

[11] *NYCD*, XIII, 63–64; XIV, 343.

[12] *Ibid.*, XIII, 70; XIV, 342; O'Callaghan, *History of New Netherland*, II, 322.

[13] *NYCD*, XIII, 68. The last mention of the prisoners occurs in a letter of the directors in September 1657 implying that only four or five children were still outstanding during the previous summer (*ibid.*, 73).

were forbidden in August 1657 to sell arms to either Christians or Indians, but this measure was taken in response to complaints from outside the province as well as within it.[14] At the same time Stuyvesant was again rebuffed in attempts to form an anti-Indian pact with New England.[15] In December 1657 the Holland directors responded to news of the three murders that year by sending over fifty soldiers and a supply of powder for the purpose of chastising at least one of the offending bands. The directors were out of touch with events, however, and although they continued to rattle the saber as late as the following May, the prospects of peace around Manhattan were becoming distinctly brighter.[16]

The Hackensack and Tappan were sufficiently reconciled by July 1657 to resell Staten Island and permit settlers to dwell there in peace. Tackapousha was still involved in land disputes with Hempstead, but this was coming to be normal, and the only casualties were livestock. Early in 1658 a new village, Harlem, was begun on the upper part of Manhattan, and settlements were re-established at Pavonia.[17] By exercising forbearance the Dutch had managed to weather the storm, which passed so gradually that its disappearance almost escaped notice. Despite a few false alarms in later years, New Amsterdam and vicinity were never again in danger of Indian attack.

There was little opportunity for rejoicing, however, because new disturbances broke out almost at once in the Esopus region, midway up the river. In 1655, after the outbreak at New Amsterdam, the few colonists who had settled at the Esopus fled their homes in expectation of a similar attack upon them. When conditions returned to normal in the spring of 1658 sixty or seventy persons returned to their scattered farms, while the local tribesmen looked on with ill-concealed resentment. On May 1 a drunken Indian murdered one of the settlers and set fire to another's house. The colonists immediately notified Stuy-

[14] *LONN*, 236–237; *Rhode Island Colonial Records*, I, 344; O'Callaghan, *Calendar of Historical MSS*, I, 171, 173, 176; *NYCD*, XIV, 373.

[15] O'Callaghan, *History of New Netherland*, II, 298; *Plymouth Colony Records*, X, 173–175; *NYCD*, XIII, 64, 70–71; O'Callaghan, *Calendar of Historical MSS*, I, 282.

[16] O'Callaghan, *Calendar of Historical MSS*, I, 165, 167; *LONN*, 234–235; *NYCD*, XIII, 75, 80.

[17] *NYCD*, XIII, 75–76; XIV, 393–394, 402, 411, 416–417; Schultz, *Colonial Hempstead*, 26–31; Brodhead, *History of New York*, I, 641–642.

vesant, reporting that they had met only derision when demanding the murderer. Already exasperated by their recent exile, they suggested that forty or fifty soldiers would make short work of these troublesome savages. After receiving two letters of this tenor the governor decided on May 28 to visit the place in person, taking fifty or sixty men with him in case they were needed.

Stuyvesant made exceptionally good time up the river and arrived the next day. Keeping his soldiers as much out of sight as he could in order not to scare off the Indians, he invited them to a conference. Meanwhile he denied the colonists' request for a preventive war. Greater provocations had occurred elsewhere, he said, and prudence had required overlooking them. Here especially, with a good harvest in the offing, it would be folly to give way to fear. Stuyvesant warned them, moreover, in no uncertain terms that he could not protect them if they retained their present mode of settlement. Either they must move together—in which case he would detail soldiers for their defense—or they could retire to Manhattan or Fort Orange. The settlers adopted the only practical course open to them, but with the greatest reluctance, and voted to form a more compact settlement. To speed the process Stuyvesant put his men to work fortifying the new village.

The Indians proved to be shy in the presence of soldiers, and only after considerable coaxing were they persuaded to meet the governor at all. Once assembled, they were quite articulate in describing their grievances, which dated back many years. Stuyvesant replied that all this was beside the point, as it had been resolved by treaty in 1645. He then upbraided them for the depredations they had committed since that time and demanded that the murderer be surrendered. When he asked the reason for the recent disorders, the Indians hesitated and then blamed them on the Dutch, who sold them brandy and made them drunk. The chiefs declared that although their own inclinations were peaceful they could not control the young men, who were spoiling for a fight. At this Stuyvesant bridled:

I told them . . . that if any of the young men present had a great desire to fight, they might come forward now, I would match man with man, or twenty against thirty, yes even forty, that it was now the proper time for it, but it was not well done to plague, threaten and injure the farmers, their women and children, who could not fight: if they did not cease doing so in future, then we might find ourselves compelled, to lay . . . hands upon old and young, women and children, and try to recover the damages, which we had suffered, without regard to person.[18]

He could seize their wives and children right now, Stuyvesant continued, but would not do so in the interest of peace. He concluded by advising them to sell their lands and move farther inland. They were too close to the Dutch, he said, and by moving away would avoid further entanglements.

Some of the Indians returned the next day and begged the director not to start a war, promising to behave well in the future. They were humiliated that none of their men had accepted his challenge to fight and asked him to say nothing of it to anyone else. They agreed to indemnify the Dutch for the damage done, but insisted that the murderer had fled beyond their jurisdiction. Finally, they promised to sell the land on which the new village was being constructed. Having secured as much as he could from the natives, and more, perhaps, than he had any right to demand, Stuyvesant quickly completed the fortifications. On June 24 he summoned the Indians again. Announcing that he was planning to leave but could easily return, he detached twenty-five soldiers as a garrison and returned with the others to New Amsterdam.

Quiet reigned for more than a month, but in August, Stuyvesant heard that the Indians were again becoming arrogant. Some young braves, just back from the hunt, boasted that if they had been present the governor's challenge would not have lacked takers. About five hundred Indians were reportedly collecting around the settlement for a purpose that the inhabitants could only imagine. Nothing happened, but Stuyvesant in October paid a return visit with fifty soldiers. Calling the Indians to another conference, he demanded all the land of the Esopus as far as he had viewed it as satisfaction for the trouble he incurred in coming and for the farmers' expense in tearing down their houses and building new ones. After his browbeating of them the Indians dutifully promised to sell the land, but they were clearly hostile whenever they got beyond the range of Dutch guns. Stuyvesant doubled the garrison and returned to New Amsterdam, leaving Ensign Dirk Smith in command. Under no circumstances was Smith to attack the

[18] *NYCD*, XIII, 77–80, 84 (including quotation), 87–88.

Indians without permission. His chief function for the present was to guard the farmers as they worked in the fields, and no one was to leave the village except under guard.

Ten days later the Indians came in to fulfill their promise of ceding the land. They presented half of the large tract around the settlement as payment for the injuries that they had committed, but expected gifts in return as a sign that the Dutch had equally good hearts. Expressing the most peaceful intentions, they invited even more colonists to come and till the land in safety, and in the future they would bring their peltry here instead of taking it to Fort Orange, as they had in the past. Such tokens of friendship, they hoped, would induce the soldiers to go home.

The Dutch had no intention of withdrawing their garrison, although Ensign Smith was soon recalled, taking some of the troops with him. The winter passed without further incident, and the Holland directors approved Stuyvesant's policies. The governor had agreed to the Indians' request for presents, but in May 1659 they complained of his failure to deliver them. In August the settlers heard rumors of a meditated Indian attack, and Stuyvesant sent Ensign Smith back with fifteen soldiers. On two occasions the sachems came in to assure the settlers that, although their intentions were entirely cordial, they still wanted to see the governor and collect the presents that he had promised. They also compensated the Dutch in wampum for various incidents dating back to 1655. All the settlers could do, however, was to promise a formal treaty as soon as the governor was able to come.

Meanwhile Stuyvesant wrote his superiors of two Indian murders on Long Island. These simultaneous threats required the dispersion of his soldiers, he said, forbidding all but defensive operations for the present. Even within a defensive context, however, Stuyvesant was taking a tougher line than he had during the troubles of a decade before. Dispatching more reinforcements to the Esopus, he provided outlying villages elsewhere with as much armament as his stores permitted. If the directors still favored a war to avenge these accumulating injuries, he wrote, he proposed to organize a cavalry troop on Long Island and Manhattan to help clear those places of the enemy.[19]

On the assumption that affairs were returning to normal at the Esopus, Stuyvesant in mid-September decided to recall Smith and

[19] *Ibid.*, 81–90, 93–108, 110–111.

eighteen of his men. The ensign had barely received his orders, however, when the colonists there precipitated a crisis. On the evening of September 20 eight Indians, having worked in the fields for Thomas Chambers, one of the leading settlers, received a bottle of brandy in payment and went off to a place in the woods not far from the village to consume their wages. When the bottle was emptied, one of the party went back to buy more. Although Chambers' supply was exhausted, one of the soldiers filled the Indian's bottle, and he returned to his friends. As the flask made its rounds, spirits rose, and the Indians began to enjoy themselves in a manner clearly audible at the village. One of them fired a gun, and the townspeople, who had been on edge for months, imagined the worst. Smith sent a few soldiers to investigate; they reported back shortly that it was only some Indians engaged in a drunken brawl. Nevertheless one Jacob Jansen Stoll organized half a dozen fellow colonists to go out and teach the savages a lesson. When they reached the scene of festivities, only five Indians remained. Without further ado the Dutchmen fired into their midst, killing one and capturing another whom they brought back to the fort. Smith had strict orders from Stuyvesant not to begin a conflict. He was distinctly unhappy at this turn of events, although he could easily have prevented it, and announced his intention to leave the next day in accord with the governor's recent command. The colonists were of another mind, however, and prevented his departure by commandeering the only available boat. The next day, letters having been written to inform Stuyvesant of the recent occurrence, a party of thirteen men went down to the river to put their letters on the boat. On the way back they fell into an ambush. The Indians, profiting by surprise and superior numbers, killed or captured the entire party. At least five hundred braves proceeded to lay siege to the fortified village, killing livestock and burning the outlying buildings.[20]

On September 22 or 23 the first messages reached New Amsterdam,

---

[20] *Ibid.*, 114–121, 124, 177–178. It is impossible to piece together a coherent narrative of these proceedings which respects all the testimony, and particularly the sequence of events, given in the sources. O'Callaghan's account (*History of New Netherland*, II, 394–397) is as reasonable as any which could be written, and the above narrative, like that of Brodhead (*History of New York*, I, 657–658), is based upon it. The evidence is comparatively clear, however, that the Dutch provoked hostilities, first by supplying the Indians with liquor and second by firing on them while they were carousing among themselves.

reporting only the original incident. As Stuyvesant was on the point of sending most of his available soldiers to meet an English threat on the Delaware, he requested La Montagne to handle the matter from Fort Orange. Many of the Manhattan and Long Island colonists took alarm at the news, however, and once more abandoned their farms. On the basis of early information Stuyvesant felt his most important job was to reassure and safeguard these residents. In spite of a fever which had troubled him for a month or more, he rode on horseback through the western Long Island towns, taking what measures he could to preserve order and allay the settlers' fears. Only on his return to New Amsterdam late in the evening of September 29 did he discover that the Esopus incident had developed into a major crisis. The next day he assembled the magistrates and militia captains, who advised that enough volunteers might be enlisted to relieve the village if all the Indians captured could be kept as prizes. But when the call was issued, almost no one responded. The colonists were alarmed for the safety of their own homes and declared that their responsibility extended no farther. Finally, after collecting what company soldiers he could from the neighboring settlements and even enlisting his own house servants, Stuyvesant conscripted one of the militia companies. On October 6, with 150 men, including twenty-five Englishmen and an equal number of Long Island Indians, he set sail up the river.

An unfavorable wind prevented their arrival until October 10, when they found that the enemy, doubtless aware of their coming, had lifted the siege a day and a half before. For twenty-three days the place had been under attack, but little harm was done to those inside the walls. As the Indians had a head start and much of the land that they would have to traverse was flooded, Stuyvesant saw no purpose in pursuing them or awaiting their return. He left supplies and the few regular soldiers that he had brought up and returned home with the militia and Indian auxiliaries.

Vice-Director La Montagne had sent a message to the Mohawk as soon as he heard of the Esopus troubles and received their promise not to aid the hostile tribesmen. But as nothing further was done to assist the colonists farther south, the Mohawk came in to ask why. "The Esopus might come now or next spring and kill the people" around Fort Orange, they said. When they offered to intercede for the purpose of arranging an armistice and ransoming the Dutch captives, La Montagne agreed. Meanwhile Smith had already parleyed with the enemy, who talked alternately of returning the prisoners and of renewing their attack with four hundred warriors. The Mohawk, Mahican, and Catskill Indians increasingly interested themselves in a cease-fire and took messages back and forth between the opposing sides. By November 1 they managed to release two of the prisoners and induced the Esopus sachems to request an armistice. Smith proving agreeable, the Indians assured him that the settlers could till their land in peace. Hostilities ceased, but Smith reported on November 13 that they still held a boy captive and had murdered the rest. The armistice, moreover, had been concluded by subordinate officials on either side—it was purely a temporary arrangement.

Stuyvesant arrived on November 28 to negotiate a peace treaty. The Indians refused to meet him, however, alleging later that they had been afraid. Smith therefore was directed to refuse them entry into the village, although they might come and trade outside. He also was authorized in strict confidence to violate the armistice by capturing hostages if he could follow this up with an immediate attack on the nearest Indian village. The best time, Stuyvesant advised, would be in the spring, when ships could come to his aid if necessary. Reports soon filtered in from friendly tribesmen that the Esopus bands were merely simulating friendship until they could collect enough allies to make another attack. They came in to trade fairly regularly, exchanging venison and corn or similar provisions for wampum. In answer to their urgent requests, and fearing that a refusal might antagonize them further, Stuyvesant agreed to furnish them with limited quantities of gunpowder as well.[21]

The governor continued to plead for more soldiers and materiel from Europe. "There is no question," he told the directors, "that if the countrymen in a new country cannot plough, sow and harvest without being molested, or the citizen and trader may not travel unhindered on streams and rivers, they will both leave and transport themselves to such a government and dwelling places, where they shall be better protected."[22] The company directors lent sympathetic attention to these appeals and gave as much aid as their slender resources allowed. Unaware that hostilities had broken out several months earlier, they nevertheless urged Stuyvesant in December to take punitive action as

[21] *NYCD*, XIII, 113, 116, 122–129, 131–135.   [22] *Ibid.*, 131.

soon as possible in the light of earlier grievances. "You ought under
no circumstances [to] settle . . . murders of Christians by composition," they warned, "but rather take the chance to fall upon them
tooth and nail." Only in March 1660 did they hear of the events of
September and October. Immediately they commanded Stuyvesant
to forbid such activities by colonists as had led to the outbreak; but
they did not excuse the Indians: "We understand perfectly well, that
these and other injuries, which we have suffered, must necessarily be
. . . avenged on this barbarous Esopus tribe, from which neither the
Company nor the inhabitants derive the least profit or advantages."
To this end they sent over more ammunition and another complement
of soldiers.[23]

Stuyvesant and his superiors were now in perfect accord. He had
already told the council in February that to restore "the almost ruined
Batavian reputation . . . it is necessary to make war on the Esopus
Indians, using all imaginable means to get the advantage of them."
At least 140 men would be required, half of whom would have to be
specially enlisted for the purpose. If necessary, he said, they should
even be raised in neighboring colonies, without regard to nationality.
To safeguard the rest of the province he proposed the retention of
sixty or seventy soldiers around New Amsterdam, the maintenance of
a mounted patrol on Long Island, re-enactment of the ordinances
regulating consolidation of settlement and approach of armed Indians,
and a renewal of peace with the neighboring bands. Losing no time, he
had the consolidation ordinance renewed the same day.[24]

As on previous occasions Stuyvesant requested his councilors' advice in writing. Again De Sille agreed substantially with the director;
but the able secretary of the province, Cornelis van Ruyven, had the
temerity to suggest that the Indians were at least partly justified in
their recourse to arms. It was the Dutch and not the Indians, he
pointed out, who had violated the compact Stuyvesant made in the
summer of 1658. Moreover, as the state of the country did not permit
a war, he favored conciliation. Strict rules of conduct should be instituted on the model that Stuyvesant had enacted in 1656, and war
should follow only if the Indians broke them. Even if this opinion did
not prevail, the secretary advocated postponing a war until August or
September when the Dutch, having gathered their own harvest, could

[23] *Ibid.*, 130, 149.   [24] *Ibid.*, 135–138; *LONN*, 368–370.

destroy that of the enemy. On February 12, in Van Ruyven's absence, the council resolved that "war was unavoidable," but deferred it until fall. By that time a hundred men at least were to be enlisted "without distinction of nationality either from Virginia or from the North [New England]." A few days later Stuyvesant sent to Curaçao for cavalry horses, money, and Negroes, the last to serve either as laborers or as soldiers. He also sent agents to Virginia to negotiate an alliance against the Indians if possible and to enlist up to thirty men, "among them as many Scots as possible." But Virginia proved no more receptive to Dutch advances than New England had been, and the commissioners brought back neither a treaty nor British mercenaries.[25]

The director had greater success in confirming the peace with the local Indians. On March 6 the western Long Island bands, the Hackensack, Nyack,[26] Haverstraw, Wecquaesgeek, and others from farther up the river sent chiefs to New Amsterdam to conclude a treaty, most of them for the first time since the outbreak of 1655. Tackapousha was so firmly attached to the Dutch, however, that he desired to be entered in the treaty on their side. The other sachems expressly denied any connection or correspondence with the Esopus bands. The treaty provided that Indians henceforth must deliver up their arms when they entered any settlement and must do their trading at two specified places in New Amsterdam. Colonists who killed Indians were to be punished with death, and the chiefs promised to deliver up any Indian murderers. The Dutch requested, furthermore, that the Indians leave some of their children to be educated. The reason given was that the natives should be able to read the agreements they had made, but the value of such children as hostages was probably not overlooked. The sachems handed over one child who was with them and promised to send more at a later date. Evidently their protestations of friendship were sincere.[27]

This treaty had the effect of isolating the Esopus Indians from many of their potential allies, and on March 15 a Wappinger chief reported that they wanted peace. Only fear, he said, kept them from announcing this desire themselves. The council was agreeable, but demanded a

[25] *NYCD*, XIII, 138–147, 163.
[26] The Nyack lived on Staten Island and were probably a portion of the Canarsee; at least some of them may have settled there after being crowded out of their lands in the Brooklyn area.
[27] *NYCD*, XIII, 147–149, 163.

guarantee that the Indians would keep it, for there were rumors that they feigned peaceful intentions in order to catch the Dutch off guard. (That such was their own policy too the councilors did not mention.) The Wappinger sachem could of course provide no such security, and the Dutch sent him back to tell the Esopus bands that they must make peace themselves.

At the same time Ensign Smith, implementing his earlier instruction, launched his first attack on the enemy. Not far from the village he encountered about sixty Indians, but they managed to escape with minimal losses. The Dutch gave up pursuit, burned the Indians' provisions, and returned to their base. There was no longer any point in prolonging the declaration of war, and Stuyvesant did so on March 25. All citizens were warned to be on guard, and boats were forbidden to sail on the river except in pairs and well armed. Smith continued the war as he had begun it, sending out two more raiding parties early in April. Stuyvesant approved of this activity and sent further reinforcements, bringing the garrison to nearly a hundred men. At the same time he asked both Smith and La Montagne to discover if any other tribes were aiding the enemy. He apparently suspected the Mahican and Catskill, but both of these were busy arranging another peace, and on April 21 they appeared at Fort Orange with propositions from the Esopus bands.

Smith's three sorties could hardly have inflicted much damage on the Indians. As Stuyvesant put it, "the expeditions of our military would have better results and the barbarians would be sooner conquered if they stood firm." This was not the way of Indian warfare, however, as the French would discover in their expeditions against the Iroquois. Nevertheless the enemy now offered in return for peace to abandon the whole Esopus tract and to return the plunder and the few prisoners that they had taken. The Susquehanna too had interceded in favor of peace, and it is plain that the pressure exerted by their neighbors was a major factor in bringing around the Esopus tribesmen. During the latter part of April they repeatedly came to the settlement to ask for peace. Stuyvesant still suspected their intentions, however, and directed that all further negotiations be held with him at New Amsterdam. If they were unwilling to go that far, then Smith must launch another attack at the earliest opportunity. The governor told friendly tribesmen that he would make no peace until he knew that the young braves as well as the chiefs intended to keep it. The Dutch now held eleven captives, whom they had taken to Manhattan for safekeeping. For some reason it was concluded that peace was impossible until these prisoners were either released or sent away beyond hope of recovery. Holding that the former course would only encourage further outbreaks, the authorities ordered instead that they be shipped to the West Indies as slaves, and this was done in July.[28]

Stuyvesant relented to the extent of ordering a cease-fire while the Mahican held another conference with the enemy, but Smith had already staged another attack before receiving his message. On May 29 and 30 he led seventy-five men on two expeditions into the interior, only to be thwarted both times by high water in the neighboring streams. His only triumph was the cold-blooded murder of an aged chief whom the Indians had left behind in their flight.

Meanwhile the other bands continued to press for a peace settlement. On June 3 Oratamin, the Hackensack sachem, and other Indians appeared at New Amsterdam to report a universal desire for peace among the Esopus tribesmen. Convinced either of the truth of the message or of the futility of pursuing such inconclusive hostilities any further, Stuyvesant now modified his position and invited Oratamin to arrange an armistice. He stipulated that the Esopus bands must move away from the vicinity of the Dutch and return the booty that they had stolen. If a firm peace resulted, he said, only then would some of the Indian captives be returned. On June 12 Smith wrote that a conference had been held; the Indians had agreed to the terms, but requested Stuyvesant's presence to formalize the treaty.

When the governor returned to the Esopus a month later, he had to wait three days, together with a delegation of Mohawk, Mahican, Susquehanna, Catskill, Wappinger, Hackensack, and other chiefs, for the Esopus sachems to make an appearance. They had decided to return to their respective homes and leave the enemy to their own fate when the sachems finally appeared on the evening of July 14. A conference was immediately held, in which the Mohawk and Susquehanna roundly rebuked the Esopus for their conduct during the past two years. Thereupon the Mohawk chief threw down a hatchet and trampled upon it, that it might never be taken up again. Stuyvesant then announced his terms, and the treaty was concluded the next day. The

[28] *Ibid.*, 150–152, 155, 157, 160–169, 178–179.

Indians agreed to indemnify the Dutch "with all the territory of the Esopus" and to remove permanently to another location. They were obliged to return the ransom that they had received for prisoners, to leave their arms behind when they came to trade, and to drink their liquor away from the settlements. Murders committed by either side were to be punished and disputes settled without recourse to war. The chiefs of the other tribes present agreed to act as surety for the conduct of the Esopus Indians, promising to assist the Dutch in subduing them if they broke the treaty. During the remainder of 1660 and the next year the Esopus bands were quiet, obeying the treaty in all its essentials. In April 1661 Stuyvesant noted this behavior and ordered the governor of Curaçao to return two of the captives who had been sent to that island. As an inducement to further good conduct he promised to redeem the rest in the course of time.[29]

Meanwhile peace, if not always friendship, persisted with the Indians around New Amsterdam. Stuyvesant was unhappy with the Navasink and Raritan regarding their failure to surrender Indian murderers, but despite the advice of the Holland directors he declined to launch a punitive expedition. With the Esopus War in mind, he felt such a course would retard colonization more than it would accomplish any positive good. In 1663 and 1664 he persuaded the Navasink to sell a great portion of their lands, which some New Englanders were attempting to buy at the same time.[30]

On Long Island disputes between the Indians and the town of Hempstead had grown so common that the town promulgated a code of procedure to regulate them, patterned after Stuyvesant's treaty of 1656. Early in 1660 Tackapousha complained to the governor that colonists were trespassing on Indian lands and had threatened to burn the natives' houses unless they moved away within eight days. Stuyvesant summoned both parties for a hearing, but Esopus matters intervened, and no settlement was reached. Hearing soon afterward that they were on the point of armed conflict, the governor once more directed them to appear at New Amsterdam. They came on May 25; the townsmen complained that the Indians would not move off the land they had sold and that their dogs were a hazard to livestock,

[29] *Ibid.*, 169–176, 178–184, 194; see also p. 202.
[30] *Ibid.*, 187, 190, 311–312, 314–317, 365; O'Callaghan, *Calendar of Historical MSS*, I, 257.

while the natives claimed they had only sold grazing rights and not the land itself. After hearing both sides the council permitted the Indians to harvest their present crop provided they fenced their fields and killed their dogs.

Tackapousha associated himself with the Dutch in the Esopus peace treaty in July and was promised protection in case of attack by the Narraganset. His relations with the Englishmen at Hempstead did not improve, however. In June 1663 Stuyvesant interrupted other pressing duties on a visit there to hear a complaint that the Indians had stolen thirty-three hogs and shot a horse which had strayed into their fields. The settlers in turn were accused of killing fifty dogs. The director tried to resolve the dispute by indemnifying the injured parties and causing the natives' fences to be repaired, but the difficulties persisted until well after the English conquest.[31]

Stuyvesant's action in shipping off the Esopus prisoners to Curaçao gradually appeared to have been a blunder. In July 1662, noting rumors that their comrades planned a surprise attack by way of revenge, he urged the company directors in the strongest terms not to diminish the force of 125 soldiers still in the province. The attack did not come, but a series of incidents or alarms in 1661 and after, many of them due to a resumption of the liquor traffic, once more put the Esopus settlers in a state of suspense. In April 1663, when a second village was being established in the vicinity, the Indians warned colonists not to settle there. When the overseers of the new village requested soldiers for their defense as well as presents to satisfy the Indians, the council authorized a large present, including guns and ammunition, and Stuyvesant sent word to the natives that he would soon come to renew his friendship. The Indians returned a friendly answer, but they soon made it clear that their real intentions were quite different.[32]

On the morning of June 7, 1663, a large number of Indians appeared at the older Esopus village (which had now been named Wiltwyck, or Indiantown) and scattered from house to house on the pretext of selling maize and beans. Scarcely fifteen minutes elapsed before several Dutchmen dashed through the gate on horseback shouting

[31] *Hempstead Town Records*, I, 87–88, 98; *NYCD*, XIV, 460, 474, 480; Henry Onderdonk, Jr., *The Annals of Hempstead, 1643 to 1832* (Hempstead, N.Y., 1878), 43.

[32] *NYCD*, XIII, 204–205, 207, 223–224, 227–229, 231–232, 237–238, 242–245, 256.

that the Indians had destroyed the new village nearby. Immediately the natives in town took up their weapons, which the inhabitants had foolishly allowed them to bring in. Colonists were shot down in their homes, others were carried off into captivity, and houses were put to the torch. Only a lucky shift in the wind saved the town from being wholly engulfed in flames. Most of the able-bodied men were out in the fields, but enough of them straggled in from various directions so that in time they managed to expel the invaders. The new village had been burned to the ground, and most of its inhabitants were either butchered or taken prisoner. The few survivors hurried into Wiltwyck, where everyone prepared for another siege. In the course of the day some forty-five persons, mostly women and children, had been captured, and more than twenty lost their lives. Only sixty-nine men, soldiers and civilians alike, remained to brave the Indians' attack.[33]

A week later Stuyvesant was on hand, issuing orders for the village's defense. On his return to Manhattan the council resolved to prosecute the war as speedily and thoroughly as possible in spite of the hostages in enemy hands. The necessary soldiers were to be enlisted "here and elsewhere, wherever they can be got." Councilor Johan de Decker was sent to Fort Orange to enlist men, including a dozen Mohawk warriors if possible, to get Mohawk help in redeeming the prisoners, and to borrow three or four thousand guilders. The governor now turned to the thankless task of raising troops among the citizenry around New Amsterdam. "Free plunder and all the savages, whom they could capture" were promised as prizes to those who offered their services. Two days later he added the remission of tithes and a schedule of compensations for injuries, as letters were sent to the Long Island villages announcing that recruiting officers would soon pay them a call. On June 27 Stuyvesant issued a warning that Esopus warriors might be heading southward. He had already forbidden travel except in properly armed parties of four or five, and an ordinance was now passed for the arrest of all natives who boarded ships in the Esopus region. Blockhouses were also erected on either side of the Narrows for the protection of Long Island and Staten Island residents.[34]

Although he had better luck raising troops than in the first Esopus War, Stuyvesant received discouraging reports from Fort Orange and

[33] *Ibid.*, 245–247, 249–250, 256–257.
[34] *Ibid.*, 248–252, 254–256, 259–260, 263; XIV, 528, 546; *LONN*, 444–445.

161

the English communities on Long Island. The Mohawk were otherwise employed, and the magistrates at Fort Orange and Rensselaerswyck were too concerned about the safety of their community to feel much urgency in sending men to the Esopus. A bitter exchange followed with Stuyvesant, who angrily quoted the golden rule for their benefit. On Long Island, where Englishmen were daily growing more dissatisfied with Dutch rule, their magistrates intervened to hold enlistments down to only five or six. By the end of June about sixty men were recruited, whom Stuyvesant sent up the river under the command of Martin Cregier, a burgomaster of New Amsterdam with military experience on the Delaware and elsewhere.[35]

The Indians meanwhile lacked the means of pursuing the advantage that they had won in their initial attack. Unable to carry a frontal assault on the village, they hovered around it, waiting to pick off any who ventured outside. The Mohawk and other tribes had ransomed only one prisoner, a daughter of La Montagne. The others, she reported, were at a fort several hours' march to the south, guarded by thirty Indians who were prepared to flee with them in case of danger. Cregier spent three weeks negotiating further with friendly tribesmen for their return, but his efforts netted only five more persons.[36]

After receiving further reinforcements, including about forty Long Island warriors whose services had been offered by Tackapousha, Cregier assumed a more active role. On July 26 he set out from Wiltwyck with a force of 210 soldiers, colonists, Negro slaves, and native auxiliaries. Their destination—to which they were guided by a redeemed captive—was the Indian fort described by Rachel la Montagne. Movement was not easy; the terrain was alternately swampy, rocky, and mountainous, and the impedimenta, including two wagons and two cannon, in some places had to be hauled over the mountains with ropes. The creeks or swamps which lay behind every hill involved further delay while trees were felled and bridges constructed. Despite these obstacles the army reached its goal on the second day out, having covered more than thirty miles in a southwesterly direction. The fort, they discovered, had been abandoned two days before, and the Dutch occupied it without further ado.

On the next morning Cregier remained at the fort with a few men while one of his lieutenants, Pieter Wolphertsen van Couwenhoven,

[35] *NYCD*, XIII, 258, 261, 268–271, 283.   [36] *Ibid.*, 257, 271–275, 324–328.

took the main force in pursuit of the enemy. After marching all day they failed to uncover anything more than a succession of abandoned camps. The Long Island natives advised that further pursuit was useless, and Van Couwenhoven led his tired army back to the Indian fort. This place, it appeared, was the center of the Indians' food supply. In addition to fields of growing corn there were pits in the ground containing a part of the previous year's harvest. The greatest blow that the Dutch could strike was to destroy these supplies, and they devoted nearly three days to it. More than two hundred acres of corn on the stalk and over one hundred pits of corn and beans went up in smoke. On July 31 the men set fire to the fort itself and the huts around it and returned to Wiltwyck.[37]

Stuyvesant was hardly less active at New Amsterdam. On June 27 he called in Oratamin and Matteno, the Hackensack and Nyack sachems, to assure himself of their continued neutrality. Oratamin, as a matter of fact, proved to be Stuyvesant's most valuable intelligence officer and intermediary, for he was just as anxious as the Dutch to keep the war from spreading. Reports had it that the Esopus bands were now reduced to eighty warriors, but at least half that number, according to one account, was planning an attack near New Amsterdam. Stuyvesant also heard that the Dutch captives had been scattered far and wide, some of them being in the custody of other bands, particularly the Catskill. On July 12 he authorized the magistrates at Fort Orange and Rensselaerswyck to pay up to one hundred guilders for each prisoner if that were necessary to ransom them. The plight of these individuals was a major object of concern, but the governor and council had already determined not to let it interfere with their prosecution of the war. Under no circumstances, therefore, was an offer of peace to be held out as a reward for their surrender. Stuyvesant warned that if the Catskill band was harboring enemy Indians or holding Dutch prisoners, it too might have to be treated as an enemy.[38]

In August the governor sent Van Couwenhoven, who had been a trader and knew the Indian language, to see if the Wappinger band could reclaim any more Dutch captives. Modifying his earlier policy, Stuyvesant authorized a provisional armistice if that would help. The Wappinger themselves were playing a close game; they obviously sympathized with the Esopus tribesmen across the river but at the

[37] *Ibid.*, 328–330.   [38] *Ibid.*, 261–262, 275–280, 282.

same time had no taste for joining them openly. Van Couwenhoven's only achievement was the release of four captives, although the Wappinger plainly had access to more. On August 27, therefore, Stuyvesant authorized hostilities against that band, asking Cregier for soldiers to defend the lower settlements as soon as a military advantage had been won. This request was lent even greater urgency on August 30, when rumors came in that no less than eight bands of Indians had united to massacre the Dutch from Fort Orange southward. However, La Montagne soon assured the director that the Iroquois, Mahican, and Catskill were friendly and had promised to harbor none of the enemy. Meanwhile Oratamin had brought in three Minisink chiefs who avowed their complete neutrality, saying that they had troubles enough elsewhere. As tributaries of the Susquehanna, they were expecting Seneca war parties at any time. Taking a cue from their allies, who had been furnished with fieldpieces by the English in Maryland, they requested a cannon from Stuyvesant, who declined as politely as he could.[39]

At Wiltwyck, Cregier and his men had attempted no major engagement since the expedition in July. The colonists were busy bringing in their harvest, which the Indians unaccountably had failed to destroy, and the soldiers stood guard while the work was being done. Tackapousha's Indians proved to be a mixed blessing. Dissatisfied with the amount of plunder that they had received, they soon wanted to come home, and Cregier vainly tried every expedient short of force to persuade them to stay. They had been invaluable on his previous foray, and their departure obliged him to retain soldiers whom Stuyvesant wanted to station around New Amsterdam. At the end of August, when news came of the construction of another Indian fort and of Van Couwenhoven's failure to rescue the captives, it was resolved to launch another attack. Rainy weather prevented a departure for several days, but on September 3 Cregier set out with fifty-five men, an interpreter, and a Wappinger guide. Again high waters impeded progress, but Cregier no longer encumbered himself with artillery. On the afternoon of September 5, having marched about forty miles in a south-southwest direction, they approached the Indians' new fort—probably near the town of Bloomingburg, Sullivan County.

The fort was palisaded and located "on a lofty plain" at the top of a

[39] *Ibid.*, 284–294, 333–337.

hill. The soldiers proceeded quietly along the side of the hill until a squaw discovered them and gave the alarm. The natives had carelessly left their weapons in their houses, a stone's throw from the fort, so that when the Dutch came upon them suddenly the fort was useless for defense. Snatching what few guns and bows and arrows they could lay hands on, they fled down the hill and across a creek. Here they turned and made a courageous stand until the Dutch crossed over and dislodged them. When the battle was over, the Indians had lost more than thirty persons, killed or captured, whereas Dutch casualties amounted to three dead and six wounded. In addition twenty-three Dutch captives were liberated. As the task of burning the Indians' corn supply would have consumed more time than the Dutch could spare in view of the condition of their wounded, they contented themselves for the present with plundering the houses. There was enough booty to fill a sloop, Cregier remarked, but much of it, including two dozen guns, had to be left behind or destroyed when the army returned to Wiltwyck on September 7.[40]

As news of the victory reached New Amsterdam, Stuyvesant was on the point of leaving for Boston to negotiate a variety of matters with the New England commissioners. A final *coup de grâce* seemed to be called for at the Esopus, and New Amsterdam was no longer felt to be in danger; the council therefore countermanded the previous orders to send soldiers down the river and promised instead to send up more reinforcements from the English and Indians on Long Island. Once more Tackapousha agreed to contribute some warriors, but on the condition that his men should fight only the Esopus Indians and should stay there only until the Indian fort and the corn around it were destroyed. The sachem himself was to receive a coat, and each of his forty-four braves was promised a piece of duffels and all the booty that he might take. In sending the Indians up the river the council urged Cregier to use them as soon as possible.

The commander obeyed his instructions, and four days after the natives' arrival he led a party of 108 Dutch and 46 Indians to the scene of the last victory. Reaching the fort on October 2, they found it deserted and contented themselves with finishing the work of destruction. On October 7 two smaller parties were sent out, one to the north and the other across the Hudson, but again no enemies were encountered

[40] *Ibid.*, 337–340.

in either place. The only result was the burning of more corn, and on October 9 Van Couwenhoven took the Long Island natives back to Manhattan.[41]

A few days later another rumor of an Indian combination to wipe out the Dutch gained currency up and down the length of the river. At least five hundred Indians, including the Mahican, Catskill, Esopus, and Wappinger, were reportedly meeting near Claverack on the east bank. The point of intended attack favored Fort Orange in the reports current there and Hoboken and Manhattan according to the stories in that vicinity, but everywhere the threat was taken seriously. If it had any basis in fact, it probably sprang from an impending rupture between the Mohawk and their Algonquian neighbors and had no relation at all to the Dutch or the Esopus War. Stuyvesant, who had now returned from Boston, had no way of knowing this, and when the reports reached New Amsterdam, he warned the inhabitants and deployed troops to meet the supposed danger. Two fully manned yachts were sent up the river under the command of Van Couwenhoven, with orders to sound out the Wappinger on tribal activity in that region. If the Indians were preparing to descend the river in canoes, he was to block their passage; if their plans had not yet reached that stage, he was to try again to release the remaining prisoners, even by exchanging Indian captives should that prove necessary; and if the Dutch could gain time for defensive measures by concluding an armistice and promising the Indians a formal peace, he was to act accordingly. Far from planning a massive attack, however, the Wappinger sachems cheerfully renewed the peace, and Van Couwenhoven was able to negotiate a ten-day armistice with the Esopus bands, looking toward an exchange of prisoners. Only three more women and children were liberated after this agreement, but it eased the tension at Wiltwyck, even after the ten days had elapsed. By mid-November, Cregier felt free to confer with the director at New Amsterdam, bringing all but sixty of the Esopus garrison with him.[42]

The winter months of 1663–1664 were a time of military quiet and diplomatic confusion as the Dutch and Indians worked cautiously toward a final settlement. In November, Oratamin and Matteno, speaking through "some of the most prominent matrons" of New Amsterdam, requested peace on behalf of both the Wappinger and the

[41] *Ibid.*, 295–296, 342–344.   [42] *Ibid.*, 299–302, 304, 345, 348–350.

Esopus Indians. These professions were probably sincere; an Esopus chieftain had told Van Couwenhoven that his people were no longer capable of sustaining the war, and the Wappinger had reportedly asked the governor of New Haven also to intercede. Stuyvesant was justifiably hesitant, however. He demanded that the sachems confer with him personally and surrender the half dozen captives who remained in their hands. Oratamin and Matteno worked diligently as always to arrange such a settlement; their major obstacle appeared to lie in the fact that the prisoners had been scattered about the countryside while the Esopus braves were out hunting. On December 29 the two sachems asked for a truce to enable the Indians to collect them and bring them in. Stuyvesant reluctantly agreed, but the truce turned out to be unproductive, as was a two-week extension into March.[43]

That the Indians were truly unable to return the prisoners at once seems plausible enough in the light of their condition. The destruction of their corn supply had been a serious blow, and apart from hunting, which unquestionably kept the men from home in wintertime, their only means of subsistence was the charity of neighboring bands. Very likely, as Stuyvesant himself remarked, it would have been hard to find more than five or six of them together. But a complicating factor was the growing hostility between the Dutch and the English at this time. It is conceivable that the Indians, though ardently desiring peace, were willing to defer it if they could get English assistance in expelling the Dutch altogether. The Wappinger request for intercession from New Haven, if it occurred at all, may therefore have had a purpose very different from mediation for peace. On March 15 the Esopus and Wappinger were reported to have been in correspondence with the English at Westchester, who had asked their help in ejecting the Dutch from the province. The Indians had been willing, so the story went, but since the English did not attack as they had promised, the natives were now threatening to make peace. Van Couwenhoven was again sent up the river to investigate and returned with testimony from several Wappinger, Esopus, and Haverstraw Indians which directly confirmed the reports. The younger Esopus warriors were still holding out for war over their sachems' objections, and one of the latter had said that the final decision would not be made until the scattered tribesmen gathered in thirty days.[44]

[43] *Ibid.*, 302, 304–306, 314, 320–322, 361. [44] *Ibid.*, 363–365, 372.

The war ended almost as suddenly as it had begun. On May 15, 1664, after the Esopus tribesmen had had time to confer, three of their chiefs appeared in the council chamber of Fort Amsterdam, flanked by a delegation of neighboring sachems. The remaining captives had been returned one or two at a time during the past few months, and the sachems were now ready to make peace. The major Dutch condition was the cession of all their territory as far inland as the two destroyed forts. They were required, moreover, to confine their contacts with the neighboring settlers to a place on the riverbank near Wiltwyck, where small numbers might come to trade if they sent a flag of truce ahead. The usual provisions for peaceful settlement of disputes were included, and the Indians, accepting all these conditions, agreed to have the rest of their chiefs ratify the treaty within a month. To avoid future misunderstanding this ratification was to be repeated at New Amsterdam every year. On the next day, May 16, the treaty was formalized, and the Hackensack and Nyack sachems agreed to act as sureties for the Esopus bands' good conduct. The disordered conditions of their existence perhaps hindered the Indians from fully observing the ratification requirement; at least this was the excuse of the single chief who finally appeared in July. He promised that the others would soon follow, but in a few weeks enforcement of the treaty had become an English problem.[45]

A contributing factor in the strife between Indian and colonist during these years was the uninterrupted course of the liquor traffic. The seeds of discontent lay far deeper, of course, than the problem of alcoholism, but that weakness and the colonists' greed for profit compounded the difficulties already inherent in their positions. Many, perhaps most, of the daily annoyances and depredations—incidents too minute to win immortalization in the records—were traceable to drunken Indians. The director and council passed two ordinances during the troubled years of 1656 and 1657 to curb this "most dangerous and damnable" traffic. As some traders by now made it a common practice to sail up and down the river peddling liquor to the Indians along the way, persons were forbidden to load this commodity on boats without a license. Enforcement of these bans was strictest at the time of their enactment, and in 1656 a married couple was banished to Holland after conviction on Indian testimony. Others were given the same sentence and later pardoned, but enforcement on the whole was

[45] *Ibid.*, 375–377, 386–387.

desultory.[46] In March 1662, after Oratamin and Matteno had complained that the liquor traffic was demoralizing their bands, the council authorized them to seize any brandy brought into their country for sale and to bring the offending traders to New Amsterdam for punishment. When they repeated the complaint a year later, specifically accusing Stuyvesant's trusted agent, Van Couwenhoven, the governor merely renewed his previous authorization with an additional reward for Indians who brought in guilty traders. In July 1663 local courts were empowered to make and enforce bans of their own on this subject, and some towns on Long Island were already doing so.[47] Later that year an order was issued for the arrest of drunken Indians on the Sabbath. Liquor had contributed mightily to the Indian troubles at the Esopus, and when peace was concluded in 1664, Stuyvesant ordered that particular caution to be taken at Wiltwyck to prevent a recurrence of the evil.[48] By this time, however, the futility of such orders should have been recognized. It is impossible to believe that the authorities were not seriously concerned with the liquor traffic, but public indifference and disobedience continued to thwart their efforts to control it.

The early ideal of converting the Indians to Christianity, and of imparting the rudiments of European civilization, never died out altogether in New Netherland but it undeniably suffered lean years. More than a decade passed after Domine Michaëlius' time before another clergyman addressed himself seriously to the problem. In 1642 Domine Johannes Megapolensis was sent over by the patroon as minister at Rensselaerswyck for a term of six years. Almost immediately he appears to have laid siege to the formidable Mohawk language, hoping eventually to preach in it. However, this tongue proved to be as much of a stumbling block as had the Algonquian dialect around New Amsterdam. The Mohawk attitude toward Christianity was equally discouraging. "When we pray," Megapolensis admitted,

they laugh at us. Some of them despise it entirely; and some . . . stand astonished. When we deliver a sermon, sometimes ten or twelve of them . . .

[46] *LONN,* 259–261, 311; *NYCD,* XII, 129; XIII, 67–69; O'Callaghan, *Calendar of Historical MSS,* I, 170–177, 199, 201, 257–259.
[47] *NYCD,* XIII, 218–219, 277; *LONN,* 446–447; Martha B. Flint, *Early Long Island: A Colonial Study* (New York, 1896), 52; *NYDH,* I, 652; *Oyster Bay Town Records, 1653–1763* (New York, 1916–1931), I, 2.
[48] *LONN,* 451; *NYCD,* XIII, 77, 105, 228–229, 237–238, 386.

will attend, each having a long tobacco pipe . . . in his mouth, and will stand awhile and look, and afterwards ask me what I am doing. . . . I tell them that I am admonishing the Christians, that they must not steal, nor commit lewdness, nor get drunk, nor commit murder, and that they too ought not to do these things; and that I intend in process of time to preach the same to them and come to them in their own country . . . when I am acquainted with their language. Then they say I do well to teach the Christians; but immediately add . . . "Why do so many Christians do these things?" [49]

By 1649, when he took up a pastorate in New Amsterdam, Megapolensis had almost certainly failed to convert a single Indian. In the same year the commonalty of New Netherland used neglect of Indian conversion as another lever with which to pry itself loose from company proprietorship. The directors defended themselves by declaring that it was "morally impossible" to convert adult Indians to Christianity. Besides, they added, it was up to the clergy and not the company to struggle with this problem. Stuyvesant sympathized with the cause and promised the classis of Amsterdam to co-operate with any suggestions that they might make to bring conversion closer to reality. He was far too busy with problems of a more earthly nature, however, and gave very little attention to the subject thereafter.[50] When an undoubtedly sincere and capable clergyman of Megapolensis' stamp made so little headway against native indifference, it is not surprising that others were no more successful. Too often the Dutch pastors sent out to America were those who had failed to get a call in the Fatherland, and once here they contented themselves with the minimum ministrations to their flocks of European birth. Domine Gideon Schaats, for instance, was sent to Rensselaerswyck in 1652 with instructions to "use all Christian zeal there to bring up both the Heathens and their children in the Christian Religion." He was also expected to take native children into his house and educate them, but there is no record in all of Schaats's forty-year pastorate that he did either.[51]

[49] *NNN*, 172, 177–178 (including quotation); Frederick J. Zwierlein, *Religion in New Netherland* (Rochester, N.Y., 1910), 268–273.

[50] *NYCD*, I, 270, 340; New York Historical Society, *Proceedings, 1844*, 64; see also *NYHSC*, 2d ser., I, 214–215.

[51] O'Callaghan, *History of New Netherland*, II, 567; Charles E. Corwin, "Efforts of the Dutch-American Colonial Pastors for the Conversion of the Indians," in Presbyterian Historical Society, *Journal*, XII (1925), 235.

Megapolensis, with his colleague Samuel Drisius, continued to work with the Indians at New Amsterdam. Both men, however, were pessimistic about the prospects of conversion "until by the numbers and power of our nation they are subdued and brought under some policy and our people shew them a better example than they have hitherto done." This opinion was based on recent experience, they reported to the classis of Amsterdam:

We have had one Indian here with us full two years, so that he could read and write good Dutch; we instructed him in the grounds of Religion; he also answered publicly in the church, & repeated the prayers. We likewise presented him with a Bible in order to work through him some good among the Indians. But it all resulted in nothing. He has taken to drinking of Brandy; he pawned the bible and became a real beast who is doing more harm than good among the Indians.[52]

That the Dutch made such a poor showing compared with the French in this field of Indian affairs was largely owing to differences between their respective faiths. Roman Catholicism, with its ritual, ceremony, and visible symbols of faith, had a stronger appeal for a people whose religion and very ways of thought were expressed in terms symbolic of the physical universe and their forest environment. How many Indians penetrated beyond the outer symbolism of the Catholic faith is another matter, but certainly very few of them at this point were ready to appreciate the introspective and unadorned Calvinism offered them by the Dutch Reformed Church. The two churches also differed in the standards required for baptism. The Jesuit fathers labored throughout Canada and Iroquoia baptizing those who requested it—and many who did not—with little regard to age or previous instruction. In accordance with general Protestant practice, however, the classis of Amsterdam ruled in 1661 that baptism should be administered only to adult Indians who had confessed their faith and to their children.[53] It is difficult to say how much evidence of regeneration ministers required before accepting such confessions, but they were certainly stricter than the Jesuits in this regard. In comparison with New England, the successes of John Eliot and others, impressive

---

[52] *NYDH*, III, 108. See also the letter of Megapolensis and Drisius of July 15, 1654, in Edward T. Corwin, ed., *Ecclesiastical Records of the State of New York* (Albany, 1901–1916), I, 326–327.

[53] Corwin, *Ecclesiastical Records of New York*, I, 508.

as they were, were attained among Indians who had already been broken on the wheel of European civilization. True conversion of the Indians, as Megapolensis and Drisius perceived and as later experience amply demonstrated, depended on their prior submission to the white man, with the attendant disintegration of their own culture. This stage of development was barely beginning in some parts of New Netherland when the province passed from Dutch hands.[54]

A common circumstance of life on every Indian frontier was the prevalence, or at least the opportunity, of miscegenation. In New Netherland as elsewhere it arose from a high proportion of unmarried men on one side, many young squaws on the other, and loose social controls on both. Mixing of the races was probably less common here than in New France or New Spain, but more so than in New England, where public disapproval was the strongest. The only known regulation of it among the Dutch occurred at Rensselaerswyck, where Indian relations were usually more cordial to begin with. In 1639 the patroon forbade his people "to mix with the heathen . . . women, for such things are a great abomination to the Lord God and kill the souls of . . . Christians." Fines were provided in an ordinance of 1643, but they seem never to have been assessed.[55] At least a few liaisons between Dutchmen and Indian women lasted for a lifetime and were entered upon with faultless precision according to Indian custom. A number of respectable citizens were born of such marriages. Perhaps the best example is offered by the descendants of Cornelis Antonisen van Slyck, a trader who settled at least temporarily in the Mohawk country about 1640, took a wife from that tribe, and raised a family that became prominent on the Mohawk frontier.[56]

Until the Indian descent upon New Amsterdam in 1655 Stuyvesant had adhered to his course of peaceful negotiation, not to say appeasement, in dealing with the surrounding tribesmen. This policy was not always popular, either with the colonists or with his colleagues on the provincial council, and after they transformed an Indian provocation into an armed attack during his absence, Stuyvesant and his superiors

---

[54] For a more extended treatment of Indian conversion in New Netherland, see Zwierlein, *Religion in New Netherland,* ch. ix, and Corwin, "Efforts of the Dutch-American Colonial Pastors," 225–246.

[55] *VRBM,* 442, 694.

[56] Nelson Greene, *Fort Plain Nelliston History, 1580–1947* (Ft. Plain, N.Y., 1947), 27; Higgins, *Expansion in New York,* 9, 18–19, and *passim.*

both reverted in theory to Kieft's policy of subjugating the natives by force. Stuyvesant was fully aware of the dangers involved in this course and of his inability to prosecute it successfully without outside aid. As this was not forthcoming, he continued to temporize, until the crisis had passed and troubles developed elsewhere. The Esopus Wars were the outgrowth in large part of Dutch encroachment on Indian lands, however legal this action may have been from the European standpoint. Again it was the local colonists who first provoked hostilities and confronted the government with an Indian war. As the tribesmen involved were fewer in number than those around New Amsterdam, Stuyvesant in this case elected to conduct the war as vigorously as possible, striving at the same time to keep it from spreading beyond manageable limits. The first Esopus War was a failure because he overestimated the enemy's willingness to submit, but the second achieved its purpose. At its end the Algonquian bands were permanently humbled, although the fact is plainer now than it was at the time. From 1664 onward the Hudson valley bands, like Tackapousha's Indians on Long Island, were hardly more than satellites of the dominant colonizing power.

By 1664 New Netherland had attained a population of close to 10,000 souls, 1,500 of whom resided in New Amsterdam. That the colony's progress had been painfully slow was due to a number of factors, not the least of which was the intermittent terror fostered by the surrounding Indians. It had been governed at the beginning as a series of trading posts, and even in Stuyvesant's time company policy was influenced by a misguided commercialism which too often sacrificed the welfare of its colonists for the sake of immediate pecuniary advantage. In the face of ever-mounting pressure from the neighboring English colonies, particularly those to the east, the only sure defense lay in a greater influx of Dutch colonists than had appeared so far or was likely to appear in the foreseeable future. No one recognized more clearly than Stuyvesant that his province was living on borrowed time. Foreclosure awaited only a concerted effort on the part of New England or its mother country. It was Stuyvesant's constant policy to avert the former through agreements between the respective provinces in America, and when the attack came, it was launched in England.

In March 1664 Charles II favored his brother James, Duke of York and Albany, with a grant of territory in North America extending from the Delaware to the Connecticut Rivers and including Long Island, Martha's Vineyard, Nantucket, and part of Maine besides. All that remained was for the duke to capture his prize. In May a squadron of four ships, carrying a complement of 450 soldiers, was dispatched under the command of Colonel Richard Nicolls to effect the reduction of New Netherland. The expedition reached the western end of Long Island early in August, just after Stuyvesant's departure for Fort Orange. As soon as the governor returned on August 25, he set about repairing New Amsterdam's defenses and parleying with messengers from the English fleet, endeavoring to the end to gain by diplomacy what he had no chance of winning by the sword. Nicolls demanded a full surrender, however, and although Stuyvesant declared privately that he would sooner be carried out dead than give up without a fight, his subjects were of another mind. The English population now constituted an openly rebellious fifth column while the Dutch, including Stuyvesant's own son, pleaded for surrender without bloodshed. The case indeed was hopeless. The fort was weak, the men and supplies were few, and the populace was on the point of revolt. The West India Company had failed its colonists; now they, having little to lose, repaid it in kind. Nicolls' terms were generous, permitting the retention of most Dutch institutions and continued intercourse with the Fatherland. Only after prolonged and acrimonious debate did Stuyvesant give in to the inevitable, and on September 8, 1664, New Amsterdam became New York. The rest of the province, now similarly renamed, was easily taken. Albany, the duke's second title, was given to Fort Orange and Beverwyck, which capitulated on September 20. The only resistance occurred on the Delaware, the west side of which was not even included in the duke's patent. The weak opposition in this quarter was overcome without difficulty by Sir Robert Carr, whose rapacity in dealings with the colonists marked the only blot on an otherwise magnanimous conquest. By the middle of October the reduction of New Netherland was complete.[57]

[57] Brodhead, *History of New York*, I, 735–745.

VII

The Submergence of the Algonquian

ONE of the first acts of the Duke of York after receiving his grant of New Netherland was to give a large part of it—forthwith named New Jersey—to two favorites, Lord John Berkeley and Sir George Carteret. This gift occurred while Nicolls and his fleet were at sea, and he did not learn of it until June 1665. Having governed the province in its entirety for almost a year, he complained strenuously to the duke of its dismemberment, and succeeding governors of New York repeatedly echoed his pleas for a reunion. After 1665, however, the Province of New York was further reduced by the transfer of the Delaware region to William Penn in 1681 and by the loss of Martha's Vineyard, Nantucket, and its share of Maine to Massachusetts. The area remaining, which will concern us henceforth, was limited to Long Island, Staten Island, and the bulk of the Hudson valley.

By the terms of the royal grant of 1664 the duke's political authority over New York was fully as broad as that which the Dutch West India Company had exercised before the conquest. The autocratic powers of Stuyvesant were undiminished in the hands of Nicolls, who wielded greater power than any other English governor on the continent. He was assisted by a provincial secretary and four councilors, all appointive, who together constituted the highest legislative and judicial authority in the colony. In Nicolls the proprietor had found very nearly the perfect man for the delicate assignment of reconciling an alien people to English rule. At once firm in establishing the essential ends of English control and conciliatory in his means of attaining them, Nicolls sought to make the transformation as painless as possible. Dutch law and Dutch local institutions were only gradually modified to fit the prevailing patterns of English colonial administration. Even the Dutch language remained in official use for many years, particularly at Albany, and subordinate officials were often permitted to remain in office on the same basis as before the conquest.

Nicolls was replaced in 1668 by Colonel Francis Lovelace, who attempted to govern in the same spirit. In 1673 his duties came to an abrupt end owing to the vicissitudes of the third Anglo-Dutch War, which England had initiated the previous year. Now, as far as New York was concerned, the tables were turned; when a Dutch fleet appeared in New York harbor at the end of July (Old Style), the city and colony proved no more defensible than in 1664. Lovelace was in Connecticut at the time, and in his absence the Dutch burghers welcomed back their fellow countrymen. The English garrison surrendered after only a token resistance, and in due course the rest of the province, along with New Jersey, followed suit. But before the year was out the hard-pressed States-General, obliged to face French armies by land as well as English fleets by sea, offered to give back their province in return for peace with England. In February 1674 a treaty was concluded at Westminster to this effect, and in October a new English governor, Major Edmund Andros, arrived at New York.

In taking up this office Andros began a long American career which eventually included also the governorships of New England, Maryland, and Virginia. The Dutch reoccupation of New York was only an interlude, and Andros, until his recall in 1681, governed the province on much the same basis as had Nicolls and Lovelace. It was two years before the duke got around to sending over a successor; meanwhile the incapacity of Anthony Brockholls, who was left in charge, and the squabbling of subordinate officials provided an opportunity for increasing agitation in favor of a popular assembly. New York was distinctly backward in this regard, for the other English colonies by this time enjoyed representative institutions with control over taxation at the very least. With the greatest reluctance James permitted his new governor, Colonel Thomas Dongan, to summon an assembly in 1683. This body met only three times, however, and ultimately all of its acts were vetoed in England.

In the next few years New York, like England herself, underwent a series of constitutional changes. When Charles II died in February 1685, his brother succeeded him as James II. By this fact New York became a propriety of the king, or, in other words, a royal colony, on the same basis as Virginia. Dongan received a new commission to this effect in 1686, but only as a temporary measure pending the enactment of a sweeping colonial reform. The fragmentation of the North American colonies, tending toward inefficiency in administration and weakness in the face of foreign powers, and particularly the near-independence of the New England commonwealths were galling in the extreme to the orderly mind and autocratic nature of the new monarch. He planned, therefore, to unite all the northern colonies under a single government, untroubled by elected assemblies and other factious popular institutions. Sir Edmund Andros (who had been knighted during his term in New York) was to head this government with essentially the same powers that he had enjoyed in New York. For two years the Dominion of New England extended only to New England proper, but in 1688 it was enlarged to include New York and New Jersey. Dongan accordingly in August of that year stepped down in favor of his predecessor. Andros remained at Boston, except for a brief visit to New York and New Jersey, and left those provinces to the immediate attention of his lieutenant governor, Francis Nicholson, who took up residence in New York.

The Dominion of New England was an artificial creation with almost no semblance of popular support and lasted no longer than the monarch who inspired it. No sooner had the news reached America in the spring of 1689 of James's flight from England and the accession of William and Mary than smaller-scale rebellions broke out in Boston and New York. The New Englanders, casting the governor into prison, resumed their former status under their respective charters; in New York the German-born Jacob Leisler led a successful revolt against Nicholson in May and June, causing the latter to return to England. By a combination of patriotic zeal against the French (with whom England went to war in 1689) and exploitation of a fanciful "Catholic menace" in New York, Leisler managed to remain in power for two years, eventually securing the allegiance of the whole province. In 1691 the new monarchs tardily sent a royal governor, Colonel Henry Sloughter, who lost no time in toppling the Leislerian regime and executing its leaders for treason. His other important action was to convene a new assembly, which continued in existence during the remainder of the colonial period. If Jacob Leisler had played the part of a demagogue by exercising power in the absence of adequate direction from the mother country, he was by no means a traitor, either to England or to William and Mary. The arbitrary course of both factions between 1689 and 1691 engendered a bitter feud between their respective partisans which dominated New York political life for a generation. Sloughter himself died after a few months in office, and his successors took sides openly with one or the other party, helping to perpetuate a controversy which they were unable or unwilling to resolve.

The population of New York grew steadily during the first generation of English control. New Netherland at the time of its conquest in 1664 numbered about 10,000 persons; by 1689 this figure, now exclusive of New Jersey and Delaware, had doubled. In part because of the effects of the first Anglo-French war (1689–1697) it fell to 18,000 by 1698, when it again began to rise. More than half of the population continued to be concentrated in and around the city of New York and on Long Island. The accessibility of this region and its proximity to the main channels of commercial activity are sufficient to explain this tendency, even without the large landed estates and a continuing Indian danger which discouraged extensive settlement in the Hudson valley. Albany, Dutchess, and Ulster Counties, comprising the northern two-thirds of that valley, contained only about 3,000 persons as late as 1698, although they grew fairly rapidly after that date. The city of New York, with about 1,500 persons in 1664, more than doubled its population by the turn of the century. It not only continued to be the commercial hub of the province but increased its economic ties with England, the West Indies, and other Atlantic ports from Boston to Charleston. To an even greater extent than before the conquest it was the most cosmopolitan, even if not the largest, city on the continent.

It is all but impossible to estimate the number of those Algonquian tribesmen who continued to live in the neighborhood of the colonial settlements. All evidence points to a continuing drop in population, a trend well established by 1664. An idea of the nature of this decline (as well as the colonists' reaction to it) may be gathered from Daniel Denton, a Long Islander writing about the Indians there in 1670:

Submergence of the Algonquian

There is now but few upon the Island, and those few no ways hurtful but rather serviceable to the English, and it is to be admired, how strangely they have decreast by the Hand of God, since the English first setling of those parts; for since my time [about 1644], where there were six towns, they are reduced to two small Villages, and it hath been generally observed, that where the English come to settle, a Divine Hand makes way for them, by removing or cutting off the Indians, either by Wars one with the other, or by some raging mortal Disease.[1]

Denton omitted to mention the mortality arising from wars with the white man, but as a killer of Indians smallpox and other diseases were probably more effective in the long run than warfare of either description. The total Indian population on Long Island was probably less than a thousand by 1664; what it amounted to thirty-five years later must be left to inference. A similar decline occurred on the neighboring mainland, although the process was probably slower in areas where English settlement was less intensified.[2]

Social and political disintegration went hand in hand with the decline in numbers. The natives continued to subsist by hunting, fishing, and farming, as Denton tells of the Long Island bands, but they grew increasingly dependent upon the white man. The Indian trade, insignificant by Albany standards, provided the Indian with the bulk of his clothing, household utensils, arms and implements, and liquor. In return for these he sold the surplus fruits of his hunting and farming or hired himself out to do odd jobs for the neighboring settlers. Long Island Indians more and more found employment in the whaling industry which developed in this period in the coastal villages. Native religious rites were still practiced, but often they degenerated into drunken orgies as the bonds of an older and simpler culture gradually gave way. The subtribal divisions tended to disappear when whole bands were decimated and their survivors consolidated with related groups. This process was probably further developed on Long Island than anywhere else in the province.[3] In the vicinity of Manhattan and

[1] Daniel Denton, *A Brief Description of New-York*, ed. by Victor H. Paltsits (New York, 1937), 6–7.

[2] In 1690 the Tappan, who may have included other tribal fragments by that time, reportedly had sixty warriors, and those in Queens County numbered forty-four in 1695 (*NYDH*, II, 237; *CSP, 1693–1696*, no. 1854).

[3] Such consolidation is suggested, for instance, by a reference in the Hempstead records of 1671 to strange Indians moving in with the Rockaway, who themselves

179

elsewhere most of the familiar bands were still present but their power and prestige had obviously waned. Political institutions remained outwardly much the same, centering in the sachem and his advisers. On Long Island, Tackapousha lived to a venerable old age, shepherding his decreasing flocks until death claimed him in 1694 or shortly thereafter. Except for some of the Delaware bands, who were fortunate enough to escape to the west, the ultimate fate of most of these native groups was extinction, and the signs of this were unmistakable by the end of the century.

Political relations between the Long Island bands and provincial authorities were almost invariably friendly, despite occasional alarms on both sides. Tackapousha and other nearby sachems followed a consistent policy of propitiating the colonial governors, in part to secure the latters' support in the recurrent disputes with local townspeople. Thus they made periodic visits to New York for no other apparent reason than to assure the governor of their continuing friendship—a practice which the governors seem to have encouraged.[4]

Distance, as well as previous alignment with New England, at first prevented such close ties with the Montauk and other bands at the far end of the island. Much to the discomfort of the New York authorities, who now claimed jurisdiction over them as well as their English neighbors, these bands continued in their tributary relationship with the Narraganset for several years. This situation precipitated a major alarm at East Hampton in 1669. Somehow the townspeople became convinced that dealings between the Montauk and Ninigret, the Narraganset sachem, were part of a widespread conspiracy against the English. They immediately disarmed the Montauk and notified Governor Lovelace of the plot. He in turn relayed the warning to the governor of Rhode Island, who summoned Ninigret before him at Newport. The sachem made such a convincing denial, however, that suspicions were soon quieted. In November, Lovelace prevailed on the Montauk to acknowledge him as their "Chiefest Sachem" in place of Ninigret, and they promised to give the latter no more of their wam-

---

constituted only about ten families at that time (*Hempstead Town Records*, I, 276).

⁴ See New York Colonial Manuscripts, 1638–1800, New York State Library (hereafter cited as Colonial MSS), XXIV, 71; XXVII, 54, 184; *CSP, 1689–1692*, no. 1380; *1693–1696*, nos. 1036, 1854; New York Council Minutes, 1668–1783, New York State Library (hereafter cited as Council Minutes), VII, 136–137, 234.

pum without the governor's consent. Henceforth their submission was almost as complete as that of the western bands under Tackapousha. By 1671, for example, the Montauk and Shinnecock permitted the governor to confirm in office the men that they had chosen as sachems and "constables" of their respective bands.[5]

Apart from what may be termed treaty relations, the ordering of Indian affairs on Long Island was wrapped up in the legal and administrative system which Nicolls established there soon after the conquest. Long Island, Staten Island, and the Bronx peninsula were organized into the County of Yorkshire, over which there was erected a court of assizes possessing legislative as well as judicial power. This court was composed of the governor, his council, and all the justices of the peace throughout the county. For several years thereafter, while other parts of the province were governed by administrative orders issued from New York, Yorkshire had its own legal code and judiciary. The code, known as the Duke's Laws, was promulgated at the proprietor's direction by the court of assizes in 1665. It dealt with practically every aspect of governmental activity above the purely local level, including Indian affairs, and was largely based on the codes of Massachusetts and New Haven. The Duke's Laws were later extended to the entire province, but they made little impression outside of Yorkshire and were superseded by acts of assembly after 1691.

For the everyday administration of Indian affairs in Yorkshire the governor relied primarily upon existing local officials; but the early years were a period of experimentation, and special officers were occasionally chosen for this purpose. In the east riding (modern Suffolk County), perhaps because it was too remote for effective supervision from New York, Nicolls established a special commission for Indian affairs in 1666. This body, consisting of five members, was empowered to hear and determine all disputes between the English and the Indians and to make such additional regulations as it saw fit for easing relations between them.[6] The commissioners functioned as creatures of the governor and subject to his authority. In 1672 Lovelace felt obliged to rebuke them for hearing cases which properly belonged to the regular

[5] Brodhead, *History of New York*, II, 155–156; *NYCD*, XIV, 627, 647; *Rhode Island Colonial Records*, II, 263–279; *Connecticut Colonial Records*, II, 548–551.

[6] Victor H. Paltsits, ed., *Minutes of the Executive Council of the Province of New York; Administration of Francis Lovelace, 1668–1673* (Albany, 1910), II, 684–685.

courts and shortly afterward stripped them of all power except a general responsibility to keep the Indians in good order. Cases of trespass and property damage involving Indians were henceforth to be heard before the town officials, with a right of appeal to the higher courts. In all likelihood the commission was soon abolished altogether or was suffered to die a natural death, for no mention of it appears after the Dutch interval of 1673–1674. A similar body was appointed for Staten Island in 1670, but its usefulness disappeared after the final purchase of that island from the natives later the same year.[7] Another early device for keeping order among the Long Island Indians was the institution of native constables who, in some instances at least, were chosen by the tribesmen themselves. They were apparently limited to the east end of the island, but whether they represented an Indian institution or one imposed by the English is unclear. Lovelace considered these officials to be a beneficial influence and urged their appointment at the Esopus and Nantucket as well.[8] Routine Indian affairs, however, came to be handled more and more by the regular local authorities; the more unusual assignments were delegated by the governor to one of the provincial council who lived nearby, such as Colonel William Smith in Suffolk and Colonel Thomas Willet in Queens.[9]

Relations with some of the northern New Jersey bands were a little more strained at the outset. Immediately after the conquest a settlement was begun between Sandy Hook and the Raritan. The land had been purchased in good faith (doubly purchased, in fact, since the Dutch also had bought it less than a year before), but the local Navasink Indians committed depredations on the new colonists. Nicolls, as yet unaware of the ducal grant of New Jersey to Berkeley and Carteret, used gifts and diplomacy, together with the presence of a large military force, to bring the Indians around peaceably.[10]

From this time the Navasink, Hackensack, Tappan, and neighboring bands remained in friendship with the authorities at New York. Most of them fell within the jurisdiction of New Jersey, but they frequently had dealings with other native groups to the north and west,

---

[7] *NYCD*, XIII, 442, 463; XIV, 663, 757.

[8] *Ibid.*, XIII, 430; Paltsits, *Executive Council Minutes*, I, 362.

[9] Council Minutes, VI, 205; VII, 93; VIII, pt. 1, 175.

[10] *NYCD*, XIII, 311–312, 314–316, 395–398; "Colonial Records; General Entries, 1664–65," in New York State Library, *Bulletin, History*, no. 2 (Albany, 1899), 169; *NYHSC, 1869*, 116–117.

and their sachems occasionally came in to discuss these matters and renew their friendship or perhaps just to visit the city. Such also was the case with the Wappinger bands north of Manhattan and the Minisink farther west. Their visits were encouraged by the governors, who managed thereby to exercise a general surveillance over them and to make sure of their continued good will. Times had changed, however; so much had the status of these bands fallen that, with a few exceptions, their names virtually disappear from the records save for these periodic courtesy calls.[11]

Indian affairs at the Esopus were handled more carefully and with greater regularity, owing to the recent strife in that quarter. Governor Nicolls visited Kingston (formerly Wiltwyck) in the fall of 1665 for the purpose, among other things, of confirming the peace and sounding out the Indians concerning a further land purchase. Soon afterward a number of the sachems went down to New York and concluded a treaty. This agreement was primarily a ratification of Stuyvesant's treaty of the year before, but in return for a sizable land cession the natives now received their former trading privileges in town. Nicolls repeated the requirement of annual ratification, but permitted the sachems to do so at Kingston instead of New York. Whether the Indians gave literal obedience to this demand is unclear, but they performed the obligation frequently and lived up to the treaty as a whole with reasonable fidelity throughout the remainder of the colonial period.[12]

By 1669 relations were on such a solid footing that Governor Lovelace ordered the disbandment of the Esopus garrison. He took pains at the same time, however, to appoint a special commission, like that on Long Island, to renew the late treaty and oversee Indian affairs generally. It was directed to appoint a constable among the Indians (who had apparently been subject to further drunken disorders) and one or two other officials to whom the Indians might have recourse. Departing somewhat from the governor's instructions, the board appointed Henry Pawling as a permanent commissioner for local Indian affairs, with

[11] For examples of such visits see *NYCD*, XIII, 428, 476, 478, 484, 551–552.

[12] *Ibid.*, 399–402, 417; Kenneth Scott and Charles E. Baker, "Renewals of Governor Nicolls' Treaty of 1665 with the Esopus Indians," in New York Historical Society, *Quarterly*, XXXVII (1953), 254; "Treaty between Col. Richard Nicolls, Governor of New York, and the Esopus Indians, 1665," in Ulster County Historical Society, *Collections*, I (1860), 62–65.

orders to carry out the governor's commands. The only specific limitation on his power was an injunction not to hinder anyone from trading with the Indians. After 1671 Pawling was apparently replaced by a new local court, which was empowered to hear cases involving Christians and Indians alike, as well as to supervise all relations with the local tribesmen. Among the recurring matters with which it had to deal were the periodic renewals of the 1665 treaty, physical violence between Indians and whites, trade relations, contracts and debts involving Indians, destruction of Indian crops by the settlers' livestock, rumors of native uprisings (these were universally exaggerated), and the harboring of strange Indians by the Esopus tribesmen. The most persistent problem in the generation after 1665 involved the boundaries of the several Indian land cessions. The court seems ordinarily to have handled these matters without interference or advice from provincial authorities, but it probably kept the governor informed on all matters of general interest.[13]

The gradual extinction of the seaboard Algonquian bands—those who found themselves directly in the path of European colonization—was unquestionably the work of the white man. It by no means follows, however, that this fate was the product of conscious planning or premeditated action, much as he might welcome it in the abstract. The provincial government and probably a majority of colonists strove to protect the Indian's rights as they saw them and looked with disapproval on attempts to take advantage of him by force or chicanery. Thus Governor Sloughter wrote to the justices of Queens County relative to a land dispute in 1691: "I desire to have Justice equally administred and will not connive at ye least Injury done to the meanest Indian in the Province." [14] Ordinary humanitarian feelings were always present, however much they might be strained in a given situation. Along the frontier it had been common for a long time to consider fair treatment of the natives a prerequisite to successful coexistence; where economic interests were a factor, as among the traders, this conviction was all the stronger. Even behind the frontier, where the Indian was seemingly at the colonists' mercy, neither law nor public opinion sanctioned ruthless spoliation. Good treatment and

[13] *NYCD*, XIII, 428–430, 432, 435, 438, 459–460; Scott and Baker, "Renewals of Governor Nicolls' Treaty," 255 ff.
[14] Colonial MSS, XXXVII, 66b.

friendly relationships were very naturally the desire of the home government too, and occasional instructions to this effect were sent to colonial authorities in 1664 and later.[15] On the other hand, there is no doubt that the Indian was relegated to a position of second-class citizenship. He was subject to racial discriminations, as well as to racial exemptions.[16] Possessing no political rights, he was at the same time free of direct taxation. Throughout the province, and particularly where he found himself in the midst of colonial settlements, a system of legal safeguards developed to assure the Indian of at least minimal human rights. In many ways his status resembled that of free Negroes in the ante-bellum south.

On Long Island the Duke's Laws provided from the beginning that "all injuryes done to the Indians . . . shall upon their Complaint and proofe thereof in any Court have speedy redress gratis, against any Christian in as full and Ample manner . . . as if the Case had been betwixt Christian & Christian." [17] The two rights here extended, equal access to the courts and free justice, were confirmed from time to time, although the latter was modified in 1669 after the people of Hempstead had complained of overlitigiousness on the part of the natives. Indian testimony was permitted in cases to which they themselves were not parties, including land disputes between colonists and prosecutions for illegal sale of liquor to the Indians. Native testimony was often held to be indispensable in such matters, but courts were sometimes reluctant to grant it equal weight with that of Christians. This was particularly true when guilt or innocence in criminal cases rested solely on evidence supplied by Indians.[18]

In the light of existing evidence it is difficult to measure very closely

---

[15] See *NYCD*, III, 53, 64, 547.

[16] An example of discrimination against Indians is provided by a council ruling of 1675 that natives discovering drift whales (in which the duke as proprietor had a vested interest) should be awarded "such reasonable satisfaction as has been usual," whereas Christians under similar circumstances were to receive a quarter of the proceeds from the whale (*NYCD*, XIV, 686). On the other hand, Indians not professing Christianity were exempted in 1695 from the provisions of a bill regulating personal conduct on Sabbath days (*Journal of the Votes and Proceedings of the General Assembly of the Colony of New York, 1691–1765* [New York, 1764–1766], I, 62).

[17] *Colonial Laws of New York from the Year 1664 to the Revolution* (Albany, 1894–1896), I, 40.

[18] *Ibid.*, 93, 99; *NYCD*, XIII, 484; XIV, 613, 632–633, 640–641.

the quality of justice actually meted out to Indians in the colonial courts. A fair proportion of the court records survive, however, and an examination of several of them, drawn from all parts of the province, warrants a few conclusions. The natives themselves, unaccustomed to litigation in the white man's courts, were generally reluctant to settle disputes in this manner. When Christians were not involved, they handled such matters in their own way; and if a complaint were to be brought against the white man, they preferred to approach the governor and council or the local magistrates as independent agents, rather than as citizens petitioning for justice according to alien forms of law. Except for a few cases on Long Island, therefore, the record of civil suits involving Indians is almost barren. Legal cases arising from Indian complaints were usually adjudicated by informal agreements outside of court or, in criminal cases, by government prosecution of colonists against whom the Indians had complained.

Cases in which the Indians themselves were accused of wrongdoing followed normal criminal procedure as nearly as circumstances allowed. On Long Island or Manhattan, where an Indian culprit like any colonist was within reach of the law, there was little variation from the standard procedure, and the same may be said for the penalties inflicted. In frontier regions, where the Indians were less subject to arrest, the only remedy was to approach the sachems and hope that the band itself would apprehend the offenders. Sometimes the natives were trusted to handle the problem in their own way, but more frequently the authorities were unimpressed with the course of Indian justice and requested surrender of the culprit for trial by the courts. These requests were ignored at least as often as not, and the only means of enforcing them was by military action. As a result Indian crimes often went unpunished unless they involved murder or some comparable offense. By and large the Indians seem to have experienced neither more nor less substantial justice under the English than under the Dutch. From their viewpoint there probably was little to choose between the two powers.

Except on the upper Hudson and perhaps along the Delaware as well, the Indian trade was no longer a major economic factor. It existed in some form, nevertheless, wherever the two races were found together and was subject to at least a modicum of official regulation, which often closely followed Dutch precedents. Ideas of *laissez faire* and free trade, with some early exceptions, were as much out of place in colonial New York as they had been in New Netherland. Not only were local monopolies an acceptable part of mercantilist doctrine, but the Indian trade in particular was open to abuses which required regulation for the good of the community. Although Nicolls and Lovelace removed some of the restrictions of Stuyvesant's time, they were largely restored under Andros and his successors.

The Duke's Laws of 1665 forbade anyone to trade with the Indians for furs without an annual license from the governor.[19] The Delaware region seems to have been under a similar regulation. These licenses were probably not hard to get, and it was stated at about this time that everyone in the province "who desires to trade for ffurs, at his request hath liberty so to doe." [20] Such latitude soon bred irregularities, both in trading methods and the sale of contraband items like liquor and armaments. In 1675, after Governor Carteret of New Jersey complained that New York traders had plundered some of the Navasink Indians, it was ordered that on no account should trade be carried on at the Indians' homes. A year later all commercial dealings with the Indians had to be registered with the local town clerk or else be transacted in the presence of a credible witness, preferably a justice of the peace. Furthermore, no Indians were to be lodged overnight in private homes, where careful supervision was next to impossible.[21] In March 1677 Andros returned to Stuyvesant's policy of confining the Indian trade to the towns and forbidding canoes or small boats to go up the Hudson without special permission.[22]

At the Esopus too all the local residents were permitted to engage in the fur trade, and there is no mention of a license requirement. They were assured a monopoly by the proclamations of 1677 and later, limiting the traffic to towns and forbidding small traders to sail up the river. After 1664 the Indians had free access to Kingston during the daytime to trade. For the convenience of those arriving after dark and with an eye to the community's nocturnal safety, a house was to be built for them just outside the gates (as at Albany) where they could stay at any time and leave their firearms. The Esopus bands had little

---

[19] *Colonial Laws,* I, 41; *NYCD,* XIV, 570, 596.

[20] *NYCD,* III, 188; XII, 459–460.

[21] *Colonial Laws,* I, 97; "New York's Colonial Archives; Transcriptions of the Records between the Years 1673 and 1675," Appendix L, in New York State Historian, *Annual Report, 1897* (New York and Albany, 1898), 388; Colonial MSS, XXV, 209; *NYCD,* XIV, 731.

[22] *NYCD,* XIII, 503–504, 553–554.

access to the sources of valuable peltry, and perhaps furs were subsidiary to other products of the forest or of Indian labor, such as venison and corn. The stakes involved in this trade were not so high as at Albany, and although it was conducted along similar lines, there is less evidence of cutthroat competition. At least one Albany habit did get established, however—that of extending credit to Indians, which led in turn to the taking of their children as hostages to ensure repayment. The latter practice, particularly when it was accomplished by force, was fraught with all sorts of danger to the community at large. Thus Governor Brockholls commended a local magistrate for restoring one of these children to his parents and warned that merchants foolish enough to trust Indians had no remedy in case of nonpayment. In no case, he declared, was force to be used against them, much less kidnaping.[23]

The liquor question was inextricably tied up with the Indian trade and with Indian relations in general. The English, who inherited the problem, came no closer than the Dutch to solving it. It was a constant source of complaint from Indians and whites alike throughout the colonial period. The Duke's Laws of 1665 prohibited the traffic on Long Island and its dependencies, but excepted the sale of up to two drams "by way of reliefe and Charity to any Indian in Case of sudden extremity sickness faintness or weariness." Moreover, the governor was authorized to license any person to sell unlimited quantities if security were pledged for the Indians' good behavior. Unlicensed persons made such a mockery of this law that it was soon amended to permit Indian testimony as a means of helping to establish guilt. Nicolls and Lovelace granted a number of these licenses, most of them, interestingly enough, to whalers for the purpose of encouraging Indians to work in this "infant industry." [24] The enforcement of the general ban was ineffectual, in spite of repeated complaints, proclamations, and renewals. The number of recorded prosecutions and convictions is so small as to imply that the Long Island magistrates gave up trying to enforce the law, and even the governor had seemingly lost interest by 1680.[25]

---

[23] "The Dutch Records of Kingston . . . 1658–1684," in New York State Historical Association, *Proceedings*, XI (1912), 168; *NYCD*, XIII, 399, 438, 566.

[24] *Colonial Laws*, I, 41, 93; *NYCD*, XIV, 596, 664; Paltsits, *Executive Council Minutes*, II, 459, 470, 473–474.

[25] *NYCD*, XIV, 645, 648, 700, 731; *Colonial Laws*, I, 97; Colonial MSS, XXVI, 68; XXVIII, 59, 61.

Submergence of the Algonquian

The city of New York was the scene of a small-scale but vigorous Indian trade, in which the natives supplied the inhabitants with provisions such as food and firewood. (Minisink tribesmen, however, occasionally brought in peltry from as far away as the Spanish frontiers.) [26] According to Jasper Danckaerts, a European visitor in 1679, rum was the chief commodity that they obtained in return. The city as he describes it was little more than a collection of speak-easies run for the purpose of fleecing the untutored natives:

The people in this city . . . are almost all traders in small articles[;] whenever they see an Indian enter the house, who they know has any money, they immediately set about getting hold of him, giving him rum to drink, whereby he is soon caught and becomes half a fool. If he should then buy any thing, he is doubly cheated, in the wares, and in the price. He is then urged to buy more drink, which they now make half water, and if he cannot drink it, they drink it themselves. They do not rest until they have cajoled him out of all his money, or most of it; and if that cannot be done in one day, they keep him, and let him lodge and sleep there, but in some out of the way place, down on the ground, guarding their merchandise and other property in the meantime, and always managing it so that the poor creature does not go away before he has given them all they want. And these miserable Christians are so much the more eager in this respect, because no money circulates among themselves, and they pay each other in wares, in which they are constantly cheating and defrauding each other. Although it is forbidden to sell the drink to the Indians, yet every one does it, and so much the more earnestly, and with so much greater and burning avarice, that it is done in secret.[27]

The mayor's court informed Governor Dongan in 1683 that both the number of Indian traders in the city and the value of their wares were slight, but as they well knew, he was looking about for new sources of revenue. He apparently thought that the traders were numerous enough to tax and henceforth required them to buy a license.[28]

The abuses Danckaerts describes were already well established by the time of his visit. Not only was the sale of liquor illegal but so was, several years earlier at least, the lodging of Indians overnight. In 1666 the mayor's court, having convicted a man of both offenses, levied a

[26] *NYCD*, XIII, 551.   [27] Danckaerts, *Journal*, 79.
[28] *Minutes of the Common Council of the City of New York, 1675–1776* (New York, 1905), I, 101–102, 108.

fine and ordered him to abandon his house, "as it is sufficiently notorious, that he resides there only for the purpose of carrying on the trade in brandy with the Indians." A year later he was threatened with banishment from the city after the sheriff found a quantity of well-watered rum at his house and other evidence of continued malpractice.[29] A Minisink sachem complained in 1681 that his fellow tribesmen came to the city to trade their beaver for winter clothing; "but finding Rumm in every house," they squandered their furs and got involved in drunken orgies, which had resulted in sixty deaths within three years.[30] In the city as elsewhere the court records indicate very few prosecutions, let alone convictions, for this offense, despite evidence of constant violations and occasional renewals of the law. Eventually the futility of this procedure led to a relaxation of the ban. After 1691 Indians were permitted to buy liquor in quantities of five gallons or more, apparently on the assumption that no more of it would be consumed in the city under this arrangement than at present.[31]

Around Kingston, where the local population depended more heavily on commerce with the Indians, the liquor prohibition was less severe. Soon after the conquest Governor Nicolls instructed the magistrates to prohibit the sale of liquor to the natives on pain of a fine of five hundred guilders. But in 1669 Lovelace required them to "regulate" Indian drunkenness in the area and investigate to see who was giving them more liquor "than is fitting or allowed of." In response heavy penalties were enacted for all persons selling the natives "such quantityes as shall make them drunk." When the Dutch took over in 1673, they granted the petition of some local residents and forbade "the sale of strong drink by the small measure" to the Indians, just as New York City did in 1691.[32] Probably this plan was retained after the English restoration.

With regard to the arms traffic too the English did very little to change the policies which had evolved by 1664. The same discrimination in favor of the Iroquois was maintained and for much the same reasons. At the Esopus as well this trade continued to take place with legal sanction as a necessary stimulant to the Indian trade. Only on the occasion of King Philip's War in New England in 1675–1676 did the

---

[29] Fernow, *New Amsterdam Records*, VI, 32–33, 76, 87.

[30] *NYCD*, XIII, 551–552.

[31] Fernow, *New Amsterdam Records*, VI, 100; *New York City Common Council Minutes*, I, 25, 223; *NYHSC*, 1868, 275–276.

[32] "Dutch Records of Kingston," 168; *NYCD*, II, 592–593; XIII, 430–431, 434.

authorities attempt to moderate the flow of guns and ammunition into Indian hands at Kingston, and this temporary measure was of doubtful utility.[33] On Long Island, where the situation was less complicated by economic considerations, regulations were somewhat stricter. The Duke's Laws forbade anyone to sell the Indians guns, ammunition, or even boats ("canooes only excepted") without license from the governor; nor were persons to "amend or repair any Gun belonging to any Indian." (In 1670 this ban was extended to the sale of horses, which the Indians were also forbidden to own.) But even on Long Island such a drastic curtailment was considered excessive, and before the year was out, the governor was prevailed upon to modify it. Henceforth the constable of each town was allowed to furnish Indians with as much ammunition "as may be thought necessary for their killing of woolves [on which there was a bounty] and provisions," and Indians were also permitted to have their guns repaired.[34] Apparently the ban, even as modified, was not uniformly enforced or obeyed; but during the first decade this seems not to have concerned the authorities overmuch. On several occasions Lovelace granted special permission to whalers to pay Indians' wages in powder and lead as well as liquor.[35]

This laxity of administration ended in July 1675 with the outbreak of King Philip's War. The Long Island tribesmen, and particularly those who were remotest from New York, had broken their agreement with the provincial authorities by paying additional tribute to the Narraganset. Fearful that this action might portend a widespread Indian conspiracy threatening his own province as well as New England, Governor Andros at once proceeded across the island, disarming the natives and reviewing the militia of the several towns. Andros had no concrete evidence of hostility on the part of any of these Indians; therefore he ordered the local authorities to protect them, while keeping them under constant surveillance. Returning to New York, he summoned the Hackensack and other New Jersey sachems, who renewed their allegiance and agreed to furnish two of their young men as hostages. With matters apparently stabilized in this vicinity he went up the Hudson in August to renew the friendship of the northern tribes.[36]

By September the fear of an Indian rising on Long Island had abated

---

[33] *NYCD*, XIII, 491–492.   [34] *Colonial Laws*, I, 40–41, 72, 78–79, 82–83.
[35] *NYCD*, XIV, 608–609, 664; Paltsits, *Executive Council Minutes*, II, 459–470.
[36] *NYCD*, III, 238, 254; XIV, 695, 699; "New York's Colonial Archives," 358; Council Minutes, III, pt. 2, 44.

somewhat. The natives' behavior was exemplary, and as the hunting season was approaching, it was decided to restore their arms. Those at East Hampton and Shelter Island, who had corresponded with the Narraganset, were excepted from this provision, however, despite a special plea by the Montauk for the return of their guns. At the same time each town was ordered to fortify a place for the safety of its inhabitants in case of attack, and measures were taken to prevent any intercourse between the mainland bands and those on the island. A group of Westchester tribesmen, moreover, was given peremptory orders to move within a fortnight to its usual winter quarters near the Hell Gate, where presumably it could be better watched.[37]

Late in October the war scare was intensified, or at least the authorities placed new credence in reports that Tackapousha and others were plotting with Indians of the mainland. Once more the Long Island bands were required to surrender their guns, on the understanding that trustworthy individuals were to receive them back again for their hunting. The Indians protested their innocence and repeated their assurances of friendship, but the process of disarmament went on over a period of several months. Local officials were ordered to investigate the natives' activities each day and to see that they remained in their usual homes. The whalers at East Hampton were required to get special permission from the constable and overseers to hire any strange Indians.[38] Hearing in December that the western bands were planning a general meeting, unusual at that time of year, Andros ordered an investigation and required them to disperse. A month later he ordered all Indians on the island to be disarmed immediately and without exception. They were not "to ramble or goe from place to place out of the Bounds they live in without a Certificate from ye Magistrate or Constable," but were nevertheless to receive justice and the full protection of the law in their legitimate pursuits.[39] In the spring of 1676, as Indian resistance was gradually crushed in New England, there was a corresponding relaxation of tension in New York. Guns were gradually returned to their native owners, and Indians again were allowed

[37] *NYCD*, XIII, 484; XIV, 696–700, 702–703, 705; *Colonial Laws*, I, 97–98.
[38] *NYCD*, XIV, 703, 706, 709, 711–712; "New York's Colonial Archives," 435; Onderdonk, *Queen's County in Olden Times*, 8; Colonial MSS, XXV, 68b; *Records of the Town of East-Hampton, Long Island* (Sag Harbor, N.Y., 1887–1905), I, 380–381.
[39] *NYCD*, XIV, 709, 712.

to go in their own boats.[40] There is no further mention of the arms traffic on Long Island; it undoubtedly persisted, however, decreasing in volume and importance as the Indians themselves fell off in number.

Just as King Philip's War marked the last stand of the natives in New England, so the false crisis which accompanied it in New York was the last Indian alarm of any consequence on Long Island or the adjacent mainland. In 1693 rumors of an intended insurrection in Queens County led to the arrest of several Indians, but the whole idea seemed improbable, and the matter was allowed to drop.[41] A year later all the sachems on the island were called before the governor and council after the natives were reported to be holding unusual meetings and making stores of bows and arrows. They apparently had fallen victim to stories of evil intent on the part of the English. Governor Benjamin Fletcher chided them for their gullibility and distrust and announced that he could easily destroy them if they were disorderly and deserved it. This declaration could hardly have allayed their fears although he coupled it with an assurance of friendship. When similar reports about the English circulated in 1700, the Indians took them less seriously, and the alarm disappeared after further official reassurances.[42]

In matters of land policy the English theoretically were less ready than the Dutch to concede Indian rights of prior ownership. Their practice, however, was not fundamentally different. By the law of nations, as the provincial council pointed out on one occasion, the title to land in a "barbarian country" was automatically vested in the prince of the state which discovered it and was subject to his ultimate disposal. "Tho it hath been & Still is ye Usuall Practice" in all colonies, they said, to pay the Indians something for their land, thus seeming to buy it from them, this was not a legal requirement. It was done, rather, "out of Prudence & Christian Charity Least otherwise the Indians might have destroyed ye first planters" or refused any "Commerce and Conversation" with them, whereby "all hopes of Converting them to ye Christian faith would be Lost." [43]

Only in the eighteenth century did the English consistently adopt

[40] *Ibid.,* XIII, 494–496; XIV, 717–718, 720–721; Colonial MSS, XXV, 165; Council Minutes, III, pt. 2, 103.

[41] *CSP, 1693–1696,* nos. 363, 386; Council Minutes, VI, 205.

[42] Council Minutes, VII, 93, 97–98; *CSP, 1700,* nos. 282, 331.

[43] *NYCD,* XIII, 487.

the Dutch practice of concentrating land purchases in the hands of the provincial authorities. Many of the Long Island towns continued to follow New England precedent in buying lands as a community project and parceling them out later to individual inhabitants.[44] After 1664 some of the Dutch towns adopted this procedure also, but most land purchases elsewhere in the colony were made by individuals. From the beginning no one was allowed to negotiate with the Indians for this purpose without a license from the governor. Once the purchase was made, both parties had to appear personally before the governor to acknowledge that a satisfactory agreement had been made. Then he issued a patent to the buyers, and the transaction was permanently recorded.[45] Admirable as it was in theory, the requirement of a personal appearance in New York was soon shown to be impractical. There were too many transactions to begin with, and the parties were often too remote from the capital to make this provision enforceable. Although governors continued to insist, without entire success, on the necessity of a prior license, they came to demand in addition only a certificate of the completed purchase before issuing a final patent.[46] By 1684 the requirement of personal appearance was dropped altogether.[47]

Beginning with Andros in 1674, every new governor was instructed to buy up such large tracts of land contiguous to settled areas or convenient for trade as the Indians might willingly part with for "small sums." Few governors did very much to implement this directive, but Dongan reported in 1687 that he had made sizable purchases along the Hudson, on the south side of Long Island, and on the Susquehanna.[48] Governor Fletcher sanctioned a number of vast purchases from the Iroquois in the 1690's which had political ramifications; these will be treated in a later chapter. The greatest land transaction around New

[44] See Charles R. Street, ed., *Huntington Town Records . . . 1653 . . . 1873* (Huntington, N.Y., 1887–1899), I, 178; II, 56–57, 81–82.

[45] "Colonial Records of the State [1664–1673]," Appendix G, in New York State Historian, *Annual Report, 1896* (New York and Albany, 1897), 340; *NYCD*, XIV, 562–563; *Colonial Laws*, I, 40; *CSP, 1697–1698*, no. 622.II; William Smith, *History of the Province of New York* (New York, 1829–1830), I, 35.

[46] Cf. *NYCD*, XIV, 569, 584–585, 635; *Huntington Town Records*, I, 178; II, 56–57, 81–82; *Oyster Bay Records*, I, 113.

[47] Colonial MSS, XXII, 136; Council Minutes, V, 60; *Colonial Laws*, I, 149.

[48] *NYCD*, III, 219, 334, 374, 406, 547.

Submergence of the Algonquian

York City was the third and final purchase of Staten Island, completed by Governor Lovelace in 1670. The Indians alleged that their first sale in 1630 had not included the whole island and that the one of 1657 was void because the Dutch had failed to deliver the goods promised in payment. It is impossible to determine the natives' sincerity in making these allegations or to know whether the goods were delivered in 1657; the patent of 1630 certainly includes the whole island, whatever the Indians may have thought. In any case one of the provisions of this final agreement was that the native occupants should leave the island permanently—a condition they soon fulfilled.[49]

The records are dotted with fragmentary references to land disputes, most of them occurring on Long Island. The population density was greater here than in any other region of comparable size, and by the turn of the century the local tribesmen were restricted to a small fraction of the island's surface. In Oyster Bay, for instance, the very last lands in the township were purchased in 1707, just fifty-four years after the original purchase and beginning of settlement.[50] After about 1710 the records of several towns are completely bereft of any reference to Indians.

By far the most persistent and troublesome land dispute on the island was the continuing quarrel between Tackapousha's tribesmen and the town of Hempstead. In this period it centered around the ownership of some necks of land along the northern coast. The town claimed to have bought them as early as 1658 from Tackapousha, but the deed was unclear and that chieftain vehemently denied having had even the right to sell them. Nicolls, Lovelace, and Andros were all forced to intervene in the matter, usually on behalf of the Indians. As soon as an agreement in principle was made to purchase (or repurchase) the lands in question, the quarrel would flare up anew over the boundaries to be drawn. In 1677 Andros peremptorily ordered the town to agree with the Indians within three months, or he would impose a settlement himself. This threat seems to have quieted matters for a while, but two years later Tackapousha was back in court over the ownership of a single neck of land in the same vicinity. In

[49] *Ibid.*, XIII, 2, 452–457.
[50] Van S. Merle-Smith, *The Village of Oyster Bay: Its Foundation and Growth from 1653 to 1700* (Garden City, N.Y., 1953), 25.

1682 he won this case in the court of assizes, and the difficulty appears to have subsided.[51]

Two years later the new governor, Dongan, had the fortitude to re-open the whole matter by summoning the Indians and townsmen before him to prove their respective titles. This action had only an incidental connection with prior events in the town; in fact, it was one of the first steps in a campaign to extort higher taxes from colonists all over the island. Beginning in 1666 Governor Nicolls had required each town to take out a new charter confirming its municipal status, boundaries, rights, and privileges. These patents provided for relatively small quitrent payments, which Dongan considered inadequate. His present plan was to have the respective towns surrender their charters "voluntarily," whereupon he would confirm them with provision for higher quitrents. A personal inducement to this course lay in the fees which governors customarily charged for issuing such documents. Dongan had no legal authority to revoke patents already granted, but in fact he had a powerful weapon at hand to force the towns' submission. This lay in a threat to buy up all the unpurchased land within their boundaries. Such action, if carried out, could have limited the present inhabitants and their descendants to the lands that they already occupied; it might also have brought an influx of strangers who had no roots in the community. Between 1684 and 1686 almost all the towns on the island submitted to new and less advantageous patents rather than face this extremity. Some, like Flushing and Hempstead, also propitiated the governor by giving him sizable tracts of land for his own use at the same time.[52]

This submission by no means eased the pressure on the Indians to sell their lands. Dongan still had his eye on quitrents and was eager to expand the amount of taxable land. Accordingly in November 1686

[51] Contemporary references to the Hempstead quarrels and lesser ones elsewhere, too fragmentary to be conclusive in most cases, appear in *NYCD*, XIV, *passim* (the most valuable); Onderdonk, *Annals of Hempstead* and *Queen's County in Olden Times;* "Colonial Records of the State" and "New York's Colonial Archives," in New York State Historian, *Annual Report,* 1896 and 1897; printed records of Hempstead, Oyster Bay, and other Long Island towns; Colonial MSS, XXIV–XXVI; *NYHSC, 1912,* 32–33. The only attempt to discuss the Hempstead affair in any detail is in Schultz, *Colonial Hempstead,* 130–133.

[52] O'Callaghan, *Calendar of Historical MSS,* II, 133; *Hempstead Town Records,* I, 487–489; Brodhead, *History of New York,* II, 109–110, 437–438; Onderdonk, *Annals of Hempstead,* 58; *Huntington Town Records,* I, 440–441, 468, 471–473.

several of the towns were ordered to buy up "for his Majesty's use" all the unpurchased lands within their boundaries. This requirement was of grave importance to the Indians, but Dongan seems to have taken care from the beginning to respect their legitimate claims and to see that they received satisfactory compensation. As a preliminary step officials were sent out with parties of Indians and townsmen to hear all claims and verify boundaries. Unfortunately the records break down at this point, and it is impossible to discover how many transactions occurred, or what lands were involved, or how fully Indian rights were respected by the time the process was completed.[53] In some cases, certainly, his purchase order was not carried out; in others he issued patents to the Indians themselves, who henceforth became owners on the same basis as their European neighbors. It is reasonable to assume, however, that this procedure effectively reduced the areas under Indian control.[54] Land disputes continued on the island, but they were less frequent. Although the natives were complaining against Hempstead as late as 1694, they continued to receive justice from the provincial authorities.[55]

Next to the problem of landownership the perennial cases of trespass and property damage, particularly on the part of stray animals, were perhaps the leading cause of racial friction on Long Island. The Duke's Laws of 1665 held the colonists themselves responsible in the first instance for whatever damage their livestock might do in the Indians' unfenced cornfields. They were encouraged to help the natives in fencing their lands, and only if such offers were refused were the Indians to be responsible for future damages. Indians, on the other hand, were held accountable for any harm that they did to the Christians' cattle as a result of such forays.[56] On occasion the governor intervened personally in disputes of this nature, at least once requiring a town to fence in the natives' land at its own expense. The recurrence of this kind of difficulty on Staten Island seems to have precipitated its final purchase with the requirement that the natives evacuate altogether. The Indians' dogs were another continuing sore point, particularly at

[53] O'Callaghan, *Calendar of Historical MSS*, II, 139; *CSP, 1685–1688*, nos. 990, 1028, 1040; *Oyster Bay Records*, II, 331; Council Minutes transcripts of Nov. 18 and 20, 1686, in "Moore–N.Y." Papers, New York Public Library.

[54] See *Oyster Bay Records*, I, 519.

[55] Colonial MSS, XXXVII, 66b; XXXVIII, 89; Council Minutes, VII, 109.

[56] *Colonial Laws*, I, 41–42.

the far end of Long Island, where they were said to be as destructive as wolves. In 1680 the natives at Southampton promised Andros to kill all but a few of them there, but neighboring East Hampton was still legislating on this problem as late as 1712.[57]

In other parts of the province, where population was thinner and land transactions were fewer, legal regulations on this subject were less thoroughly enforced. The governor kept a fairly close watch over land matters, but necessarily left the primary responsibility to local officials. One of Nicolls' purposes in visiting the Esopus in 1665 was to confirm the Indians' promise to Stuyvesant of the year before to cede most of their remaining lands in that vicinity. His treaty, like Stuyvesant's, provided for the purchase of a large tract west and southwest of Kingston, which he hoped would serve as the basis of a large settlement.[58] The treaty was subject to annual ratification, but this did not prevent disputes from arising later over the boundaries involved. By 1675 there were rumblings of discontent among the tribesmen, and two years later it was ordered that a perambulation of the bounds be made publicly in the presence of both Indians and Christians. Furthermore, the white population in the area was growing, and pressure was being exerted on the natives to sell still another large tract, partly for the accommodation of some newly arrived French Huguenots. When the Indians proved reluctant, the council refused to let the matter drop and invited settlers to try their luck at individual negotiations. A month later Andros came up to add his voice to the clamor, and Indian resistance collapsed. The sachem Kaelcop, one of Stuyvesant's old antagonists, was prevailed upon to cede the northernmost part of the tribal domain, and the other Indians claimed to be satisfied with the negligible compensation that he requested for himself: a blanket, a shirt, a loaf of bread, and some cloth. The next day Andros permitted the Huguenots to negotiate with the Indians for a separate tract of their own, which resulted soon afterward in the settlement of New Paltz, several miles south. Other sales followed in the years to come, and there was occasional friction over their terms, as well as some irregularity in the procedures followed.[59] These difficulties were ap-

[57] *NYCD*, XIII, 441–442; XIV, 589, 756–757; *East Hampton Town Records*, II, 118, 287–288.

[58] *NYCD*, XIII, 400; Smith, *History of New York*, I, 36.

[59] *NYCD*, XIII, 492–493, 503–507, 515, 571; Scott and Baker, "Renewals of Governor Nicolls' Treaty," 262.

parently minor however, and had no serious consequences save the gradual but remorseless contraction of Indian freedom.

One of the most interesting economic enterprises to develop in colonial New York was the Long Island whaling industry, which assumed importance shortly after the English conquest. From its beginnings until its decline more than a century later, the local Indians played an important role in carrying it forward. Interest in drift whales washed up on the island's beaches was stimulated at an early date by the proceeds to be made from selling the oil and bone. As early as 1644 Southampton provided for the patrolling of beaches, the division of labor, and the distribution of profits arising from drift whales found within the town limits. Apparently the Indians were the first to take to the sea in order to harpoon whales that they had sighted from shore. A major industry developed only after the colonists adopted and improved upon this example by initiating longer voyages. Southampton again seems to have led the way. In 1667 a number of residents agreed to fit out a boat manned by thirteen men and a boy for a whaling voyage of six to eight months. Within three years the business had become highly profitable and constituted a major activity in Southampton, East Hampton, Huntington, and other towns near the eastern end of the island.[60]

The Indians were particularly adept at capturing and killing the whales, and as a result they seem from the beginning to have provided a large part of the labor force. In order to attract even more of them Governor Lovelace permitted whalers to promise at least part of the wages in liquor and gunpowder. The Indians were ordinarily hired in the spring or early summer, well ahead of the whaling season, which lasted from October to March. They contracted for the entire season, binding themselves by a written contract to do such work as their employer might require, in return for specified wages. He was to furnish the boat and apparently most of the equipment. Indians who were willing and able to do this kind of work were in short supply and hence in a relatively good bargaining position. In some cases they were able to demand part of their pay in advance, and the wage level rose as a result of competitive bidding by prospective employers.[61]

[60] For a fuller discussion of this industry see Flick, *History of New York*, II, 278–280, and Adams, *History of Southampton*, 227–233.

[61] *NYCD*, XIV, 608–609, 645–646, 648, 664, 707–709; Paltsits, *Executive Coun-*

Under these circumstances the strong arm of seventeenth-century law was bound to intervene on behalf of Christian property interests. Southampton provided in 1672 "that Whosoever Shall Hire an Indyan to go a Whaling shall not give him for his Hire above one Trucking [trading] Cloath Coat for each Whale . . . hee or his Company Shall Kill or half the Blubber, without the Whale Bone." This regulation appeared so wholesome to Lovelace that he extended it to all other towns which might find it practicable.[62] Complaints that some of the Indians at East Hampton had broken their contract to accept better terms from other employers brought an order from Andros forbidding such actions and warning that the Indians should not be trusted or paid beforehand.[63] Undoubtedly the natives suffered discrimination, but much of it was common to laboring classes of all descriptions in colonial America, and the whale fishery provided an opportunity of a sort which most Algonquian tribesmen never enjoyed.

For at least a generation the English were no more willing or able than the Dutch to work for the religious conversion of the Indians. Despite the usual talk in official and unofficial quarters about the responsibility for bringing the heathen to the light of Christian truth, the proddings of conscience on this account were not particularly severe. Except at Albany the only formal action by the government was to restrain Indians in the performance of their own religious rites, which were looked upon primarily as disturbances of the peace. The Duke's Laws proclaimed in 1665 that "no Indian whatsoever shall at any time be Suffered to Powaw or performe outward worship to the Devil in any Towne within this Government." Such goings on were idolatrous, of course, and they became insupportable when the natives, thoroughly primed with illicit rum, performed them virtually in the citizens' back yards. In 1671, after complaints to this effect from the far end of Long Island, the council reaffirmed the previous order along with the liquor ordinance and warned the natives to hold their powwows well away from the towns.[64]

The only man who labored actively with the Long Island Indians

---

cil Minutes, II, 459, 470. For examples of Indian whaling agreements see *East Hampton Town Records*, I, 378–379, and *Huntington Town Records*, I, 295–296.

[62] *NYCD*, XIV, 675. [63] *Ibid.*, 756–757.

[64] *Colonial Laws*, I, 42; *NYCD*, XIV, 648.

before 1700 was the Rev. Thomas James, minister of the church at East Hampton. Personally and theologically James was a product of New England, with which he maintained close relationships for many years. In 1660 the commissioners of the New England Confederation, hearing that he was interested in working with the tribesmen around East Hampton, granted him an allowance of £10 for an interpreter and other expenses and appropriated further sums for at least three years thereafter.[65] In time he became proficient in the local Algonquian dialect, with the result that his services were solicited in all quarters. Persons in Connecticut asked him to move there and continue the work of conversion begun by another; Governor Winthrop of the same colony offered him full support if he would devote himself entirely to Indian work; and some residents of Long Island suggested that he serve as official interpreter there. James frequently acted in this capacity and as an intermediary between Indians and colonists, particularly on behalf of the Montauk at East Hampton, but he refused all offers which would have taken him away from home permanently. Governor Lovelace took an immediate interest in James's work and asked for a copy of the Indian catechism which the minister had found time to compose, so that he could send it to England to be printed. He also promised to solicit the duke for support and to find another minister for East Hampton so that James could give his full time to Indian work, but none of these projects bore fruit.[66] Nor did James's labors have any appreciable or lasting affect on the Indians, so far as is discoverable. The number of his converts is unknown, and no one appears to have taken up the work after his death in 1696. Although Lovelace's interest in conversion of the Indians extended beyond Long Island to the work of the Mayhews on Martha's Vineyard, Andros was less enthusiastic, and the subject rarely if ever occupied his attention.[67]

Dongan and succeeding royal governors received standardized instructions from home "to find out the best means to facilitate & encourage the Conversion of Negros & Indians to the Christian

[65] *Plymouth Colony Records*, X, 247; Thompson, *History of Long Island*, II, 124.

[66] Massachusetts Historical Society, *Collections*, 4th ser., VII (1865), 485–486; *NYCD*, XIV, 610–611; Thompson, *History of Long Island*, II, 124–126.

[67] See Paltsits, *Executive Council Minutes*, I, 364–365, and *NYCD*, XIV, 699–700, 713.

Religion." In no case, however, did they interpret this as one of their major responsibilities.[68] Only with regard to the Iroquois, where political considerations were predominant, did the subject receive particular attention. But even at Albany the work of conversion had to wait for another clergyman like James to undertake it first on his own initiative.

There are scattered references to the existence of Indian slavery in New York over a long period of time, but it was always comparatively rare. The English governors, probably because a comparable motivation never arose, did not follow the course of Stuyvesant and the New England colonies in reducing Indian prisoners of war to slavery. Many of the natives who were held as slaves in New York seem to have originated elsewhere, particularly in the Caribbean. Generally referred to as "Spanish Indians," they arrived with shiploads of Negroes from the West Indies, and very likely many of them had Negro blood. Slavery, or something like it, existed among many of the North American Indian tribes, who sometimes enslaved their prisoners of war. A few of these persons may have been taken to the white settlements, where they were held either as slaves or as indentured servants. Local tribesmen too were occasionally held to service for specified terms, but the practice was never common.

The provincial government mildly discouraged Indian slavery and on several occasions took ineffectual action to prohibit it altogether. The reasons for this attitude are not entirely clear. The practice aroused no apparent resentment on the part of the neighboring tribesmen, and if there were humanitarian objections, they certainly did not extend to the Negro. In 1679 and 1680 the provincial council resolved that "all Indyans here, are free & not slaves" and that no one could force them to become servants against their will. An exception was made of "such as have beene formerly brought from the Bay of Campechio & other foreign parts," but even these were to be liberated if not removed from the province within six months. The only reason given for this enactment was that Indian servitude was "contrary to former custome, & practice."[69] Several years later Governor Dongan twice reaffirmed this ruling, but with respect only to such Spanish In-

---

[68] Leonard Woods Labaree, ed., *Royal Instructions to British Colonial Governors, 1670–1776* (New York, 1935), II, 505–506.

[69] *NYCD*, XIII, 537–538; *New York City Common Council Minutes*, I, 80.

dian slaves as could give an account of the Christian faith and repeat the Lord's Prayer.[70] Thus a man was forbidden in 1688 to retain an Indian slave whom he had procured in Honduras, and a resident of Connecticut was prevented from recovering two young Indian "servants" who had fled to New York. In the latter case the local tribesmen with whom the runaways had taken refuge agreed with the owner to purchase their freedom.[71] Nevertheless there is evidence that Indian slaves continued to be held and sold in various parts of the province.[72] They were probably Algonquian for the most part, and their servile status, even if exceptional, provides further evidence of the degradation to which these Indians were subjected by the end of the century.

[70] Council Minutes transcript of Oct. 11, 1687, "Moore–N.Y." Papers; Council Minutes, VI, reverse side, first pagination, 35.

[71] Colonial MSS, XXXV, 169b; *ARSCM,* III, 367.

[72] For references to specific cases of Indian servitude see *Hempstead Town Records,* II, 60–61 (a deed of sale); Onderdonk, *Queen's County in Olden Times,* 8, and *Annals of Hempstead,* 60; *New York City Common Council Minutes,* I, *passim.* The best account of the subject is in Almon Wheeler Lauber, *Indian Slavery in Colonial Times within the Present Limits of the United States* (New York, 1913), 112–115, 193, 201, 316–319; see also A. Judd Northrup, *Slavery in New York: A Historical Sketch* (New York State Library Bulletin, History, no. 4; Albany, 1900), 305–309.

VIII

The Management of Indian Affairs

at Albany

DURING the first generation of English rule Albany began to emerge from the relative isolation that it had enjoyed under the Dutch, and its political if not economic importance was gradually enhanced. Meanwhile the town grew very slowly in population, its exposed frontier position repelling all but the most hardy immigrants. Such immigration from Holland as had taken place before 1664 was now largely cut off, and Englishmen found more congenial places to settle, even if the provincial land policies did not discourage them from entering the colony altogether. There are no population figures before 1686, but at that time Albany County, which included nearly all of the province north of Kingston, numbered only 2,143 persons. A majority of these lived in small villages or isolated farms, most of them south of Albany. During the first intercolonial war the county's population dropped from 2,016 to 1,449—a decrease of more than 25 per cent— owing to the economic as well as military dislocations which that conflict engendered. By the turn of the century, however, these losses had been made up, and the population approximated that of fifteen years before.

Jasper Danckaerts, who visited Albany in the spring of 1680, described it as nearly square in shape, lying "against the hill, with several good streets, on which there may be about eighty or ninety houses. . . . The town is surrounded by palisades, and has several gates corresponding with the streets." By 1676 the old Fort Orange, standing below the town on the riverbank, had been abandoned in favor of another "high up on the declivity of the hill" behind town, near the site of the present Statehouse. Fort Albany like its predecessor was built of wood and defensible only against Indians. It was garrisoned with English soldiers, but ordinarily by no more than a company until the 1690's. Governor Dongan reported in 1687 that it had nine large guns and enough small arms for forty men. The palisades, both at the fort and around town, were subject to rotting and had to be replaced every six or seven years. The weakness of the town's defenses was the subject of nearly constant anxiety after the outbreak of the intercolonial wars. Dongan urged that the fort be rebuilt of stone, but neither the colony nor the mother country made the necessary appropriations before the turn of the century.[1]

Schenectady, only three years old in 1664, was the most exposed settlement in the province. A blockhouse was built there about 1670, and twenty years later the village was surrounded with palisades. However, carelessness in keeping watch at that time rendered them entirely useless when the place was subjected to a French and Indian attack. In 1698, at the end of the war which saw the village destroyed, it numbered 238 inhabitants.[2]

In several respects Albany was poorly qualified to serve as an outpost of the English empire. The town and its environs were perhaps less affected by the transition to English rule than any other part of the province. It remained overwhelmingly Dutch in composition and character until well into the eighteenth century, and for a generation after 1664 its residents were as little interested in furthering British imperialism as the English on Long Island had been to preserve the integrity of New Netherland. This is not to say—regardless of English suspicions at the time—that the Albanians constituted a fifth column; their primary interest before and after 1664 was to advance their own material prosperity through the fur trade and farming. If the path of short-run gain departed from that of imperial advantage, they were apt to take the former. Only gradually did a feeling of identity develop between them and their fellow New Yorkers to the south.

[1] Danckaerts, *Journal*, 216–217; *NYCD*, III, 255; *NYDH*, I, 89, 150; *ARSCM*, II, 384; III, 41.
[2] *ARSCM*, I, 177; II, 39.

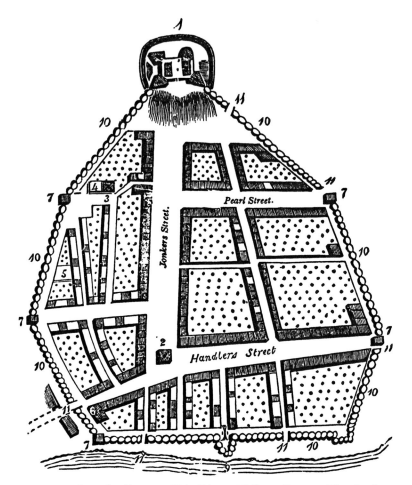

Map 4. Plan of Albany, 1695. (From William Barnes, *The Settlement and Early History of Albany*, 1864.)

1. The fort
2. Dutch church
3. Lutheran church
4. Its burial place
5. Dutch church burial place

6. Stadhuis, or City Hall
7. Blockhouses
[8. Missing in the original]
9. Great gun to clear a gully
10. Stockades

11. City gates, 6 in all

Management at Albany

Ultimate control of Indian affairs at Albany was, of course, in the hands of the governor, but as elsewhere in the colony the details were necessarily left to the local magistrates. These officials—the schout (sheriff) and schepens (burgomasters or commissaries)—continued for the next twenty-two years to be chosen according to the Dutch method established by Stuyvesant. The governor filled vacancies from a double list of names submitted by the remaining magistrates. The commissaries, sitting together after 1665 as a court for Albany, Rensselaerswyck, Schenectady, and other nearby settlements, were almost invariably Dutchmen who continued for many years to transact their business in the language of the Fatherland. Although the English military commander was ordered after 1668 (if not before) to sit with and preside over the court in matters concerning the Indians,[3] it continued to be dominated by and responsive to local interests. In matters of general concern the governor expected to be informed, and his voice was usually decisive, but at a distance of more than a hundred miles he had to rely on local agents:

He was dependent always for information, which was given in a form colored by Albany interests and prejudices; dependent often for a policy, since many of the governors had no policy of their own and left the management of Indian affairs almost wholly in the hands of the commissioners; and dependent also for aid in carrying out any policy of his own. In case the policy of the governor was not favored by the commissioners, the chances of its success were small, for the governor seldom had any trustworthy means of communicating with the Indians except through them. . . . Governors came and went, reflecting temporarily the policy or lack of policy of the British government, or developing one of their own; but the one constant factor in British Indian policy was the policy of Albany.[4]

In 1675 Governor Andros is said to have organized "a local board of commissioners for Indian affairs, composed of some of the Albany officers."[5] Probably this action amounted to little more than a confirmation of the powers enjoyed by the magistrates before the Dutch reoccupation of 1673–1674. Later writers have sometimes referred to the Albany officials after 1675 as commissioners for Indian affairs.

[3] Joel Munsell, ed., *The Annals of Albany* (Albany, 1850–1859), VII, 99–100.
[4] Arthur H. Buffinton, "The Policy of Albany and English Westward Expansion," *Mississippi Valley Historical Review*, VIII (1922), 335.
[5] Brodhead, *History of New York*, II, 287.

There is no indication, however, that this term was used at the time or that such a board was formally created before 1696. Until then the management of Indian affairs was held to be one of the duties attached to the local magistracy, and no special commissions or instructions seem to have been issued to define the responsibility more clearly. In 1698, after a brief experiment with a special board of four commissioners, the members of the local court regained their former powers; but henceforth they received specific instructions from the governor and the additional title of commissioners for Indian affairs —an arrangement which lasted well into the next century.

At the English restoration Andros further confirmed earlier practice by requiring the Albany town clerk to keep a separate record of Indian transactions. Until 1686 this office was held by the secretary of Rensselaerswyck. Domine Nicholas van Rensselaer, whose manorial rights were confirmed by the English, appointed Robert Livingston to this post in 1675. From that time forward the Albany Indian records were kept more systematically, owing to Livingston's personal interest as well as the growing importance of the transactions themselves.[6]

A further step in defining the administration of Indian affairs was taken by Governor Dongan when he granted Albany a city charter in 1686. This document converted the town in form from a Dutch to an English municipality. Political power henceforth was vested in an elective council and in a mayor, recorder, clerk, and sheriff appointed by the governor.[7] By confirming Albany's monopoly of the western fur trade and empowering the local authorities to regulate it, the charter also strengthened their control of Indian affairs as a whole. However, the document made no formal grant of this power, and the new magistrates, like the old, continued to supervise political and diplomatic relations with the Indians by virtue of the governor's will and subject to his authority.

Under the new dispensation Robert Livingston was retained as city clerk and ex officio secretary for Indian affairs; but he managed to hold down as well the offices of clerk of the peace, clerk of the common pleas, subcollector of the excise, and receiver of the quitrents for Albany County. Only twenty years old at the time of his initial appointment in 1675, Livingston had just arrived in the province. His

---

[6] *LIR*, 5–6, 8. [7] *Colonial Laws*, I, 195 ff.

father was a Scots Presbyterian clergyman who had been exiled to Holland in 1663. The son, who followed him there, acquired a command of the Dutch language which was to serve him well in the unique environment at Albany. Not long after his arrival in Albany he won the hand of Alida Schuyler van Rensselaer, who was the widow of his recent benefactor and brought connections with some of the colony's most prominent families. In succeeding years he used these relationships, together with his local offices, as steppingstones to one of the most notable careers and substantial fortunes in colonial New York.

Equally prominent on the local and provincial scene for many years was Livingston's brother-in-law, Peter Schuyler. The son of an early settler at Fort Orange who had accumulated a modest fortune in the fur trade, Schuyler was born into the local aristocracy which dominated Albany for most of the colonial period. He received the first appointment as mayor in 1686 and retained the office for eight years. In this and later political capacities and as major (later colonel) of the local militia during the first two wars with France, Schuyler was thrown into constant contact with the Iroquois. In both spheres of activity he won their respect and devotion, retaining it all his life. As a result he was indispensable to succeeding governors, who made him their chief lieutenant in matters diplomatic as well as military on the Albany frontier. By virtue of his long tenure on the provincial council Schuyler also served as acting governor on occasion after the turn of the century.

The lives of Livingston and Schuyler, whose personalities in some respects were complementary, ran parallel until their deaths in the 1720's. Livingston, as his biographer suggests, was the man of vision whereas Schuyler was the man of action. Both men acquired fortunes from the fur trade and land speculation, and both enjoyed considerable political power at various times. Livingston was the more clever and acquisitive of the two and by material standards was more successful. Schuyler, on the other hand, was far more popular. His physical courage and personal integrity contrasted markedly with the shrewdness of his brother-in-law which savored more of the court and the countinghouse. Schuyler managed to stay in the good graces of every successive governor—a feat requiring supreme tact as well as agility

—whereas Livingston's initial good impression often soured on longer acquaintance.[8]

The governor and local magistrates alike made it a constant policy to limit all political or diplomatic dealings with the Indians to the properly constituted authorities. This rule applied to representatives of other colonies seeking to confer with the Iroquois as well as to private citizens. Firm and prompt correction was meted out to those who attempted on their own responsibility to negotiate or even discuss matters of public concern with the natives. By the same token, although it was not always enforceable, no one was permitted to go into the Indian country without special permission. Apart from the danger that private negotiations might subvert official policy, it was considered dangerous in principle for colonists to mix in Indian affairs.[9]

The transaction of Indian affairs was ordinarily centered at Albany itself, where Iroquois and other tribesmen continued to come on missions of trade and diplomacy. Here, as they put it, the council fire was kept burning, and the covenant was periodically renewed. But as the years passed and Indian relations grew in political importance, it became more and more common to send special envoys to the Mohawk villages, to Onondaga, or even into the Seneca country. Members of the local court traveled on such missions if they were deemed important enough, but ordinarily an interpreter or a local trader versed in the Iroquois language was dispatched with more or less explicit instructions as to what he was expected to do. Toward the end of the century such persons were occasionally sent for longer periods of time in order to observe and report on Iroquois activity and, if possible, to direct it in conformity with Albany policy. The first recorded envoy of this sort was one Gerrit Luycasse, who spent the fall of 1690 at Onondaga. Arnout Cornelisse Viele, an official interpreter, was sent to succeed him and apparently spent the following winter there.[10] The benefits of a more or less permanent embassy among the Five Nations were not lost on official policy makers, and much attention was given to the problem of recruiting suitable ambassadors. The major obstacle

[8] For Livingston's life see the sketch by Lawrence H. Leder in *LIR*, 5–10, and the forthcoming biography by the same author. Schuyler has no recent biographer, but much information about him as well as Livingston is to be found in George W. Schuyler, *Colonial New York: Phillip Schuyler and His Family* (New York, 1885).

[9] *ARSCM*, I, 94, 102, 223; II, 37.   [10] *NYDH*, II, 314–315.

lay in the continuing reluctance of Albanians—who alone had the necessary acquaintance with the Iroquois and their language—to abandon the comforts of home for extended residence among the Indians. The same problem extended to the stationing of gunsmiths at the Indian villages. After war broke out in 1689, the Iroquois repeatedly asked for such persons in order to save them the necessity of going to Albany every time repairs were needed. A young man seems to have been sent for this purpose with Luycasse or Viele in 1690; but he was primarily interested in trade, and after he acquired a store of peltry, he returned home again, leaving his anvil behind. Another man was dispatched on this service in 1693, but recruits were always hard to find.[11]

As Indian affairs became more important politically, the office of Indian interpreter grew correspondingly and was gradually institutionalized. It was not usually a full-time job and most of those who held it were traders, but the position often involved much more responsibility than its title implied. The official interpreters—there were often two or three on call at a given time—were actually the field representatives of the Albany magistrates in their dealings with the Five Nations. As such they were required not only to interpret at conferences, but eventually to serve as messengers and diplomatic agents to the Indian country, sometimes for extended periods of time. Two or three of these men ultimately became trusted agents of English diplomacy. On occasion they also assisted ministers in their work of educating and converting the Indians. For the most part the interpreters were drawn from Dutch families of Albany or Schenectady, and at least two seem to have been the offspring of mixed marriages between the Dutch and the Mohawk. None of them ranked very high in the social spectrum—neither the job itself nor the prerequisite experience could be regarded as meeting the standards of even frontier gentility in the seventeenth century.

One of the first persons mentioned as a regular interpreter, in 1682, was Akus Cornelis of Schenectady, described in the records as "formerly an Indian," who performed most of his service in the time of Governor Dongan.[12] Arnout Cornelisse Viele, whose name appears even earlier, was more prominent and had a longer tenure. Even interpreters were caught up in the factional controversies of the 1690's,

[11] *NYCD*, III, 775–776, 844; IV, 22–23, 43, 76.   [12] *Ibid.*, III, 323, 431.

and Viele lost his position after the overthrow of Jacob Leisler in 1691. Although he spent a second winter at Onondaga in 1694–1695, his regular service lapsed until the return of the Leislerians in 1698. During the interval he led a trading party into the Ohio valley—the farthest penetration of the interior which New Yorkers had made until then—and returned with a large contingent of Shawnee Indians. Recalled as interpreter by Lord Bellomont, his last service seems to have been in 1699.[13] The only woman to hold the position with any regularity was Hilletie van Olinda, the daughter of a Dutch father and a Mohawk mother, who left the Mohawk country to become a Christian convert and the wife of a Schenectady Dutchman sometime before 1680. Her service as interpreter seems to have begun after Viele's dismissal in 1691. She received a salary of £20 per year and continued to serve off and on until 1702. Unlike most of her male counterparts she was seldom called upon to leave the Albany vicinity in performing her duties.[14] Jan Baptist van Eps, another interpreter, had been captured as a boy in 1690 during the attack by the French on Schenectady. When they descended upon the Mohawk villages three years later, the French brought him along, probably as a guide, and he managed to make his escape.[15] Serving as interpreter after 1698, he and Lawrence Claessen, who first appears in the records two years later, were trusted agents among the Iroquois until well into the next century.

Indian conferences at Albany were usually held in the fort until the 1670's, and after that in the courthouse in town. They were almost invariably conducted in the Indian tongue, and the interpreters, who knew little or no English, rendered everything into Dutch. The transactions were then recorded in that language by the secretary—after 1675 Robert Livingston or a deputy—and were retranslated into English only if they were deemed important enough to forward to the governor. Most conferences were irregular meetings between the magistrates and one or more Indians who might come in at any time of year. More important were the full-dress councils attended by the governor and his retinue on the one hand and a full panoply of Iroquois sachems with their official speakers and leading warriors on the other.

[13] *Ibid.*, 323; IV, 198, 329; Colonial MSS, XXV, 184.
[14] Danckaerts, *Journal*, 201–206; NYCD, III, 777; CSP, 1689–1692, no. 2541.
[15] NYCD, IV, 16; IX, 551.

Management at Albany

These occasions were not unknown in Stuyvesant's time, but they occurred more frequently after 1664 and became annual affairs after
1690. The drafting of the governor's propositions, or speech, to the
Indians became a significant matter as Iroquois relations gained in
importance and conferences became week-long affairs. The governor
often delegated this job to others, particularly when he was new to the
colony and ignorant of the policy details in question, as well as of the
ritual and procedure appropriate to such occasions. Sometimes the
propositions were drawn up by the provincial council, and at least once
by the assembly, but here too the Albany magistrates often had a
dominant voice. Dependent on them for information and on two of
their translators for every word he exchanged with the Indians, more
than one governor suspected rightly or wrongly that he and the sachems
heard only what Albany wanted them to hear.

Another feature of Indian conferences, large or small, was the exchange of presents. This was considered mandatory among the natives
themselves and long antedated the white man's coming. No meeting
could be held, no agreement concluded in their eyes, without sealing
the transaction with mutual tokens of sincerity. The Indians' offerings
usually took the form of peltry and were looked upon by colonial
officials as one of the perquisites of office. They were seldom very considerable except at large conferences. Although estimates vary widely
as to their value, Lord Bellomont reported selling his gift in 1698 for
£88.[16] Far grander were the presents which the natives expected in
return. These were composed of all the familiar trading goods, but
especially woolen cloth, rum, powder, and lead. The sachems often
received laced coats, hats, shirts, and other accouterments of gentility
in the white community, which they cherished as marks of their own
social and political status. Guns too were given out as presents; in the
early years they were distributed a few at a time, mostly as personal
gifts to the sachems, but later they were given in larger quantities as a
political and military subsidy. The governor brought his gifts with him
to the larger conferences; they were paid for by the colony, though
the royal treasury eventually lent a helping hand. Before 1689 they
never exceeded £150 in value, but they grew steadily in amount, and
by the end of the century appropriations for this purpose totaled more
than £500 a year.

[16] *Ibid.*, IV, 183, 186, 522, 876.

Indian Affairs in Colonial New York

The money laid out in presents was only part of the cost of a major Indian conference. As these meetings became more elaborate, several hundred pounds more were often required to transport the governor and his entourage to Albany and to maintain them there for a week or two during the conference and its preliminaries. Some governors were unduly lavish on these occasions, but within limits this expense was unavoidable. Furthermore, the natives expected to be fed and entertained while in town, and they too were not always of Spartan tastes. Apart from the cost of conferences a relatively constant expense was entailed in sending messages back and forth between Albany, New York, the Iroquois country, and elsewhere. Together these items constituted the financial burden Albany and the colony bore as a result of their peculiar position in Indian affairs. The price was high in relation to the colony's resources, and in later years it is questionable if the returns justified the expenditure.

The Colony of New York was not long in asserting a claim to all territory between the Hudson, the St. Lawrence, and Lakes Erie and Ontario. A natural outgrowth of this claim was the further assertion that all Indians in this region, especially the Iroquois confederation, were under its exclusive jurisdiction. Sovereignty over the Iroquois was first advanced tentatively by Nicolls and then more explicitly by Andros; under Dongan and his successors it became the foundation of an ambitious and comprehensive western policy which sought to use the Iroquois as agents of English imperialism. In dealings with the Indians themselves this claim was expressed in terms of their being under the protection of His Majesty and of his Province of New York. In dealings with the French it rapidly became a leading bone of international contention, for it ran directly contrary to their own continental aspirations. New York was able for many years to enforce her claim against neighboring English colonies, who, because of the far-flung activities of the Five Nations, often felt a pressing need to consult or remonstrate with them. Under Andros it became well established that Iroquois affairs were a New York monopoly and that dealings with them were normally confined to Albany. This did not preclude conferences between the natives and delegates from other provinces—New York was happy to adjust disputes between her Indians and sister colonies—but such negotiations could be held only with the provincial authorities' consent and in the presence of the

Albany magistrates.[17] Even the Indians found it expedient on occasion to stipulate that conferees must come to them at Albany.

Most of the Indian lands purchased within the Albany court jurisdiction were acquired from the Mahican and other River Indians who were in the process of extinction. White settlers had entered the Mohawk country only around Schenectady, and serious incursion upon their lands was just beginning by the turn of the century. That this problem was so long delayed among the Iroquois is explained by the factors inhibiting population growth as a whole in this part of the province. An additional restraint, however, was exercised by Albany itself, which regarded westward settlement as a potential threat to its own trade monopoly.[18] By and large the same land regulations applied as elsewhere in the province, but there seems to have been a temporary relaxation here of the rule that all purchasers must secure a license from the governor before treating with the Indians. Although governors repeatedly granted such licenses, they apparently were also issued by the local court in the time of Lovelace.[19] In 1675, however, Schenectady was denied a patent to certain lands that it had bought from the natives three years earlier, because no record was found of the town's having procured a license beforehand.[20] Recorded land disputes between Indians and white men in this period are almost nonexistent. The only ones of any consequence, in the 1690's, developed into a major political issue and will be reserved for a later chapter.

The advent of English control had no appreciable effect on the nature of the fur trade by which Albany largely subsisted. The Indians continued to bring their peltry into town and carried back with them the same variety of trading goods. The passing of Dutch political authority brought with it, according to the mercantilist regulations of the day, a substitution of English woolens and West Indian rum for corresponding items of Dutch manufacture. The articles of surrender had guaranteed a continuance of normal trade relations with Holland for at least six months, but the outbreak of war between the two powers

[17] *Ibid.*, XIII, 502, 529–530.
[18] *CSP, 1697–1698*, no. 988.XVIII; *NYCD*, IV, 874.
[19] *ARSCM*, I, 175; III, 166; Council Minutes, V, 60. An Act of Assembly of 1684 regulating land purchases makes no exception of Albany in the requirement that purchasers must have a prior license from the governor (*Colonial Laws*, I, 149). For examples of such licenses see *NYCD*, XIII, 395 ff.
[20] *NYCD*, XIII, 464–465, 490.

had largely nullified this privilege. After the Peace of Breda in 1667 Stuyvesant petitioned the English government for a restoration of free trade between the colony and the former mother country. One of his arguments was that the Indians, being deprived of the Holland duffels and other trading goods to which they had grown accustomed, might turn to the French instead. The upshot of his petition was a royal relaxation of the Navigation Acts that permitted three Dutch ships to visit New York annually for seven years. Even this privilege was revoked a year later, and there is no record that the Indians were unduly put out with the altered source of trading goods. Most of the complaints came rather from New York merchants who were directly affected by the change in the course of trade.[21] Stuyvesant, who had decided to spend his last years on his Manhattan bowery, was undoubtedly acting as their spokesman.

The size of the fur trade at Albany can only be guessed at during the first generation of English rule. In 1656 and 1657 the annual peltry shipments down the Hudson had approximated 46,000 skins. Thirty years later, as a result of hostilities between the French, the Iroquois, and the western tribes, this figure had fallen to 14,000 or less.[22] The decline seems to have begun in the early 1680's, after the Iroquois had gone to war with the western Indians,[23] but it got even worse in the next decade when they found themselves at war with Canada too. Until about 1700, when these conflicts drew to a close, the number of skins exported from New York fluctuated between five and fifteen thousand a year.[24] Meanwhile the cost of trading goods and especially of powder had gone up in response to wartime demand and the greater hazards and scarcity of shipping. The Indians, who needed powder more than ever, were caught in the squeeze and repeatedly asked for "better penniworths" at Albany. To make matters worse, beaver hats were going out of style in Europe, and when the Indians were freer to go back to their hunting, prices had fallen by nearly two-

---

[21] *Ibid.*, II, 251; III, 163–167, 175–179, 187.

[22] Curtis P. Nettels, *The Money Supply of the American Colonies before 1720* (Madison, 1934), 75n.; "Chalmers–N.Y." Papers, 22, New York Public Library. In 1689 Edward Randolph estimated the value of Albany's Indian trade at £40,000 per year (*CSP, 1689–1692*, no. 482).

[23] *NYCD*, III, 476, 599, 693, 705; XIV, 772; *LIR*, 98; *CSP, 1699* (Addenda), no. 1155. Cf. Flick, *History of New York*, II, 333, where the Seneca alone are said to have brought 10,000 beaver skins to Albany in 1685.

[24] Nettels, *Money Supply of the American Colonies*, 75n.

thirds, and their skins were a glut on the market. For this reason they sent ten beavers to the king on one occasion, praying His Majesty to make a hat of them so that "all his good subjects will follow his example and were [*sic*] Beaver hatts again as the fashion was formerly." If beaver were no longer a commodity, they said, they would not bother to hunt them.[25] Obviously the traders too were hurt by these conditions; Lord Bellomont reported in 1700 that whereas half a dozen men at Albany had "competent estates . . . all the rest are miserable poor." He seconded the Indians' request for government action to restore beaver hats to favor and asked for a repeal of all the duties on peltry exported from the province; but neither request got much attention.[26]

One of the few bright spots for the Albany traders was their consistent ability to outbid the French—an advantage which the latter had to compensate for by war and diplomacy. A comparative price schedule of 1689, for example, indicates that the Indians were receiving two to four times as much for their peltry at Albany as at Montreal.[27] The reasons for Albany's competitive advantage are many. Manufacturing costs were higher in France than in England, although English goods were usually superior in quality, and the cost of transporting the goods

[25] *NYCD*, III, 775, 806–807; IV, 571–572, 733, 741, 789, 905, 920.

[26] *Ibid.*, IV, 718, 834, 855.

[27] This list, compiled in Canada, indicates the comparative prices an Indian had to pay at the two cities in 1689:

	Albany	Montreal
8 pounds of powder	1 beaver	4 beavers
A gun	2	5
40 pounds of lead	1	3
A blanket of red cloth	1	2
A white blanket	1	2
4 shirts	1	2
6 pairs of stockings	1	2

The English gave six quarts ("pots") of rum for one beaver, the informant continues, but the French never gave as much as one quart of brandy for the same return. The English, furthermore, did not discriminate in the quality of the beaver, taking all at the same rate, which augmented the price difference by an additional 50 per cent. See *NYCD*, IX, 408–409; see also the longer list in Benjamin Sulte, "Le Commerce de France avec le Canada avant 1760," in Royal Society of Canada, *Proceedings and Transactions*, 2d ser., XII, sec. 1 (1906), 45–46. Prices at Montreal appear to have been lower at this time than they had been in 1665, but comparable figures are not available for Albany. Cf. *Collection de Manuscrits Relatifs à la Nouvelle-France* (Quebec, 1883–1885), I, 179–180; see also *NYCD*, IX, 198, 253.

to America was higher for the French. In this respect the English‛ and the Dutch were able to outsell the French almost anywhere in the world. In Canada, furthermore, the Indian trade was subject to a tax of 25 per cent, forcing the traders to raise their prices proportionately.[28] In New York the fur trade was also taxed, but somewhat less heavily. Trading goods brought into the colony were liable in the first place to a general import levy which amounted to 5 per cent ad valorem in 1674 and 10 per cent by 1683. Rum, firearms, and ammunition were taxed separately when entering the province and shipped up the Hudson. Another duty, with less direct effect on prices at Albany, was charged on all furs leaving the province. Finally, all Indian traders were subject by 1687 to a tax of 10 per cent on the value of their annual trade.[29] Most of these impositions, it may be noted, were less easily collected than enacted.

Despite its ups and downs the western fur trade continued to be Albany's mainstay. Local residents made it a central policy, therefore, to retain and strengthen their long-standing monopoly. Governor Nicolls apparently confirmed this arrangement soon after the conquest, and it was repeatedly renewed in later years.[30] Apart from the fact that it was a well-established vested interest and therefore deserving of respect, successive governors undoubtedly agreed with Stuyvesant that it was good to limit the fur trade to a few places where it could be more easily regulated.

Enforcing the monopoly was another matter, and the major cause of its reiteration lay in the persistent attempts of outlying settlers to muscle in on the traffic. The inhabitants of Schenectady remained particularly obdurate on this score, despite Nicolls' confirmation of the trade ban at their village. The local court repeatedly passed ordinances to the same effect, as did succeeding governors at its request. Other laws forbade the shipment of trading goods to Schenectady, and several times the sheriff went there to search houses for such

---

[28] Innis, *The Fur Trade in Canada*, 52 ff.

[29] *Colonial Laws*, I, 117–118, 170–171; *NYCD*, III, 217, 400. For an example of nonenforcement of one of these duties see *ibid.*, 499.

[30] *NYCD*, II, 595; III, 117; Arthur H. Buffinton, "The Policy of the Northern Colonies towards the French to the Peace of Utrecht" (Ph.D. dissertation, Harvard University, 1925), 133–134; *ARSCM*, I, 17, 91; II, 246, 394; III, 251, 461, 476, 498–499.

contraband. These visitations led to a number of convictions and fines.[31] The difficulty seems to have abated during the 1680's, but it never disappeared altogether. In 1686 Albany complained of similar violations of its "antient right & priviledge" by residents of Rensselaerswyck. It was without doubt in response to this plea that Dongan included a clause in his city charter that year confirming to Albany "forever . . . the Sole & only Managmt of the Trade with the Indians as well within this whole County as without the same to the Eastward Northward and Westward thereof so farr as his Ma[jes]ties Dominion here does or may extend." [32] During the factional controversy in 1689 and 1690 Leisler and his adherents sought to win popular support for their cause by threatening to end the monopoly, but nothing seems to have come of this.[33]

In 1700 the Iroquois themselves endorsed the city's monopoly and asked that traders be forbidden to come into their country since the prices they charged were higher than at Albany. Trading in the Indian country had been facilitated by the sending of official agents. Some of these envoys, nearly all traders by profession, either engaged in the traffic themselves while on public business or took others with them who did so. On one occasion Peter Schuyler himself had to deny a charge of sending goods to be sold by the Mohawk delegates at a league council at Onondaga. The trading privilege was once offered as an official inducement to secure such envoys, but the Albany magistrates normally opposed it. By prosecuting offenders and convincing successive governors of the wisdom of their monopoly they managed to keep the practice from becoming widespread.[34] The city's greatest worry in these years was how to stem the increasing competition from outside the province.

[31] *ARSCM*, I, 75–76, 145, 148–150, 172–174, 267; II, 24, 123, 129, 361–364, 370; III, 68, 251; *NYCD*, II, 675; XIII, 426, 466, 486, 533; XIV, 559; Paltsits, *Executive Council Minutes*, I, 385; II, 748–749; Munsell, *Annals of Albany*, II, 95–97; Arthur J. Weise, *The History of the City of Albany, New York* (Albany, 1884), 155; Jonathan Pearson *et al.*, *A History of the Schenectady Patent in the Dutch and English Times*, ed. by J. W. MacMurray (Albany, 1883), 413–414.

[32] *LIR*, 97–98; *Colonial Laws*, I, 211 (including quotation).

[33] *NYDH*, II, 66; *NYCD*, III, 708.

[34] *NYCD*, IV, 733, 741, 753–754; *CSP, 1693–1696*, nos. 1328, 1374; Munsell, *Annals of Albany*, II, 114, 118–119, 129–130, 134; Cadwallader Colden, *The History of the Five Indian Nations of Canada* (New York, 1902), I, 137–138.

Indian Affairs in Colonial New York

Although the question was settled as to where the Indian trade might be conducted, there was a long record of argument as to who could engage in it. For several years it remained open to all inhabitants of the province, and at least a handful of New York merchants came up the river during the trading seasons to take part. The Albanians regarded such persons with a jealous eye and considered petitioning the governor for a monopoly. Hearing of this intention, three New Yorkers in 1668 got the backing of the mayor's court there for a continuation of free trade at Albany. Two years later the governor and council expressly permitted residents of Schenectady to trade with the Indians at Albany, whereas New Englanders and others from outside the province could do so only by special order from the governor. In 1676 the magistrates finally got Andros' permission to restrict the trade to burghers and free persons of Albany, with a provision that outsiders desiring the privilege must pay a tax on the value of the goods they brought with them.[35] This discrimination was hardened into a flat prohibition two years later, when trading privileges were limited absolutely to burghers who "keep fire & Candle, watch & ward here [at Albany] the whole year throw." In return for this concession the Albanians were constrained, much against their will, to concede New Yorkers a similar monopoly of overseas trade.[36] The local fathers had further reason to thank Governor Dongan when this vested interest was also permanently embodied in the municipal charter of 1686. Henceforth the Indian trade was limited to "the ffreemen being Actuall Inhabitants" of the city, and its conduct was restricted to the area "within the Now Walls or Stockados thereof." All other persons were forbidden to trade with the Iroquois or other tribes to the north, east, or west, and provision was made for the apprehension of offenders and confiscation of their goods by the local authorities. The governor promised, furthermore, not even to grant passes for hunting in that part of the province without the magistrates' consent.[37]

There was less change after 1664 in the rules and methods by which

---

[35] Fernow, *New Amsterdam Records*, VI, 138–139; *NYCD*, XIII, 458; *ARSCM*, I, 173–174; II, 135–138, 256, 336.

[36] *ARSCM*, II, 336–337, 403–404, 406–408, 413; *NYCD*, XIII, 532; Brodhead, *History of New York*, II, 318; Jerome R. Reich, *Leisler's Rebellion: A Study of Democracy in New York, 1664–1720* (Chicago, 1953), 49.

[37] *Colonial Laws*, I, 211–213; *LIR*, 96–97.

the trade was conducted. Although the traders as a class were becoming more sophisticated and used kidnaping and violence less often to secure native customers, they were by no means universally respectful of the local ordinances. Some of these laws forbade trading on Sunday or after dark; [38] others required the Indians to leave town when the evening bell rang at eight o'clock and to spend the night in houses which had been constructed for them at public expense outside the gates.[39] The first mention of these "Indian houses" occurs in 1666. They were apparently a recent introduction at that time, and for a number of years the magistrates required their use only by larger groups of natives. After 1672 the laws were tightened up, and the only exceptions allowed were sachems visiting on diplomatic missions.[40] Few regulations came in for more constant evasion by the traders, and the court records are full of convictions for lodging Indians.[41] The magistrates eventually had their way, however. After two additional houses were provided in 1676, they seem to have been more generally accepted, the traders even being assessed to provide firewood for their visitors' convenience.[42] The houses fell into disrepair during the lean years after 1689, and the old abuses reappeared. In 1699, therefore, three new structures were built at the traders' expense, but the natives were not required to stay in them during the slack season from December 1 to April 1. Sachems were still exempted from the requirement altogether, as were the River Indians and Mohawk, who probably were well known as individuals by this time.[43]

As in Stuyvesant's day no trader was to solicit business, let alone transact it, outside his own house. To this end the magistrates repeatedly forbade trading outside the gates, running up the hill to meet Indians on their arrival, going to the Indian houses, or sending children to do the same things. The employment of Christian or Indian

[38] *ARSCM*, II, 394; III, 147–148, 251–252, 462, 498–499; Munsell, *Annals of Albany*, VIII, 209.

[39] A. J. F. Van Laer, ed., "Albany Notarial Papers, 1666–1693," in Dutch Settlers Society of Albany, *Yearbook*, XIII (1937–1938), 2; *LIR*, 30; *NYCD*, III, 68; XIII, 480.

[40] Van Laer, "Albany Notarial Papers," 2; *ARSCM*, I, 148, 162, 280, 303; II, 108, 244–245, 394; III, 339, 430–431, 462; *LIR*, 110.

[41] *ARSCM*, I, 96, 160–161, 167, 211, 214; II, 62; III, 69.

[42] Danckaerts, *Journal*, 217; *ARSCM*, II, 106–107, 187, 376; III, 26, 204, 317, 515; Munsell, *Annals of Albany*, II, 97.

[43] Munsell, *Annals of Albany*, II, 121; III, 47–49, 51, 53; IV, 110–111.

brokers remained under a consistent ban, and persons were still fined for stepping outside and calling to Indians in the street. Violations of these ordinances were frequent, but many of the individuals named were chronic offenders. Probably a majority of the traders had learned by this time to conform to the law in most of its essentials.[44]

Traders persisted in extending credit to Indians, and although the court never forbade this practice, it did seek to curb some of its evil effects. After 1677, for instance, persons were forbidden to take anything but wampum as a pledge of repayment. In the collection of debts all resort to force was condemned, as was any attempt to seek repayment outside of town. If friendly persuasion were insufficient, the trader must either resort to the normal legal channels or write off his debt altogether.[45] Such were the alternatives in theory, but the river bands still had occasion to complain of beatings on the part of the less scrupulous traders.

Another reflection of stiff competition was the offering of gifts to the natives as a means of drawing their business. This was obviously a form of price cutting, and in 1681 some of the traders petitioned for a return of official controls, whereby the "scandalously cheap" prices then being offered could be raised to a more comfortable level. The court was apparently unimpressed, for it made no attempt to deal with the problem for another five years. There is no indication that the magistrates attempted to restore the price controls of the 1640's, and when they acted in 1686 it was only to limit these gifts to half a pound in value.[46]

In September 1686 the Albany court enacted a lengthy trading ordinance to implement the powers recently granted it by Dongan's charter. Intended as a comprehensive code of regulations governing the conduct of the Indian trade, it re-enacted a number of the rules already in force and added some others which the terms of the charter or recent experience seemed to make necessary. In language parallel to the

---

[44] For ordinances on these subjects see *ARSCM*, I, 162–163, 280; II, 17, 91, 107–108, 394; III, 251–252, 368–369, 461–462, 476, 498–499; Munsell, *Annals of Albany*, II, 141; VIII, 207–213; *NYDH*, II, 221. For prosecutions under them see *ARSCM*, I, 111–112, 160; II, 159, 241–242, 262–263, 270–271, 277, 345–346, 353–354; III, 544–546.

[45] *ARSCM*, I, 160, 280, 318; II, 37, 246, 394; III, 251–252, 475; Munsell, *Annals of Albany*, VIII, 208; Council Minutes, VIII, pt. 1, 121; *NYCD*, IV, 577.

[46] *ARSCM*, III, 143–144; *LIR*, 97; Munsell, *Annals of Albany*, VIII, 209.

charter, it confined all trading activity to the city limits except for transactions involving Indian corn, venison, and dressed deerskins, which had no commercial importance in the province. No one was allowed to keep trading goods or valuable peltry in his house if it lay outside Albany or to transport out of the city and county any wampum or other items having money value among Indians. The ordinance also substantially repeated an older restriction which forbade Indian traders to procure their goods directly from overseas. This regulation was designed to protect not only the regular overseas merchants but also the smaller Indian traders who could not afford to compete on these terms. As early as 1678 it was alleged that twenty to thirty persons at Albany had secured control of the greater part of the trade. In order to protect the remainder the magistrates now sought to create a separation of functions between them. In the interests of

a more equall distribucon of ye Indian Trade amongst ye Inhabitants of this Citty, its hereby ordered that no Trader who hereafter shall sell Duffells, Strouds, Blanketts, and other Indian goods of value . . . may sell . . . to any Indian . . . [the following smaller wares]: Knives, Looking Glasses, Painting stuff, Boxes, Aules, Tobacco Pipes, Tobacco, Tabocco [sic] Boxes, flints, Steels, Sizers [scissors?], Wire of any sort, Ribboning, Bottles, Thread, Salt, Sugar, Prunes, Apples, Razins, Juiseharps, Bells, Thimbles, Beedes, Indian Combs and Needles.

Finally, to permit better enforcement of these various orders, the magistrates adopted a recent recommendation of the local grand jury and recognized Indian testimony as sufficient to justify an indictment. The accused, following Dutch legal forms, was permitted to clear himself on oath; if he refused to take the oath when tendered, it was deemed proof of his guilt.[47] These regulations governed the conduct of the fur trade for three years, when they were replaced by a similar but less comprehensive code which was renewed periodically thereafter.[48]

Both the provincial authorities and the local magistrates continued after 1664 to impose restrictions on the liquor traffic in and around Albany. One of the articles of agreement made with the local officials in that year confirmed the former order against selling "Brandewine

---

[47] *ARSCM,* II, 407; Munsell, *Annals of Albany,* VIII, 207–213 (quotation from p. 212); *LIR,* 97.
[48] Munsell, *Annals of Albany,* II, 108–109; III, 13–14, 50–51; IV, 110–111.

or strong Liquors" to the Indians. Continued violations of this rule led by 1671 to a modification which left the traffic freer than before but subject to an excise tax. This proving unsuccessful, the governor and magistrates tried restricting Indian liquor sales to members of the local court itself, thus hoping to satisfy both the minimum demands of the natives and a need for revenue. When this policy fared no better, the court adopted a fourth plan, similar to that used in other parts of the colony. Henceforth no inhabitant of Albany or Rensselaerswyck was permitted "to tap to the savages," but larger amounts of liquor could be sold to Indians for consumption off the premises.[49] Although special exemptions or temporary bans of a more rigorous character were occasionally enacted, particularly at the time of large Indian conferences, this policy remained in effect until 1688.[50] The dispensing of liquor to sachems and others for diplomatic purposes was not affected by these ordinances. Governor Andros, for example, ordered at the end of an important conference in 1678 that an anker of rum be sent as a personal gift to each of the Iroquois and Mahican castles, and this practice became standard in later years. In furtherance of Albany's trade monopoly no strong liquor at all could be sold to the Indians at Schenectady or other outlying settlements, but this rule too was frequently violated.[51]

After the outbreak of war in 1689 more stringent regulations seem to have alternated with almost complete liberty. The Indians were as inconsistent in their desires as the magistrates were in establishing a policy. In 1691 the sachems asked that warriors might be supplied with free rum "to comfort their hearts and to encourage them in this present war." But less than two years later they asked Governor Fletcher to prohibit rum sales "whilst the warr is soe hott, since our soldiers cannot be kept within bounds when they are drunk." Whatever the official policy at a given time, its restrictions were persistently

[49] *NYCD,* IX, 883; XIV, 559; Van Laer, "Albany Notarial Papers," 2; Paltsits, *Executive Council Minutes,* I, 83; ARSCM, I, 237–238, 245–249, 280–281.

[50] ARSCM, II, 76–77, 88, 123–124, 244, 246, 257; III, 272–274, 475–476; O'Callaghan, *Calendar of Historical MSS,* II, 139; Munsell, *Annals of Albany,* II, 95.

[51] *NYCD,* III, 479; IV, 753–754; XIII, 486; ARSCM, II, 24, 95, 246; III, 273; Munsell, *Annals of Albany,* II, 129–130; *Wraxall's Abridgement,* 31. A temporary lifting of the Schenectady ban was made in the case of Arent van Curler's widow, who was allowed to sell rum to Indians for a period of fourteen months. This permission, granted by Lovelace in 1673, was confirmed by the Dutch occupation authorities some months later. See *NYCD,* II, 652; XIII, 469–470.

violated throughout this period of nearly forty years, if one may judge by the preambles to the many ordinances. Recorded prosecutions are almost nonexistent, however, and the magistrates eventually gave up; by the turn of the century they were forbidding the traffic only on special occasions and for short periods of time.[52]

Meanwhile the trade in guns and ammunition assumed larger proportions than ever before. Because of its importance both to the fur trade and to the increasingly ambitious imperial policy, neither the governors nor the local officials took any steps to discourage it. The trade ordinance of 1686 guaranteed Indians the freedom to visit without hindrance whichever of the Albany gunsmiths they pleased, and the later practice of sending smiths to the Iroquois country has already been mentioned. In addition to the regular sale of guns, powder, and lead as a part of the fur trade, visiting delegations of tribesmen were frequently sent home with gifts of these items from the authorities. Such presents increased in quantity and frequency as hostilities with the French became a more distinct possibility in the 1680's, and they were partly financed by the crown after 1690. The French, who were fully aware of the arms traffic at Albany, rightly regarded it as the major cause of Iroquois power and prestige.[53] Although the Five Nations were by far the greatest recipients of these materials, all neighboring friendly tribes were served in the same fashion and for the same reasons.

Albany in these years was surrounded by a succession of intercolonial, intertribal, and Indian-white conflicts which were a source of constant concern to the community. Yet relations with the neighboring tribesmen were always comparatively placid. When the English arrived in 1664, they exchanged promises with the Iroquois to punish promptly and fully all persons who committed interracial crimes. The other nearby tribes were included in the agreement, although they were not present at the time. These pledges seem to have been carried out with reasonable faithfulness, to judge by the surviving record. The number of reported cases in which Indians were accused is about equal to those involving white men, but many in the latter category

[52] *NYDH*, II, 91–92, 220–221; *NYCD*, III, 775; IV, 15, 24; Munsell, *Annals of Albany*, II, 106–107, 119–120, 141; III, 30, 38.

[53] Munsell, *Annals of Albany*, VIII, 212; *NYCD*, III, 506; IX, 281–282. For a brief defense of the economic and political importance of the arms trade, written about 1682, see *CSP, 1681–1685*, pp. 365–366.

probably were never reported.[54] The offenses committed by colonists against Indians included theft, assault, manslaughter, and murder. In most of these cases the authorities seem to have proceeded less harshly than when similar crimes were committed among white men.[55] The natives were not, of course, versed in Anglo-Dutch law and perhaps were unaware of discrimination. In 1678, after one of the settlers had shot a Mahican squaw, the sachems were invited to a hearing in which testimony indicated that the death had been accidental. They received fifty guilders in wampum as reparation and expressed themselves well satisfied. The court took no steps to punish the offender save confining him to his house until it heard from New York. The council approved the proceedings and required only that the defendant pay the costs. Twenty years later the Iroquois themselves interceded with the governor, and apparently with success, for the pardon of a soldier who had murdered one of their sachems.[56]

Indians generally were prosecuted with greater vigor, although there were no flagrant miscarriages of justice. Two "Northern Indians," for instance, were sentenced to death by a special court in 1673 for murdering an English soldier. On the other hand, only a payment of atonement seems to have been required nine years later for a drunken attack on a Negro slave which might still have proved fatal when the crime was punished. In 1683 a young Mohawk was held for attacking a white boy with a tomahawk. Throughout the proceedings the sachems were kept fully informed, and they declared that if the boy died the Indian must die too. This was also the opinion of the governor and magistrates; when the victim recovered, they returned the prisoner to his tribe on condition that he never return to the Albany jurisdiction. The Indians were assessed fifty beavers in costs. In another case the same year two River Indians were imprisoned for beating a white man who had slept with a squaw. The court felt that their action was a serious offense, "but as they are heathen and ignorant of our laws," it was decided to let them off with a payment of four beavers.[57]

A major source of annoyance in the 1690's was the old Iroquois habit

[54] NYCD, III, 67–68; ARSCM, III, 363.
[55] ARSCM, I, 101, 168–169; II, 335–336; III, 134.
[56] Ibid., II, 324–327; NYCD, IV, 364–365, 428–429, 453–454.
[57] ARSCM, I, 326–328; III, 274–277, 281, 331–334, 342–343, 362–364, 369–371, 376–377; NYCD, XIII, 570. For another case in which Indian murderers were severely punished see Brodhead, *History of New York*, II, 87.

of attacking settlers' property on their way to and from Albany. Governors made this a subject of almost annual complaint at their regular conferences. The chief targets were corn and livestock, which the Indians appropriated to their own use, but there were many acts of vandalism as well, such as destroying fences and burning the deserted houses in Schenectady which the French had left standing after their attack in 1690. The sachems sometimes agreed to make reparation, but as often as not they got off with an admonition not to repeat the offense.[58]

Many causes for mutual irritation must have arisen almost daily. Nevertheless the two races continued to live in close proximity with no real danger to the good understanding which trade and diplomacy required of them both. Acts of individual violence or fraud were comparatively infrequent, and when they did occur, something approaching justice was done in almost every case. So far as the white man's records indicate, the Indians never contested the workings of his justice except to ask greater leniency for white criminals.

[58] *NYCD*, III, 773–774, 779; IV, 41, 44, 735; *LIR*, 164–166.

IX

Anglo-Iroquois Relations

in Transition

WHEN the English took Albany, they inherited with it the problems arising from the surrounding Indian warfare which had recently broken out between the eastern Iroquois and the Algonquian tribes. One of the first objectives of Colonel George Cartwright, Nicolls' deputy here, was to put the English on the same friendly footing with the Five Nations as the Dutch had enjoyed. This was equally acceptable to the Iroquois, and a treaty was concluded on September 24 and 25, 1664, with representatives of the Mohawk and at least three of the other tribes. Two clauses guaranteed a continuance of accustomed trade relations at Albany, and others dealt with the punishment of interracial crimes. The extent of Mohawk difficulties at this time is reflected in a number of additional propositions for which the Indians secured Cartwright's approval. He agreed not to aid the New England tribes with whom they were at war and to "accommodate" the Iroquois if these tribes should defeat them. Cartwright promised finally to make peace for them with the Indian bands farther down the Hudson, who had apparently been drawn into the hostilities on the side of their Mahican and New England kinsmen.[1]

The Mahican themselves were not mentioned in the treaty, and their conflict with the Mohawk continued at least sporadically for

[1] *NYCD*, III, 67–68; Beauchamp, *History of the New York Iroquois*, 216.

several years. In the spring or early summer of 1665 a new outbreak between them resulted in the death of some Dutch settlers near Albany. Nicolls, having requested Governor Winthrop of Connecticut to help mediate a peace between the two tribes, paid a visit to the community shortly afterward, but made no headway in arranging a settlement. By 1666, when the English as well as the Mohawk found themselves at war with France, there was even more need to end this intertribal dissension, and Connecticut officials joined actively in the quest for a settlement.[2] The Mohawk were so frightened by a French invasion of their territory early in this year that they were more willing than ever to co-operate. English persistence brought about a treaty between the Mohawk and the Mahican at the end of August, but it was broken almost immediately.[3]

Although Cartwright had promised the Iroquois an agreement with the Algonquian bands to the south, no such treaty was apparently made. Early in 1669 it was the turn of the Esopus, Hackensack, and other Indians nearby to request English mediation, which was willingly granted. By this means the Mohawk made peace in July with all or most of the bands living west of the Hudson. The Mahican were not a party to the agreement, and the Mohawk also refused to include the Wappinger bands, probably because of their close relationship with the Mahican and New England tribes.[4]

Meanwhile the Mahican had sent a war party of three hundred men to attack the palisaded Mohawk village of Caughnawaga. When relief came from the other Mohawk castles, the attackers were forced back with heavy losses and the next day were completely routed. The Mohawk, reinforced with Oneida, Onondaga, and Cayuga warriors to the number of four hundred, then launched an attack of their own on an unidentified Mahican town in the direction of New York. When this attack also failed, the Iroquois appealed to Governor Lovelace, who once more sought the aid of Winthrop in making peace. After two years of negotiation the governors managed to produce another agreement between these tribes in August 1671.[5] Mutual suspicions did not

---

[2] Brodhead, *History of New York*, II, 87; Winthrop Papers, Alphabetical Volumes, Massachusetts Historical Society, VI, 167; VII, 3, 6; *NYCD*, III, 117.

[3] *LIR*, 29–30, 33–35; Massachusetts Historical Society, *Collections*, 5th ser., VIII (1882), 99–100; *NYCD*, III, 120, 137–138.

[4] *NYCD*, XIII, 423, 427–428.

[5] *Ibid.*, 427, 440, 458, 460; Winthrop Papers, Connecticut State Library, 143;

quickly evaporate, and a third treaty had to be arranged in the fall of 1675. By this time King Philip's War had broken out, and the English were encouraging the Mohawk to strike at hostile New England bands with whom the Mahican remained closely affiliated. The treaty of 1675 and subsequent negotiations with the Mohawk and the Mahican may only have been precautionary measures, therefore, designed to prevent a recurrence of the conflict around Albany.[6] Two years later, when Mohawk warriors attacked the Mahican as well as some New England Indians who had taken refuge with them, the sachems disavowed this action, and nothing seems to have come of it.[7] All evidence suggests that the Mahican were badly depleted by this time, both in manpower and in resources. Mohawk pressure had perhaps induced some of them to move eastward to the Berkshires and out of New York's jurisdiction. Those who remained near Albany ceased to be a major power factor, and their subsequent relations with both the Mohawk and the English were marked by greater friendship and increasing dependence.

The English conquest of New Netherland wrought less change than might be expected in relations with New England. The Duke of York's charter, like the early Dutch territorial claims, extended to the Connecticut River, and Governor Andros in particular did not allow his neighbors to forget the fact. Moreover, a common allegiance did little to remove the grievances arising from the Albany arms traffic and forays of the Mohawk to the eastward. This tribe remained friendly with the New England colonists themselves, but its war parties persisted in attacking natives whom the New Englanders had assured of protection and in appropriating livestock and crops. Except for a short breathing spell after the Indian treaty in 1671, these visitations continued to vex relations between New York and New England for nearly a generation.[8]

King Philip's War began toward the end of June 1675 in the vicinity

---

Winthrop Papers, Alphabetical Volumes, Massachusetts Historical Society, V, 167–168; VII, 15–17; Brodhead, *History of New York*, II, 161, 167, 181.

[6] *LIR*, 35–38; *NYCD*, III, 254; XIII, 491; Colonial MSS, XXV, 97.

[7] *NYCD*, XIII, 508–509; *LIR*, 40–42; *ARSCM*, II, 245–246.

[8] *CSP, 1661–1668*, no. 1052; *NYCD*, III, 120–121, 137–138; *Massachusetts Colonial Records*, IV, pt. 2, 359–361; Winthrop Papers, Alphabetical Volumes, Massachusetts Historical Society, V, 167–168; VI, 167; VII, 3, 6, 15, 17; Brodhead, *History of New York*, II, 127.

of Narragansett Bay. It spread rapidly to the north and west, as band after band took to the warpath in the greatest Indian uprising of New England history. Although Governor Andros took steps to prevent New York tribesmen from joining the rebellion, that colony did not escape involvement. On the first news of disturbances to the east, Andros gathered a supply of arms and ammunition and took them to the mouth of the Connecticut River, expecting to take an active part in suppressing the revolt. As it happened, this action came shortly after he had demanded that the Connecticut authorities surrender the western half of their province to New York. Under the circumstances they refused to have any dealings with him at all, lest he use the Indian war as a cover for territorial aggrandizement at their expense. Andros returned home, therefore, after sending some of his armament to the more receptive Rhode Islanders.

As the rebellion spread during the month of August, the New Englanders were driven reluctantly to ask for Mohawk intervention, if only against such enemies as happened to pass into New York.[9] The Mohawk, however, had other irons in the fire and probably hesitated to commit themselves to further adventures in New England. For the present they seem to have adhered to a policy of benevolent neutrality toward the eastern colonists. Andros, on the other hand, continued to interest himself in the conflict despite his initial rebuff. He paid his first visit to Albany in August and, together with the local magistrates, sought to keep the Mahican and other neighboring tribesmen away from the scene of hostilities. In December, when some of Philip's warriors approached Albany, the authorities tried to free their Christian prisoners. The local inhabitants, moreover, were forbidden to buy any goods which had been plundered from Christian homes.[10] On one occasion Andros was able to warn the Connecticut authorities of a rumored attack on Hartford. In October he forbade the sale of powder and lead to the Indians at Albany and the Esopus in order to prevent their falling into the wrong hands. This order was rendered almost meaningless, however, by the exceptions it contained. The Iroquois were exempted from the ban—he had just assured them of his full support against the French—as were any other tribesmen known personally to the authorities, who might be allotted small

[9] *Connecticut Colonial Records*, II, 350, 377.
[10] *ARSCM*, II, 17, 48–49, 56, 65.

quantities for their hunting.[11] With loopholes the size of these it is more than likely that some contraband found its way, at least indirectly, to the New England tribesmen. Whether this leakage assumed significant proportions is more questionable, but New Englanders were convinced that it did. In December the Massachusetts government declared publicly that Philip had supplied himself with ammunition from Albany, and a month later the Connecticut council insinuated the same thing to Andros. "We are confident," they wrote, that "you have already taken the most effectuall course imaginable to restraine the supplying [of] the comon enemy with either armes or amunition, especially the Dutch people, who you know are soe much bent vpon their profit." [12]

These accusations infuriated Andros, who took them as a personal attack upon his own administration as well as on the residents of his province. He wrote a blistering reply to Hartford, praying for an explanation and the names of the guilty parties. As for the Dutch, he said, there are "none in this Gouernment but his Ma[jes]ties subjects, which obey all his lawes, the penalty of which shall certainly bee inflicted on any transgressors." A similar protest was sent to Boston, but both governments, though clearing the New York magistrates of any complicity, were unshaken in their conviction of chronic wrongdoing at Albany. They had every reason, including past performance on the part of the Albany Dutchmen, to sustain this belief; but in the nature of the case they were unable to substantiate their charges. These were based largely upon Indian reports which, even if true, were lacking in detail and not susceptible of proof.[13] Somewhat more convincing were accusations originating in Albany itself. Two men, both with English names, were sent down to New York in November 1675 for "writing false storeys to Boston," and in the following March one William Loveridge was arrested for accusing the provincial interpreter, Arnout Cornelisse Viele, of supplying armaments to hostile Indians. Little was

[11] *Connecticut Colonial Records,* II, 377–378; *NYCD,* III, 254; XIII, 491–492.

[12] Charles Henry Lincoln, ed., *Narratives of the Indian Wars, 1675–1699* (New York, 1913), 64; *Connecticut Colonial Records,* II, 398.

[13] *Connecticut Colonial Records,* II, 404 (including quotation), 472, 478; *NYCD,* III, 242, 254, 257–258; XIV, 711; Thomas Hutchinson, ed., *Collection of Original Papers Relative to the History of the Colony of Massachusetts-Bay* (Boston, 1769), 476; *CSP, 1675–1676,* no. 876; cf. Douglas Edward Leach, *Flintlock and Tomahawk: New England in King Philip's War* (New York, 1958), 176–177, and George W. Ellis and John E. Morris, *King Philip's War* (New York, 1906), 167.

done, apparently, to check on the veracity of these reports, and Loveridge, unable to prove his case, was fined by the court.[14]

Andros' conduct did nothing to allay New England suspicions, which continued to be widely aired. So sensitive was the governor on this score that during a visit to England in the spring of 1678, nearly two years after the war, he petitioned the king for a formal hearing. Massachusetts had agents in London at the time, but they had come on other business. Three thousand miles distant from whatever evidence may have existed, they could give only a halting reply to Andros' argument and added nothing to the previous accusations. To the best of their knowledge, they said, their government had never heard charges against specific persons. The upshot of this rather one-sided inquest was a royal order completely vindicating Andros and the Albany traders, and the subject was never clarified any further.[15]

Mohawk neutrality might have continued indefinitely had not Philip and several hundred of his followers spent the winter of 1675–1676 in the vicinity of Albany. Whatever their purpose may have been, they came in December, apparently in two parties, to a point on the Hoosic River less than forty miles northeast of town. As their numbers increased and became known at Albany, the inhabitants were thrown into a panic. Since the river was frozen, they sent runners down to inform Andros. Much of the evidence as to what followed is lacking, but soon afterward Captain Brockholls, whom the governor had left in charge at Albany, managed to enlist the Mohawk against the unwelcome visitors. While the warriors were away, he seems to have sheltered at least part of their noncombatants at Albany.[16]

Meanwhile Andros had sent news of Philip's whereabouts to Connecticut. The Hartford authorities replied that this was the perfect opportunity for the Mohawk "to gratify . . . New England" and settle their own scores as well by destroying "all their old enymys together." They expressed joy that Philip was now in a position to be annihilated "without adventuringe any of his Majesty's subjects in the designe." Andros carried a chip on his shoulder in all dealings with Connecticut and interpreted this statement as one of relief that the

---

[14] Brodhead, *History of New York*, II, 290, 292; Colonial MSS, XXV, 90, 184.
[15] *NYCD*, III, 254, 257–258, 266–267.
[16] *ARSCM*, II, 48–49; *NYCD*, III, 255; Lincoln, *Narratives of the Indian Wars*, 68; *Connecticut Colonial Records*, II, 397.

warriors were now in New York instead of Connecticut. In his answer, therefore, he accused them of trying to dump the whole Indian problem in his lap. Early in February he wrote to ask if Christian or Indian forces from New York, and particularly Iroquois warriors, would be allowed to pursue the enemy into Connecticut. Once more the Hartford officials urged him to foster a Mohawk attack on the enemy near Albany. They had had too much experience already with allegedly friendly Indians in their towns and would welcome Iroquois visitors only in the last extremity.[17]

Having received notice by this time of Mohawk co-operation against Philip, Andros went up to Albany with reinforcements. Here he found three hundred Mohawk warriors, just back from a successful foray. They were eager to pursue the enemy all the way to Connecticut, he later claimed, but he was put to great expense to restrain them because of New England's nonco-operation. In any case he sent a messenger warning Philip and his men to leave the province, and this they seem to have done. Before returning to New York, Andros supervised the construction of a new stockaded fort on the hill above town. This was the structure which served Albany until the turn of the century.[18]

Hearing toward the end of May that the Massachusetts Indians were on the point of submission, the New York authorities resolved to put a stop if possible to further Mohawk depredations in that area. They also decided that any New England tribesmen who were inclined to enter the province and submit to its authority should be invited to settle down permanently in the neighborhood of Albany. This decision gave birth to a long-standing and somewhat unique policy in colonial New York; for many years to come the provincial and local authorities would bend every effort, not only to keep the local Indians from emigrating, but to induce outside tribes or tribal fragments to settle in the province. A larger Indian population would enhance trade at the same time that it cushioned the frontier settlements against attack from the French or other outside enemies. Lacking a large white population, Andros and his successors were ready to use Indian mercenaries, particularly when their trade might go far to earn their keep. In accordance with these resolutions he summoned

[17] *Connecticut Colonial Records*, II, 397–398, 404, 406–407; *NYCD*, III, 255.
[18] *NYCD*, III, 255, 257; XIII, 494; XIV, 717; Lincoln, *Narratives of the Indian Wars*, 97; Brodhead, *History of New York*, II, 291–292.

the Iroquois to meet him at Albany and requested the Mahican to bring their eastern kinsmen there at the same time.[19]

At Albany the governor found the Mohawk as curious as he to know if peace had been concluded. In answer to his request for further information the Hartford authorities assured him that the war was still on and that Mohawk aid would still be appreciated as long as their warriors kept well away from the settlements. Meanwhile Andros welcomed about twenty New England Indians, including women and children, who had apparently accepted his offer of asylum. Probably in their company he went to Scaticook (the present Schaghticoke), on the Hoosic River about twenty miles northeast of Albany. Here, near the site of Philip's recent camp, he "planted a Tree of welfare" to shelter all New England tribesmen who might settle in the province and enjoy the protection of his government.[20] About two hundred of these Indians seem to have settled here within the next year or two and were known henceforth as the Scaticook Indians. Apart from the fact that they were New England refugees, their precise origin and previous tribal affiliation are unknown. They may have belonged to eastern Mahican bands; certainly the New York Mahican were primarily responsible for getting them to accept Andros' invitation. The two groups maintained separate organizations, but they lived relatively close together, and as time passed they became more or less indistinguishable in the white man's records.

The officials in New England by no means agreed with Andros concerning the proper treatment of the Indian refugees. Having suffered at the hands of these tribesmen, they demanded severe punishment, extending in some cases to death or enslavement. During the summer of 1676 several groups of defeated Indians retreated westward, out of their reach. When Connecticut warned of the flight of one such party toward the Hudson and requested their apprehension or annihilation —preferably the latter—Andros did nothing. Other requests from Boston and Hartford for the surrender of prisoners were similarly ignored or rejected. New York co-operated only to the extent of ordering that less desirable refugees be delivered to the Mohawk. In March 1677 it was provided that "all strange Indyans" entering the province

---

[19] *NYCD*, XIII, 496–497; XIV, 721; Colonial MSS, XXV, 121; Council Minutes, III, pt. 2, 101.

[20] *Connecticut Colonial Records*, II, 461–462; *NYCD*, III, 565; IV, 744, 902, 991; Brodhead, *History of New York*, II, 294–295.

might live and be incorporated with the Mohawk, Mahican, Esopus, or other New York tribes and receive equal protection from the government.[21]

In October 1676, after native resistance had collapsed in southern New England, Massachusetts again sought Iroquois aid against the Abnaki in Maine. At the same time she and Connecticut were faced once more with the problem of making peace between the Mohawk and friendly Indians, like Uncas and his Mohegan tribe of Connecticut, who had remained loyal to the English during the war. Although Andros seconded their peacemaking efforts, they were not notably successful. New England delegates renewed the covenant at Albany in April 1677, but the Mohegan were not included in this treaty, and shortly afterward a Mohawk raiding party seized Uncas' son. Andros was already having difficulties of his own with the Mohawk, who had captured some Mahican and New England tribesmen around Albany. The local authorities managed to release nearly all the captives, including Uncas' son, but peace with the Connecticut Indians was no closer than before.[22]

The last stages of King Philip's War or, more properly, a simultaneous but unrelated conflict along the Maine coast dragged on until August 1677. Massachusetts was no more successful in getting the Mohawk to intervene in this contest than she was in having them desist from the other. It was in this theater, nevertheless, that Andros performed his greatest service to New England. The Duke of York continued to claim all of Maine east of the Kennebec River by virtue of the royal grant of 1664. As governor of this region Andros in the summer of 1677 sent about one hundred men under Captain Brockholls to retake Pemaquid from the Indians. Soon after their landing the neighboring Indians submitted and concluded a peace settlement. Massachusetts was not overly happy about this interference in a region which she too claimed, but she accepted the peace and followed it up with a more comprehensive treaty the next spring.[23]

[21] *Connecticut Colonial Records*, II, 466–467, 469–470, 477–478, 480, 492, 494–495, 508; Ellis and Morris, *King Philip's War*, 281; NYCD, XIII, 501–503.

[22] *Massachusetts Colonial Records*, V, 123; *Connecticut Colonial Records*, II, 480, 485, 491–496, 499–500, 502; NYCD, XIII, 501–502, 504, 509; LIR, 39–42; ARSCM, II, 245–246.

[23] *Connecticut Colonial Records*, II, 496; *Massachusetts Colonial Records*, V, 123, 134, 165, 167; NYCD, III, 258, 265; John G. Palfrey, *History of New England* (Boston, 1858–1890), III, 213–214.

Anglo-Iroquois Relations

In September 1677 some unknown Indians attacked the towns of Hatfield and Deerfield in western Massachusetts. The Connecticut authorities jumped to the conclusion that the attackers were Mohawk and complained accordingly to New York and Albany. This provoked another quarrel with Andros, until it was discovered that the culprits were from Canada. The Mohawk were unquestionably responsible, however, for depredations against John Eliot's "Praying Indians" at Natick, near Boston, who were under the protection of Massachusetts. That government immediately protested the action as a violation of their recent peace agreement at Albany and invited the Mohawk instead to fall upon those who had attacked Hatfield. Both colonies requested, for the protection of the Mohawk themselves, that they approach English settlements in the company of white men, or at least with credentials to identify them as friendly Indians. This plan was never seriously adopted, however, and several Mahican as well as Mohawk were mistakenly apprehended by local authorities in each colony.[24]

Other Mohawk forays took place in the summer of 1678, including a second attack upon the Natick in which they took more than twenty prisoners. This time Massachusetts, without consulting New York beforehand, sent agents directly to the Mohawk to demand the prisoners' release and arrange for a full treaty conference in New England. The Mohawk were quite aware of New York's attitude toward such outside dealings and on this occasion found it expedient to insist that Albany was the place ordained for all their conferences. Captain Brockholls, acting as governor while Andros was in England, was furious at Massachusetts' presumption and reprimanded the Albany commandant for letting her agents enter the Mohawk country in the first place. When Andros returned shortly afterward, he informed Boston of his willingness to co-operate in reaching a settlement, but insisted that all negotiations be conducted in his presence by fully accredited agents. As far as the Natick prisoners were concerned, it was of little importance, however. News reached Albany that most of them had been put to death—probably burned at the stake—soon after their capture.[25]

---

[24] *Connecticut Colonial Records,* II, 506–509; *Massachusetts Colonial Records,* V, 165–168; *NYCD,* XIII, 516–518.

[25] *NYCD,* III, 271–276; XIII, 519–531; *Connecticut Colonial Records,* II, 258–259, 262–264, 491, 494–495, 503–504.

Indian Affairs in Colonial New York

The Mohawk, according to reports from Albany, had been thoroughly frightened by this incident, especially as it was coupled with threats of retaliation from Massachusetts. The number of war parties going in that direction apparently fell off sharply, yet the Bay Colony had to send to Albany on a similar mission in 1680. This time, however, it took care to apprise the New York officials in advance. The Mohawk now alleged that they "neuer had any delight in this warr" and fought it only "as servants and souldjers" of the English. However unconvincing this argument was, they finally announced a readiness to "lay doune the axe," and New Englanders as well as their native wards henceforth breathed more easily.[26] Throughout this affair colonial authorities, and particularly those of New England, had sought to use the Mohawk for their own ends. Perhaps it was only justice that they paid a high price in return.

New England was but one of the theaters of Iroquois activity, and it was of far less consequence to the western tribes of the confederacy than to the Mohawk. Elsewhere the Seneca and Cayuga had been waging an intermittent war with the Susquehanna since the late 1650's. They were ultimately to win this contest, but after a decade of fighting both tribes had suffered such grave reverses that some of their number took refuge north of Lake Ontario. The Mohawk had originally held aloof from this struggle, maintaining closer relations for a time with the Susquehanna than with their Seneca confederates. Although Mohawk war parties went out against the Susquehanna in 1667, indicating a *rapprochement* within the league, they had so much to do elsewhere that they took little part in this war or later Iroquois involvements to the south. Among the English colonies only Maryland involved herself directly in the contest, siding actively with the Susquehanna. The English of New York, like the Dutch before them, apparently regarded the war primarily as a commercial opportunity and supplied armaments to both sides, on the Delaware and the Hudson respectively. Certainly there was no desire at this time to protect the Iroquois or assist them militarily in their hard-fought contest. Governor Nicolls had none of the solicitude which his successors came to feel for the western Iroquois after they had emerged as a buffer against the French. At one point he even contemplated an Anglo-Indian alliance to make war on them, after they had killed several colonists in

---

[26] *Massachusetts Colonial Records*, V, 299–300, 319–320.

Maryland and around Albany. Only after Governor Andros' arrival did the Susquehanna war receive much attention in New York. Hoping to negotiate a peace settlement, Andros found on his first visit to Albany in 1675 that the Seneca were determined to pursue the enemy until it was utterly defeated. The fortunes of war had altered considerably by this time, and that objective was achieved to all intents and purposes the next year.[27]

In 1677, as peace negotiations were afoot between the Mohawk and New England, Andros made himself similarly useful to the government of Maryland. When its agent, Colonel Henry Coursey, came to make peace with the Iroquois, Andros and the officials at Albany sent messengers as far as the Seneca country (apparently the first Albanians to reach that far) to summon the sachems to a conference. Andros as usual was careful to guard his colony's prerogatives and severely restricted Coursey's activities and his statements to the Indians. This conference culminated in a peace treaty which included both Maryland and Virginia as well as their local Indians.[28] The tribesmen of these two colonies were under English protection, but they enjoyed no more security from Iroquois attack than the hapless Natick of Massachusetts. A year later Andros intervened in the wake of further depredations along the Maryland and Virginia frontiers, committed by the Oneida and Onondaga. At his insistence the four western nations promised again to withhold their war parties and surrender the prisoners that they had taken. In the summer of 1679, thinking another treaty might prove helpful, Virginia sent agents northward to renew the covenant.[29]

Lord Baltimore complained to New York in March 1682 of still another incursion and suggested that a trade boycott be imposed on the Iroquois until they learned to keep their covenants. Andros by this time had left the province permanently, and Brockholls was again serving as interim governor. He had no intention of complying with

---

[27] Benjamin Sulte, "Le Fort de Frontenac, 1668–1678," in Royal Society of Canada, *Proceedings and Transactions*, 2d ser., VII, sec. 1 (1901), 50–51; Hunt, *Wars of the Iroquois*, 103, 134–135, 137–144; Winthrop Papers, Alphabetical Volumes, Massachusetts Historical Society, VII, 13, 18; *NYCD*, XIII, 491.

[28] *Maryland Archives*, V, 243–258, 348–349; XV, 149 ff.; *NYCD*, XIII, 507–508; *LIR*, 42–48.

[29] *NYCD*, III, 271–272, 277–278; XIII, 536–537; Colden, *History of the Five Nations*, I, 24–31; *LIR*, 48–61.

such a drastic proposal, but he ordered the Albany magistrates to send the Indians another warning. At his suggestion, furthermore, Maryland decided to renew the 1677 treaty again, and Coursey, with Colonel Philemon Lloyd, was appointed to make the return trip to Albany. Lord Baltimore was gravely offended at the way that Andros had circumscribed Coursey's activities in 1677. On this occasion, therefore, he instructed his agents to choose their own interpreter and manage their business in their own way. The proprietor also drew up a list of arguments which he hoped would induce New York out of self-interest to exercise greater control over her Indian allies.

Coursey and Lloyd arrived at New York in June and immediately sought Brockholls' permission to treat with the Indians in whatever form and manner that they should consider most proper. They proposed that New York, as a sister colony, join Maryland in these negotiations, making it plain to the Iroquois that an offense against English subjects in one colony would not be tolerated in another. This proposition, if accepted, would have constituted a first step toward an imperial Indian policy. But as it would have restricted New York's peculiar prerogatives and perhaps have entailed such punitive action as a trade boycott at Albany as well, it was not accepted. Brockholls, who was determined not to deviate from the policies and precedents laid down by Andros, side-stepped the question altogether. He was completely willing to let Coursey and Lloyd treat with the Indians, but only as long as they confined themselves to a renewal of the previous treaty. Unable or unwilling to accompany them himself, he wrote to the Albany magistrates cautioning them to be present at all the Marylanders' transactions with the Indians and to see that these were conducted in public.[30]

As soon as the agents reached Albany, they discovered a similar intransigence on the part of the local officials. Amidst reports that war parties were again heading southward, the magistrates contented themselves with a warning to the Indians to stay home. They also refused to join directly in any Maryland treaty with the Five Nations, promising only to tell the Indians that they could expect no "relief or assistance" from Albany in case of further violations of the covenant.

[30] *Maryland Archives*, V, 347–349; VII, 110–111, 269–271, 290–291, 295–296, 305–307, 320; XVII, 85–86, 89–90, 95–104, 197–200; *NYCD*, XIII, 555–556; *LIR*, 68–69.

Complaints to Brockholls proved unavailing. He refused to let the agents send messages to the Iroquois themselves, told them to stick to the business of renewing the old treaty, and turned down their request that Albany at least stop furnishing the Indians with arms and ammunition until they had recalled their warriors.[31]

When the Iroquois finally arrived, Coursey and Lloyd, properly chaperoned, cleared the Seneca at the outset of any complicity in the southern depredations. That tribe, in fact, was fully occupied in the west, and the chief guilt clearly fell on the Oneida and Onondaga. None of the sachems really defended the actions of their unruly braves, and all but the Seneca promised to contribute toward an indemnity of five hundred beavers which the agents demanded. They thanked the Marylanders for not making war upon them, agreed to recall their warriors, and made the usual promises for the future.[32] Certainly the Iroquois sachems were not the main obstacle which Coursey and Lloyd had faced at Albany. Returning home after the conference, the envoys heard that a party of Oneida, who had gone south before the conference opened, had taken more than fifty prisoners among the Maryland Indians. Coursey immediately wrote to Brockholls, who went up to Albany himself in the middle of September and got the Indians to promise the prisoners' release. At least fourteen of them were sent back, and Lord Baltimore professed himself well satisfied with the governor's service.[33]

Troublesome as these forays were to the English, they lacked the strategic and commercial significance of Iroquois relations to the north and west. The substitution of English for Dutch control on the Hudson had no immediate effect on either the basic objectives or the tactics of the French and Iroquois. Anglo-French rivalry along the New York frontier developed only gradually, and even a war between the two powers in the late 1660's did little to alter the relations which had prevailed in the time of Stuyvesant. For more than a decade English policy at Albany, like that of the Dutch, was limited to an essentially commercial rivalry with Canada for the good will of the Indians and the proceeds of their hunting. For Nicolls and Lovelace the main task

[31] *ARSCM*, III, 264–266, 271–272; *Maryland Archives*, XVII, 203–209; *NYCD*, XIII, 557–562; *LIR*, 64.
[32] *Maryland Archives*, XVII, 210–215; *NYCD*, III, 321–328.
[33] *Maryland Archives*, VII, 334; XVII, 215–216; *NYCD*, XIII, 563–565.

was that of assimilating an alien province and defending it against reconquest by the Dutch. The Netherlands, and not France, was England's primary rival in these years.[34]

When the English arrived at Albany, the eastern Iroquois had been engaged in desultory warfare with the French and their Indians for about six years. Governor Nicolls paid little attention to this contest at first, except to hope that Mohawk losses in the north would "be a good Ingredient of peace" between them and the New England tribes.[35] Canada meanwhile came under new royal management at this time. The Marquis de Tracy arrived at Quebec in June 1665 as viceroy of all French America and soon was followed by the Sieur de Courcelle and Jean Talon, who were to serve as governor and intendant respectively of New France. With them came a thousand French troops and royal orders "totally to exterminate" the Iroquois confederacy. To implement this plan forts were now built on the northern approaches to Lake Champlain, and preparations were made for a full-scale invasion of Iroquoia.[36] These activities generated considerable alarm among the intended victims, and the four western nations hastened to make peace at Quebec in December. Acknowledging French sovereignty once more, they asked that Jesuits and French colonists be sent back to their villages to lead them in the path of light.[37]

The Mohawk were conspicuously absent from these negotiations, and Courcelle determined to humble them without further delay. With a force of three hundred French regulars and an equal number of Canadians he set forth on an adventure which would have been arduous at any time, but was doubly so in midwinter. His army tramped southward on snowshoes over the ice of Lake Champlain, thence to Lake George and the upper Hudson. At this point, suffering from cold and exhaustion, they went astray; on February 9, to the great surprise of everyone concerned, they found themselves within two miles of Schenectady. The Dutch inhabitants had little choice but to receive them kindly. They said that most of the Mohawk were away from home fighting another tribe, but a small party of French-

---

[34] See Buffinton, "The Policy of Albany and English Westward Expansion," 331 ff.

[35] *Winthrop Papers*, Alphabetical Volumes, Massachusetts Historical Society, VI, 168.

[36] *NYCD*, IX, 25, 29, 36; Francis Parkman, *The Old Regime in Canada* (27th ed.; Boston, 1892), 184.

[37] *NYCD*, III, 121–125; IX, 37–38; *NYDH*, I, 64–65.

men fell into a Mohawk ambush nevertheless and was severely mauled before it retreated back to the main body. As soon as the Albany magistrates learned of the French invasion, they sent to inquire its meaning. Finding that the Mohawk were the sole target, they not only accepted the French explanations, but actually helped to replenish their supplies and care for their wounded. Courcelle refused invitations to take his men into Schenectady, however, partly for fear that in their demoralized and half-starved condition they might never leave again. The French, in fact, were no longer in condition to take on the Mohawk, who had begun to rally in self-defense. The only course left was to retreat, and the army's withdrawal degenerated into a near-rout by the time that it reached Canada. Mohawk warriors picked off stragglers as they fell behind, and the winter itself took a toll of sixty men.[38]

Although Courcelle failed utterly to accomplish his immediate objective, he did not fail to impress the Five Nations with the potentialities of French power. His expedition, along with reverses sustained at the hands of the Susquehanna, undoubtedly reinforced the determination of the western nations to maintain peace with Canada. The Seneca renewed their submission in May, and the Oneida followed in July. The latter took with them a letter from the Albany magistrates, written on behalf of the Mohawk, who had pleaded for English intercession. The French replied that the Mohawk would have to make their own application, but at least part of that tribe was still far from penitent. When further depredations were committed, apparently in violation of pledges that the sachems had made at Albany, the French prepared for even greater punitive measures.[39]

Nicolls, in New York, had feared that Courcelle's expedition was aimed primarily at Albany. When the event proved otherwise, he had seconded Albany's attempts to make peace for the Mohawk. Early in the summer, however, he received a royal letter announcing the outbreak of war between England and France. As the king now directed the English colonies to combine in reducing Canada, Nicolls reversed his position and sent orders to Albany to obstruct all negotiations with

[38] *NYCD*, III, 118–119, 126–127, 152; Colden, *History of the Five Nations*, I, 16; *NYDH*, I, 65–67; Parkman, *Old Regime in Canada*, 186–190.
[39] *NYCD*, III, 125–135, 153; *NYDH*, I, 67–68; *LIR*, 29–32; Winthrop Papers, Alphabetical Volumes, Massachusetts Historical Society, VII, 3; Parkman, *Old Regime in Canada*, 191–192.

the French. If the Mohawk would make peace with the eastern Indians, he continued, he would assist them himself against the French, or at least furnish them with ammunition. At the same time he asked Massachusetts and Connecticut for help in repelling another reported invasion of the Mohawk country. Both colonies turned down this request, partly because of Mohawk depredations in New England; but Connecticut co-operated to the extent of sending a scouting party to Lake Champlain. Although Nicolls' information proved to be erroneous, he had evidenced during this crisis, as Stuyvesant had on earlier occasions, a readiness to combine with savages against Christians if it were necessary to the defense of his province.[40] He reached this decision with great reluctance, but later governors were to be less squeamish.

By early October the French were ready for their second invasion of the Mohawk country. Tracy, despite his more than seventy years, determined to lead this expedition in person. With more than a thousand men, including a hundred Indian auxiliaries, he followed the same route that Courcelle had taken the previous winter. Weather conditions were better, but the difficulties of conducting such an army through 120 leagues of lake, forest, river, and mountain terrain were almost staggering. No such operation could long remain unknown to the Indians, and the alarm was spread before the French had left Lake Champlain. The Mohawk, with roughly 350 warriors, could not hope to stop them. Thus the invaders advanced with little opposition to the Indian villages, only to find them deserted. In their flight the Mohawk had followed the invariable practice of abandoning their grain and other provisions. These stores, together with all the houses and unused fortifications, were consigned to flames as the French moved from one castle to the next. Tracy could do no more against the Mohawk, and he was unwilling to risk an attack on the English. Before leaving, however, he took formal possession of the Mohawk country on behalf of the king of France and posted his arms before the remains of each castle. Retiring northward the way that it had come, the army returned to Canada without major incident.[41]

---

[40] Winthrop Papers, Alphabetical Volumes, Massachusetts Historical Society, VII, 1, 5–6; *NYCD*, III, 120–121, 133, 137–138, 141–142, 154–155; *LIR*, 29–31.
[41] *NYDH*, I, 68–71; *NYCD*, III, 135; IX, 56; Parkman, *Old Regime in Canada*, 192–199.

Anglo-Iroquois Relations

The French were no closer than before to their real objective of destroying the Mohawk, but they had certainly given that tribe additional cause for worry. Hoping to capitalize on these fears, they now demanded that the Mohawk accept French peace terms by the middle of June if they wanted to avoid further punishment. The Indians sought advice at Albany and proposed moving their settlements nearer the town for protection. Nicolls discouraged this idea, but on the other hand he strongly opposed any peace settlement which would leave the Mohawk as French satellites. He recognized that a primary French objective was "ingrossing the Beaver trade by destroying and interrupting ours at Albany" and advised the magistrates to keep this in mind in counseling the Indians. The Mohawk, he said, should insist upon the destruction of the French fortifications near Lake Champlain and should inform the French that they were subordinate to the king of England. Thus, it should be noted, Nicolls departed from Dutch policy and took a first step toward the assumption by New York of sovereignty over the Five Nations.[42]

The French were prepared to invade the Mohawk country a third time, but that tribe finally sent agents to Quebec in June 1667 in compliance with Tracy's command. The treaty imposed upon them provided that they as well as the Oneida should receive Jesuit missionaries and leave hostages as pledges of good faith. When the Indians returned home in July, the black robes went with them. The other tribes had already made their submission, and during the next several years the Jesuits labored among the Iroquois with little sustained opposition from either the Indians or the English. Both Nicolls and Lovelace extended the hospitality of their province to the missionaries, whom they accepted for some time entirely at face value. Only in 1670 did Lovelace voice apprehension that it was the Kingdom of France, not the Kingdom of Christ, which they sought most to advance. He did not know that in this same year Charles II and Louis XIV abandoned their halfhearted war in favor of a secret alliance in which his own sovereign became a pensioner of the Grand Monarch.[43]

The peace with Canada left the Iroquois free to extend their ac-

[42] NYCD, III, 144–148, 151; Winthrop Papers, Alphabetical Volumes, Massachusetts Historical Society, VII, 9, 11.

[43] Parkman, Old Regime in Canada, 204–206; Brodhead, History of New York, II, 127–130, 146–148, 168, 170, 235–236; NYCD, III, 162–163, 190; IX, 883.

tivities westward. More than ever before the French complained of Iroquois hunters who were taking furs north of the lakes in the territory of other tribes and selling them at Albany for higher prices than Montreal could offer. More troublesome still were the increasingly frequent raids on Ottawa trading parties which forcibly diverted much of the latters' peltry to the Hudson. The paradox of Franco-Iroquois relations, it was long ago suggested, lay in the fact that although the Iroquois constituted the greatest economic and military threat to Canada they were also the only factor keeping Albany from opening direct relations with the Ottawa and thus crippling the Canadian fur trade.[44] The price differential between Albany and Montreal was a source of constant danger to the French. When they prevailed on the Iroquois to send peace envoys to the Ottawa in 1670, the latter, hearing the facts, were so eager to share in the Albany trade that they persuaded the Iroquois to conduct them there the following spring. The French did all that they could to frustrate this plan, even to the point of provoking further hostilities between the tribes, but a group of Ottawa managed to reach the Iroquois country anyway.[45] They did not get to Albany, but their effort suggested later attempts by the English themselves to reach the Ottawa country.

Canadian traders, defying their own government, had greater success in carrying peltry to Albany. Unlike the Albany Dutchmen many merchants at Montreal had found it possible to send their own agents into the Indian country to trade, thus assuring a greater flow of peltry to the east. Moreover, many of these *coureurs de bois,* who were often half-breeds and already familiar with the natives, began to operate in the west on a free-lance basis. This practice was repeatedly condemned by the French authorities for the same reasons as it was among the Dutch and English, but the number of *coureurs de bois* continued to grow. There were reportedly four or five hundred of them by 1676. As

[44] The Baron de Lahontan, writing about 1700, concluded therefore that " 'tis the interest of the French to weaken the Iroquese [*sic*], but not to see 'em intirely defeated" (Louis Armand, Baron de Lahontan, *New Voyages to North America* [1703], ed. by R. G. Thwaites [Chicago, 1905], I, 394). A modern student, W. J. Eccles, makes the same point, basing his conclusion in part on the Iroquois' supposed position as middlemen ("Frontenac and the Iroquois, 1672–1682," *Canadian Historical Review,* XXXVI [1955], 1). The league's persistent hostilities with the western tribes, whatever their cause, had the same result, however, both in disrupting French trade and in preventing Ottawa peltry from reaching Albany.

[45] *NYCD,* IX, 84–85.

their activities were illegal to begin with, the *coureurs de bois* were hardly inclined to be scrupulous about considerations of national policy. Beginning in the 1670's they came to Albany in increasing numbers, apparently of their own volition at first, but soon with ample encouragement. The Canadian officials regarded them as deserters and were equally furious at the English authorities who harbored them.

The French were in an almost impossible competitive position, and their whole policy was aimed at diverting the natural channels of trade and diplomacy. They found themselves wanting simultaneously to prevent Iroquois raids on the Ottawa and to prevent peaceful intercourse between these tribes. Short of conquering or annexing New York, the perennial dream of Canadian officialdom, or of securing the Iroquois trade for themselves, which was economically and politically impossible, the only policy left as they saw it was to so weaken the Five Nations that they could be kept in permanent subjection. Although Frenchmen now and then expressed a fond wish for the complete destruction of the confederacy, it was perhaps fortunate for them that they were never able to accomplish this.

Courcelle, who hoped to overawe the Iroquois with demonstrations of French power, planned the construction of a fort at the junction of Lake Ontario and the St. Lawrence. This post would serve the triple purpose of keeping a military force within striking distance of the western Iroquois across the lake, of providing a convenient trading place for both the Ottawa and the Iroquois, and of frustrating commerce on the lake between these tribes. Courcelle was recalled in 1672 before undertaking this project, but he convinced his successor, Frontenac, of its importance, and the work was done in the summer of 1673. The new post was named Fort Frontenac, but the Iroquois always referred to it by their own name of Cadaraqui. Initially welcomed by them as an additional place to trade, the fort almost immediately became a springboard for further French penetration of the west. The Iroquois were not long in changing their minds, therefore, and came to regard it as a threat to their very existence.

The Comte de Frontenac was a farsighted, vigorous, and devoted exponent of French imperialism—undoubtedly the ablest governor of Canada since Champlain. His ultimate objective was to extend French domination to the entire North American interior. With the limited resources at his disposal he could achieve this only in conjunction with the Indian tribes who lived there. A cornerstone of his policy was therefore to win their allegiance, both political and commercial, by use of the carrot rather than the stick wherever possible. One of his chief lieutenants in this process was the Sieur de la Salle, whose western explorations and empire building Frontenac in large measure made possible. After the construction of Fort Frontenac the governor envisioned a chain of French posts extending from Quebec through the Great Lakes region and the Mississippi valley as far as the Gulf of Mexico. In 1679 he built a fort at Niagara and encouraged La Salle's construction of similar posts on the St. Joseph and Illinois Rivers. Ambitious and imaginative as it was, Frontenac's western policy was subject to the same basic contradictions which had plagued his more conservative predecessors. On the one hand, he desired a general Indian pacification that would ensure the uninterrupted flow of peltry from the interior. But no sooner had he effected such a settlement than he proceeded to undermine it with his westward expansionism which antagonized the Iroquois and the English. With each successive step that the French took in this direction the rumblings of Iroquois discontent became more audible, particularly after the Susquehanna were finally crushed in 1676. French activity in the west probably contributed to the Iroquois invasions of the Illinois country in 1677 and afterward, as well as the subsequent renewal of their hostilities with the Ottawa. It certainly was a factor in the Iroquois-French rupture of 1682.[46]

The English at New York were only dimly aware of Frontenac's activity and at first were little concerned with it. By 1673 the contortions of European diplomacy had brought England and France into an alliance against the Dutch, which in turn led to the reconquest of New Netherland. One of the effects of this reconquest at Albany was a more belligerent attitude toward the French. The local authorities now went out of their way to renew the Iroquois alliance and gave a substantial present to counteract Jesuit influence among the Indians.

---

[46] Benjamin Sulte, "Guerres des Iroquois, 1670–1673," in Royal Society of Canada, *Transactions,* 3d ser., XV, sec. 1, 85–95; "Le Fort de Frontenac," 47–96; Buffinton, "The Policy of Albany and English Westward Expansion," 339–343, and "The Policy of the Northern Colonies towards the French," 150–152; Eccles, "Frontenac and the Iroquois," 1 ff.; Hunt, *Wars of the Iroquois,* 149 ff.; Innis, *The Fur Trade in Canada,* 50–54; Francis Parkman, *La Salle and the Discovery of the Great West* (12th ed.; Boston, 1892), *passim.*

Mohawk sachems were even brought down to New York to view the victorious Dutch fleet. That tribe at least was happy to reciprocate Dutch good will, and they exchanged promises of mutual assistance in the event of a French attack. The Dutch authorities, moreover, repeatedly tried to stop the visits of the French *coureurs de bois* to Albany, regarding this traffic as a reprehensible trade with the enemy.[47]

The occupation by the Dutch was only an interlude, but when Governor Andros arrived in 1674, his French and Indian policy remained closer to theirs in some respects than it was to that of his English predecessors. This was partly in keeping with attitudes back home, where, in the public mind at least, France was rapidly replacing Holland as the national enemy; but it was also the result of increased French activity among the Indians. Andros assumed from the beginning that the Iroquois constituted a part of his province and were under his protection, and he acted on this assumption in most of his dealings with the French as well as his English neighbors. When a dispute broke out between the French and the Mohawk, he offered to mediate on behalf of the French, but warned them against prosecuting any of the Indians in his government. Moreover, he summoned the Jesuit missionary who lived with the Mohawk to meet him at Albany and explain "his being & Actings in those parts"; the priest was told that if he expected to continue there he would have to give proper assurances concerning his future conduct. In August 1675 Andros took the unprecedented step of visiting the Mohawk at their own castles in order to impress them with his role of friend and protector. (It was on this occasion that they first bestowed the title of Corlaer, which they applied to Andros and all his successors.)[48] Andros consistently denied French claims of jurisdiction over the Iroquois and occasionally got the Indians themselves to admit English sovereignty. In 1679, for instance, an Oneida speaker declared that his fellow tribesmen were subjects of Corlaer, who "governs the whole Land from New York to Albany & from thence to the Sennekas Land."[49] Such statements were usually made for diplomatic purposes, in order to conciliate the English and win their support. On most occasions the Iroquois continued

[47] *NYCD*, II, 594, 608, 618, 659, 662, 712–713, 716–717.
[48] *Ibid.*, III, 254, 559; XIII, 483–484; *CSP, 1681–1685*, no. 874, p. 365.
[49] *Wraxall's Abridgement*, 9 (including quotation); *NYCD*, XIII, 503; *ARSCM*, II, 211–212.

to regard themselves as politically independent of all Europeans, as they were in fact, and to act accordingly.

Although the governors of New York and Canada received repeated instructions to maintain friendly relations, both London and Paris backed up the Indian policies of their respective agents. The Duke of York approved Andros' policy of supporting the Iroquois, without specifically claiming them as English subjects, however. He also urged a Franco-Iroquois settlement that would keep the French north of Lake Ontario and the St. Lawrence, but the French obviously had no intention of limiting themselves in this way. At the same time Andros' support of the Five Nations was more verbal than active. Despite a warning to the French in 1677 against trading with the Iroquois south of Lake Ontario, almost no opposition was encountered from either the Seneca or New York when the French built their fort at Niagara in 1679. Andros had had several months' notice of their preparations and fully understood the consequences of a French garrison in the Seneca country, but he had little power to prevent it. Fortunately for New York and the Iroquois, the fort burned down within three years.[50]

The French frequently gave Andros greater credit for thwarting their plans than he really deserved. Such was the case with the *coureurs de bois,* whose continuing visits to Albany they attributed to the governor's encouragement. Frontenac accused Andros in 1679 of harboring one of these renegades named Péré, along with some others, in order to use him to open a direct English trade with the Ottawa. Actually Andros was striving almost as hard as Frontenac himself to put an end to these traders' visits, and Péré was arrested and sent to London, where he spent eighteen months in jail. In the same year New York not only forbade all trade with Frenchmen at Albany, but ordered that any persons of that nationality who entered the province without passes should be secured and sent to the West Indies. Although this policy was reaffirmed by Brockholls and Dongan in 1683, it was never fully observed at Albany. The local traders were in fact the proper objects of Frontenac's wrath. The town continued to be a haven for *coureurs de bois,* who frequented it more often still under Frontenac's successor. Moreover, a substantial number of Iroquois

---

[50] *NYCD,* III, 233, 278; XIII, 531; Brodhead, *History of New York,* II, 308; Frank H. Severance, *An Old Frontier of France: The Niagara Region and Adjacent Lakes under French Control* (New York, 1917), I, 41–42.

whom the French induced to resettle in Canada did not change their trading habits because of this removal. They came to Albany so frequently that Frontenac requested additional troops to block their passage.[51]

From the standpoint of English imperial interest the Albany-Canada trade could be approached in opposite ways. While the Canadian traders enlarged the Albany trade by bringing peltry which otherwise would have gone to Montreal, they also carried trading goods back with them, some of which were exchanged for peltry which found its market in Canada. The English therefore could stimulate the trade between Albany and Canada or attempt to prohibit it, in either case using imperial advantage as the pretext. Since both governments chose at this time to interpret the trade as harmful, it was driven underground; and it is even more difficult now than it was then to discover its real effects.

It was during these years that the Jesuits scored their greatest triumphs among the Iroquois. The degree of success that they attained as a result of unrelenting missionary labors among each of the Five Nations cannot be measured. Certainly the number of their converts, measured in terms of a genuine and deep-felt alteration in life and outlook, was relatively small. The black robes managed to create a French faction among the Iroquois, however, which weakened the league's resistance to French expansion. Probably their greatest success lay in persuading hundreds of Iroquois over a period of two decades to abandon their traditional homes, families, and allegiance and to settle instead on missionary reservations in Canada. The impulse and significance of this movement were political as well as religious in character.

The Jesuits had found from the very beginning that their missionary labors were frustrated by the environment in which they had to work. The long and laborious hours spent in the instruction of an individual convert were constantly being undermined as a result of his continued association with the pagan tribesmen around him. The white man's liquor contributed to backsliding, and converts were frequently

---

[51] Buffinton, "The Policy of Albany and English Westward Expansion," 340–341; Helen Broshar, "First Push Westward of the Albany Traders," *Mississippi Valley Historical Review*, VII (1920), 231–232; Severance, *An Old Frontier of France*, I, 29–30; ARSCM, II, 422–423; Council Minutes, V, 1.

subject to resentment if not actual persecution from members of their own families. No sooner were missions founded, therefore, than the priests felt it necessary to remove their wards to a more congenial atmosphere in Canada if their work was to reach fulfillment. In the case of the Iroquois not only did such a policy promise greater success in propagating the faith but, as Courcelle quickly perceived, it could also be of great value in weakening the Five Nations and undermining the English interest among them.

The first Iroquois village in Canada was founded in 1669 by Father Pierre Raffeix, who chose as its site the Prairie de la Madeleine on the south bank of the St. Lawrence, opposite Montreal. To this mission, which was named St. Francis Xavier des Près, came a small but constant stream of adherents, attracted by the stories of the priests and previous emigrants and by the opportunity to practice the new religion in peace. After one year it contained sixty souls, and chieftainships were instituted. The first adherents were largely Oneida, but before long all of the Five Nations were represented, together with a scattering of Mahican, New England, and other tribesmen. In 1676 a prominent Mohawk chief by the name of Kryn, who had already defected to the settlement, brought at least forty of his fellow tribesmen to the village, and in later years it became primarily Mohawk in composition. The mission of St. Francis, which the Indians came to call Caughnawaga, was supplemented by another in the same vicinity, usually referred to as the Mountain, which was tended by the Sulpician order. By 1680 each village could boast at least two hundred residents. The Catholic piety of some was questionable; that of others could not be doubted. But all of them showed firm devotion to the cause of France. Meanwhile the Jesuits by no means abandoned their work in the Iroquois country, where often they had to brave the resentment of the Indians who remained. The Mohawk sachems, for instance, accused their missionary, Father Bruyas, of depopulating the tribe, but they seem to have done nothing to terminate his activity.[52]

The Iroquois exodus was neither large enough nor sudden enough to provoke much notice at Albany for several years. Apparently it was not until his return from England in 1678 that the matter came to Gov-

[52] John G. Shea, *History of the Catholic Missions among the Indian Tribes of the United States, 1529–1854* (New York, 1855), 261–262, 268, 271–272, 296–311.

ernor Andros' attention. Robert Livingston and two of the Albany magistrates warned him at that time that the Mohawk, Mahican, and Scaticook Indians were likely to be drawn away from the English by repeated French offers of land and other privileges in Canada. The religious motivation for removal was not mentioned at all. Andros wanted to offer similar inducements to keep these Indians at home; however, he made no real attempt to implement this policy or to counteract the work of the Jesuits.[53] When the priests finally found life among the Iroquois too uncomfortable and returned to Canada one by one after 1680, it was due more to hostility on the part of the Indians themselves than to active intervention by the English.

English policy toward the Iroquois only gradually diverged from that which the Dutch had followed before 1664. The fur trade, with the attendant arms traffic, was still the major factor in New York calculations, with embarrassing consequences so far as relations with New England and the southern colonies were concerned. Only in the growing rivalry with France were significant modifications made in the colony's established Indian policy, and even here the new elements were by 1683 hardly more than foreshadowed. It was during the succeeding administration of Governor Dongan that Andros' claim to sovereignty over the Iroquois was carried to something like its logical conclusion.

[53] *NYCD*, XIII, 531–532.

X

Governor Dongan and the Iroquois

THE YEARS 1680–1683 brought new leaders to office in New York and Canada. At the same time both provinces as well as the Five Nations embarked on new policies, or at least contributed new emphases, which made this period a turning point in the history of relations between them. It was in 1680 that the Iroquois, spearheaded by the Seneca, launched a full-scale war on the Illinois tribes. Soon afterward they resumed hostilities with the Ottawa and Miami and gradually became embroiled once more with the French. In 1682 Frontenac was succeeded in Canada by Lefebvre de la Barre, who adopted a far more bellicose tone toward the Iroquois. Governor Andros had returned to England in 1681, leaving New York in the hands of Captain Brockholls, whose most fervent wish was for the early arrival of a successor. This event was delayed until the summer of 1683, when, with the advent of Colonel Thomas Dongan, New York Indian policy became infinitely more aggressive.

As French and Iroquois affairs assumed greater importance, New York's relationship with the Five Nations continued to complicate her dealings with the other English colonies. Dongan had hardly set foot in the province when he found Albany's western trade monopoly threatened by the new colony of Pennsylvania. William Penn's royal grant of 1681 embraced the territory west of the Delaware River as far north as the forty-third parallel—considerably beyond the present New York–Pennsylvania line. This limit had never been surveyed, and its location was very much in doubt, but Penn wanted to extend his settlements as far north as possible before someone else anticipated him. Most of the territory in question was claimed by the Five Nations as a result of their defeat of the Susquehanna. In July 1683, therefore, he sent two agents to Albany to negotiate with the Indians for a large tract along the upper Susquehanna River.[1] The agents had already arrived at Albany when Dongan reached New York late in August. Hearing of their mission, the governor hurried up the river as soon as possible, probably to investigate its ramifications. He seems to have returned to New York very shortly, without having talked to the Indians. But on September 7 the local court interviewed a Susquehanna and two Cayuga tribesmen and questioned them closely as to the location of the lands in question and their proximity to the Iroquois country. The magistrates were told that the region was only ten days' journey from the Seneca country, and the Indians assured them that it was far more convenient to reach than Albany for purposes of trade. In reporting to Dongan the magistrates forwarded the Indians' remarks, together with a map of the Susquehanna lands, and pointed out that a settlement here by outsiders might prove prejudicial to the colony.[2]

Dongan responded to this warning with orders to halt Penn's proceedings with the Indians pending a determination of the boundary between the two colonies. The Indians themselves were apparently delighted at the prospect of traders settling on the Susquehanna, an attitude which caused even greater alarm among the magistrates. If Penn were to buy this land, they wrote Dongan,

it will tend to ye utter Ruine off ye Bev[e]r Trade. . . . Wee Presume that there hath not anything ever been moved or agitated from ye first seteing of these Parts, more Prejudiciall to his Royall highnesse Intrest, and ye Inhabitants of this his governm[en]t, then this businesse of ye Susquehanne River. The french its true have Endevourd to take away our trade, by Peace meals but this will cutt it all off att once.[3]

On their own responsibility, therefore, and before receiving Dongan's orders, the local court undertook successfully to frustrate Penn's ef-

---

[1] Samuel Hazard *et al.*, eds., *Pennsylvania Archives* (Philadelphia and Harrisburg, 1852–1949), 2d ser., VII, 3.

[2] *LIR*, 69–70; ARSCM, III, 379–381; Brodhead, *History of New York*, II, 375–376.

[3] *Pennsylvania Archives*, 1st ser., I, 74–75; ARSCM, III, 388 (including quotation).

forts. In return for some presents and a promise of more ample payment by the governor the Onondaga and Cayuga sachems (who claimed sole jurisdiction over the Susquehanna lands) were prevailed upon to cede this territory to Corlaer. Contrary to normal procedure this conveyance was made to Dongan personally rather than to the province or the Duke of York. Whether this was done at the governor's own suggestion or on the magistrates' initiative is unclear, but he accepted the conveyance in this form and apparently paid an additional sum for it later.[4]

When Penn again sent agents to New York in April 1684, Dongan accused them of conspiring to take away Albany's trade. Pennsylvania had more than enough land already, he declared, and he advised that colony to take up its argument with the Duke of York. A few months later he prevailed on the Indians to renew their grant and to prevent Pennsylvanians from settling on it.[5] Had the agents followed Dongan's advice, they would have gotten no more comfort from the duke, who had just warned Dongan to use great care in preventing Penn and the inhabitants of New Jersey "from obstructing ye Peltry trade of New York." He repeated this injunction on later occasions, and Dongan's action with regard to the Susquehanna lands was specifically confirmed in August. "My desire," the duke wrote, is "to preserve the Indian Trade as entire as I can for the benefitt of the Inhabit[ant]s and traders of New Yorke preferably to all others."[6] In time Dongan came to begrudge the very existence of Pennsylvania, just as all New York governors deplored the separation of New Jersey and Delaware from the ducal propriety. He reported in 1687 that a flourishing Indian trade was developing on the Schuylkill. If this were not prevented, he warned, his government could no longer hope to maintain itself financially, and both New York and Albany would be wholly depopulated.[7]

If the Indians expected Albany to send traders of its own to the Susquehanna country, they were doomed to disappointment. Instead, the provincial council offered a reward in 1687 to Indians who should apprehend and bring in trespassers seeking to establish themselves on this land without the government's permission. Pennsylvania was warned not to send persons to the upper Susquehanna, and the council

---

[4] *NYDH*, I, 396–397, 400–401; *NYCD*, III, 393, 406.

[5] *Pennsylvania Archives*, 1st ser., I, 81; *NYDH*, I, 399–403.

[6] *NYCD*, III, 341, 348–350, 373.   [7] *Ibid.*, 393–394, 416.

threatened to remove the few Indians living there if they did not bring their trade to Albany as formerly.[8]

So the matter stood until 1697, some years after Dongan's return to England. At that distance and for reasons that have never been satisfactorily explained, he reversed his earlier position by selling the lands himself to William Penn. This transaction was eventually confirmed by the Indians, and in 1736 Pennsylvania bought the tract all over again.[9] Dongan's motives in this affair are open to legitimate question. The fact that he accepted a personal conveyance in the first place, together with his comparable record in the Long Island land controversies, indicates strongly that in serving the province he was also serving himself. The most that can be said in extenuation of the sale in 1697 is that perhaps he was aware by then that most of the Susquehanna land fell within the boundaries of Pennsylvania. In any case the original cession could hardly have done more than postpone the settlement of this region, since squatters would probably have moved in regardless of title.[10] There is no record of the Indians' turning in such trespassers, but in 1699 they were rebuked for sounding out the governor of Pennsylvania about trading prospects there.[11] In spite of halfhearted efforts by Dongan's successors to prevent it, residents of both Pennsylvania and New Jersey found means of carrying on a small-scale trade with the Iroquois during all of this period.[12]

Iroquois hostilities with the Indians of Maryland and Virginia, which had become a major source of concern after the conquest of the Susquehanna, increased in frequency and intensity during Dongan's administration. The Maryland treaty of 1682, in which Virginia had been associated, was hardly a year old before Iroquois warriors were back on the frontiers of Virginia, harassing colonists as well as the neighboring tribesmen. The newly arrived governor there, Lord Howard of Effingham, decided in 1684 to visit New York himself in

[8] Colonial MSS, XXXV, 60; Letter from Governor and Council of New York to President and Council of Pennsylvania, April 15, 1687, in *Pennsylvania Magazine of History and Biography*, XI (1887–1888), 242.

[9] *Pennsylvania Archives*, 1st ser., I, 121–123, 133, 494–497.

[10] Cf. Charles P. Keith, *Chronicles of Pennsylvania, 1688–1748* (Philadelphia, 1917), I, 111–113; Henry Allain St. Paul, "Governor Thomas Dongan's Expansion Policy," *Mid-America*, XVII (n.s. VI; 1935), 178–181; John H. Kennedy, *Thomas Dongan, Governor of New York (1682–1688)* (Washington, 1930), 37–38.

[11] *Wraxall's Abridgement*, 33; *CSP, 1699*, no. 747.

[12] *NYCD*, III, 689–690, 798, 822–823; IV, 289; *CSP, 1693–1696*, no. 289.II.

order to set matters aright. He was not so demanding as Coursey and Lloyd, nor was Dongan as unsure of himself as Brockholls had been. He received his visitor toward the end of June with all the pomp and ceremony that New York could muster, and soon afterward the two governors sailed up the river to Albany, where the Iroquois had been summoned to meet them.[13]

When the Indians arrived, Effingham recalled their repeated violations of the covenant and declared that he had asked Colonel Dongan to assist him in a war against them. But, he continued, their governor had offered to mediate, and therefore he had come to Albany to talk instead of fight. He promised to forget the past and forge a stronger covenant chain if they would withdraw their men from Virginia and Maryland and keep them west of the mountains. In order to confirm this agreement he would send an agent with some Virginia sachems to ratify it at Albany the next summer. Effingham's leniency probably arose from the imminence at this time of a French attack upon the Iroquois. Dongan undoubtedly informed him of this threat and of the league's strategic importance as a counterweight to French power. Much of the present conference, in fact, was devoted to strengthening Anglo-Iroquois ties with this situation in mind. By the same token the sachems went out of their way to conciliate the English. The Mohawk, declaring themselves innocent of any wrongdoing in the south, roundly rebuked the Oneida, Onondaga, and Cayuga for violating their agreements. These tribes thanked the governor for forgetting their misdeeds and promised better conduct in the future. They concluded by delivering three hatchets, one for each tribe, which were solemnly buried in the courthouse yard.[14]

Iroquois polity being what it was, neither outside pressure nor the policy of the sachems could prevent war parties from setting out wherever and whenever it pleased them. Like most Iroquois conflicts these southern quarrels tended to be self-perpetuating until the weaker ad-

[13] *NYCD*, IX, 228; *LIR*, 70–71; Brodhead, *History of New York*, II, 396.

[14] Colden, *History of the Five Nations*, I, 34–44, 49–50; *LIR*, 71–74. Colden was apparently mistaken in dating Effingham's speech and the Indian reply on July 13 and 14, respectively, instead of July 30 and 31. The editor of the *Livingston Indian Records*, on the other hand, while drawing attention to this error (p. 71n.), seems also to be mistaken in attributing the Indian reply, as printed by Colden, to the conference of 1685 with Colonel William Byrd. Internal and external evidence both support Colden on this point. Cf. *CSP, 1681–1685*, nos. 1822, 1823; *LIR*, 87–89; *Wraxall's Abridgement*, 10.

versary was reduced to complete submission. The Cayuga were reported in mid-September to have captured or killed five colonists on
one of these forays, and Dongan warned them again to recall their
men and obey the covenant. As the depredations multiplied in 1685,
Virginia lost no time in sending agents back to Albany, with several
of the local sachems, to ratify the treaty.[15] Further incidents in Virginia were reported in 1687, however, this time implicating at least
the Mohawk and Oneida. Dongan met the Five Nations at Albany in
August of that year, following a full-scale French invasion of the
Seneca country. The governor, whose primary interest related to the
contest with Canada, was thoroughly exasperated with these southern
forays which uselessly complicated the main issue. Moreover, Effingham had returned to New York—though he did not venture to Albany
this time—and was trying once more to put an end to these diversions.
Dongan therefore did not mince words with the sachems:

Doe the Brethren think they can Warr with all the Christians in America . . .
it seems you make no difference between your Friends and your Foes . . .
The Christians [would not have endured] it from one another, much lesse
from you that are Indyans[,] if it was not for mee who have protected you
these fouer yeares past . . . I must tell you plainly, that if you will not
forbear doeing of Mischeife there hereafter, I will dig upp the Axes againe,
and give them in the hands of My Lord Howard, and I myselfe will joyne
with him & warr upon you, and then you will be totally ruined; for the
Governor of Cannada himselfe makes his complaint of me to the King att
home, that I protect people, that murders the King of England's subjects in
Virginia and Maryland and breaks all the Covenant Chaines they make;
therefore, doe this noe more, nor goe neere Virginia. . . . I will strive to
stopp My Lord Effingham's mouth, that he makes noe complaint of you to
the King, by promising him that you will make him satisfaction, ass soon,
as the warr with the French is over, and I doe not doubt, butt you will
make good whatsoever I promise, that I may not be found a Liar.[16]

The sachems were fully aware that "promising will not doe without
a performance" and expressed thanks for Dongan's intercession. They
unanimously agreed to warn the young warriors once more, but after
that they would no longer take their part. Although the Oneida were

---

[15] *NYCD*, IX, 259, 261; *LIR*, 75, 84–91; H. R. McIlwaine, ed., *Executive Journals of the Council of Colonial Virginia, 1680–1739* (Richmond, 1925–1930), I,
70–71, 506; cf. *CSP, 1685–1688*, nos. 154, 241.

[16] *LIR*, 112–115, 121–126, 135–136; *NYCD*, III, 440–441 (including quotation).

reprimanded in September for another attack on Virginia, Iroquois inroads in that direction were discontinued for several years.[17] Either the French menace finally diverted their attention elsewhere, or Dongan's hard talking had had its desired effect.

Dongan was not the first governor of New York to realize the value of the west, at least as a source of peltry. It was he, however, who sought for the first time to win control of this vast area for England. Dongan was an Irish Catholic whose service came at a time of profound peace between England and France; nevertheless he proved to be a pugnacious English imperialist in his dealings with the Catholic Frenchmen to the north. By substituting the influence of New York for that of Canada among the western tribes, he hoped to beat the French at their own game. To this end he was prepared to use both the Five Nations and the Albany fur trade as positive instruments of English policy. Whether this policy or the means he used in pursuing it were always sound is another question, but it is probably safe to say that he had greater support from the traders and magistrates at Albany than any other governor of his time.

Dongan did not create the anti-French feeling which marked his administration. The seeds were sown before his arrival, and the initiative actually lay with the Iroquois, although the French thought otherwise. Frontenac, his successor La Barre, and the generality of Canadian officialdom seem to have been convinced that Iroquois depredations against the Illinois, Ottawa, and Miami were inspired by the English, who hoped thereby to intimidate these tribes into trading with Albany. Their belief was based on the incontestable fact that Albany regularly supplied arms and ammunition to the Five Nations. This practice was hardly new, however, and Albany in fact was more interested in furthering her trade by smoothing over intertribal conflicts than by inciting them. There is no convincing evidence that the Iroquois' westward expansion was not their own idea, pursued for their own objectives.[18]

Iroquois relations with Canada had become increasingly cool after their invasion of the Illinois country in 1680, and within two years the Indians began to commit depredations against the French them-

---

[17] *NYCD*, III, 441–443; *LIR*, 138n.
[18] *NYCD*, IX, 147, 162–163, 184, 191, 194, 197; Buffinton, "The Policy of Albany and English Westward Expansion," 343.

selves. The French, on their part, stirred up bitter resentment among the Five Nations every time that they encouraged a group of tribesmen to desert to the Christian missions near Montreal. They also provoked the Iroquois by assisting their western allies who were the objects of Iroquois attack. (On the other hand, both Frontenac and La Barre were criticized by their own countrymen for the extent to which they withheld this support in order to appease the Iroquois.) The French could not afford to see these tribes in subjection to the Iroquois, and Frontenac continued to hope that a mere show of force might remove or at least postpone the threat. La Barre's original instructions from the king were based upon Frontenac's recommendations, but the new governor convinced his home government in 1683 that a serious military expedition against the Iroquois was necessary to preserve the colony. The Seneca were singled out for attention since they possessed about half the population and military force of the confederation and had been the prime offenders in the west. Having secured additional men and supplies from France, La Barre prepared for a grand invasion of the Seneca country in the summer of 1684.

As early as November 1682 the French governor had asked his superiors to intercede with Charles II and the Duke of York to prevent any further Iroquois support from Albany. His request was forwarded to the English government, which apparently rejected it. According to a draft reply which may have been given to the French ambassador, the king upheld Andros' claim of English jurisdiction over the Iroquois, defended the supply of firearms to these tribes, and asked that La Barre himself be ordered to let them alone.[19]

This was the state of affairs when Dongan entered the scene in August 1683. Early in October a Mohawk deputation came down to New York at his invitation, and the governor took this occasion to set forth a large part of his future policy toward the French and the Iroquois. He reaffirmed Andros' contention that all territory south of Lake Ontario belonged to the Province of New York. As this comprehended the Iroquois country, he now expected their submission; moreover, if he should want to build a fort or trading post near their castles, he hoped that they might be willing to sell the necessary land. He disclaimed knowledge of any French threat to the Iroquois, although the noisy preparations in Canada had begun to reach Indian ears, but he

---

[19] *CSP, 1681–1685,* no. 1059; *1685–1688,* no. 2072; *NYCD,* IX, 197–198.

promised to warn them if he heard any threatening news. Meanwhile he asked the Mohawk to trade no more with the French and not to go to Canada without the consent of his government. The Indians should permit no one to trade or settle among them except the Jesuits, who should be limited to one missionary per village, or persons carrying a pass from him. The Mohawk should also try to persuade their disaffected brethren to return from Canada. As all his predecessors had done (contrary to French belief), Dongan requested the Mohawk to make peace with their Indian enemies and trade with them instead. They were urged in particular to establish friendly contact with the western tribes and give them free passage to Albany. If they wished, he would send a white man with them to help arrange such a settlement. Having set forth the terms of the Iroquois protectorate that he wanted to establish, Dongan now admonished the Mohawk to transmit his propositions to the other four nations.

The Mohawk envoys were agreeable guests—probably more agreeable than they had any intention of being when they returned home. They voiced great optimism about redeeming the Christian Iroquois in Canada if they and the governor could "go hand in hand to promote it." The Indians were more noncommittal when it came to making peace with their enemies, but promised to call a general council on the subject when they got home. With greater regard for present expediency than historical fact, the Mohawk now claimed that they had always belonged to the government of New York; they took this opportunity, therefore, to put themselves again under Corlaer's protection. They promised to harbor no straggling Frenchmen and even offered to send away the remaining Jesuits if he desired, but described them as "very good men and very quiett." Although they had not answered all of Dongan's points, the Mohawk certainly did not displease him, and soon afterward they were dispatched homeward on a sloop furnished by the government.[20]

This conference was of greater significance for what was said than for the material results that it brought. The Seneca and Cayuga continued their western operations without letup and early in 1684 launched what was to be their last great invasion of the Illinois country. They failed to differentiate on this occasion between the French and their native allies and made an unsuccessful attack upon La Salle's

[20] *NYCD*, XIV, 771–774.

Governor Dongan and the Iroquois

Fort St. Louis on the Illinois River. This incident, added to the multiplying depredations inflicted upon the French farther east, confirmed La Barre's intention to launch an offensive of his own. Dongan had already written him, claiming English jurisdiction over the Iroquois country, but La Barre was no more ready than Frontenac to admit any such pretension. On June 15 he informed Dongan of his intent to attack the Iroquois and asked the New York governor to refrain from aiding them. The Mohawk and Oneida would not be disturbed, he said, but an attack on the western nations was the only way of reducing them to order. "When they see the Christians united on this subject," he continued hopefully, the Indians "will shew them more respect than they have done hitherto." [21]

Thoroughly alarmed at the prospect of another French invasion, Dongan wrote back immediately, repeating his claim of jurisdiction over the Iroquois and all the territory south of the St. Lawrence. If La Barre would prevent Frenchmen from coming south of the lakes, he in turn would forbid New Yorkers to venture north of them. He was "so heartily bent to promote the quiet and tranquility of this country and yours," Dongan continued, that he would go to Albany forthwith and require the Indians to do what was just to satisfy the French. (Dongan had already planned to meet the Iroquois on account of depredations in the south.) If they refused this satisfaction, he would no longer protect them; but meanwhile La Barre must commit no act of hostility. By the third of July Dongan was at Albany, where he heard a false report that the invasion might already have begun. The governor wrote again to La Barre, expressing surprise that he would "invade the Dukes Territories, after so just and so honest an offer" as he had recently made. If they could not adjust these disputes peacefully, he said, they should refer them to their respective superiors in Europe. Meanwhile, he announced, he had ordered the duke's coat of arms to be erected in the Iroquois castles to make plain the fact of English sovereignty there.[22]

There were some in Canada who had felt all along that La Barre's preparations were merely a bluff. The Iroquois could hardly afford to assume this, however, and the Onondaga, with Oneida and Cayuga support, strove to avert the invasion by diplomacy. By mid-July they per-

[21] *Ibid.*, III, 447–448; IX, 226; Brodhead, *History of New York*, II, 395.
[22] *NYCD*, III, 448–449; *ARSCM*, III, 470.

suaded the Seneca to accept their mediation and decided to request a conference with La Barre. Father Jean de Lamberville, the Jesuit missionary at Onondaga, also labored diligently to this end, warning La Barre repeatedly that his plans would inevitably lead to a war with the whole confederacy which would endanger the entire Canadian frontier.[23]

Dongan hoped to emerge from this crisis as the acknowledged protector of the Iroquois. From his point of view the risks involved in a French attack were almost preferable to the possibility of their submitting to the French peacefully. Therefore, when he met the sachems at Albany late in July, with Lord Howard of Effingham also in attendance, Dongan warned them to make no agreement with the French without his approbation. As their self-appointed guardian he even offered to compose such difficulties as might occur among the Five Nations themselves. The Iroquois were prepared to go a long way to conciliate the English governors, but they were not ready to yield the substance of their own policy, recently settled upon at Onondaga. They patched up their quarrel with Virginia, renewed their cession of the Susquehanna lands, and, so far as the Onondaga and Cayuga were concerned, made their submission to the English as complete as words alone could convey it. "Wee have putt our selves under the great Sachim Charles that lives over the great lake," these tribes asserted, and they presented two dressed deerskins which were to be sent to the king as a formal acknowledgment of the fact, so "that he may write upon them, and putt a great Redd Seale to them." They welcomed Dongan's suggestion that the duke's arms be posted in their castles as a deterrent to French aggression and promised "neither [to] joyn Our selves nor our Land to any other Governm[en]t then this." Although the Mohawk, Oneida, and Seneca held aloof from the most extravagant of their confederates' statements, all five tribes expressed great attachment to the English as allies.

What the Indians sought in return for these concessions and promises was English military support in case the forthcoming conference with La Barre should miscarry. Their true sentiments were probably best expressed when the Onondaga and Cayuga sachems declared at the end of their speech that "we are a ffree people uniting our selves to what sachem we please." Dongan, on the other hand, was in no posi-

[23] *NYCD,* IX, 252–257.

tion politically or militarily to meet the French in battle in the Iroquois country. Despite his talk about English protection, therefore, he probably had no intention of backing the Iroquois with men. Short of such a promise—and perhaps even with it—the Indians were determined to make their own terms with the French.[24]

Meanwhile the Canadian governor, who apparently had not heard of the Iroquois peace movement, wrote Dongan again to say that his invasion of the Seneca country would be launched in August. This helpful information Dongan immediately forwarded to the Indians, with a message commanding them once more not to confer with the French. He also sent an account of his proceedings to England, where eventually they were fully approved. (One of the major advantages to Dongan of Effingham's two visits to New York was that they both coincided with French armed threats to the Iroquois. The Virginia governor was so impressed with the Indians' strategic importance that he strongly backed Dongan's Indian policies in his own province and in letters to England.) The duke's instructions for Dongan's future conduct were somewhat enigmatic. On the one hand he was to "incourage . . . ye Indians upon all occasions," that they might continue to trade with the English instead of the French; but on the other he was "to act soe prudently" with respect to the French that they would have no just cause for complaint against him.[25]

Less than a week after sending his letter to Dongan, La Barre received news that the Iroquois were eager to make peace and wanted him to send an agent to Onondaga for preliminary negotiations. Having collected an army of 1,200 men with the greatest fanfare, La Barre now hastened to comply with the Indians' request, thereby fulfilling the worst expectations of his critics in Canada. The French envoy and Arnout Viele, the Albany interpreter entrusted with Dongan's message, both converged on Onondaga in the middle of August. As the sachems had already made up their minds about conferring with La Barre, Viele's mission was doomed to failure. The Indians told him that they were brethren, not subjects, of Corlaer and must take care of themselves. Accordingly they prepared to send delegates, as La Barre had

---

[24] *Ibid.*, III, 347, 417–418; *Wraxall's Abridgement*, 10–13; Colden, *History of the Five Nations*, I, 34–51.

[25] *NYCD*, III, 351–352, 450–452; IX, 243; Colden, *History of the Five Nations*, I, 56–58; Brodhead, *History of New York*, II, 400–401.

requested, to confer with him at La Famine, the mouth of the Salmon River in Oswego County.[26] The French governor meanwhile had been waiting with his army at Fort Frontenac. Even if he had wanted to prosecute the war, he probably was no longer capable of it. His supplies had run down, and the men were succumbing to fever. As soon as he heard from Onondaga, therefore, he sent word to Niagara to turn back the hundreds of Frenchmen and western Indians who had been summoned to participate in the glorious enterprise and immediately embarked with a part of his force for La Famine. Here on August 26 he conferred with Onondaga, Cayuga, and Oneida delegates who claimed to speak for the entire league.

Opening with a lengthy résumé of Seneca misdeeds, La Barre still threatened the Iroquois with war unless they made reparation and restored the prisoners that they had taken from the western tribes. The sachems were surprised at this belligerence in view of the soft words which had passed at Onondaga; what is more, they knew that the governor was bluffing and proceeded to turn the conference into a diplomatic rout. Their speaker replied with exquisite sarcasm:

Yonnondio [or Onontio—their name for the governors of Canada], you must have believed, when you left Quebeck, that the Sun had burnt up all the Forests which render our Country inaccessible to the French, or that the Lakes had so far overflown their Banks, that they had surrounded our Castles, and that it was impossible for us to get out of them. Yes, Yonnondio, surely you must have dreamt so, and the Curiosity of seeing so great a Wonder has brought you so far. Now you are undeceived, since . . . I and the Warriors here present are come to assure you, that the Senekas, Cayugas, Onondagas, Oneydoes, and Mohawks are yet alive. I thank you, in their Name, for bringing back into their Country the Calumet [peace pipe]. . . . It was happy for you, that you left Underground that murdering Hatchet, that has been so often dyed in the Blood of the French.[27]

Although La Barre had threatened war, the speaker continued, it was evident all around that sickness had tied his hands and saved his men from a worse fate. He denied that the Seneca had given sufficient provocation for war and promised only vaguely that that tribe would make reparation. The Indians' only concession was a promise to cease hostilities with the French and all of the western tribes except

[26] *NYCD*, IX, 242, 257–258, 261; Colden, *History of the Five Nations*, I, 61–63.
[27] Colden, *History of the Five Nations*, I, 67.

Governor Dongan and the Iroquois

the Illinois. In return for this La Barre agreed to make peace with the Iroquois on the spot, to accept La Famine as a place of future conferences between them, and to take his army back to Canada immediately. The Iroquois asked for a return of the Jesuit missionaries, who in several cases had either fled or been expelled from their posts during the recent troubles. The governor naturally agreed to this request, but with the novel stipulation that he would send missionaries to the Seneca only when they had begun to make amends for their past infractions.

La Barre had cut a sorry figure at La Famine. In the words of Cadwallader Colden, "a very chargeable and fatiguing Expedition (which was to strike the Terror of the French Name into the stubborn Hearts of the Five Nations) ended in a Scold between the French General and an old Indian." Returning to Canada, the governor was subjected to scorn and ridicule. He was accused of abandoning the Illinois to their enemies and forfeiting the respect and trade of all the interior tribes. When his king learned of the fiasco, La Barre was abruptly removed from office and summoned home to France.[28]

The Iroquois had managed to outmaneuver both the English and the French, a feat that they were not often to repeat. In October, Dongan sent a message to the Five Nations thanking the Mohawk and Seneca for refusing to treat with the French and rebuking the others. It was not the peace that they concluded or anything else they had done by themselves, he announced, but rather the threat of English intervention which had prevented the French from attacking.[29] In his letters home the governor was equally immodest in describing his achievements with the Iroquois. His superiors could hardly have avoided the impression that the league was now completely under his thumb.

The Five Nations in fact had never been friendlier with the English than at this time of diplomatic triumph. But there was as little willingness as ever to sacrifice their essential independence on behalf of this friendship, and Dongan clearly exaggerated its importance. The Iroquois continued to let Onontio call them his children and repeatedly referred to themselves as subjects of the English Crown, but just as often they affirmed their own freedom of action. "We are born free," they declared to La Barre at La Famine; "we neither

[28] Ibid., 63–71; NYCD, IX, 236–239, 242–248, 269.   [29] LIR, 74–75.

depend on Yonnondio nor Corlaer. We may go where we please, and carry with us whom we please, and buy and sell what we please."[30] The Iroquois' submission to England was in reality no more than a facet of their independent diplomacy. They admitted Corlaer's jurisdiction in order to get his support against the French; but their admissions and promises at Albany never prevented them from acting as they later saw fit. The Seneca now made no effort to pay the reparations La Barre had demanded, although they did heed his injunction to stop fighting the Ottawa and Miami. The result was an upswing in the Albany fur trade in 1685 which was as warmly welcomed there as it was deprecated in Montreal.

The disillusionment and contempt for the French, which extended to the western tribes as well as the Iroquois, now enabled the English to take the initiative for the first time. Dongan had several ideas for taking advantage of this situation, which he offered to the Duke of York for approval. One of these involved the construction of English forts in the Indian country, a matter that will be dealt with later. A second proposal—that the duke should persuade the French government to restrain its people from trading with the Iroquois—was properly rejected as "wholly impracticable, for the Fr[en]ch will never forbid their people a beneficiall trade." Nevertheless Dongan was encouraged to use all the arts at his disposal to attain this goal in his dealings with the Indians. His only limitation was to avoid all actions that might "run us into disputes w[i]th the Fr[en]ch who in our present circumstances are not to be made enemyes." These instructions were obviously contradictory, and doubtless the officials in England were as aware of this as Dongan himself; but in view of the foreign policy of Charles II and James II there was little else that they could say. For whatever comfort it may have afforded, the governors of Canada were under similar orders.[31] The governor's third project was apparently undertaken on his own initiative. It called for a reversal of Albany's traditional policy by sending traders directly to the Ottawa country, near the Straits of Mackinac. His hope was to divert

[30] Colden, *History of the Five Nations*, I, 69.

[31] *NYCD*, III, 352–353; Dongan to Duke of York, Dec. 9, 1684, in "New York— MSS, Letters, and Docs.," New York Public Library; Labaree, *Royal Instructions to British Colonial Governors*, II, 464; St. Paul, "Governor Thomas Dongan's Expansion Policy," 262.

the major part of Canada's western trade to Albany. It was an ambitious plan and potentially a dangerous one.

The idea of sending Albany traders to the western tribes probably did not originate with Dongan. For more than a decade Albany had been using the French *coureurs de bois* for this purpose, and it was only a small additional step to send a few Dutchmen or Englishmen along with them. There is little evidence as to when this step was first taken; La Barre wrote in the spring of 1683 that the English had hired a large number of French deserters to show them the way to the Ottawa country. At La Famine the next year he taxed the Iroquois with performing the same service. They defiantly admitted the charge, saying that they had brought Englishmen to the lakes in order to trade with the Ottawa and Huron and that this was their prerogative.[32] Although Dongan said later that no inhabitant of the colony had gone beyond the Seneca country before he took office, he was trying at the time to impress his superiors with his own activity. It is likely, therefore, that the idea of striking directly at the western fur supply originated with the Albany traders and magistrates, not with Dongan himself as is usually imagined.[33] It fitted in perfectly, however, with the governor's own expansionist policies, and he took it up wholeheartedly.

In the fall of 1684 the governor began granting passes to individuals or groups of men "to hunt unmolested among the Indians in the province." Dongan took a broad view of the provincial bounds, and some of these passes permitted the recipients to go as far as the Ottawa country. Most important was the trading party which he organized in 1685 under the leadership of Johannes Roseboom of Albany. This group succeeded in reaching the Ottawa country near Michilimackinac, where they found the Indians so delighted with English prices that they were invited to return every year. As in 1670, the Ottawa also asked that the Seneca open a path for them so that they might come to Albany themselves.[34]

This request was not granted, and the Seneca were soon on the warpath again, fighting both the Ottawa and the Miami. They made no

[32] *NYCD*, IX, 197; Colden, *History of the Five Nations*, I, 64–65, 68–69.

[33] *NYCD*, III, 395, 476; cf. Buffinton, "The Policy of Albany and English Westward Expansion," 345–346.

[34] O'Callaghan, *Calendar of Historical MSS*, II, 131, 136, 139; Colonial MSS, XXXIV, pt. 1, 64–65; *NYCD*, III, 395, 476; IX, 275, 287, 297, 302, 324.

attempt to discourage the Albany traders, however. In view of this fact and the success of Roseboom's expedition, plans were made to repeat the experiment on a larger scale the next year. Some persons were so eager to take advantage of the newly discovered opportunity that they departed for the west without the governor's authorization. Dongan rather foolishly asked the Indians to apprehend them, saying that if they—but presumably not the licensed traders—once found the way to hunt and trade as the Indians did, the latters' own trade would suffer. The Iroquois apparently did not recognize this danger and refused to take the responsibility of arresting white men.[35]

In 1686 Dongan granted more passes and organized a much more elaborate diplomatic and commercial invasion of the west. His plan called for two large parties. The first, consisting of twenty-nine Christians and five Indians under Roseboom's command, left Albany in September. It was composed for the most part of Albany youths, including members of some of the town's leading families. They were to spend the winter in the Seneca country and then proceed toward Michilimackinac in the spring. The second division, of about the same size, was under the command of Major Patrick Magregory, a recent Scottish immigrant who had won the governor's confidence. This group was to leave Albany early in the spring, overtake Roseboom's party, and accompany it through Lakes Erie and Huron to the Ottawa country. After concluding their trade they were to return under Magregory's command to Albany. Dongan tried to have Iroquois delegates accompany the expedition in order to exchange prisoners with the Ottawa and arrange for a peace conference. But the Iroquois were not ready for peace, and only a handful of them and their prisoners actually went. The traders were ordered not to disturb any Frenchmen whom they might meet, and when word was received of a new French garrison at Detroit, Roseboom was ordered to stay in his winter quarters until Magregory's party caught up with him.

Apparently Roseboom failed to get this message, and the French were distinctly annoyed as his party moved on from the Seneca country in the spring of 1687. They were making their way northward in Lake Huron early in May when they encountered a much larger party of French and Indians coming down from Michilimackinac. The French promptly took them into custody and confiscated all their

[35] *LIR*, 99–100; *NYDH*, I, 403–405.

goods. Magregory's party, which had left Albany early in April, was similarly intercepted not long afterward on Lake Erie. As it happened, the French were converging on Detroit just at this time with hundreds of Indian allies in order to take part in another attack upon the Seneca. Had this mobilization not coincided with the New Yorkers' voyages, they might have reached their destination. The French took their prisoners with them to Niagara, whence they were eventually sent to Quebec. After four months in prison, when it was too late for them to embark on a new expedition that year, they were released and sent home.[36]

Dongan's plan to wrest control of the western fur trade, as it was conceived and executed, might have worked once or twice under more favorable circumstances. But it could not have become an annual affair without French acquiescence. Dongan's hope that the French would not molest his traders indicates that he took too seriously his own claims of English sovereignty over all the territory south of the lakes. He should have recognized that the French had too much at stake in the west to permit this dangerous experiment to succeed. Dongan's plan required a greater military force than the French could bring to bear on the Great Lakes, but he had no such force at his command. The English were never able to match French power in the west until, nearly a century later, they had removed its foundation by reducing Quebec. It may be said in Dongan's behalf that he did not repeat this experiment.

In August 1685 La Barre was replaced by the Marquis de Denonville. The new governor brought instructions to humble the Iroquois, by war if necessary, and above all to assist the Illinois and other western tribes whom La Barre had virtually abandoned to Iroquois rapacity. At the same time Denonville was admonished to preserve a good understanding with the English. Like his predecessor the new governor was not long in concluding that the safety of his colony required a war with at least the Seneca. First, however, he would have

---

[36] Colonial MSS, XXXIV, pt. 1, 113, 115; *LIR*, 83–84, 106–108, 110–111; *NYCD*, III, 395, 436–437, 442–443, 473, 476, 489, 512–513, 516, 520; IX, 300, 302, 308–309, 318–319, 348, 363; *CSP, 1685–1688*, nos. 886, 1262.II; Thwaites, *Jesuit Relations*, LXII, 281–283. It seems probable that the conference (printed in *LIR*, 83–84) between the Albany magistrates and a group of Iroquois sachems who had just been with the governor at New York took place in September 1686 rather than a year earlier, as the published record is dated.

to regain his western allies and prepare his defenses, lulling the Iroquois with peace talks in the meantime.

Denonville was thoroughly alarmed at the English eruption into the lakes and made a vain attempt to intercept Roseboom's first party. If these traders should make permanent contact with the Ottawa and if other English incursions should continue around Hudson Bay, he wrote to his superiors, the entire trade of Canada would be ruined. Thus he requested permission to build another fort at Niagara, which would close the road to the Ottawa country for the English and Iroquois alike. Furthermore, it would serve as a check on Iroquois activity in general and provide a retreat for friendly Indians who now were afraid to attack them. Without waiting for a reply he went ahead and ordered the construction of a small fort at Detroit in the summer of 1686. In a further revival of Frontenac's policy Denonville reestablished a garrison on the Richelieu River to prevent the flow of men and goods to Albany.

Lulling the Iroquois took the form of encouraging peace negotiations between the Iroquois and Denonville's Huron and Ottawa allies. Father Jean de Lamberville, still in charge of the Onondaga mission, was indefatigable in his alternate role of French ambassador to the Iroquois. He spent the whole summer of 1686 in reporting and offsetting Dongan's activities at Albany and carrying messages back and forth to Canada. While the Jesuit thus strove for a genuine Franco-Iroquois settlement—his long-time goal—he remained blissfully unaware of the governor's real intentions. Reversing La Barre's procedure, Denonville spoke softly as he readied his big stick. Father Lamberville, he wrote in November,

has gone back with orders from me to assemble all the Iroquois nations next spring at Cataraqui to talk over our affairs. I am persuaded that scarcely any will come, but my principal object is to attract [some of them] to that place whilst the Jesuit Father remains alone. . . . [He] knows nothing of our designs. . . . I am very sorry to see him exposed, but should I withdraw him this year the storm will . . . burst sooner upon us, for the Iroquois would surely discover our plans by his retiring.

Canada must be put down as lost, he added, if war were not waged the next year.[37] Denonville had a healthy respect for the enemy and

[37] *NYCD*, IX, 271–272, 282–291, 297–300 (including quotation); Francis Parkman, *Count Frontenac and New France under Louis XIV* (28th ed.; Boston, 1893), 128.

realized the futility of merely chasing the Indians from their cabins and destroying their corn as Tracy had done in 1666. In March 1687 the king approved of an expedition against the Iroquois, and two months later a force of eight hundred French regulars arrived in Canada under the Chevalier de Vaudreuil.

Dongan's efforts had meanwhile been directed toward keeping the Iroquois at peace and strengthening his own influence over them. In the fall of 1685 the Seneca heard reports that the French were planning to violate La Barre's peace agreement. Instead of waiting for the blow to fall where it would, they approached the other tribes in order to launch a combined attack of their own before the French had time for preparations. On this occasion both Dongan and Father Lamberville persuaded the Indians that the rumors were groundless (and they may have been at that early date). But as the winter gave way to spring, reports of unaccustomed French activity became more frequent, and the Indians grew increasingly restless. Dongan was also disturbed by the reports and by news that Denonville contemplated a fort at Niagara. For this reason he invited the sachems to meet him at Albany in May 1686, at the same time assuring the apprehensive Father Lamberville that his only purpose was to prevent the Iroquois from disturbing Canada.[38]

At Albany, Dongan informed the sachems that the French had sent provisions and ammunition to Cadaraqui, or Fort Frontenac. This was ominous news, and he warned them to be watchful; but he charged them at the same time not to make peace or war with the French without his approval. He also admonished them in the strongest terms not to permit the French to build a fort at Niagara or in any other place which might obstruct their hunting. They should make no trade agreements with Christians without his consent but continue instead to bring their peltry to Albany, where they would always be assured of support. The Indians were in no position to refuse Dongan's demands. They recognized as well as he the danger of French forts in their territory and agreed to the unpleasant necessity of preventing their construction, even to the point of tearing down such forts if the French tried to build them. They promised not to take up the hatchet unless the French attacked them first, but in that case they expected Dongan's help. "If one member suffers the whole body is in pain," they pointed out. They also promised solemnly "never to listen to any

[38] *NYCD*, III, 453, 464; IX, 311; *LIR*, 91–94.

proposals of any Christians unless they are made in this house" at Albany.[39]

Denonville's worst fear was that the Iroquois would attack before his own preparations were complete. In a sense, therefore, Dongan had played into his hands by consciously preventing the Indians from taking the initiative. Short of letting the Iroquois carry out their own policies, however, a possibility which seldom occurred to English governors after this time, it is difficult to see what alternative was open to him. To incite the Iroquois to attack Canada before there was definite information of French intentions would certainly have constituted a violation of his repeated instructions to maintain a good correspondence with the French.

Denonville's projected fort at Niagara was particularly alarming to Dongan because he had formulated similar plans of his own at least as early as 1684. The control of Niagara had obvious advantages for both nations, whose objectives in circumscribing Iroquois activity and channeling the western fur trade were closely parallel. The Duke of York had given Dongan full discretion in building forts in the Indian country wherever they might seem most practicable, subject always to the condition that no legitimate offense be given to the French.[40] For Dongan, Iroquois consent was a necessary prerequisite to any construction at Niagara. The whole English policy was dependent upon the friendship and trade of the Five Nations, and unlike the French their only communication with Niagara was overland through the Iroquois country. Dongan had deferred mentioning this matter to the Indians, perhaps because of the almost insurmountable task of provisioning and garrisoning so remote an outpost. The French governor, who got wind of Dongan's idea, thought that he was deterred by the certainty of Indian refusal. In any case the very fact of his interest in such a project, together with the simultaneous appearance of English traders on the lakes, drove Denonville into a fury. "I am disposed to go straight to Orange [Albany], storm their fort, and burn the whole concern," he fumed, at the same time repeating his own requests for permission to build at Niagara.[41]

---

[39] *LIR*, 99–102.

[40] *NYCD*, III, 353, 363, 394; Dongan to Duke of York, Dec. 9, 1684, in "New York—MSS, Letters, and Docs.," New York Public Library.

[41] *NYCD*, IX, 298, 306–310, 314–315, 321.

Governor Dongan and the Iroquois

A day after his conference with the Indians, Dongan wrote to inform the marquis that the Five Nations were apprehensive of an attack. "I know you are a man of judgement," he said, "and, that you will not attack the King of England's subjects." Any construction at Niagara, furthermore, would constitute an equal invasion of the king's territory. If these matters could not be amicably adjusted between them, Dongan said once more, they should be referred to the home governments in Europe. Meanwhile he pledged that if war should break out he would not be its initiator. On receiving this letter, Denonville was convinced that the English governor had side-stepped his instructions and assembled the Iroquois to incite them against Canada. In the ensuing correspondence between them, however, he adopted a conciliatory tone. After upholding French territorial claims, he appealed to his fellow Catholic on religious grounds to support the valiant work of the Jesuits in taming these savages. If the Indians feared a French attack, it was only the fruit of their consciences, he said, "since I have not done the least thing to make them believe that I want any thing else from them than to see peace well established throughout all the country." In another vein he inferred that Dongan was guilty of harboring renegade *coureurs de bois*. Friendly relations, he suggested, could best be served by sending these "rogues, vagabonds and thieves" back to Canada. Nothing came of this request, and Dongan denied hotly that he had incited the Iroquois against Canada. There was also an exchange over the evils of liquor among the Indians. "Certainly our rum doth as little hurt as your Brandy," wrote Dongan in answer to a criticism of the Albany liquor traffic, "and in the opinion of Christians is much more wholesome; however to keep the Indians temperate and sober is a *uery* good and Christian performance but to prohibit them all strong liquors seems a little hard and *uery* turkish." [42]

Denonville had unwittingly emphasized in Dongan's mind the danger of permitting the Jesuits to remain any longer among the Iroquois. The only missionaries left by this time were Father Lamberville and his younger brother at Onondaga, but for some time past their political as well as religious services there had been well known at Albany. As a Catholic himself Dongan hitherto had been unwilling to jeopardize their avowed purpose of advancing the faith. When Lamberville

[42] *Ibid.*, III, 455–459, 461–463; IX, 296–297.

wrote him of unkind treatment from the Indians, for instance, Dongan had asked them at his next conference to treat the missionaries civilly.[43] It was probably at the time of Dongan's visit to Albany in May 1686 that he received a petition on this subject from the local magistrates. After describing the evil effects of the priests' "debauching" Indians to Canada, they asked Dongan to petition the king for English priests to replace them. Such persons might regain the natives who had left, while continuing the good work begun by the French.[44] This subject must have been discussed at some length during the governor's visit, and the local officials suggested land which had recently been purchased at Saratoga as a home for such Indians as could be persuaded to return from Canada. The Mohawk sachems were consulted, and they agreed to send a message to these Indians mentioning the offer of land and promising a priest to instruct them there. In August the Mohawk envoy reported that the Christian Iroquois were willing to return, but Denonville refused to let them go until he had received a letter from Dongan. About three weeks later, after Dongan had returned to New York, representatives of each of the Five Nations came down to see him and reiterated the request that he write to Canada for this purpose. The Mohawk in particular were delighted at the prospect of a Christian Iroquois settlement at Saratoga because, as they said, most of those coming would be of their tribe. There is no record of Dongan's sending such a letter or of his reasons for failing to do so. The whole thing may have been a hoax on Denonville's part or a mistake on that of the Indians. It is hard to conceive of the French permitting such an exodus after they had worked so hard to bring the Indians to Canada in the first place. On the other hand, Dongan may have been reluctant to go on record as asking for the intercession of the French governor, whose jurisdiction over the Iroquois he always made it a point to deny. In any case he now asked the Indians to dismiss their French missionaries altogether, promising to replace them with English Jesuits.[45]

It was one thing to promise English Jesuits and quite another to deliver them, as Dongan soon found. He wrote home for six priests, three to live with the relocated Christian Indians and three to travel

---

[43] *Ibid.*, III, 454, 464; *LIR*, 100.   [44] *LIR*, 97–98; *NYCD*, III, 418–419.
[45] *LIR*, 104; *NYCD*, III, 394, 489; *NYDH*, I, 404; Brodhead, *History of New York*, II, 442.

from castle to castle ministering to the rest. By that means the French missionaries would be forced to return to Canada, he hoped, depriving the French of any claims to the Iroquois country and allowing the English to enjoy the fur trade unmolested. He repeated the request on several occasions, but no priests were ever sent. Two or three English Jesuits were apparently in the province already, but they were occupied with a Latin school in New York and do not seem to have been called upon for missionary service.[46] As far as the Canadian Iroquois were concerned, the deficiency probably mattered very little, for Denonville effectively stopped their return to New York. Although the Albany magistrates had hit upon an ingenious answer to the problem posed by the Jesuits, Dongan was certainly unwise to raise Iroquois hopes when he had no assurance that he could fulfill his promise. The Indians unquestionably wanted missionaries, for both political and religious reasons, and broken promises on this score were bound to diminish his credit with them.

In February 1687 the Mohawk reported at Albany that Denonville had invited the Five Nations to meet him at Cadaraqui in the coming spring. This was the bogus conference that he had devised to pacify the Iroquois while he made ready to invade them. The Mohawk and Seneca refused to heed the invitation, but as in 1684 the other three tribes agreed to attend. The magistrates reminded them of their earlier promises, and Dongan again sent a special messenger to warn them against going. This matter was so important that he sacrificed his long-standing policy of furthering Indian pacification and promised powder and lead to each nation for use against the Miami, whom they had singled out as their major enemy for the time being. For one reason or another Dongan's appeal was successful. The Indians announced that they were planning a general council about the first of June and that the central tribes had given their votes to the Mohawk and Seneca. They soon had occasion, moreover, to discover Denonville's real frame of mind when a number of their warriors, returning home from hunting, were arrested near Cadaraqui and shipped off to France to serve in the king's galleys.[47]

[46] *NYCD*, III, 394–395, 463, 478, 511; *CSP, 1685–1688,* no. 1262; St. Paul, "Governor Thomas Dongan's Expansion Policy," 266.
[47] *LIR*, 109–117, 120–122; *NYCD*, III, 440, 445; IX, 331, 341; Parkman, *Count Frontenac and New France,* 139–142.

Indian Affairs in Colonial New York

Just as Denonville was making his final preparations to attack the Seneca, news reached America that France and England had concluded a treaty of friendship and neutrality in November 1686. This treaty arose from a variety of disputes involving their respective American colonies from Hudson Bay to the West Indies. Although it did little to clear up many of the points at issue, it provided for a later discussion in Europe of such questions as the colonial governors were unable to settle on the spot. These officials meanwhile were to keep a good understanding and to preserve the peace in their own regions, even if hostilities should break out between the two mother countries. One article required "that the officers of neither king shall molest the subjects of the other in establishing their respective colonies or carrying on commerce and navigation." This was as close as the treaty came to mentioning the Iroquois problem. The dispute as to which nation had jurisdiction over them was presumably one of those questions to be settled in later talks.[48]

Dongan received a copy of the treaty, with orders to enforce it, in June 1687. Denonville had received Louis XIV's similar instructions about two weeks earlier, in the same letter which conveyed royal approval of his war on the Iroquois. Dongan immediately informed the French governor of his determination to observe the treaty "to the least title." He expected the latter's compliance as well, which to Dongan meant no further correspondence with the Five Nations except through him. And "as for those further nations," he continued airily, "I suppose that to trade with them is free and common to us all until the meers and bounds bee adjusted" in Europe.[49] Denonville, however, had already left for the Seneca country.

As Dongan was writing, in fact, the Indians came to Albany with ominous reports that the French were about to strike. They now wanted to collect the ammunition which Dongan had promised them and asked for his protection. The local authorities immediately sent word to New York, where the council resolved that if a French attack took place it would constitute a violation of the treaty and that the Iroquois as English subjects ought to be defended. A message was

[48] Frances Gardiner Davenport and Charles O. Paullin, eds., *European Treaties Bearing on the History of the United States and Its Dependencies* (Washington, 1917–1937), II, 309–323.
[49] *NYCD*, III, 388–389, 465; IX, 322–324; *LIR*, 117–118.

sent to this effect, urging them not to be afraid and to remain on guard. The Indians were not to treat with Denonville, but to inform him that they were subjects of the king of England, who would protect them. Dongan promised to come up to Albany himself within twenty days. Meanwhile they should send their wives and old people to Albany for safety, refusing to fight the French until they saw a chance to attack them south of the lake; for good measure he sent additional coats of arms for any castles that were still without them.[50]

This message had hardly gone forth when nearly 3,000 French and Indians converged on Irondequoit Bay in the Seneca country on June 30. Their timing was perfect, for Denonville, bringing the main Canadian force from Cadaraqui, arrived the same day as the western contingents which had been resting at Niagara after their trip through the lakes. (It was they who had intercepted the Albany traders.) Irondequoit, with its sheltered harbor, was the best port of entry to the Seneca country, with the main villages lying about twenty-five miles to the south. Denonville spent two days constructing a small fort to guard the boats. Then he began his march southward through the hilly and heavily wooded country, his men carrying their provisions on their backs. In the vanguard were eight or nine hundred western Indians and Christian Iroquois, the latter invading their former homeland in the service of their new masters; the main body consisted of more than a thousand French regulars and Canadian militia, and Indians and loyal *coureurs de bois* brought up the rear. On the second day out they made contact with the enemy. Some 450 Seneca warriors had been lying in wait, hoping for an opportunity to make a surprise attack. Their chance came as the advance guard approached a large marsh near the present village of Victor. The Seneca suddenly swooped down, piercing the air with yells and brandishing every species of weapon. The Ottawa auxiliaries gave way before this attack, but as the main body of troops under Denonville pushed forward, the Seneca found themselves hopelessly outnumbered. This battle was no Thermopylae; the Seneca had neither the necessity nor the inclination to make martyrs of themselves when avenues of escape lay all about them. They chose the course of discretion and retreated—retreated so far, in fact, that the French saw no more of them during the entire campaign.

[50] *LIR*, 118–120; Colonial MSS, XXXV, 71.

Denonville made no attempt to follow; his men were exhausted, and he feared further ambushes. As it turned out, his losses were probably less than those of the attackers, who suffered at least forty casualties. On the next day, July 4, the army resumed its march and approached the first of the Seneca villages. The French found it not only deserted but burned to the ground except for the usual corn supplies. As soon as the army had destroyed these, it moved to a hilltop fort nearby, similarly abandoned, and did the same work there. Three other villages in the vicinity were visited in turn, the work of destruction occupying ten full days. The only Seneca that they encountered were four or five women and old men who somehow had been left behind in the general exodus. The remainder had fled to the Cayuga country where, behind a barrier of marshy terrain and the largest two of the Finger Lakes, they were virtually inaccessible. The French were suffering from sickness and fatigue, furthermore, and their Indian allies were eager to disband.

After taking formal possession of the Seneca country, the invaders returned to Irondequoit Bay on July 14. From here they proceeded by boat and canoe along the lake shore to the mouth of the Niagara. On the east side of this stream, overlooking the lake, Denonville set his men to work on his long-projected fort. At the beginning of August, when the work had advanced sufficiently to require the presence of his full army no longer, Denonville left a garrison of one hundred men behind and returned to Montreal.[51]

The French campaign was only a qualified success, for the Seneca were no more crushed than the Mohawk had been a generation earlier. They must have suffered privation in the winter of 1687–1688, depending on their confederates for scanty corn supplies, but their economy had never rested solely upon agriculture. To defeat the Seneca overwhelmingly and permanently, Denonville found out, was beyond the power of Canada to effect. His major achievement was the re-establishment of a French outpost at Niagara.

On July 4, while the French laid waste the first Seneca village, Dongan was at Albany conferring with the Seneca war chief and a group of Onondaga and Cayuga tribesmen. He had already received a premature and inaccurate report of hostilities in the Seneca country,

---

[51] *NYCD*, III, 433–435, 445–447; IX, 334–335, 337–339, 358–369; Parkman, *Count Frontenac and New France*, 147–157.

together with Mohawk appeals for help. To the Seneca he now recommended the same tactics which in fact were customary with them and which they were using at that moment. If their corn were destroyed, he would supply them and meanwhile would send other Indians to their defense. On July 8, as more accurate reports began to arrive, he ordered the other four nations to go to the relief of the Seneca while he gathered warriors from the Scaticook and Mahican tribes. If necessary, the Indians should retreat toward Albany, sending their old men, women, and children ahead. Although he was apparently still skeptical of the truth of the invasion, Dongan conferred next day with the Scaticook tribesmen and required them either to join the Mohawk warriors or to post themselves at Schenectady until further orders. After sending similar requests to bands as far away as the Minisink, Dongan repaired to Schenectady where he could keep in closer touch with events. Here on July 14, the day Denonville returned to his base at Irondequoit, Dongan was sending word to the Iroquois of his recent actions, repeating his earlier advice about defensive tactics, and promising additional ammunition when it was needed.[52]

Throughout these proceedings the governor carefully avoided any mention of direct English military support. Although he had sent to New York to alert the militia for any emergency, Dongan could not put Englishmen into the field against the French without openly violating the treaty of neutrality. He was sure in his own mind that Denonville had flouted the treaty by attacking the Seneca, but since that agreement had failed to mention the Iroquois as English subjects, the case was open to question. Except to defend the English settlements themselves, therefore, Dongan refused to commit his own troops without orders from home.[53] The French had in fact unintentionally called Dongan's bluff with the Iroquois. His previous assurances of protection had led them to expect more substantial support than ammunition and a handful of Algonquian warriors. If they felt resentment, they seem not to have voiced it; but when the invaders withdrew to Niagara, the anti-French unity of the league began to evaporate. As in 1684 one faction, including the Seneca, favored continuing the war with the French, whereas others called for an immediate peace. Dongan warned against any independent negotiations and, hearing of a general council to be held at Onondaga, dispatched

[52] *LIR*, 126–131.   [53] *NYCD*, III, 428.

envoys to present his argument more forcefully. If the Iroquois made an agreement with Canada, he threatened, "I will not trouble my Self any longer w[i]th ye Brethren but goe doune to N: Yorke . . . wee can live without ye Brethren," he said, "but can Scarcely beleive they can live without us; haveing Everything thrice as cheep here as Elsewhere." Hoping that they would thus associate the continuation of trade relations at Albany with the continuance of the English alliance, Dongan required one of the sachems and war chiefs of each nation to meet him at Albany in order to make plans for the future.[54]

The governor was not disappointed, and when the chiefs gathered at Albany on August 5, he blamed the Indians themselves for their recent afflictions. Had they followed his original advice and refused to deal with the French except through him, Dongan assured them, the French would have looked upon them as English subjects and would not have dared to attack. For the future he advised them to make peace with the Ottawa, Miami, and other western tribes and "open a path for them this way, they being the King of England's subjects likewise." By this means they would come freely to trade at Albany, and the Iroquois could receive an annual "acknowledgement" from them for the right of way. Then, the governor continued, the Iroquois might join those tribes in an alliance against the French. Dongan urged them once more to reclaim their brethren in Canada and to receive no more French Jesuits, since he had requested English priests to replace the departed missionaries. (Father Lamberville, the last of the missionaries to remain, had made his escape to Canada on the eve of Denonville's invasion.) Having heard of Denonville's work at Niagara, Dongan deemed this the most favorable opportunity to broach the matter of an English fort on Lake Ontario. In doing so he stressed the protective value of such a post and asked what location would be most convenient.

By comparison with Dongan's arraignment of Iroquois misdeeds their reply was a model of self-restraint. The war resulted, they said, from the French interfering unjustly in a conflict between the Iroquois and other Indians. "Why should you not joyne with us in a just cause," they chided him, "when the French joynes with our Enemies in an unjust cause." The French intended to kill the Iroquois and divert the whole beaver trade to Canada. The "great King of England" would

[54] *LIR*, 131–135.

lose his land likewise; "therefore, o Great Sachim beyond the Great Lake, awake and suffer not those poor Indians that have given themselfs and their Lands under your protection to bee destroyed by the French without cause." Having justified themselves, the Indians were otherwise entirely compliant, for they still hoped for positive English military support. They expressed greater willingness now to make peace with the Ottawa, and even with their "mortal Enemies" the Miami, and requested the help of the Mahican and other River Indians to bring it about. Promising also to open a path to Albany for the western tribes, they pledged themselves "to wadge warr with the French as long as wee have a man left" and to make no peace without the governor's consent. The best site for an English fort, they said, would be at La Famine. The sachems would do their best to persuade their brethren in Canada to return and would receive no more French Jesuits; if any of the Five Nations wanted English priests, however, they would let the governor know. To most outward appearances the Iroquois had rebounded from the French attack directly into Dongan's arms.[55]

From Dongan's point of view the subsequent Iroquois performance against Canada was exemplary. By the end of August they were sending war parties in the direction of Montreal. These groups, some of them numbering at least two hundred men, attacked outlying settlements, burned houses and barns, and murdered colonists whom they found in the woods and fields. By the spring of 1688 the French around Montreal found themselves more closely besieged and more fully exposed to the horrors of Indian warfare than at any time since the 1650's, when Stuyvesant was predicting the downfall of Canada. The attackers struck so silently and retired so swiftly that there was no opportunity to fight back. As Denonville remarked, it was like warring against wolves in the forest whose lairs were known to no man. Only the largest settlements were safe, and even around them the fields went untilled as the inhabitants cowered within their fortifications. Denonville was afraid to use the hundreds of soldiers that he had on hand, and meanwhile they ate up precious food supplies. Trade languished, and it was said that no shipment of furs got through from Michilimackinac for two years.

The French governor was furious with Dongan for having armed

[55] *NYCD*, III, 438–444.

the Iroquois and, as he thought, for having incited them against him in the first place. A bitter exchange of letters took place, in which each governor accused the other of violating the treaty of neutrality and defended his own claim to the Iroquois and the western tribes. Seeking to justify English sovereignty over the "far Indians," Dongan now claimed that they had "traded with Albany long before the French settled att Montreall." This statement was open to considerable doubt, however, and Dongan had sent to Albany only two days before to collect evidence on this point.[56]

In September 1687 he sent a special envoy to England with a full account of the recent invasion, his own proceedings to counteract it, and his proposals for long-range action to curb the French. The Iroquois, he said, were "a better Bullwark against the French and the other Indians than so many Christians" would be, and if they were not sustained, the French would soon be masters of the whole interior. To prevent this and to secure the peltry trade he urged the construction of forts on Lake Champlain, at La Famine, and at Niagara, with two or three smaller posts between Schenectady and Lake Ontario to protect the lines of communication. This program would require four or five hundred men from Europe, he said, unless substantial aid were forthcoming from neighboring colonies. About 1,500 Indians were prowling in Canada, he reported later, but there was danger nevertheless of another French invasion by spring.[57]

Dongan had already begun to get reports that the French were preparing another expedition and that Albany itself would be attacked if it continued to arm the Five Nations. The French had made 1,500 pairs of snowshoes, it was said; if this were true, it could only mean another winter foray in the manner of Courcelle. Because of these reports he ordered Albany and Schenectady to prepare for an attack and directed Mayor Peter Schuyler to enlist thirty or forty Indian scouts to patrol Albany's northern approaches. The Iroquois were to be warned of the danger and requested to send all their noncombatants to the Hudson valley for safety before winter set in. They were to bring as much of their corn with them as possible, and all persons were forbidden to take corn or peas from the upper part of

---

[56] *Ibid.*, 466–475; *NYDH*, I, 266.
[57] *NYCD*, III, 428–430, 475–477; *CSP, 1685–1688*, no. 1479.

the province. Dongan could no longer afford to leave the fighting to the Iroquois alone. Their continued allegiance and the safety of Albany seemed to require more positive English action than he had been willing to provide before. By September 12 Dongan had decided to take two hundred men to Albany and spend the winter there himself. Believing that a winter attack would have to come by way of Lake Champlain, he asked each of the Five Nations to send a quota of men, three hundred in all, to Schenectady, where they should spend the winter in a position to join his forces if necessary.

When the governor's orders reached Albany, some of the Indians were then in town. The Mohawk, who had not participated so far in the Canadian forays, had just announced their preparations to do so and were encouraged in this action by the magistrates. The Onondaga, requesting cannon for the defense of their castle, felt now that the best site for an English fort would be at the mouth of the Oswego River —the best spot for warding off an attack upon their own village. They were overjoyed with the governor's plans of defense and promised to acquaint all the nations with his message.[58] Dongan soon changed his mind about the probability of a French attack that winter, but he nevertheless proceeded to Albany, arriving near the end of October with an even larger body of militia—between three and four hundred—than he had originally planned. Writing again to Denonville, he demanded reparation for the trading goods seized on the lakes, the release of Iroquois prisoners in French hands, and the demolition of the fort at Niagara. In another letter to England he said that if the king had any regard for the beaver trade or for any part of America beyond the Atlantic seaboard this was the time to act.[59]

The Indians were dilatory in sending warriors to Schenectady, and fresh rumors came to Albany of an impending attack. In November, Dongan sent another message to the Five Nations as well as an appeal for reinforcements from his predecessor Andros, who was now in Boston as governor of the newly created Dominion of New England. To the Indians, Dongan repeated his request for two or three hundred warriors to stay at Schenectady and pledged his support if they were attacked. Meanwhile they must not listen to the French, who were

[58] *NYCD,* III, 477–486; *NYDH,* I, 266, 272.
[59] *NYCD,* III, 516–517; *CSP, 1685–1688,* nos. 1479, 1494.

trying to split the confederacy by promising peace to all but the Seneca and Cayuga. The only place to make peace, he said, was at Albany, where he was already interceding on their behalf with the governor of Canada. The warriors subsequently arrived—800 of them, Dongan said, although this figure seems rather high. Andros, who was by no means a stranger to Dongan's problems, replied that he was willing to send all the men asked for whenever they were needed. He was evidently unimpressed with the immediacy of Dongan's appeal, and probably with reason. The rumors of a winter attack turned out to be false, but Dongan's preparations could hardly have avoided creating a favorable impression among the Iroquois.[60]

Meanwhile, pursuant to the treaty of 1686, negotiations had been taking place in London for a settlement of Anglo-French differences in America. In October 1687 the French ambassadors had charged Dongan with using the Iroquois to wage war on Canada in violation of that agreement. At this point Dongan's dispatches arrived from New York, putting an entirely different light on the matter. Denonville's invasion of the Seneca country and Dongan's energetic policies to combat him forced the London government either to support its governor or to repudiate him publicly. It chose the former course, apparently without hesitation, and on November 10 a royal letter was addressed to Dongan, acknowledging the Five Nations as English subjects and fully endorsing his policies to date. He was required to notify the French governor of this decision and to demand the release of the western traders with all of their goods. "And in case the People of Canada shall . . . persevere in invading our Dominions and annoying those Indians," the king continued, "you are with the utmost of your power to defend and protect them." Dongan was empowered to build any forts that he felt necessary to carry out this policy, and the other American governors were notified to send such help as he might require. Several days later the English commissioners proposed a treaty to settle the boundaries between their respective colonies. The French, however, were unwilling to commit themselves to specific boundaries without further information from America. The only result of these conferences was an agreement providing merely that until January 1, 1689, and afterward until further order, no English or French governor in America should commit hostilities against subjects of the other.

[60] *CSP, 1685–1688*, nos. 1548–1548.II, 1684; *LIR*, 140–143.

Governor Dongan and the Iroquois

This document was even vaguer in its terminology than the 1686 treaty, but both kings instructed their governors to abide by it.[61] When King James's letter reached Dongan in February 1688, he was still at Albany, engaged in negotiations of his own with the French. Denonville had sent a former Mohawk missionary, Father François Vaillant, to see if some agreement could not be worked out with the English to ease the pressure on Canada. Iroquois depredations, famine, and sickness were taking a heavy toll, and the colony was apparently on the verge of paralysis. Father Vaillant proposed a fifteen-month truce, looking toward a pacification embracing all Indian tribes involved in the present hostilities. Dongan's answer was to reiterate the conditions that he had made before: reparation for the goods taken from Roseboom and Magregory, demolition of Niagara and any other forts erected in the Iroquois country since November 1686, and restoration of all Iroquois prisoners, including those sent to France. To these demands he later added a fourth, that the Christian Iroquois in Canada be permitted to return home freely at their own desire. Dongan decided nevertheless to submit the French proposal to a group of Iroquois sachems who were then in town. He acquainted them at the same time with the king's decision to protect them and left it to them whether or not to accept the truce. The Indians not only reaffirmed Dongan's demands, but called for the abandonment of Cadaraqui as well. As long as the French retained these forts on the lakes, they said, they would be under a continual state of siege and would lose their beaver hunting besides. The sachems ended by leaving the whole matter in Dongan's hands. His decision was to adhere to the original demands, and the priest, being unable to accept them, was escorted back to Canada.[62]

When Dongan returned to New York in March, his major problem was no longer diplomatic or military, but financial. He had already written to England that the provincial revenue had fallen to £3,000 in 1687, owing to the effects of the Franco-Indian war on the fur trade. The colony was unable to maintain itself in normal times, he said, much less bear the brunt of a war with Canada, which received

[61] NYCD, III, 503–510; IX, 371; Davenport and Paullin, *European Treaties Bearing on the History of the United States*, II, 324–329; Brodhead, *History of New York*, II, 492–494.
[62] NYCD, III, 510–512, 517–536.

constant financial aid from France. Not only did the winter's expenses at Albany have to be met, but forts in the Indian country continued to be an urgent if expensive necessity. Dongan's own remedy had long been the annexation of Connecticut and the two colonies of East and West New Jersey to New York; the king's, as he would soon discover, was the annexation of New York and the Jerseys to a consolidated New England. Meanwhile, having James's permission to solicit aid from other colonies, Dongan wrote letters to his fellow governors asking for contributions. The cost of the winter's expedition, he informed them, was over £10,000—far more than New York alone could afford. (The council had earlier estimated this expense at less than £9,000, and the final tally seems to have been closer to £6,000.) Virginia, Maryland, Pennsylvania, and the Jerseys were requested to send money, and Andros in New England was again called upon for men. The response to these letters was disappointng. Andros still held himself ready to send as many men as possible when they should be needed, but obviously felt that that time was not now. East New Jersey promised money, but seems never to have paid it. Pennsylvania withheld aid for the present, and Maryland refused altogether until the king specifically commanded it. In Virginia, Lord Howard of Effingham and the council, thankful for Dongan's past services with the Iroquois, finally remitted £500 out of the quitrents after the House of Burgesses had refused two appeals for an appropriation.[63]

This discouraging response necessitated a curtailment of Dongan's plans and imposed a tremendous tax burden on the thinly populated Colony of New York. The governor's dependence on freewill offerings from neighboring provinces meant in effect that their estimates of New York's needs and of their own ability to pay became controlling factors in imperial relations with the French and Indians. The home government's failure to assume responsibility for these expenditures and its shifting of the burden to the several colonies were to be a chronic feature of imperial policy for many years. It was a godsend

---

[63] *Ibid.*, 511, 566; Brodhead, *History of New York*, II, 496, 505; *CSP, 1685–1688*, nos. 1665, 1678, 1684.I; *Pennsylvania Archives*, 1st ser., I, 104; *Maryland Archives*, VIII, 26–29; H. R. McIlwaine and J. P. Kennedy, eds., *Journals of the House of Burgesses of Virginia* (Richmond, 1905–1915), *1659/60–1693*, 292–294, 298–300, 302; McIlwaine, *Executive Journals of the Council of Colonial Virginia*, I, 92–94.

to the French, who could never have retained Canada in the face of concerted opposition by the overwhelmingly stronger English colonies; furthermore, these colonies were encouraged by the lack of effective imperial control to follow a course of increasing self-reliance and independence of the mother country.

In the spring of 1688 the Iroquois relentlessly pursued their war on Canada. The true state of affairs there was not appreciated in New York, where fears of a French attack persisted. An alarm reached Dongan late in April, stirring him to renewed activity. He again urged the Iroquois to send their women, children, and old people to safety —this time he suggested the Mohawk country—and encouraged them to stand up to the French. Several days later he decided to return to Albany himself and to send men to each of the Five Nations to watch for French activity. The Minisink and all other available Indians in the province were called upon to assist the Iroquois, and Dongan considered sending again for the troops Andros had promised.[64] Only on reaching Albany did he discover that this was a false alarm.

At Albany, Dongan also received his first word of the Anglo-French agreement concluded at London in December. In his view the French attack on the Seneca had nullified the treaty of 1686, and Iroquois operations in Canada were in pursuance of a war Denonville himself had started. The December agreement in itself added nothing to that treaty, but the governor interpreted his orders to observe it as a royal command to call off the Iroquois now that they, as English subjects, were on the offensive. He sent a copy of the agreement to Denonville in June and requested the Iroquois to withdraw their parties from Canada. Denonville had urged this in February and was delighted to co-operate. He even consented to Dongan's renewed appeal for the demolition of the fort at Niagara. This order had in fact already been given, and the fort was destroyed in September. Although Denonville did not admit it, the truth was that the Iroquois attacks on Canada had made Niagara untenable. Cut off from all communication with the east, its original garrison of over one hundred had been reduced by sickness to only seven men.[65]

Many colonists were convinced that this cease-fire had played into

---

[64] Colonial MSS, XXXV, 148 (translation by A. J. F. Van Laer); *CSP, 1685–1688*, no. 1744.

[65] *NYCD*, III, 504–505, 556, 563–564; IX, 386–388, 391.

French hands and constituted a grave setback for the English. Their appraisal was correct, except for the fact that a peace movement had reappeared among the Iroquois. The Mohawk and Seneca continued to send out war parties through the summer, but the other three tribes had grown increasingly restive under Dongan's commands. Before his cease-fire order was issued, they had already responded to peace feelers from Denonville and sent a large party of sachems and warriors to confer with him at Montreal. Conscious that they were negotiating from strength, the Iroquois made it plain that they were not humble suppliants. Any treaty that they might conclude here, it was intimated, would not extend to the western tribes, as Denonville desired. They denied Dongan's pretensions to sovereignty over them and reaffirmed their independence of both European nations. They would be friends of both and would observe a perfect neutrality between them. In the absence of the Mohawk and the Seneca, Denonville asked them to return at a later date with powers to conclude peace for the whole confederacy. This peace was never made, however. The Canadian Indians did all that they could to undermine it, since they did not relish being deserted by their French allies; moreover, the Iroquois themselves proved reluctant in the end to abandon so successful a war.[66]

On August 11, 1688, Sir Edmund Andros returned to New York as governor. Dongan had received intimations of his recall nearly a year before and now retired to a farm on Long Island, where he remained until the Leislerians forced him to flee the province in 1690. Louis XIV knew of the replacement as early as February and delightedly informed Denonville that he would soon be relieved "of the embarrassment which the cupidity and bad faith of that man were causing you." If the French believed that Dongan's recall was owing to his conduct in office or that Andros would modify his Indian policy more than Dongan himself had just modified it, they were soon disappointed. The change in governors resulted from James II's broad policy of colonial reform which brought the annexation of New York and New Jersey to the Dominion of New England. The king expressed "entire satisfaction" with Dongan's services and made no effort to alter the main outlines of the governor's policy, which he had already

[66] *Ibid.*, III, 556; IX, 384–386, 390–391, 393–396, 402; Parkman, *Count Frontenac and New France*, 170–177.

adopted. His instructions to Andros relative to supporting and defending the Iroquois were identical to those received by Dongan, including the injunction to keep on a friendly footing with Canada. In fact,
one purpose of the Dominion of New England was to enable the
English to confront Canada with greater resources and solidarity.
From the standpoint of colonial "states' rights" and self-government
the Dominion of New England, with its suppression of elected assemblies, represented a temporary setback, at least in New England
proper; in terms of imperial foreign policy it was a challenging experiment which unfortunately disappeared before it could be put
to the test.[67]

One of Andros' first actions was to notify Denonville of his orders
to protect the Iroquois as English subjects. He promised to make
reparation for any injury that they might do the people of Canada, so
long as the latter did not provoke it by acts of hostility. In September
he went up to Albany, where he had summoned the Indians to meet
him. They were already conferring among themselves about Denonville's peace offer, but they interrupted their proceedings and came
in great numbers to welcome him back. Andros' advice to them did
not differ in most respects from Denonville's. Reminding them of the
truce with Canada, he urged them to exchange prisoners with the
French and make peace with the far Indians, as well as recall their
brethren who had moved out of the province. As usual, the sachems
promised more at Albany than at Montreal and agreed to these propositions. It was only with the greatest reluctance, however, that they
promised to surrender their French prisoners before Denonville returned the tribesmen that he had shipped to France. Having gotten the
answers he wanted, Andros returned to Boston, where most of his
work would lie in the months ahead. Although his conference was a
diplomatic success, the French probably overrated its magnitude.
When the Iroquois failed to appear in Canada to negotiate a peace,
they mistakenly attributed it to the new governor's urging. Denonville
sent nevertheless for the Iroquois prisoners in France, and the frontiers
remained quiet until the following summer.[68]

In 1689 the Iroquois were absorbed into the larger war between
England and France which resulted from the English revolution.

---

[67] *NYCD*, III, 548–550; IX, 372–373.
[68] *Ibid.*, III, 553–555, 557–561, 568–571, 722; IX, 402.

Indian Affairs in Colonial New York

Thanks in large measure to Dongan, the transition from peace to war was less abrupt on the New York frontier than in Europe. His "cold war" with the French in fact set the stage for the conflict which followed. Inheriting from Nicolls and Andros a claim of sovereignty over the Iroquois, he went much farther than they in pushing it to its logical conclusion. Nevertheless he failed to achieve any of his major objectives because the policy itself was basically unsound no matter how vigorously it was pursued. Dongan rashly promised English priests to the Iroquois when he had none to deliver; he sent Albany traders into the western lakes when he should have foreseen that the French would inevitably retaliate in such a way as not only to frustrate the plan itself, but also to bring on a crisis which he was unready to meet; furthermore, he assured the Indians of protection which he was both unable and unwilling to provide when they requested it. Calculated risks are often necessary in war and diplomacy, but they make sense only when the odds permit a sporting chance of success. Dongan's policy was impulsive rather than calculated; failing to compute the odds beforehand, he was doomed to frustration from the outset.

French power in the west, based upon direct access from Canada by way of the St. Lawrence and the Great Lakes, was stronger than any power that the English could have exerted there, dependent as they were upon an overland approach through the Iroquois country. Any English attempts to penetrate the interior were bound to arouse French opposition, as they did, and the possibility of Iroquois opposition as well. Dongan's projected line of forts in the Iroquois country would have been prohibitively expensive to construct and maintain with the resources at his disposal, and in the face of this opposition he could not have secured enough of the western trade to equal the cost. English control of the west required at least one of the following conditions: full economic and military support by the English government; concerted support of the same nature from all the northern English colonies; the full co-operation (or the complete subjection) of the Iroquois confederacy; or, most satisfactorily of all, the elimination of the French from Canada. None of these conditions was present and none was feasible at the time for reasons which were beyond Dongan's power to alter. A policy of friendship with France was in the ascendant in England, in spite of the king's verbal support of Dongan's policy; the colonies had great latitude in their own affairs and were

Governor Dongan and the Iroquois

little concerned with the New York frontier; and the Iroquois, well aware of their own best interests, were determined to pursue them as far as possible in their own way.

The governor's objectives were economic as well as political. He hoped to enhance the province's wealth by increasing the volume of the Albany fur trade. That trade supported Albany and a number of merchants in New York and England; it also provided a substantial proportion of the colony's revenue. Unlike Canada, however, New York was not basically dependent upon the fur trade for its continued existence and prosperity. It is unfortunate that Dongan, perhaps under the influence of Albany, chose to emphasize it as much as he did. This traffic, like the governor's diplomacy, was dependent on factors—in this case the Indians—which were beyond the colony's control, and hence it was a fundamentally unstable enterprise. By emulating his English and Dutch predecessors and letting the trade take care of itself, Dongan could probably have encouraged a greater flow of peltry than by enmeshing it in power politics. The Franco-Iroquois conflict was not of Dongan's making, nor in all likelihood did he markedly affect its course; but insofar as he deterred the Indians from making a separate peace with the French, he accentuated its disruptive effect upon trade and hindered its resumption on a normal basis.

Even if Dongan's policy is regarded as purely defensive, as an attempt to keep the Indians and their trade from going over to the French, it hardly seems justified by the situation as known at the time. With comparative prices what they were, the Iroquois would not voluntarily have taken their trade to Montreal or Niagara. The French, moreover, had demonstrated that they lacked the power to compel them to do so. The Five Nations and the English were natural business partners, and Iroquois self-interest was the best possible insurance of a continuance of the Albany fur trade. Securing the trade of the western tribes could best have been achieved by a more concerted effort to make peace between them and the Iroquois. If Dongan was unrealistic in thinking that he could deter the French from exerting pressure on the Iroquois, he was doubly so in thinking that his measures could preserve the Indians in case of a direct attack. When the attack came, he went to great expense to defend his own settlements (which would not have needed defense save for his policy) and to persuade the Indians of his support. But apart from the normal arms traffic the actual military assistance he gave, and intended from the beginning to give, was negligible, consisting only of a few Indian auxiliaries who arrived too late to see any action. Even if he had committed the New York troops at his disposal, as he may have intended to do in case of another attack in the winter and spring of 1687–1688, they were far too few to have prevailed against an army the size of Denonville's. If the Indians had really needed such forces as Dongan could deploy for their defense, they would have been in a sorry condition indeed, and from his point of view probably not worth defending at all.

The immediate results of Dongan's policy were a crisis with the French which his home government was unwilling to sustain and an equally futile expense of over £6,000, nearly all of which was borne by the taxpayers of New York. The province was chronically under-populated and overtaxed by comparison with its neighbors, and the two factors were closely related. According to Dongan and later governors the high tax rate, arising in large part from Indian expenses, caused would-be immigrants to go elsewhere and residents of the colony to follow them. Dongan might have performed a more lasting service to the province and its revenue had he encouraged economic enterprise of a less ephemeral nature and opened more lands to settlement on a freehold basis, instead of creating additional landed estates and servile tenures on the pattern of the old patroonships.

Some of Dongan's efforts to win control of the western tribes and their trade proved to be too ambitious or of too little value for most of his successors to imitate. On the other hand, the unrealistic claim of sovereignty over the Iroquois and the constant effort to manipulate them against the French, which he developed, became the keystone of New York Indian policy in the years ahead.

XI

The Iroquois as English Allies

AS stadholder of the Netherlands, William of Orange had taken a leading part in forming the League of Augsburg, directed against the French expansionism of Louis XIV. When he ascended the English throne in February 1689, that country, hitherto a protégé of France, joined the league and in May entered the war against France which had already begun on the continent. The repercussions of this revolution were soon felt in America. Andros was overthrown at Boston in April, and Jacob Leisler seized full control of New York after the flight of Lieutenant Governor Nicholson in June. His rule was contested only at Albany, where the local oligarchy, headed by Peter Schuyler and Robert Livingston and abetted by refugees from New York, retained a firm hold on affairs for the better part of a year. A series of almost incomprehensible delays in England prevented the arrival of Governor Henry Sloughter until 1691. Meanwhile Leisler prosecuted the war with France and stirred up the bitter political feud which plagued the colony for a generation. Sloughter compounded the troubles by executing Leisler and his chief lieutenant, Jacob Milborne, for treason. The governor's early death brought a successor in 1692, Colonel Benjamin Fletcher, who continued to support the faction which had opposed Leisler. But with the arrival in 1698 of the Earl of Bellomont the Leislerians, now with injuries of their own to avenge, secured official favor which they enjoyed until Bellomont's death and the accession of Lord Cornbury as governor in 1702.

The American extension of the War of the League of Augsburg, which dragged on until 1697, is usually known as King William's War. This conflict was dependent on that in Europe, but at the same time it had causes and complications which were largely American in origin. On the New York frontier it was really a continuation of the troubles between the French, English, and Iroquois which had marked Dongan's administration. This new phase of the contest, moreover, was initiated by the Iroquois in the spring and summer of 1689, independently (and probably in ignorance) of the shift in Anglo-French relations in Europe. As far as the Five Nations were concerned, the war ended, not with the Treaty of Ryswick in 1697, but four years later when they too finally made peace with the French and their Indian allies.

As early as January 1689 the Chevalier de Callières, the astute commander at Montreal, who was then in Paris, warned the French government that the Iroquois had no intention of honoring the previous year's truce any longer than it suited their convenience. He therefore regarded a renewal of the war as inevitable. Looking upon the English as the real source of Iroquois inspiration as well as supply, Callières urged an overland expedition against Albany and New York to end this threat for once and all.[1] Louis XIV was much impressed by the proposal, but he was unwilling to implement it until the English themselves declared war in May. Diplomatic obstacles now removed, he recalled Denonville and sent Frontenac, the ablest man he could have chosen, back to Canada with orders to launch simultaneous attacks on the English at Hudson Bay and New York. When Frontenac left for America in June, New York was in the throes of Leisler's Rebellion, and poorly prepared indeed to make any concerted resistance against the French.

The Iroquois, furthermore, had fallen prey to baseless rumors that Governor Andros was plotting against them with the French.[2] Both Nicholson and the Albany magistrates hastened to reassure the tribesmen, and the lieutenant governor, who was expecting news any day that war had broken out with France, sent a barrel of powder to each

[1] *NYCD*, IX, 403 ff.
[2] In the tension which prevailed in New England and New York in the spring of 1689 no accusation against the "popishly inclined" governor was too fantastic to win believers among the English and Dutch Calvinists in his jurisdiction. In the Westchester region reports had it that Andros had bribed local tribesmen to attack New York itself (*NYCD*, III, 659).

nation. He urged them to have no dealings with the French and, like Dongan, offered to protect their noncombatants near Albany if they wanted to fight their enemies. Although Nicholson did not specifically ask them to fight the French, he made no effort to preserve the truce any longer. However, he did refuse the petition of at least sixty Albany traders—veterans of the Roseboom and Magregory expeditions—who sought permission to recoup their losses from that venture by a raid on Canada.[3]

Connecticut too was alarmed at reports of a general Iroquois defection and sent agents to Albany in May to renew the covenant and set the Indians at ease. This mission was a success, especially as it headed off a league council which was to have discussed peace feelers put out by Denonville to gain time. The Iroquois were not really in favor of peace at this time—too many grievances were still outstanding—and they were delighted to hear of a new belligerency on the part of England.[4] Probably it was shortly after this conference that they made plans among themselves for a large-scale resumption of hostilities. Accordingly they spurned an Abnaki request to join in an Indian coalition against the English and instead collected warriors for an attack on Canada. The French later blamed the English for inspiring this attack, but the evidence suggests that the English were ignorant of it until the warriors had already departed.[5]

Before dawn on July 26 warriors to the number of 1,500 landed at the village of Lachine, on the St. Lawrence, six miles upstream from Montreal. No one was awake to give warning, and the Iroquois braves quietly scattered through the settlement. At a signal they began their attack, killing or capturing all the colonists on whom they could lay their hands and burning their homes. The massacre took place almost under the noses of three garrisoned forts and an encampment of two hundred regulars. The only attempt at retaliation was checked on orders of Denonville, who commanded the troops to remain on the defensive. The Iroquois therefore remained in the vicinity, enjoying the stores of French brandy that they had taken and spreading terror to settlements for twenty miles around. On the second day nearly eighty men from one of the garrisons were butchered in full sight of five

[3] *Ibid.*, 592–593; *NYHSC, 1868,* 256–258, 266–267, 285–286.
[4] *Connecticut Colonial Records,* III, 462–464.
[5] *NYDH,* II, 19–20; *NYCD,* III, 599, 611; *LIR,* 150–153, 157.

hundred regulars and militia whom they were trying to join at a nearby fort. The forts themselves and Montreal, which was protected by a wall of palisades, were not attacked, but Iroquois control of the open country was undisputed until they voluntarily withdrew several days later. Suffering negligible losses, they had killed about two hundred colonists in the massacre and its aftermath; at least 120 others were carried off to face a more leisurely death later or, if they were fortunate, adoption into one of the Five Nations.

Denonville knew that the Lachine massacre would be followed by other attacks in the weeks ahead. Feeling that the safety of Canada required further consolidation of its inhabitants and military forces, he now ordered the abandonment and demolition of Fort Frontenac, or Cadaraqui. This command was being carried out in October when the fort's builder and namesake arrived at Montreal to survey the damage and resume the government. The old governor, who looked upon Fort Frontenac as the cornerstone of French supremacy in the west, was furious to hear of its impending destruction and sent quickly to countermand Denonville's order. He was too late, however, and the affair ended more unfortunately than even Denonville had expected. Although the soldiers had burned much of the fort's contents before evacuating it, the charges that they had planted on leaving failed to go off. In their haste to get away they enabled the Iroquois to take possession of the fort as well as a substantial amount of its munitions and stores.[6]

The Iroquois were at least partially responsible for Frontenac's abandonment of the grandiose scheme devised in France for the conquest of New York. Instead he sought to confine hostilities to raids on the New York and New England frontiers, trying by diplomacy to win over the Iroquois to a policy of neutrality. This course, if successful, would not only facilitate later full-scale warfare against the English and forestall any Anglo-Iroquois attack on Canada, but would also restore a semblance of order to that province and help to recover the fur trade. Having brought the Iroquois captives from France, Frontenac therefore used a promise of their release to lure the sachems to a peace conference with him the following spring. Meanwhile the Iroquois staged another successful attack near Montreal in November.

[6] Parkman, *Count Frontenac and New France*, 177–181, 192–193; Brodhead, *History of New York*, II, 583.

The Iroquois as English Allies

New England was having similar difficulties at the hands of the Abnaki and Pennacook Indians in Maine and New Hampshire. In August, New England delegates returned to Albany to ask for Iroquois help against these enemies. The sachems engaged privately to attack the Pennacook and Abnaki as soon as they had scouted their villages, but they declined the request in their public conference and seem to have done nothing in the matter thereafter. The Mohawk, fearful of French retaliation after the Lachine attack, were in the process of moving one of their villages, with the help of men and horses from Albany, to a more defensible location. They had been at peace with the Abnaki for several years and were probably reluctant to renew hostilities in that quarter as long as the French conflict persisted.[7]

The prospect of a French attack was at least as frightening to the Albanians as to the Iroquois. French Indians had killed three colonists near Schenectady, and in August the magistrates forbade anyone capable of bearing arms to leave the city. Soon afterward they swallowed their pride and appealed to Jacob Leisler for aid; but when he demanded their submission in return, the magistrates looked elsewhere. Asking for scouts from the Esopus Indians and others, they wrote to Massachusetts and Connecticut for men to help garrison the city during the coming winter. The Iroquois, while singing "Courage! Courage!" to their Albany brethren, were persuaded to second this request in their conference with the agents of New England. Although Massachusetts needed her men elsewhere, Connecticut responded with eighty-seven soldiers, twenty-five of whom were posted at Schenectady.[8]

Meanwhile Leisler redoubled his efforts to gain control of Albany. Unwilling to boycott the city by closing its Hudson River life line, he tried instead to reduce it by force and by subversion from within. His lieutenant, Jacob Milborne, was sent up the river early in November with about fifty men, under the pretext of reinforcing the garrison. Milborne entered the city with no difficulty and did his best to win

[7] *LIR*, 147–148, 150–158; *NYCD*, III, 611, 621; Colden, *History of the Five Nations*, I, 119–125; *CSP, 1689–1692*, no. 509; *Connecticut Colonial Records*, IV, 2; Robert N. Toppan and Alfred T. S. Goodrick, eds., *Edward Randolph* (Boston, 1898–1909), V, 66–67; Brodhead, *History of New York*, II, 583–584.

[8] *LIR*, 155; Toppan and Goodrick, *Edward Randolph*, VI, 299–300; Brodhead, *History of New York*, II, 584–585, 589.

over the populace, but to little avail. The magistrates, headed by Mayor Schuyler, retained control of the fort and its garrison and refused Milborne's summons to surrender. When a party of Mohawk braves threatened to open fire on him if he tried to take over by force, Milborne retired to New York in defeat. A few days later the Connecticut reinforcements arrived and were received with open arms.[9]

In December the Iroquois received Frontenac's invitation to a peace conference to be held at Cadaraqui in the spring. They were interested enough to summon a league council to consider the matter, but invited Schuyler and others from Albany to come and advise them. The magistrates had so little faith in their allies, however, that they were afraid to send anyone lest he be put in danger if the Indians decided to co-operate with the French. Instead they entrusted their answer to the Mohawk envoys. This message announced that Albany was "the Prefixed house to speake of Peace and all Publike affairs and not Onondage," and it urged the Indians in the strongest terms not to heed Frontenac's invitation. Albany had finally gotten definite news of the Anglo-French war, and a Franco-Iroquois agreement at this time would have been particularly inopportune. A few days later, in January 1690, the magistrates recognized the insufficiency of their previous action and decided to risk their interpreter, Arnout Cornelisse Viele, to make sure that their message was heard. Extending the hope this time of "rooting out" the French altogether from Canada, they renewed their earlier plea and requested the services of three to four hundred Indian scouts in the vicinity of the European settlements.[10] The Albany message carried the day, coinciding as it did with the Iroquois' real desires. For the first time they were offered the prospect of a complete French defeat now that the English were willing to co-operate with them. The league council refused to send delegates to a conference and urged the English to join in a concerted attack on Canada. "Strike at the Root," they admonished Massachusetts when they heard that she was proposing to attack the eastern Indians; "when the Trunk shall be cut down, the Branches fall of Course. Corlaer and Kinshon [their name for Massachusetts, signifying "fish"], Courage! Courage! In the Spring to Quebeck, take that Place, and you'll have

[9] *NYDH*, II, 130–132; *NYCD*, III, 646–647, 655, 675; Brodhead, *History of New York*, II, 585–589.
[10] *NYDH*, II, 137–144.

The Iroquois as English Allies

your Feet on the Necks of the French, and all their Friends in America." [11]

Frontenac was already organizing his own offensive operations against the English. They called for three parties, which were to strike almost simultaneously at the frontiers of New York and New England. The main force was to attack the New York frontier from Montreal, while the others, based on Three Rivers and Quebec respectively, were directed at New Hampshire and Maine. These two parties accomplished the destruction of Salmon Falls, New Hampshire, and Casco Bay (Portland) early in the spring. The first expedition met similar success almost at the gates of Albany. It was composed of 210 men, about half Canadians and half Praying Iroquois from the Caughnawaga mission. Moving down the frozen shore of Lake Champlain and then overland, they came to within a few miles of Schenectady on February 8. This village had probably been chosen in preference to Albany because of its weaker defenses. Indeed, if Schenectady itself had been properly on guard, the exhausted and benumbed invaders might well have surrendered on the spot as Courcelle's men had almost done in 1666. Schenectady was not on guard, however; of the inhabitants and the Connecticut militiamen stationed there, not a soul was on duty that night, and the village gates were wide open. Shortly before midnight the French and Indians quietly entered the town and fell upon the sleeping inhabitants, who were blissfully unaware of any enemy force within a hundred miles. In the next two hours, sixty persons were killed outright, and eighty or ninety were taken prisoner. Many were treated to the horrors of Indian torture, which the French could not or would not stop. A lucky few escaped to spread the alarm to Albany. On the next day the victors set fire to the village and began a hasty retreat homeward before opposition could form against them. It was two days before the Mohawk got word of the attack, and a war party, joined by fifty young men from Albany, set out in pursuit. By the time they caught up, the enemy was almost in sight of Montreal, and they were able to inflict only a few casualties.

Whatever their value in lifting Canadian morale, Frontenac's forays won him no material advantage against the English. He had hoped to forestall such a combined attack on Canada as the Iroquois were then

[11] Colden, *History of the Five Nations*, I, 127–136; *Wraxall's Abridgement*, 14–16.

advocating; but in fact he brought this even closer. The French danger now created a unity within and among the northern English colonies which had not existed before and which might not otherwise have been formed at all.

On February 15 the Albany magistrates resolved to write to the governments of Massachusetts, Connecticut, Maryland, and Virginia, as well as to Leisler in New York, asking for a sea-borne attack on Quebec in the spring. Albany itself took on the air of a town besieged. Most of the women were sent to New York for safety, and it was decided to invite the Mohawk and River Indians to settle nearer the town to aid in its defense. The Mohawk themselves were less alarmed at the French menace than at Albany's reaction to it. Coming to condole the English on their losses, they noticed the exodus southward and asked the townspeople not to "pack and goe away," but to take heart and rebuild Schenectady. Once more they requested the co-operation of New England in an attack on Canada, promising to warn the other nations to hold themselves in readiness. The magistrates were in hearty agreement with these sentiments, and they appointed Robert Livingston to carry the proposals to Boston and Hartford. An agent was sent to New York with a similar message, in both cases requesting further aid to Albany as well as the attack upon Quebec.[12]

Jacob Leisler was just as eager for the reduction of Canada, and he threw himself wholeheartedly into the cause, writing for military assistance from Maryland and Virginia. But he was still determined to suppress the "rebels" at Albany and tried unsuccessfully to get Livingston apprehended in New England as a traitor. He also sent Milborne up the river again with 160 men, ostensibly in response to Albany's cry for reinforcements. This time the magistrates were frightened into submission. The Schenectady massacre and rumors of another French attack in the spring were largely responsible, but Connecticut was also insisting on the withdrawal of her contingent. Thus the magistrates accepted Leisler's reinforcements and acknowledged his authority as acting governor; in return they were confirmed in their own positions of local authority. When Milborne returned to New York, he took two Mohawk sachems along for a *rapprochement* with Leisler himself. Almost everyone, including the Indians, seemed happy with the new arrangement. Milborne brought up further rein-

[12] *NYDH*, II, 162, 164–167; Brodhead, *History of New York*, II, 609–611.

forcements and supplies in April, and Leisler persuaded the Tappan and other tribesmen around New York to send some of their men to co-operate in Albany's defense.[13]

In New England, Livingston found a great deal of interest and several plans afoot for striking at the French in Canada. Despite their political enmity he and Leisler were working for the same goal, and their efforts were in large measure complementary. As a result of their labors the New England colonies sent delegates to New York in May for the purpose of planning an invasion. The plan that they agreed upon was substantially what Livingston had been advocating: a two-pronged offensive involving an overland expedition against Montreal, which would be based on Albany and use the Iroquois, as well as a sea-borne attack on Quebec. The colonies agreed to raise 855 men, including four hundred from New York and another hundred from Maryland, which had sent no delegates. Meanwhile Connecticut had already promised to send two hundred men to Albany to replace her previous garrison there.[14]

A conference was held almost simultaneously at Albany, in which the Indians reiterated their support of such a campaign as the colonies were organizing. Soon afterward, as the magistrates took steps to refortify Schenectady, the Iroquois gave further evidence of their hostility to the French. Frontenac had decided to try peace negotiations once more and with this objective in mind sent the Chevalier d'Aux and several attendants to the Iroquois country. The Indians gave them a warm reception: two of the Frenchmen were roasted over a fire, and the chevalier himself was turned over to the English after he had been forced to run the gauntlet.[15]

At New England's insistence the command of the overland expedition was entrusted to Fitz-John Winthrop of Connecticut. Massachusetts and Plymouth withdrew their promise of men after the intervening French attack on Casco Bay, but Winthrop marched to Albany with the Connecticut contingent in July. Here he was to join with the New Yorkers and Iroquois for the march on Montreal. Meanwhile Massachusetts, having taken Port Royal in Nova Scotia with little difficulty,

[13] *NYDH*, II, 236–237.

[14] Brodhead, *History of New York*, II, 612–617; Herbert L. Osgood, *The American Colonies in the Eighteenth Century* (New York, 1924), I, 80–82.

[15] *NYCD*, III, 712–714, 732–736; *NYDH*, II, 224; Parkman, *Count Frontenac and New France*, 200–201.

prepared a fleet for the assault on Quebec. Command of this force was given to William Phips, the leader of the Port Royal venture. The mother country provided no aid in either undertaking. William of Orange was fully absorbed with the contest in Europe and particularly with a landing by James II in Ireland.

When Winthrop arrived at Albany, he was dismayed to find that the promised New York contingent of four hundred men had dwindled in reality to no more than 150. Other preparations lagged correspondingly, and the town, he said, was a scene of extreme disorder. After considerable delay the troops were able to start their northward march toward the end of July, although they were dangerously short of provisions. They reached Wood Creek, near the lower end of Lake Champlain, on August 7. Here they sat for nine days, vainly waiting for further supplies and reinforcements. Arnout Viele arrived from the Seneca country with news that a smallpox epidemic had broken out among the Indians, preventing any effective aid from them. As it turned out, only the Mohawk sent warriors to co-operate with the expedition. The same disease, moreover, had struck in Winthrop's own camp, and it was liable to spread. The army had less than half the canoes needed to move forward, and the season was so far advanced that bark would no longer peel, thus preventing the construction of any more. Winthrop therefore bowed to the inevitable. He sent a raiding party of forty English and a hundred Indians under John Schuyler, Peter Schuyler's brother, to do what damage it could in Canada, and returned with the bulk of his army to Albany. Except for thirty-odd casualties which Schuyler's men inflicted on the Praying Iroquois at Caughnawaga, the expedition was a complete failure.[16]

The Iroquois' excuse for their nonappearance was undoubtedly genuine. There was a general prevalence of smallpox in North America between 1688 and 1691, among Europeans as well as Indians. According to reports reaching Canada the Iroquois had contracted the disease from the very Englishmen who came to solicit their help in the forthcoming invasion. These same reports, probably exaggerated, stated that three or four hundred lives were lost among the Five Nations and one hundred among the tribesmen closer to Albany, causing the Iroquois to refuse any further co-operation with the expedition.[17]

[16] *NYCD*, IV, 193–196.
[17] *Ibid.*, IX, 460–461, 490; John Duffy, *Epidemics in Colonial America* (Baton Rouge, 1953), 72.

The Iroquois as English Allies

Epidemics of this sort constituted the greatest single threat to Indian survival, cutting down more individuals in a few weeks than the French and their allies could normally dispose of in as many years. At least as important in contributing to the expedition's failure were the lack of co-ordination and the inefficiency of the English themselves. For this the New Yorkers seem to have been primarily responsible, although Winthrop was made the scapegoat. Leisler was enraged at the commander's ignominious return to Albany and clapped him in jail, along with several other officers, until Connecticut intervened to secure their release. As it happened, the failure of the overland expedition was deprived of most of its significance by an equally spectacular failure on the part of the New Englanders to take Quebec. Taken collectively, the American campaigns of 1690 suffered from a lack of co-ordination, if not of military and naval support, which only the mother country could have supplied.

These failures did not weaken the Anglo-Iroquois alliance, however, or the joint determination to carry the war to the French. In August, in order to concert future measures between New York and the Iroquois more fully, Leisler commissioned several Albanians who were acquainted with the Indians to reside temporarily at Onondaga. Later Arnout Viele was sent to take charge of this mission during the coming winter. In effect these agents were ambassadors whose function was to promote the English interest among the Five Nations, particularly with reference to the war against Canada.[18]

When Governor Henry Sloughter arrived at New York in March 1691, he brought royal instructions to maintain the Iroquois alliance; he also brought £100 from the king, to be laid out in Indian presents. After devoting his first two months to leveling the Leislerian regime and creating another in its place, Sloughter went up to Albany late in May. Here he held a series of conferences with the Five Nations, assured himself of their continuing fidelity, and distributed his presents. The Indians for their part urged another attack upon Canada, this time with support from the king's navy. In the meantime they agreed to furnish warriors to accompany a raiding party which Sloughter planned to send out in about two weeks.[19]

This force, consisting of more than a hundred colonists and sixty

[18] *NYDH*, II, 314–315.

[19] *NYCD*, III, 618–619, 622, 690, 773–780; *Calendar of Treasury Books, 1685–* (London, 1904–), XVII, 543.

River Indians under the command of Peter Schuyler, was ready to start by July 2, but the promised Iroquois warriors had not arrived. One of the Mohawk castles was mourning a deceased sachem, it appeared, and the Indians were in no hurry to cut short the ceremony. Furthermore, they resented the lack of a present to help wipe away their tears. They had waited for the English to get started a year ago, they said, and the English could wait for them now. Delays of this sort were to tax English patience almost to the breaking point in the years ahead, although the Indians had equal causes for discontent. "I wish to God we had such a force that we needed not to court such heathens," Robert Livingston wrote on this occasion. "They are a broken reed to depend upon; but for the present there is noe help for it, they must be tenderly handled." [20]

When the Mohawk finally appeared, Schuyler took his party toward Montreal, where it fought a pitched battle with the French and Indians. Both sides lost heavily, and in fact the benefits of the raid hardly equaled its cost. The Iroquois now registered increasing impatience, blaming the English for sending out small parties when only a full-scale invasion could dislodge the enemy. The Indians themselves had uniformly failed to provide the assistance promised beforehand, as the magistrates pointed out, but their argument was unanswerable. [21]

The failure to conduct the war properly was not Sloughter's fault. He had already written to the neighboring provinces, asking closer cooperation and planning as well as men and supplies for the Albany garrison. New York required outside aid for its own defense, let alone for offensive operations. The replies, which came after his death in July, were almost uniformly negative. No colony sent men, and only Virginia—whose new governor, Francis Nicholson, had himself served in New York—sent any money. This amounted to £102 and was used for Indian presents. [22] Under these circumstances another expedition was out of the question. The New York Assembly in September 1691 appropriated only enough money to station 150 men at Albany until the following April. Under subsequent acts this garrison, occasionally raised to as many as three hundred men, was retained until the end of

[20] *NYCD*, III, 783; *CSP, 1689–1692*, no. 1610.

[21] *NYCD*, III, 800–805, 807–808; Parkman, *Count Frontenac and New France*, 289–295.

[22] *NYCD*, III, 784–789; McIlwaine, *Executive Journals of the Virginia Council*, I, 190–191, 526; *CSP, 1689–1692*, nos. 1680, 1681, 1733; Council Minutes, VI, 59.

the war. Its physical maintenance was inadequate, however, and the men were subjected to scandalous conditions, leading to a constant problem of desertion.[23]

Insofar as the war was waged at all in this quarter in the following months, the Iroquois conducted it by themselves. Their raiding parties, often several hundred strong, continued to prowl along the Ottawa and St. Lawrence Rivers, sometimes going as far east as Three Rivers. They not only terrorized the Canadian *habitants* but resumed their western blockade of Montreal for another two years. These operations were costly, however, to all parties concerned. The Iroquois suffered the casualties, which were considerable, and the fur trade languished as they neglected their hunting. For this reason Albany was to suffer a decade of economic depression and dwindling population. The English colonies also lost prestige among the Indians; the tribesmen became more and more disillusioned with their erstwhile allies who spurred them on to ever greater efforts against the French while doing nothing themselves. Repeatedly they drew attention to the disparity between English professions and actions and called upon the other colonies to honor their covenant obligations and take up the hatchet once more. The Indians also complained of a shortage of guns and ammunition. The more they needed these items to prosecute the war, the scarcer and more expensive they became. It is no wonder, therefore, that Albany repeatedly got word of restiveness and an increasing inclination toward peace among the Five Nations.[24]

Reports of this nature led Major Richard Ingoldsby, Sloughter's interim successor, to confer with the Indians in June 1692. Although Ingoldsby seems to have exaggerated the danger of a rupture in order to magnify his success in renewing the covenant, he was justifiably concerned about their continued participation in the war. His position was by no means easy. Everyone favored a Canadian invasion in principle, but Ingoldsby was no more able than his predecessors to command the necessary outside assistance. Thus he followed the only course open to him and continued to subsidize the Indians with ever larger presents of guns, ammunition, and trading goods. These gifts had totaled about £700 in value in 1691, and £500 more were added

[23] *Colonial Laws,* I, 258–383, *passim.*
[24] *CSP, 1689–1692,* nos. 2229, 2242, 2256; *NYCD,* III, 837, 842–844; *LIR,* 162–168.

by the end of May 1692. At the same time he had to support the province's own defense establishment, which amounted to more than £10,000 between March 1691 and September 1692. It may well be that a defensive policy was more expensive in the long run than one of attack. Despite the fact that New Yorkers were subjected to an increasing tax burden, the provincial resources soon proved inadequate. The colony's credit was strained to the breaking point as Ingoldsby borrowed the necessary funds wherever he could get them, often at exorbitant interest. New York and the Five Nations were in fact joint victims of colonial particularism and the lack of direction or support from England.[25]

The autumn of 1692 brought temporary hopes of improvement. Governor Benjamin Fletcher arrived at the end of August bearing the same royal instructions regarding the Iroquois, and the same money for Indian presents, as Sloughter had brought.[26] What was more important, the crown now took halting steps for the first time to relieve New York of a part of its frontier burdens. In October, after receiving appeals from New York for help, Queen Mary wrote to the governors of Virginia, Maryland, Pennsylvania, and the New England colonies, asking them to contribute as much aid to New York as the state of their respective provinces permitted and to agree upon a system of quotas for continuing support.[27] Fletcher, moreover, was given the governorship of Pennsylvania following the crown's confiscation of that province from Penn in 1692. With both colonies under a single royal governor it was hoped that a larger measure of co-operation between them might be forthcoming. Another source of hope was the governor himself, who immediately infused new life into the administration. Fletcher's official dispatches give the impression of an outspoken soldier—a vigorous and dedicated servant of the crown, whose repeated pleas for royal and colonial assistance were lamentably unsuccessful through no fault of his own. This impression is partially

[25] *NYCD*, III, 837, 840–842; *CSP, 1689–1692*, nos. 1990, 2228, 2243, 2256, 2462, 2463; *Journal of the Legislative Council of the Colony of New-York (1691–1775)* (Albany, 1861), I, 17–18; Council Minutes, VI, 92, 94; *Maryland Archives*, VIII, 326–327, 330, 334; McIlwaine, *Executive Journals of the Virginia Council*, I, 259–260.

[26] *NYCD*, III, 823; *CSP, 1689–1692*, no. 2094; *Calendar of Treasury Books*, IX, pt. iv, 1582, 1585.

[27] *CSP, 1689–1692*, no. 2462; *NYCD*, III, 836–837, 855–856; *Maryland Archives*, VIII, 381.

correct, but it fails to reveal the political and financial corruption which Fletcher and his favorites engaged in at the same time, ranging from exorbitant land grants to the harboring of pirates. In the realm of Indian affairs he proved on the whole to be a zealous and moderately effective defender of the national interest. He charged a high price for this service, but it does not seem to have altered much the course of events.

Within a month of his arrival, and against the council's advice, the governor paid a quick visit to Albany to survey the frontiers and discover the temper of the Indians. He found the latter to be satisfactory, and the most significant result of the visit was probably the friendships that he made among the Albany magnates.[28] This cordiality persisted, with one major exception, throughout his administration, and it was an important factor in the conduct of Indian affairs during the remainder of the war. In 1696, breaking with tradition, Fletcher took the management of Indian relations out of the hands of the city magistrates and appointed instead a board of three commissioners. The men chosen were Peter Schuyler, who by now was serving on the provincial council, Mayor Dirck Wessels, and Domine Godfrey Dellius of the local Dutch church. Soon afterward this group was increased to four with the addition of Evert Banker, Wessels' predecessor as mayor.[29]

Robert Livingston, on the other hand, fell from grace at almost the time of his friends' elevation. For some years Livingston had lent money to the provincial government in times of emergency, in expectation of repayment from revenue collections. He was careful to charge adequate interest for this service and won a reputation as an insistent creditor. When Fletcher failed to satisfy his demands for repayment in 1695, Livingston decided to seek redress in England. Once there, he did not confine himself to the collection of past debts; with an eye to future security as well he requested confirmation for life in his local offices at Albany, with the customary salaries and fees, and a life appointment with salary as official secretary or agent to the Five Nations. In pursuing these objectives, Livingston effectively blackened the governor's reputation and imposed upon the ignorance of the lords of trade and the king concerning affairs in New York. With a little help from Dongan, who testified to his valuable services in Indian negotiations, Livingston persuaded the authorities that a separate

[28] *CSP, 1689–1692*, nos. 2444, 2541.   [29] *NYCD*, IV, 177–178, 362–363.

office of secretary for Indian affairs existed at Albany, that he had served in this capacity for twenty years without compensation and at great financial loss, and that only the king's protection could save him from the vengeance of a corrupt governor. None of these statements was more than half true, but they appear to have been wholly convincing. The result was a series of royal orders awarding his financial claims, some payable in England and the rest in New York; confirming him as town clerk, clerk of the peace, clerk of the common pleas, receiver of the quitrents, and collector of the excise at Albany; and appointing him agent or secretary to the Five Nations with a salary of £100 per annum.[30]

When Livingston returned to New York the next year to present Fletcher with his new commission and warrants for payment, his apprehension of the governor's wrath was immediately realized. With the council's concurrence (Schuyler not voting or perhaps not present) Fletcher suspended him as Indian secretary and revenue agent until the other side of the story could be told in England. "All that Mr Livingston can pretend to have done" with the Indians, the council declared in a formal statement, "was to render from Dutch into English what passed at the conferences, which has, for more than fourty years past, been the duty of the Town Clerke of Albany as appendant to his Office; nor was . . . Livingston sent on any publick message or ever had any power . . . to treate with the Indians, having no knowledge of their language" or any influence with them. Pushing the argument further, Fletcher wrote home accusing Livingston of profiteering at the colony's expense. Beginning as "a little Book keeper, he has screwed himself into one of the most considerable estates in the province." Fletcher was determined to stop him, he said, and in any case there was no expectation of paying his accounts as long as the war lasted. For the next year and a half, until Fletcher's recall, Domine Dellius recorded the Indian conferences at Albany while Livingston struggled in vain to make good his claims.[31]

By January 1693 Frontenac had decided that Canadian morale and French prestige among the western tribes required retaliation against the Iroquois. The Mohawk had figured most prominently in the at-

[30] *Ibid.*, 127–141; *CSP, 1693–1696*, nos. 2241, 2247, 2258.
[31] *NYCD*, IV, 201–206, 251–254.

tacks on Canada, and he chose them as his target. On January 25 an army of about four hundred French and Canadians, together with two hundred mission Indians, left Montreal on the familiar route to the Mohawk country. As this was the hunting season, most of the Mohawk warriors were away from home, and the tribe was taken completely by surprise when the French reached their villages on February 8. The invaders, meeting next to no resistance, captured and burned all three towns in succession, took about three hundred prisoners, and totally destroyed the tribe's winter food supply. The French had no thought of attacking the English settlements, and on February 13 they were prepared to return home as quickly as possible.

Albany was informed of the attack almost immediately, but Major Ingoldsby, whom Fletcher had placed in command here, refused to commit his troops until he had raised the local militia and sent to the Esopus and New York for reinforcements. Whatever justification this policy may have had from the English point of view, it infuriated the Indians. The most that Ingoldsby would do immediately was to move some of his troops cautiously to Schenectady, while sending Peter Schuyler to pacify the natives and organize what resistance he could on the spot. Schuyler soon discovered that the enemy were still at the Mohawk castles, but Ingoldsby turned down his pleas for permission to attack them. By February 13 the Indians were so close to open desertion that Schuyler proceeded without orders, taking with him a force of about 275 colonists and an equal number of Indians.

So much time had been lost that the French would have escaped unharmed if the weather had not interfered. They counted on an easy retreat over the frozen lakes and streams as they had come, but a sudden thaw now transformed these into major obstacles. With progress thus impeded Schuyler's party caught up on February 17, and a running fight ensued for several days until the pursuers felt obliged to turn back. The English hesitated to go farther without more provisions, and the Mohawk themselves lost their ardor after the French threatened to kill the prisoners with them. The French had attained their objective, but they paid a high price. Between thirty and eighty men had been killed in combat, with many others wounded, and the survivors, suffering from starvation and exposure, had to free most of the captives before reaching Canada. This was the last wintertime invasion of New York; the elements were too severe and unpredictable.[32]

The first news of the French attack did not reach New York until the night of February 12. Fletcher immediately called out the militia and prepared to take them up to Albany, arranging for both land and water transportation in case the river should be frozen. Luckily it proved to be open, and he embarked on Febuary 14 with enough men to fill eight sloops, the rest having orders to follow as soon as possible. The council meanwhile sent word of the attack to the neighboring colonies with renewed pleas for financial assistance. Meeting favorable winds, the governor reached Albany in the unprecedented space of three days. The soldiers were marched at once to Schenectady, where they began crossing the Mohawk River on their way to join Schuyler's party; at the same time fresh arrivals poured into Albany from New York and Long Island. On February 21 Fletcher got word that Schuyler was returning after his partially successful chase. He therefore recalled his own forces and sent them back home.[33]

Fletcher now invited the Indians who had accompanied Schuyler's party to meet him at Albany. Pending their arrival, he ordered the frontier settlers to consolidate their homes and received an address of thanks from the magistrates for his speedy assistance, "which was more then ever could be expected in this winter season." The Indians were equally amazed and gratified—so much so that they bestowed on him the special name of Cayenquiragoe, or Lord of the Great Swift Arrow, which they used in addressing him henceforth. (Peter de la Noy, a political foe, later sought to discredit the governor by saying that this title had been intended by the Indians as a sarcastic pun on Fletcher's real name, meaning arrow maker; although the Indians may have taken his name into consideration in choosing a title, the fact remains that they regarded such a bestowal as a signal honor.) In his conference Fletcher rebuked the Mohawk for letting the enemy catch them off guard. He also took steps to rally them, however, providing a supply of corn and ordering Schuyler to find them a temporary home. The tribe decided to build three new villages, this time on the less accessible south side of the Mohawk River. They promised to continue

---

[32] *Ibid.*, 6–7, 16–19, 41; W. J. Eccles, "Frontenac's Military Policies, 1689–1698: A Reassessment," *Canadian Historical Review*, XXXVII (1956), 208–209.
[33] *NYCD*, IV, 14–15; *CSP, 1693–1696*, nos. 82, 124.

the war as soon as they were able; meanwhile they repeated their demands for a large-scale attack on Canada and complained again of a shortage of arms and ammunition. On his return to New York the governor could boast with considerable justice that he had preserved the Iroquois alliance. That he had reached Albany too late to do any good against the French was not his fault. His spectacular trip averted a diplomatic crisis with the Indians which would surely have arisen from Ingoldsby's hesitation and transparent willingness to sacrifice them.[34]

Fletcher's activity was not enough to prevent some of the Iroquois from agitating for peace again. Almost three years had elapsed since the expeditions of 1690, and Indian demands for another invasion of Canada had been unavailing. Furthermore, the Oneida at least had been exposed to French diplomacy for some time past. Father Pierre Millet, who was living with that tribe as a nominal prisoner, but actually as an honored guest, served as an able spokesman and source of information for Frontenac. The governor himself now reverted to his favorite role of peacemaker with the Iroquois, trying as always to neutralize the confederacy since he could not (and probably would not) destroy it.

In order to head off Frontenac's overtures Fletcher prepared for a full-dress conference with the sachems as soon as warm weather returned. He spared no effort to retain their favor, although the cost was almost prohibitive, and departed for Albany in the middle of June laden with presents. By this time Frontenac had already approached the Iroquois through Father Millet, and they reportedly were planning a league conference at Onondaga to which delegates from New York and the River Indians would be invited. Fletcher's immediate objectives were to squelch this movement and secure the expulsion of Millet from his position among the Oneida. At Albany the natives made it very clear that their willingness to listen to the French did not signify impatience with Fletcher himself. Thanking him again for his swift assistance in February, the sachems expressed hope that this governor, who understood and sympathized with them, would not soon be called away to a new assignment. In reply Fletcher said that he would doubtless be there long enough to see Canada subdued. After speaking his piece about negotiating with the French and tolerating a Jesuit

[34] *NYCD*, IV, 19–24, 40, 222; *CSP, 1693–1696*, no. 161.

spy in their midst, he renewed the covenant and distributed his gifts. Following the main conference he gave "two fatt bulls" to the young braves who were present and then invited several of the sachems and war captains aboard his boat. Here he "treated them to their Extraordinary Satisfaction," recounting some of His Majesty's recent victories over the French in Europe and on the seas. The governor urged upon them once more the importance of remaining true to the covenant and finally bade them good night with a five-gun salute. Thus wined and dined, the sachems accepted most of his propositions with enthusiasm. They joyfully renewed the covenant and promised to have no dealings with the French. Though reluctant to get rid of Father Millet, they promised nevertheless to intercept all messages between him and Canada and to bring them to Albany. Fletcher received similar assurances of support from the River Indians and returned to New York on July 14 to report that the Indians appeared better satisfied than ever before. In appreciation of his services the mayor and common council of New York presented him with a gold cup.[35]

Outward appearances to the contrary, Fletcher's speeches and entertainment had done nothing whatever to alter the Indians' fundamental position. The Oneida in particular proved to be far from won over. Less than three weeks elapsed before they notified Albany of plans for a conference at Onondaga to consider Frontenac's message. This news came as a great shock to Fletcher, who lost no time in sending a message to the sachems repeating his former demands. Signing himself "yor freind and elder brother Ben Fletcher Caijenquiragoe," he assured them that he was "still true & stedfast" in his promises of continuing support.[36] Dirck Wessels was sent to Onondaga with this message, and the negotiations with Frontenac temporarily broke down. The Iroquois dilemma was well stated to Wessels by Aquadarondo, the chief sachem of the Onondaga:

The Mohaques are as if conquered, the Oneijdes wavering, the Senekes have great force but [are] more inclined to bever hunting than warr so that the Onondages ly in the greatest danger. You hear in your ears the cry of the women & children for the losse of their husbands & relations[;] great promises were made now neer five years agoe that Quebeque should be taken by Sea

---

[35] *NYCD*, IV, 32, 38–47; *LIR*, 170–172; *CSP, 1693–1696*, nos. 457, 481, 501.II–III.

[36] *CSP, 1693–1696*, nos. 478, 501.II–III; *NYCD*, IV, 47–51.

but I dont hear that it is done. I speak not in reference to Our Brother Caijenquiragoe[;] he behaves himselfe like a soldier and hath not been long here. New England, Virginia & Maryland doe nothing that we hear of. Our Brother hath renewed the Covenant for them but that doth not knock the enemy in the head, so my senses are as drunk not knowing what to doe.[37]

The inclination to peace remained, therefore, and fostered a continuing state of anxiety in Albany and New York.

This situation, together with enemy forays near Albany and reports of military preparations at Montreal, led Fletcher to consider spending the winter in Albany as Dongan had done. In the meantime he had entrusted Peter Schuyler with the main responsibility for Iroquois affairs. A French attack was continually expected, and at more than one point Schuyler almost despaired of Iroquois fidelity. That a breach did not occur was partly the result of his own diplomacy. Schuyler's constant plea in his letters to New York, like that of Fletcher to his own superiors and fellow governors, was for more money—money to send out Indian scouts, to pay messengers and informants, to support and supply the Indians, and to buy the goods and services needed to defend Albany itself. Given his lack of resources, Schuyler made the most that he could out of a very difficult situation.[38]

The royal letter asking for help from other colonies brought an increase in the amount given, but it still fell short of New York's demands and legitimate needs. Virginia and Maryland sent £900 in all; the much smaller province of East New Jersey contributed money as well as men for the Albany garrison; but despite Fletcher's pleas and threats his Quaker subjects in Pennsylvania refused to contribute a penny. Massachusetts and Connecticut were similarly deficient, the Bay Colony pointing out quite properly that it had trouble and expense enough in defending its own frontiers.[39] When a meeting was

---

[37] *NYCD*, IV, 62.

[38] *CSP, 1693–1696*, nos. 538, 571, 582, 587, 606, 613, 667, 698, 733, 854, 867, 991.VI; *NYCD*, IV, 55–57, 59–67, 74–83, 85–93, 96–98.

[39] Nevertheless both provinces sent agents to participate in Fletcher's conference with the Iroquois in August 1694, Massachusetts sending £200 for Indian presents too. Her delegates wanted this gift to be given separately in Massachusetts' name, but Fletcher adhered to New York policy and presented it to the Indians himself on behalf of the king and queen. A year later Massachusetts contributed another £50 for the same purpose. By 1696 Maryland and Virginia had contributed a total of £2,260. See *CSP, 1693–1696*, nos. 1103, 1133, 1191, 1221, 2075; *1696–1697*, no. 6; *Connecticut Colonial Records*, IV, 130.

held at New York in October 1693 for the purpose of setting quotas of assistance for the respective colonies, several of them refused to send delegates. Those who attended used this failure as a pretext for taking no action themselves.

Fletcher's repeated requests for the annexation of Pennsylvania, the Jerseys, and Connecticut to New York brought him only the command of Connecticut's militia. But when he tried to assume this command at Hartford, hoping to take the militia to Albany, the Connecticut Yankees refused to surrender their forces, and the governor returned to New York in a state of extreme frustration. Although the French alarms persisted over the winter, they were never so urgent as to require prompt military action. With considerable reluctance, therefore, Fletcher agreed at the council's insistence to stay at home.

Fletcher was subjected to personal criticism by the Five Nations for the first time in the spring of 1694. Schuyler had conducted a holding operation over the winter, trying as hard as he could to dissuade the Indians from listening to Frontenac's overtures until the governor could meet them himself and perhaps come up with a new solution. He was pessimistic for the future, however, and in March it was learned that the sachems had reopened peace negotiations. Fletcher now cut short a session of the assembly and hastened to Albany to meet the Indians. After keeping him waiting until May 4, the Indians promptly admitted that they had broken their promises by sending envoys to Canada. Fear had driven them to this extremity, they said, along with English inaction. Furthermore, the sachems accused Fletcher of having meddled in their internal affairs the previous year by persuading the Mohawk and others to boycott and thus frustrate a league conference. They later retracted this charge and parted from the governor as friends, but it was clear that they intended to follow their own course. Fletcher acquiesced as gracefully as he could, merely calling another conference for the summer to discuss the progress of affairs by then.[40]

Meanwhile the Iroquois deputies in Canada demanded that Frontenac go to Albany for a formal peace conference, which should include New York as well as the French and Indians. Frontenac naturally repudiated this suggestion, but he tacitly agreed to include

[40] *Journal of the Legislative Council*, I, 55; *NYCD*, IV, 84–85; *Wraxall's Abridgement*, 22–24; Colden, *History of the Five Nations*, I, 211–216.

The Iroquois as English Allies

New York in the peace settlement by promising not to attack that province during the coming summer. Before leaving, the envoys also made arrangements for a treaty with the western Indians and warned Frontenac not to refortify Cadaraqui, a course which they knew that he was considering.

The peace party now in the ascendancy among the Iroquois seems to have been aiming at a permanent neutrality in the larger Anglo-French war—a neutrality in which they were anxious to include New York as well. The Jesuit historian Charlevoix, in speaking of this period, attributed a different motive to Iroquois policy. In his view the confederacy's basic aim was to keep the English and the French evenly balanced in America, fearing the consequences to themselves of a complete victory by either nation. This, he said, was the reason for their sporadic peace missions to Canada, which he felt were insincere.[41] Such deep diplomacy does not appear in the Indians' dealings with New York, however, where they unquestionably spoke more fully and freely than in Canada. The Iroquois' fondest hope was clearly the expulsion of the French from Canada, but by now it was apparent that they lacked the power to do this themselves. As the English repeatedly ignored their appeals for joint action to this end, the war no longer promised anything but continued tribulations. Thus they were prepared to accept peace as the best alternative, restoring the imperfect but at least tolerable conditions which had prevailed in the 1670's.

In August 1694 the sachems returned to Albany to report their proceedings to Fletcher. Also on hand were Governor Andrew Hamilton of the Jerseys, a loyal supporter of Fletcher's frontier policies, and agents of Massachusetts and Connecticut. The English listened as Decannisora, an influential member of the Onondaga tribe, described his transactions in Canada. Fletcher had no further cards up his sleeve, and again he acquiesced in the main outline of the Indian program, hoping thus to avoid antagonizing them further. He was careful to exempt New York from their peace negotiations, but otherwise contented himself with a warning about French duplicity and the danger of a reoccupation of Fort Frontenac.[42]

[41] Pierre François X. Charlevoix, *History and General Description of New France*, ed. by J. G. Shea (New York, 1868–1872), IV, 247–248.

[42] *Wraxall's Abridgement*, 25–27; Colden, *History of the Five Nations*, I, 218–229; Colonial MSS, XXXIX, 184a–b, 185a–b; CSP, *1693–1696*, no. 1340.

Unfortunately for Iroquois policy and apparently through no effort of Fletcher's, this peace negotiation went the way of the last one. The circumstances are not entirely clear, but by fall the more belligerent elements in the league seem to have regained the initiative. War parties again set forth, with or without official sanction, and Frontenac terminated the peace talks. Reports of military concentrations around Montreal and Frontenac's announcement in January 1695 that he intended to refortify Cadaraqui were enough to seal the doom of several months' diplomacy. Hearing that the French had embarked upon this mission in February and planned to use the post as a springboard for an attack on the Onondaga, the sachems sent posthaste to Albany for reinforcements. The alarm was relayed to Fletcher, who made instant preparations to send three hundred soldiers to the Onondaga country. The emergency proved to be false, but several sachems came down to New York, where they expressed due appreciation for his preparations and good intentions. While there they partook of Fletcher's hospitality and witnessed the armed might which England seemed able to bring to bear everywhere except in the Iroquois country and Canada. They went aboard the greatest ships in the harbor, and as their visit coincided with the king's birthday, Fletcher ordered all the guns to be fired as they looked on. Before sending them home with "considerable presents," the governor also treated them to a drive around the city in his private coach.[43]

Reports of French activity continued to reach Albany during the summer of 1695. Fletcher was detained at New York by alarms of a possible sea-borne attack on that city, but he ordered Schuyler to march with some men to the Mohawk country as a demonstration of continuing English support. Late in August the Indians brought definite word that the French were reoccupying Cadaraqui. Decannisora now requested that a colonial force of five hundred men, with siege artillery, be sent up to dislodge them.[44] By September 18 Fletcher was at Albany in conference with the sachems. Difficulties of transportation and supply would have ruled out such an expedition even if Fletcher had had the necessary men. The king had just sent over two companies of royal troops for the Albany garrison, supplementing a company which Sloughter had brought, and he had also assigned

[43] *NYCD*, IV, 118, 123, 275; *CSP, 1693–1696*, nos. 1716, 1768.
[44] *CSP, 1693–1696*, nos. 1956, 2014, 2040; *Maryland Archives*, XX, 332–333.

definite quotas of men to the other colonies. The latter made little effort to comply with these orders, however, and New York was still limited very largely to its own resources. Having no intention of granting the Indians' wish, Fletcher could only reply that the season was too far advanced to send a proper body of men to dispossess the French. He rebuked them, moreover, for their own alleged deficiencies: "I must tell you since I have had the honour to serve the Great King of England my Master in this Province, all your misfortunes have been occasioned by your own Drunken, supine, Negligent & Careless humours." How the natives could have prevented the French action he did not say, but the only course left was to station warriors to cut off supplies for the post. Softening his answer with a sizable present of arms and ammunition, Fletcher sent the sachems back home to continue the war by themselves. This they did, sending out small raiding parties and intercepting similar groups of enemy Indians, who infested their own country as well as the frontiers around Albany. Despite their disappointment at Albany, Schuyler could report in May 1696 that their allegiance seemed secure.[45]

One of Frontenac's aims in refortifying Cadaraqui was, as the Indians suspected, to use it as a base for another invasion of the Iroquois country. Its possession enabled him once more to deal with the upper nations of the confederacy as he had done with the Mohawk in 1693. His objective this time was the Onondaga village, and in June 1696 he assembled at Montreal nearly the whole military force of Canada, together with all available Indian auxiliaries, to a total of about 2,200 men. Frontenac commanded the army in person this time and marched it to Cadaraqui, where the men boarded boats to cross the lake. They reached the mouth of the Oswego River on July 18 and immediately proceeded upstream toward the Iroquois capital. Four days later, as the French approached their destination, they found the Indians in the process of burning the village preparatory to their flight. Like the Mohawk before them, the Onondaga suffered no casualties to speak of, although most of their food supply was left behind. The French were destroying this when a messenger came from the Oneida, suing for peace. Frontenac agreed to this appeal, but only on condition

<hr>

[45] *Wraxall's Abridgement,* 27–28 (including quotation); Colden, *History of the Five Nations,* I, 234–235; *CSP, 1693–1696,* nos. 2082, 2124; *NYCD,* IV, 150–152, 157–158, 449, 486.

that the whole tribe emigrate to Canada. To enforce this demand he sent seven hundred men to destroy the Oneida village and bring back hostages. In three more days the destruction was complete at both towns, and the French returned to Canada without incident. By now it was transparently clear that they had the power to invade the Iroquois country virtually at will and to destroy their villages and corn supplies; but it was also plain that the Indians were not to be crushed by these operations and that they may not have been worth the effort.[46]

Definite word of the French preparations, even including their destination, had reached New York more than a week before Frontenac and his army got to Oswego. On hearing this news, Fletcher again proposed to take several hundred soldiers to the defense of Onondaga. But for three weeks he allowed himself to be overborne by the council, who urged delay because of a shortage of funds. On the last day of July, learning that the French had begun their march and that the Indians were calling for help, several councilors pledged their private credit for the sum of £200 to fit out a relief force from Albany. Two days later news came that the enemy were in the Iroquois country (actually they had already left it by this time) and that Albany itself was fearful of attack. Hearing at the same time from England that the French were planning some major venture in America, Fletcher at last departed for Albany, arriving there August 7. He now proposed sending about ninety men to help cover the Indians' retreat, but his advisers knew that by this time it was the French who were retreating and that such action was unnecessary. At this point several Mohawk and Oneida sachems arrived with the full story of what had transpired. There was nothing left but to pat the Indians on the back, encourage their future endeavors, and provide for their present needs. A message was accordingly sent to the upper nations stating that the governor had come up to assist them "upon the first news . . . of the French invasion," only to find the enemy in retreat. Summoning them to a conference at Albany in two months, Fletcher returned hastily to New York, where a French attack by sea was still feared. Soon afterward he ordered corn to be supplied to the Oneida and Onondaga at public expense during the coming winter and forbade its shipment down the river until their needs were met.[47] Had Fletcher

---

[46] Colden, *History of the Five Nations*, I, 242–249; Parkman, *Count Frontenac and New France*, 410–415.

[47] *NYDH*, I, 323–325, 345; *NYCD*, IV, 173–178.

followed his first impulse and taken troops up the river on July 9, it would still have been nearly impossible to put them into action in the Onondaga country before the enemy had retreated beyond reach. Moreover, the men at his disposal, perhaps five hundred at most, could scarcely have accomplished much against Frontenac's larger army. Once again, therefore, it was demonstrated for all who cared to see that New York neither could nor would back up its promises to protect the Iroquois.

The French threat to New York City failed to materialize, and Fletcher returned to Albany in the middle of September. He took with him a large Indian present from the king, supplemented with items which the colony had added and amounting to £500 in value. Every Iroquois conference seemed to be crucial, but this unprecedented gift indicated the importance attached to the present one. The Indians, it developed, were more agreeable than Fletcher had any right to expect. They were not to be put off from their long-standing grievance, however, and repeatedly brought up the subject of a land and sea attack upon Canada. They had even prepared a map of that colony on the outside of a bundle of beaver skins, to show the Englishmen how unprotected and accessible it was. They demanded that the map and their accompanying propositions be sent to the king, so that he too might see for himself and send out an expedition in the spring. The Indians would brook no further delay in this matter, and to ensure the delivery of their message they offered five beaver skins to pay for the necessary pen, paper, and ink to transmit it. Fletcher protested that there was too little time to send their message over the ocean, to make the necessary arrangements, and then to transmit the news back to America, all by spring; but the Indians were unmoved. Only after he had promised to write the king as soon as possible did they renew the covenant and return home. Two of the sachems, in fact, were so earnest in their desire to reach the king's ear that they followed the governor to New York with the intention of going to England themselves, although they changed their minds at the last minute. No one attending this conference could have entertained the least doubt at its end that the Iroquois desired the complete expulsion of the French from Canada. Fletcher sent their message to England as he was asked to do and also repeated earlier requests for a supply of light-weight guns which the Indians strongly preferred.[48]

[48] *NYCD*, IV, 198, 234–241, 276.

Indian Affairs in Colonial New York

The fall of 1696 brought more than the usual crop of rumors that the French intended to attack Albany in the coming winter. They were taken so seriously that Fletcher this time did what he had wanted to do three years before. He arrived in November and remained until March, when the alarm had obviously passed. At Albany he sent messages of encouragement to the Five Nations and conferred to the same purpose with the River Indians. The latter had been doing yeoman service as scouts, stimulated by a reward of £6 which the government had offered to any Christian or Indian who brought in an enemy scalp. Fletcher also urged them to emulate the Five Nations in consolidating their settlements for safety. The Oneida, who had long since given up their Jesuit adviser, refused to honor the terms which Frontenac had wrung from them at gunpoint and promised their continued loyalty to New York. At least thirty members of the tribe deserted to Canada, however, and the missions near Montreal continued to receive a trickle of converts from most if not all of the nations. When Fletcher returned to New York in the spring, the Iroquois were apparently secure, and he could boast without too much exaggeration that he had "as much of their esteem as any Governor ever had" before him.[49]

Despite this esteem the Onondaga, who had not yet fully recovered from the last year's attack, announced in June 1697 that they had been considering another peace offer from Frontenac. Except for the Oneida most of the tribes seemed willing to continue the war a while longer, and the Onondaga themselves may have brought this message primarily to test its reaction. They were unwilling to alienate the English, but hoped that permission to negotiate with the French might be extended now as it had been two years before. The Albany commissioners had asked Fletcher in January to arrange a peace between the Iroquois and the French Indians as a means of sparing Christian blood along the frontiers. The effect of such a settlement in restoring at least part of the fur trade could not have escaped them either. But peace with the French at this time was another matter, and Schuyler and his colleagues dutifully rebuked the Indians for taking steps in that direction without the governor's permission.[50] The Onon-

[49] Ibid., 232–235, 243, 245, 247–249, 256, 275; Maryland Archives, XXIII, 66–68; CSP, 1696–1697, nos. 521, 1008; Colden, History of the Five Nations, I, 249.
[50] Colonial MSS, XLI, 21, 38; NYCD, IV, 279–282.

daga seem to have accepted this answer, and for several more months the war dragged on as before.

In October 1697 the Anglo-French war came to an end with the Peace of Ryswick. Louis XIV and the League of Augsburg headed by William of Orange had fought each other to a draw, and the peace treaty only perpetuated the stalemate. It settled none of the major causes of war, either in Europe or in America, and left things essentially where they had been in 1689. For the English and French colonists hostilities automatically ended with the receipt of orders from home, which arrived in New York in December. But contrary to all expectation the Indians, who for several years had been straining at the leash to make peace, found it far more difficult to attain for themselves. Even in the process of peacemaking the Iroquois were to suffer as unwilling pawns in the game of international politics.

To Albany as well as to the Iroquois and the world at large the war had been as costly as it was inconclusive. The danger to outlying settlements and to the city itself, combined with the virtual disappearance of the fur trade, had brought a striking loss of population. According to a census taken in 1697 or 1698, more than four hundred men, women, and children had departed the city and county of Albany since 1689 —a decrease of about 25 per cent. Nearly forty had died natural deaths, eighty-four had been killed by the enemy, and sixteen had been taken prisoner. These experiences and the lessons they taught about frontier warfare were not lost on the Albanians in the years to come. For the Five Nations the situation may have been far worse. According to an estimate of their numbers at the time of the Albany census they had declined from 2,550 men at the beginning of the war to only 1,230. On the other hand, a modern authority, George Snyderman, feels that both figures are exaggerated, and that the league's "total war potential never rose to a figure greater than 2200 or decreased to less than 1800." [51] That the Iroquois suffered heavy losses in these years can hardly be disputed, however, in view of the constant activity of their war parties and those of the enemy, the desertions to Canada, the smallpox epidemic in 1690, and the destruc-

[51] In the contemporary estimate the Mohawk dropped from 270 men to 110; the Oneida from 180 to 70; the Onondaga from 500 to 250; the Cayuga from 300 to 200; and the Seneca from 1,300 to 600. The River Indians, chiefly Mahican, are said to have declined from 250 to 90 men. See *NYCD*, IV, 337–338; cf. *ibid.*, 420–421; Snyderman, "Behind the Tree of Peace," 41.

tion of tribal food supplies. Even if most of the losses were ultimately made up by adoption, as was probably the case, the war would not soon be forgotten.

The war with Canada dominated, but fell short of monopolizing, Indian affairs in these years. The renewal of hostilities in 1689 called a temporary halt to the efforts which Dongan had sponsored to establish trade relations between Albany and the western Indians. This objective was not abandoned, however. Traders at Albany and the Esopus were eager to break through to the Ottawa country once more, if only to recover their losses from the expedition of 1687. The provincial council discouraged them in May 1689 because of the then uncertain relations between England and France. It was ready to sanction an attempt two years later, although the party which was authorized to go at that time seems not to have done so.[52] The Iroquois were often of mixed feelings concerning such trips. Some historians have attributed their lack of enthusiasm to a desire to safeguard their alleged position as middlemen in the western trade. But in the absence of proof that they actually held or seriously aspired to that position, reliance must be placed on their own explanation, which was simply that they were at war with the western tribes in question, did not trust them in the Iroquois country, and were reluctant to send their own people into enemy territory. The authorities at Albany repeatedly encouraged the Iroquois to make peace with the far Indians so long as the French were not included in the negotiations. In 1690 some Ottawa tribesmen even came to the Esopus to propose a free trade, only to die in the smallpox epidemic that year. Both the Iroquois and the western tribes intermittently desired peace, the latter partially to enable them to trade at Albany, but the French always managed to frustrate such arrangements.[53]

The most ambitious attempt to establish a western trade involved the Shawnee tribe in the Ohio valley, who were less under French influence than the tribes farther north. The Mahican or Minisink seem to have opened this trade, perhaps with English co-operation. They were reported to the French as having distributed English trad-

[52] *NYHSC, 1868,* 266–267, 285–286; *NYCD,* III, 599; *Journal of the Legislative Council,* I, 14.

[53] *NYDH,* II, 142; *Wraxall's Abridgement,* 15, 23–24, 26; *NYCD,* III, 776, 778, 842, 844; IV, 45, 124; Colden, *History of the Five Nations,* I, 198, 224–227; Buffinton, "The Policy of the Northern Colonies towards the French," 300; *LIR,* 168–169.

ing goods among tribes in the Ohio region, probably in 1692, and in August of that year a hundred Shawnee appeared on the upper Delaware River. Learning of their arrival, Major Ingoldsby sent Arent Schuyler, a brother of Peter Schuyler, to escort them to New York. The Shawnee were interested in trade, but they also wanted to settle the next year in the Minisink country. The council welcomed this suggestion and promised to send Schuyler and a party of thirty traders back with them, to return in the spring with the whole band. The Iroquois were at war with the Shawnee, and when they heard of these talks, they inquired about them suspiciously. At this point Governor Fletcher arrived in the province. Falling in with the arrangements already made, he nevertheless required the Shawnee to make peace with the Iroquois before he would extend them his protection. Moreover, Arnout Viele, now out of his job as interpreter, replaced Arent Schuyler in command of the traders. The Shawnee conferred at Albany with the Iroquois sachems, and soon afterward the party left for the Ohio country with Iroquois blessings.[54]

Viele and his companions are the first known Europeans to have explored the Ohio region—a type of distinction more often reserved for the French and Spanish than the Dutch and English—but they left no journal of their trip, and it is impossible to know exactly where they went or what they did. They were gone for two years, during which time they suffered some losses at the hands of the Miami. An advance group reached Albany in February 1694 to report that Viele would arrive that summer with at least seven hundred fur-laden Shawnee. Peter Schuyler was hard put to keep most of the able-bodied men in town from going to meet them. The main party seems to have arrived in August, when Fletcher conferred with some of them at the Esopus. On the return trip a number of them, Christian as well as Indian, had been killed by hostile tribesmen, and they brought fewer peltry than expected. As a trading venture the expedition was not very successful, and it was not repeated. Several hundred Shawnee settled in the Minisink country, however, the two bands forming the basis for the later Munsee group.[55]

The welcome which New York extended to these Algonquian tribes-

[54] Council Minutes, VI, 117–118, 126, 130; *CSP, 1689–1692*, nos. 2444, 2479; *NYCD*, IV, 43, 51; IX, 569–570; *LIR*, 168–169; Charles A. Hanna, *The Wilderness Trail* (New York, 1911), I, 137–139.

[55] *CSP, 1693–1696*, no. 1403; *NYCD*, IV, 90, 96–99; IX, 586; Colonial MSS, XXXIX, 188; Hanna, *Wilderness Trail*, I, 4, 139–143.

men was in accord with well-established provincial policy. Each succeeding governor, with active co-operation from Albany, continued Andros' policy of supporting the refugee New England Indians at Scaticook and encouraging more tribesmen from outside the province to join them. Similar favor was extended to the Mahican and other groups who were native to the region. This reversal of common frontier attitudes toward the Indian arose from the same necessities that dictated support of the Iroquois, although the latter, commensurate with their greater strength and numbers, received much more attention. The French continually threatened to draw these other tribesmen as well as the Iroquois to missions in Canada, and New York's policy was partly a negative reaction to those attempts. Dongan, on the other hand, seems to have persuaded a group of 150 who had fled to Canada after King Philip's defeat to desert the French and settle at Scaticook in 1685. For the most part, however, recruitment took place among those Mahican, Pennacook, and other Indians who had remained in New England at the end of that conflict. The Scaticook and Mahican groups in New York had the most to gain by this policy, and it was they who usually took the initiative in persuading kinsmen to join them. Their efforts were only moderately successful, however. The Algonquian population around Albany continued to drop, although the rate of decline was less than it would otherwise have been. The English failed to distinguish any more between the various tribal groups, simply lumping them together as River Indians. In 1689 this category, living in scattered settlements, was estimated at 250 men—slightly less than the Mohawk at that time—indicating a total population of little more than a thousand.[56]

The River Indians, along with the Tappan and other bands around New York, played a subsidiary role in the war against Canada. As they had submitted to the Mohawk as well as to New York, their involvement in that contest was almost automatic. They performed valuable service in scouting, sending out small raiding parties, and cutting off similar bands of Canadian Indians who prowled in the vicinity of their own and the English settlements. The River Indians were in no sense a single tribe, and on several occasions the Albany officials as well as the Mohawk desired them to move closer together at strategic places in order to increase their usefulness. For this

[56] *LIR*, 77–79, 82, 95–96, 108–109; *NYCD*, IV, 337.

reason the Scaticook band moved in 1691 to a place known as the Half Moon on the Mohawk River, nearer Albany, where Sloughter supplied them with corn and promised help in building a fort.[57] The efforts of Massachusetts and New Hampshire to stamp out hostile tribesmen within their borders were not entirely consistent with New York's standing offer of hospitality to such Indians. The Scaticook, furthermore, were almost constantly under suspicion of aiding their New England brethren in depredations on the towns of western Massachusetts. Fletcher regularly met with the River Indians on his trips to Albany, and complaints on this score were often among the matters discussed. The natives persistently denied these charges and requested the governor's intercession on their behalf, either to clear their good name or to release individual tribesmen who had been caught and imprisoned in New England. Despite orders that they were not to go into New England at all, the depredations and complaints continued until after the war.[58] These years were at least as hard on the River Indians as on the Iroquois, with smallpox as well as the war the major contributors to their decline. By 1698 they were estimated to have only ninety men, or about four hundred persons in all.[59]

Nearly two generations after Domine Megapolensis left Fort Orange, a successor finally arrived to take up his work of preaching to the Mohawk. Apart from a handful of tribesmen or half-breeds like Hilletie van Olinda, who came of their own initiative to Albany or Schenectady, such Iroquois as received Christian doctrine during that interval got it from the French. The first Protestant to deserve any mention in this connection was Domine Godfrey Dellius, who came to the Albany Reformed Church from Holland in 1683. Dellius lacked the aura of saintliness which characterized John Eliot or Father Jogues, and he maintained a deep interest in matters temporal as well as spiritual. Political involvements, in fact, caused him to flee the province on two occasions, and his tempestuous extracurricular activities eventually overshadowed and brought to an end his substantial work with the Indians. He appears to have played no active part in affairs of either description until 1689, when he began preach-

[57] *LIR*, 81, 149; *NYDH*, II, 162, 166, 169–170, 236–237; *CSP, 1689–1692*, nos. 1555, 1569; Council Minutes, VI, 57; *NYCD*, IV, 46–47, 247–248.

[58] *LIR*, 150; *NYCD*, IV, 38, 47, 248; Council Minutes, VII, 146; *CSP, 1696–1697*, no. 749; *1697–1698*, nos. 567, 689, 822.I, IV.

[59] *CSP, 1689–1692*, no. 1555; *1697–1698*, no. 822.I; *NYCD*, IV, 337.

ing to the Mohawk. By the spring of 1690 his efforts had resulted in one Indian baptism, and others followed in the next few years. The elders and deacons of his church testified that he had undertaken the work "at his own expense, and of his own motion and out of pure love." His success, they said, was a cause of general astonishment among the Albanians, who were unused to such enterprise. There seems no reason to question this evaluation, but unfortunately Dellius got embroiled in partisan politics just as his religious work was well under way. He seems never to have been more than lukewarm about the Glorious Revolution in England, despite his Dutch and Calvinist affiliations, and he became an outspoken critic of Jacob Leisler. When Albany capitulated to Leisler in 1690, Dellius went to New Jersey, and eventually to Boston, where he intended to embark for England.

Dellius won a substantial following among the Indians as well as his own congregation, and both groups desired his return. At Governor Sloughter's request he came back to Albany in 1691. For several years thereafter he received a regular annual salary of £60 in consideration of his work with the Indians.[60] In 1693 Dellius boasted to the classis of Amsterdam of two hundred "converts," although the number who had been accepted as members of the church and taken into communion was apparently only sixteen. To do this work effectively a knowledge of the Mohawk language was required—the major stumbling block of his predecessors. How familiar Dellius was with this tongue is unclear, but he seems to have made frequent use of Hilletie, the interpreter. Probably with her help he translated "several prayers, the Ten Commandments, the Confession of Faith, and eight or ten Psalms." Like Eliot he used the Roman alphabet in approximating Mohawk phonetics; the Psalms were set to music, and the Indians, he reported, sang them "with sweet melody." This work was time consuming, and for optimum results it required more attention than he alone could give it. Furthermore, Dellius said, he could "easily perceive into what straits the [Indian] church would come, both as to services, and policy (of winning the Indians) if I should die or leave; as there is yet nobody who could take charge of it." [61]

The political implications of Dellius' work were fully as significant

[60] *NYCD*, III, 696, 771–772; Corwin, *Ecclesiastical Records of New York*, II, 1003–1004; Colonial MSS, XXXVII, 163b; Council Minutes, VI, 134, 215.

[61] Corwin, *Ecclesiastical Records of New York*, II, 1065–1066, 1087; *NYCD*, IV, 364.

to the provincial and local officials as the religous aim. As early as March 1690 agents from Albany had asked Massachusetts for some of their "young divines" to supplement Dellius' efforts with the Mohawk. The Jesuits, they said, had gone among the Iroquois "not so much to convert their soules as their bever and other trade to Canida." Like Dongan they intended to follow the same course themselves in order to keep these commodities at Albany. The next year, after the Christian Mohawk had asked Sloughter for ministers at their villages, the governor and council forwarded this request to the king in a formal address, again urging the importance of countering Jesuit influences. As Dongan had discovered, little outside help was to be expected. Despite repeated solicitation no ministers were available in either Old or New England to serve in this hardship post, and requests for financial aid from the Society for the Propagation of the Gospel in New England, which had underwritten similar projects there, were largely unavailing.[62] After a while Dellius himself seems to have devoted less time to the Indians, and there is no record of his receiving a salary for that purpose after 1693. His political activity increased proportionately, however, as he won the favor of Governor Fletcher. This favor brought his appointment as a commissioner for Indian affairs in 1696; the next year it involved him in a land transaction which eventually contributed to his downfall and speedy departure for Europe.

Fletcher and most of his predecessors had received the following royal instructions on assuming the government of New York: "when any opportunity shall offer for purchasing great Tracts of Land for us [the crown] from the Indians for small sums you are to use your discretion therein as you shall judge for the convenience or advantage which may arise unto us by the same."[63] The most reasonable interpretation of this passage would suggest that these tracts were to be purchased at a mutually satisfactory price in the name of the crown (as had been the official policy since New York became a royal colony) and that afterward the governor could grant them in the crown's name to such persons as were willing to settle them and pay the annual quitrent. The size of each grant was a matter for the governor to determine in accordance with his conceptions of proper land policy.

[62] *NYCD*, III, 696, 771–772, 799; IV, 184, 230, 254; Colonial MSS, XXXVII, 160a.
[63] *NYCD*, III, 823.

Previous executives had not always been consistent on this score, and the baneful effect of large landed estates on New York's development is well established. On at least one occasion Fletcher himself nullified a land purchase because it was too big, trimming it down from 100,000 to 2,000 acres.[64] This action was not typical, however, and he proved to be one of the worst offenders, granting at least half a dozen gigantic tracts to important persons whose favor he hoped to attract or retain. Nearly all of these grants, it is interesting to note, were made in 1697 when Fletcher knew that he was being recalled to England and that a successor was on his way. None of them contained adequate provision for quitrent payments or actual settlement of the lands, nor were their bounds clearly defined, much less surveyed. At least three are of interest here because the governor's generosity took too little account of the rights of the Indians and the privileges of the Albany trading community.

The most controversial was a grant in 1697 of extensive lands in the Mohawk country to the Albany Indian commissioners. These men—Schuyler, Dellius, Wessels, and Banker—were given permission in June of that year to buy from the Indians a tract fifty miles long and two miles wide on each side of the Mohawk River, extending roughly from modern Amsterdam to Little Falls. Fletcher's only condition was that the recipients include in their transaction one William Pinhorne, a councilor and supreme court justice who had had no connection with that part of the province, but who was one of the governor's foremost supporters. This condition was met, the evidence of purchase was presented, and the patent was issued on July 31. In addition Dellius was favored with a separate grant which lay east of the Hudson and of Lakes George and Champlain, measuring about seventy miles north and south by twelve miles east and west. Hendrick van Rensselaer received a patent for a tract six miles square near the Indian village at Scaticook, although he had not bought all of it from the Indians and fifty acres of it already belonged to the City of Albany. Finally, Nicholas Bayard, another councilor and favorite, acquired a strip of the Mohawk country twenty-four to thirty miles long, embracing most of the Schoharie valley.[65]

The first and last grants, it later appeared, were acquired from the

[64] *CSP, 1693–1696*, no. 2009.
[65] Council Minutes, VIII, pt. I, 3, 11; *NYCD*, IV, 391–392, 447–448.

Mohawk for no consideration at all in the one case and for a trifling amount of trading goods in the other. Mohawk lands belonged to the tribe as a whole and could be alienated only by tribal consent, yet both transactions were concluded by a handful of Indians without the knowledge of the rest of the tribe. Dellius appears to have been the prime mover in securing the deed for the lands on the Mohawk River. He acquired it through eight of his proselytes, whom he convinced that his only purpose was to protect them against the French and any others who might try to take away their lands. He and his colleagues, Dellius explained, would serve only as guardians or trustees, reserving for the Indians the full use of their land as long as the Mohawk nation existed. The deed itself specified no such thing, however, except as it reserved certain plots for the natives' use; otherwise it was a simple transfer of title to Dellius and his four associates. When the grant was later called into question, the patentees continued to maintain that it had been acquired in good faith and for the purpose stated. The evidence, nevertheless, together with the character of the other grants Fletcher made at this time, points strongly in the other direction. Moreover, the governor himself, in defending the grant after his return to England, argued its usefulness in extending frontier settlement.[66] All of the grants, including several in which the Indians did not figure, created a major political storm as soon as Fletcher left the province.

[66] *NYCD*, IV, 345–346, 447–448; *CSP, 1697–1698*, no. 822.II–III; Corwin, *Ecclesiastical Records of New York*, II, 1401–1408, 1416.

XII

The Iroquois Quest for Neutrality

IN England the subjects of Indian affairs, colonial defense, and inter-colonial co-operation had received increasing attention as the war with France dragged on. This was due in no small measure to Governor Fletcher himself, who for five long years had subjected London to a steady barrage of requests for men, money, ships, armaments, Indian presents, and more control over the resources of other colonies. The New York governor was not alone in this respect, and Massachusetts in particular faced similar problems on its northern frontier. The lords of trade were sympathetic with these pleas and complaints, and their intercession with the king was largely responsible for the small diversion of men and money from the main theater of war which did take place. The system of colonial quotas was a further attempt at solving the problem, but it broke down at the outset because of the nonco-operation of the colonial assemblies. By 1697 the home government was convinced that the only feasible way of mobilizing colonial resources against Canada was to revive in a modified form King James's plan for the Dominion of New England. Assemblies were not to be abolished, nor were existing colonial charters to be forfeited, but insofar as possible the northern colonies were to be united once more under a single executive. New York, Massachusetts, and New Hampshire were therefore placed under a single royal governor, who was also given command of the militia of Rhode Island, Connecticut, and the Jerseys. (Pennsylvania had been restored to Penn in 1696 and was not included in this arrangement.) The man chosen to fill this unenviable

332

position was Richard Coote, Earl of Bellomont, who reached New York, his first destination, in April 1698.

Although Bellomont's multiple office had been conceived in time of war, primarily to answer wartime needs, his appointment coincided with the return of peace. Furthermore, his death three years later took place on the eve of a renewal of the conflict. Thus his responsibilities were those arising in the wake of war, and he never had to exercise military command. Unlike Andros after 1688 he was to find that most of his pressing problems were centered in New York, where as a result he spent most of his term as governor. Bellomont was an intelligent and conscientious servant of the crown, possessing a breadth of vision and a degree of personal integrity which contrasted favorably with the shortcomings of his predecessor. These advantages were partially offset, however, by a propensity for self-righteousness and contentiousness in his dealings with other people. From the time of his appointment he was well aware of the allegations of corruption brought against Fletcher and was prepared to accept them at face value. Thus it did not take long to discover substantiating evidence once he had arrived in the colony and taken counsel with his predecessor's enemies. Most of Fletcher's associates, on the other hand, became *persona non grata,* and the new governor devoted much time and effort to driving them from power and bringing to justice those who could be proved guilty of wrongdoing. Where Fletcher had aligned himself with the opponents of the martyred Jacob Leisler, Bellomont perpetuated the factionalism by adopting the Leislerians. He made a partial exception of Peter Schuyler and a few others at Albany, who were well-nigh indispensable to a strange governor in need of cultivating the Indians. Relations between New York and Albany were perceptibly chillier, however, than they had been under Fletcher or Dongan.

Indian affairs, direct or indirect, proved to be Bellomont's greatest responsibility and most constant source of anxiety in governing New York. With the return of peace in 1697 relations among the English, French, and Iroquois again approximated those in Dongan's time. Bellomont's ideas and policies were essentially those of Dongan, warmed over and freshened with a few new ingredients. In the end he was no more effective than Dongan had been and for much the same reason; even with his broader jurisdiction and a more co-operative government at home his power was still limited. Furthermore, he seemed to lack the innate aptitude, which Dongan possessed in a greater degree, of translating his ideas into effective action.

Bellomont had received enough briefing in England to know something of the Iroquois' past performance. Even before his arrival, therefore, hearing of Indian hostilities on the Maine and New Hampshire frontiers, he intended to use the Five Nations against the offending tribesmen. Although the New Englanders had vainly approached Dongan for such aid in 1684, they were not ready now to see Iroquois warriors prowling again through their countryside. Bellomont, misunderstanding their position, thought that they were overly squeamish about using "the devil to destroy the devil," but he did not broach the subject to the Iroquois.[1] Two years later he was equally unsuccessful in encouraging an alliance between the Mohawk and the Abnaki and Pennacook Indians. As this would have entailed submission to Mohawk guidance and protection according to the Iroquois way of doing things, it did not appeal to the eastern tribes, and with ample encouragement from Canada they continued to harass the New England frontier.[2]

Immediately on his arrival at New York, Bellomont sent Peter Schuyler and Domine Godfrey Dellius to transmit news of the recent peace to Canada and to arrange for an exchange of prisoners. The transactions of Schuyler and Dellius in Canada foreshadowed the course of diplomacy among the English, French, and Iroquois for some years to come. At Montreal the local commander, Callières, informed the New Yorkers that the Iroquois were expected very soon to conclude a peace and that they would exchange prisoners at that time. Schuyler and Dellius replied that it was unnecessary for the Iroquois to make a separate peace since they were subjects of the king of England and as such were included in the Treaty of Ryswick. Callières insisted, on the other hand, that the Iroquois were subjects of France. French missionaries, he said, had lived and worked among them for years before the English had arrived on the scene, and furthermore they habitually addressed the governor of Canada as "Father."

This debate was repeated at greater length when the envoys reached

[1] *CSP, 1698*, no. 159; *1699*, no. 769; *NYCD*, IV, 315; Brodhead, *History of New York*, II, 393–394.
[2] *CSP, 1700*, nos. 345.XV, 883; *1702*, no. 184.I; *NYCD*, IV, 726, 758–759.

Iroquois Quest for Neutrality

Quebec and conferred with Frontenac. The governor readily agreed to return such Englishmen as had been detained in Canada, but refused to release his Iroquois captives until the Five Nations sued for peace as they had promised to do. Objecting that these promises had been made without the sachems' approval, Schuyler and Dellius repeated their claims of English sovereignty. The Jesuit missions, they continued, "had been tolerated by the English merely through indulgence." The English, on the other hand, had acquired their rights by conquest from the Dutch, and "it cannot be disputed but the Dutch had the Five Nations under their dependence." After both sides had disposed of Iroquois independence to suit their respective purposes, Frontenac sensibly concluded that he and Bellomont would never agree on the point and that it would have to be settled by the two crowns. Meanwhile he had precise orders from his king on the subject, and if the Iroquois "did not come to him to make peace, he knew the way to their country, and would go and force them to do so." Schuyler and Dellius had already received a visit from the Jesuit superior and other clerical officials at Quebec, who said that they hoped soon to re-establish their missions among the Indians. The envoys asked them to spare themselves that trouble; Dellius himself had the natives under his care, and the king and the bishop of London would amply provide for their further needs. The Jesuit fathers, they said, had shown only too often during the war that they "were prompted rather by the desire to seduce our Indians and to enfeeble us, by attracting them hither with a view to strengthen themselves, than by charity and a design for their salvation." Following these conferences the envoys returned home, accompanied by a number of English captives but not by the Iroquois prisoners whom they had also hoped to release.[3]

Schuyler and Dellius had already heard of the latest Iroquois peace mission in Canada before their departure from Albany and had warned the sachems against it. Despite the Indians' denial of any such intention Bellomont felt it necessary to repeat the injunction in person and made arrangements for a formal conference in the summer. Moreover, he had a considerable present for the Indians—again a joint effort of the king and the colony—and the natives were beginning to look askance at any new governor who did not within a few

[3] NYCD, IV, 338–341, 343–345, 347–351.

335

months of his arrival formally renew the covenant and seal the transaction with proper gifts. The governor also proceeded to get affidavits from old residents of the colony, as Dongan had done in similar circumstances, to support his contention that the Iroquois had been wards of the Dutch prior to 1664. Writing to England, he called further attention to the French menace and suggested that Protestant missionaries be sent to the Iroquois to "oblige them to the interest of the Crown of England as well as save their souls." [4]

The obstacles confronting Bellomont were even greater than those which Fletcher had faced. When Fletcher had sought to keep the Iroquois from making peace, the English and French were nominally at war; now they were at peace, their prisoners had been exchanged, and the Iroquois in name as well as fact were facing Canada alone. The new governor had no opportunity to impress the natives with a grand military gesture, and his unmilitary bearing was not apt to dazzle the tribesmen in any case. As he embarked for the conference in July, Bellomont reported, he was suffering from an attack of gout, "by which means, and a cold taken upon Hudson's River, I had like to have dyed when I came to Albany." The Indians were surly at first and did not make his task any easier. When he blamed part of the Indians' losses on their own neglect and lack of watchfulness, they retorted with an attack upon Fletcher. Citing chapter and verse, they detailed the occasions on which Fletcher had failed to keep his promises by neglecting to bring timely relief in answer to their appeals. On the other hand, the sachems had nothing but praise for Quider—Peter Schuyler—whom they singled out as the only person who had actually come to their assistance in time of need.

Apart from their zeal in justifying their own record and attacking Fletcher's, which they may have realized would not overly offend the new governor, the sachems were outwardly co-operative. They omitted to mention a new round of Canadian negotiations that they had just inaugurated and promised solemnly to heed the governor's warning about treating for a separate peace. They also agreed not to receive any more Jesuit missionaries. Like most of his predecessors on such occasions Bellomont was convinced that he had won a diplomatic victory.[5]

[4] *Ibid.*, 333–334, 336–337, 341–342, 352–353; *CSP, 1697–1698*, no. 632.
[5] *CSP, 1697–1698*, no. 822.I; *NYCD*, IV, 362–364.

Iroquois Quest for Neutrality

Closely related to the Jesuit problem was that of winning back the converts who had already gone to Canada. Although Schuyler had requested the Five Nations in 1692 to persuade their brethren to return, Fletcher seems to have ignored the matter altogether. Meanwhile the attrition continued. On their return from Canada in June 1698 Schuyler and Dellius brought back forty "French Indians" and their families, with a sizable amount of peltry, despite French attempts to prevent them. Bellomont does not seem to have mentioned this subject during his conference, but he broached it to three Praying Iroquois who arrived in Albany to trade during his stay there.[6] These Indians lost no time in resuming the commerce which the war had interrupted. They continued to visit Albany for many years, but they proved more reluctant to return to their former homes. This goal became another constant element in New York Indian policy.

Bellomont's first trip to Albany was memorable for several reasons. This was his first opportunity to meet the Albany magnates on their home ground and to discover at first hand the alleged mismanagement of Indian affairs by Fletcher's favorites. The governor by no means came to Albany with an open mind on this subject. He had sent Schuyler and Dellius to Canada in the spring because he found them in charge of Indian affairs, and at that time he had no reason to do otherwise. But since that time he had been confronted with evidence of malfeasance on the part of Fletcher and his appointees all over the province. The present conference hardened Bellomont's suspicion into a firm conviction that the Indian commissioners at Albany were abusing their trust. The most flagrant abuse seemed to be that involved in a complaint by the Mohawk that the commissioners had defrauded them of part of their lands. The sachems' initial coldness was further evidence to Bellomont that they had been tampered with by men who were seeking to perpetuate their own influence and fortunes at the public expense.[7] Although the second charge is impossible to prove or disprove at this distance, the case of the Mohawk lands was more substantial.

The Albany magistrates had opposed at least three of Fletcher's exorbitant land grants, basing their objections on grounds of general Indian policy as well as immediate self-interest. The Mohawk grants

[6] LIR, 163–164, 167; NYCD, IV, 351; CSP, 1697–1698, no. 822.I.
[7] NYCD, IV, 362–364.

threatened to have serious consequences for relations with the entire confederacy, they felt, as soon as the Indians learned of them. Furthermore, settlers who might establish themselves on these lands and on Van Rensselaer's tract at Scaticook would threaten the city's trade monopoly in the same way that the residents of Schenectady menaced it. As long as Fletcher remained in office, these complaints were hardly expressed, much less acted upon. But with Bellomont's arrival the recorder and common council petitioned him to void the Mohawk River grant, and at the same time they took steps to purchase Van Rensselaer's tract for the city. Before Bellomont could hear arguments on the Albany petition, Schuyler and Wessels resigned their shares in the Mohawk grant, claiming that their only purpose in acquiring it had been to hold the lands in trust for the Indians. When the hearing was held at New York soon afterward, the remaining grantees failed to appear. Bellomont nevertheless took testimony from the Albanians and from two Mohawk converts that they had brought along. These Indians, who claimed that Dellius had duped them into signing the deed, joined in calling for the revocation of this grant as well as Bayard's purchase at Schoharie.[8] When Bellomont went to Albany in July, the Mohawk repeated their plea and complained that Dellius had abused them for appealing against the grant. Bellomont then confronted Dellius with the evidence against him and found the minister's defense unimpressive. Moreover, his "proud and insolent" attitude, together with the sachems' chilly demeanor at the beginning of the conference, convinced the governor that the five patentees had been guilty of fraud and backstairs intrigue. Schuyler and Wessels had partially redeemed themselves by their "frank and genteel" renunciation, however, and although they remained under suspicion, they continued to perform important Indian assignments. Dellius was singled out as the major offender, and his functions at Albany were considerably curtailed. Bellomont promised the Indians to try to have the grant revoked and urged them in any future difficulty to apply to Schuyler and Livingston.

Robert Livingston was now restored to favor, but the arguments against his full pretensions, especially the Indian secretaryship at

[8] Munsell, *Annals of Albany,* III, 30–36; *NYCD,* IV, 330, 345–346; *CSP, 1697–1698,* no. 859.II–IV, VI–VII; *Acts of the Privy Council of England, Colonial Series, 1613–1783* (London, 1908–1912), VI, 64.

£100 per year, were so strong that Bellomont refused on his own authority to reverse Fletcher's action suspending him. Livingston's case was left hanging for the remainder of Bellomont's term. He resumed his former duties at Albany and even joined Schuyler on the provincial council, but his financial arrears continued to pile up, to his intense discomfiture. Before leaving Albany, the governor removed Fletcher's commissioners for Indian affairs and returned this function to the city magistrates as a whole, although that body included Schuyler and Wessels, two of the four commissioners involved. Henceforth the magistrates served in this capacity by virtue of a special commission from the governor, a change from the less formal arrangement which had prevailed before 1696.[9]

Bellomont lost little time in attacking the Mohawk land grant. In fact, several of Fletcher's larger grants seemed to him so fraught with evil that he determined to strike at them simultaneously. The home government sanctioned this move, calling upon Fletcher to account for his actions, and in the spring of 1699 Bellomont urged the assembly to nullify the grants by legislative action. The lower house, now packed with Leislerians who regarded this as a means of striking back at their enemies, was quite agreeable. The council was divided, however. Composed of the colony's leading grandees, some of them carry-overs from Fletcher's administration, it disapproved of such action in principle. Moreover, several members correctly sensed the governor's intention to put their own estates to the test if the present motion should carry. The bill passed, but only by the narrowest of margins, Bellomont casting a vote himself to break a tie. The grants thus revoked included all of those previously mentioned except Van Rensselaer's tract at Scaticook, which he had sold to the City of Albany. The lower house, furthermore, had insisted upon a provision suspending Dellius from all his ministerial functions at Albany.[10] The domine soon found it expedient to depart for Europe, where he made sure that both the classis of Amsterdam and the bishop of London were acquainted with his side of the controversy.

The vacating act of 1699 naturally became one of the bitterest

---

[9] *NYCD*, IV, 331–332, 362–366, 716, 782–784, 869, 911; *Wraxall's Abridgement*, 29–30; *CSP, 1697–1698*, no. 822.I–III; *1700*, no. 780; *1701*, nos. 114, 431.III.

[10] Munsell, *Annals of Albany*, III, 55–56; *NYCD*, IV, 363–367, 391–398, 411, 425, 447–448, 462, 472–473, 479, 484, 510, 528–529, 535, 622; *Assembly Journal*, I, 97, 101–104; *Colonial Laws*, I, 412–417.

partisan issues in the province, and a later assembly eventually repealed it. Although the crown had approved Bellomont's policy in advance, it neglected to pass on the act specifically until 1708, when it was finally confirmed and the repealer disallowed. The act of 1699 vested title to the lands in the crown instead of returning them to the Indians. Technically, according to English law, uncivilized Indians never had legal title to their lands, and it would have been difficult to convey these tracts to the natives formally. Little or no effort was made to protect the Mohawk rights of possession, however. The future disposition of the lands was up to the governor—a fact which some of his enemies were quick to point out. After the act had been passed, Bellomont assured the Mohawk that they now possessed their lands as fully as if the contested deed had never been written; yet three months later he proposed to the Board of Trade that these lands be distributed among the officers and soldiers at Albany as a means of preventing desertion and furthering frontier expansion. Nothing came of the plan, and frontier expansion in this vicinity was still several years in the future, but the Mohawk owed no thanks to Bellomont. In 1700 his agents secretly persuaded them to give up all the timber rights on their lands as part of a program of producing naval stores for the king.[11] Under his aegis, therefore, the process of encroachment upon the first of the Iroquois tribes got under way.

The Indians had neglected to inform Bellomont in their conference of July 1698 that they had already sent messengers to Canada requesting an exchange of prisoners. In August they learned that Frontenac would not only be delighted to exchange prisoners, but that he had threatened to attack them if they failed to do so. Resolving upon a general council, the sachems sent word of their transactions to Bellomont with an invitation to send an English delegate. Dirck Wessels now returned to Onondaga with instructions to hold the Indians firm to the promises made at Albany and to assure them once more of English protection. At the same time Bellomont sent Lieutenant Governor John Nanfan to Albany with a company of soldiers. He had orders to march to the Indians' relief with all the forces at his disposal should they request it. The governor also sent a blunt warning to Frontenac that he was prepared to defend the Five Nations against any French attack. Captain John Schuyler, who carried this message, was to report back

[11] *NYCD,* IV, 553, 565–566, 622; *CSP, 1700,* no. 953 ff.; *1701,* no. 3, 38 ff.

immediately if he found that the French were preparing an invasion.[12]

Reaching Canada, Schuyler could discover no such preparations, and after more futile debate with Frontenac he returned home. On the way back he stopped long enough to talk with some of the Praying Indians. They seemed willing to return to New York, he reported, if Bellomont could supply them with missionaries. Wessels met only partial success at Onondaga, where the Indians decided to return their prisoners to Canada via Albany. From there they hoped to proceed with English agents to conclude a joint agreement with the French. (The Mohawk, firmly attached to Albany, refused to be a party to any of these decisions, and they remained aloof from their confederates' ensuing actions.) When the sachems of the four upper nations appeared at Albany in October with a few of their prisoners in tow, the magistrates had orders from New York to discourage their proceedings as strongly as possible. John Schuyler had acquired the impression in Canada that Frontenac might return his Iroquois prisoners even if they failed to negotiate with him. Nanfan now used this idea, together with the usual promise of protection, to dissuade the sachems from their projected trip to Canada. After his speech, in which he also urged them to discontinue all hostilities with the French, they obediently returned home, leaving their captives at Albany for safe-keeping.[13]

This latest submission to English direction was a tribute to Iroquois loyalty and to the power of Albany diplomacy; furthermore, it illustrated an overestimation by the Indians of the value of the English alliance. The fear of offending Corlaer and his government exercised a constant curbing effect on most of their proceedings with the French. Had they asserted their independence, however, and established peace with the French, the few solid benefits that they received from the Albany alliance could hardly have been denied them. The English would still have strained every resource to keep them from going over to the French altogether. Instead of pursuing an independent course openly, the sachems did so secretly; then they subverted their own efforts by informing the English and allowing the latter to talk them into submission for a brief period, after which the

[12] *CSP, 1697–1698*, no. 749; Toppan and Goodrick, *Edward Randolph*, VII, 541; *NYCD*, IV, 369–372.
[13] *NYCD*, IV, 373–374, 404–409; *CSP, 1697–1698*, nos. 837, 877.

process would start over again. Far from pursuing a complicated game of balancing the English and the French against each other, as the latter often suspected, the sachems' policy at this time was still relatively simple. The difficulty was that they lacked either the decision or the power to follow it consistently. Anglo-Iroquois diplomacy continued for several years, therefore, to be inconclusive and frustrating for both parties. The death of Frontenac late in 1698 had little effect on this situation since Callières, his successor, continued his policies.

Another diplomatic round took place early in 1699, when the three central tribes called a league council at Onondaga to consider the results of another mission that they had sent to Canada. This action resulted in a great deal of coming and going between New York, Albany, and Onondaga, but the Indians ended by terminating their Canadian talks and asking for a conference with Bellomont. The governor had departed for Boston, and Nanfan, now in New York, entrusted the negotiations to the Albany magistrates. In response to orders from France, Callières had gradually released his Iroquois captives, and by the time that the sachems reached Albany in June 1699, they had all been freed. No longer having any pressing reason for consulting with the French, the Indians once more hearkened to the English and permitted their own captives at Albany to be released.[14]

The Indians soon found that the exchange of prisoners did not automatically bring peace. The French had orders from home to abstain from hostilities for the time being, but their western allies did not feel similarly bound. In September, Ottawa war parties were reported to have inflicted a number of casualties in the Seneca country. Instead of sending to Canada to discover the cause of these raids, the Iroquois pleased Albany by asking the English to procure redress for them. Bellomont refused to intercede with the French, however, because he feared that such action would constitute recognition of French sovereignty over the Ottawa.[15]

There was little, in fact, that the English could or would do on behalf of the Iroquois as long as the confederacy's political status remained in debate between England and France. The Treaty of Ryswick

[14] *NYCD*, IV, 487, 491–500, 558–565, 567–574; *Journal of the Legislative Council*, I, 124–126; *Assembly Journal*, I, 99–101.
[15] *NYCD*, IV, 590, 596–598.

had reserved for later negotiation such outstanding disputes between the two crowns as the status of Hudson Bay, sovereignty over the Iroquois, and the boundaries of Acadia. Commissioners appointed for this purpose held sessions during 1699, and in the following year their work was continued through normal diplomatic channels. These discussions produced no solution of the Iroquois problem, and until their conclusion neither governor was to engage in hostilities or to debate the matter unduly in America.[16]

In the spring of 1700 Bellomont, still in Boston, was alarmed by rumors that all the northern Indians were plotting a general insurrection against the English. Although these reports originated in New England, where they eventually proved to be unfounded, he at once suspected that the Iroquois were involved in the conspiracy and that the safety of all the northern provinces was in jeopardy. He was led all the more to this conclusion by his consciousness of Iroquois dissatisfaction. Not only were they eager to placate the French by concluding a firm peace in Canada—a course which the French continued to urge upon them—but Bellomont recognized all too well his own inability to protect them in case the French tried to enforce their demands. Worst of all, he feared that recent experience under Fletcher as well as the obvious weakness of the New York frontier would make the Indians as aware of this incapacity as he. If they had not already succumbed to the French, therefore, he feared such action was only a matter of time; the results for the English colonies, he felt, would be incalculable.[17]

The realization of English and Iroquois weakness was not new to Bellomont. He had hardly arrived in New York before he was sending home lengthy and urgent letters pleading for the resources that he needed to strengthen the frontiers against future attack. His first concern was to replace the rotting stockaded forts at Albany and Schenectady, which he compared to cattle pounds, with more permanent buildings of stone. These projects remained high on his priority list, but by April 1699 he was suggesting forts in the Iroquois country as well, one in the Mohawk country and another at Onondaga. Such posts would not only protect the Indians militarily but would also be permanent centers of English influence among the Five Nations. At

---

[16] *Ibid.*, 453, 475–478, 580, 608; IX, 697–699; *CSP, 1699*, no. 130.
[17] *NYCD*, IV, 606–609, 637–638.

Onondaga he envisioned a sod and stockade structure with a garrison of a hundred men which he hoped would provide the nucleus of a substantial English settlement. To the same end he revived the earlier efforts to secure English missionaries for the Five Nations—persons who would thwart both the political and religious designs of the Jesuits and stop the flow of Iroquois to Canada.[18] This program would have gone far to make the Iroquois English wards in fact as well as name. To implement it, however, the governor had not only to obtain the necessary resources in England or America, but to persuade the Iroquois themselves that it was in their best interest. As so often before, convincing the Iroquois was perhaps the lesser obstacle.

As early as May 1698 the Christian Mohawk had asked Bellomont for another minister, who would live with them in their own country. Knowing that the Jesuits were on the point of resuming their Iroquois missions unless he could stop them, Bellomont forwarded the request to England with the suggestion that necessary funds might be available from the Society for the Propagation of the Gospel, which New York had approached for the same purpose several years before. That organization informed the Board of Trade, however, that its money was earmarked for New England alone.[19] Nevertheless Bellomont and his subordinates fell into Dongan's error of promising the Iroquois missionaries when they had none to provide, because that seemed the most effective method of stemming another Jesuit influx. In May 1699, when the sachems as a whole were first consulted about missionaries and forts in their country, they were evasive. Regarding missionaries they promised only to consider the matter when "all things are well and settled." The need for forts, they said, had passed when the war ended, but they would be welcomed in case of another conflict. A month later, however, when all their captives had been released by the French, they showed definite interest in both propositions.[20]

As soon as Bellomont heard of the reported insurrection early in 1700, he ordered Schuyler, Livingston, and former Mayor Hendrick Hansen of Albany to go to Onondaga. There they were to sound out

---

[18] *Ibid.*, 504–505, 513, 609–610; *CSP, 1699*, no. 1011.

[19] *NYCD*, IV, 333–334, 346–347, 455; *CSP, 1697–1698*, no. 958. This oranization, originally chartered by Parliament in 1649 and reorganized after the Stuart Restoration, should not be confused with the Anglican group of similar name formed in 1701, which subsequently sponsored Iroquois missions.

[20] *NYCD*, IV, 500, 564–565, 573.

the Indians and invite them to a conference in August. When the emissaries reached the Iroquois country in April, they found the natives in a state of demoralization. They knew nothing of a plot to extirpate the English; on the contrary, many of them had fallen victim to French-inspired rumors that the English were planning a similar fate for them. The tribes were more deeply torn than ever between those who urged compliance with the French and those who continued to stand firm with Corlaer. The Mohawk, nearly two-thirds of whom according to Livingston had already fled to Canada, were as usual the most steadfast in the English interest. Two sachems of that tribe agreed to become Christians themselves if missionaries should come to their country, and they promised to set aside land for a minister's support. They did not comment on a fort in their country because the English themselves had dropped this project in favor of concentrating on the one at Onondaga. The other nations failed to commit themselves on either point, but the envoys did much to quiet their fears of the English, if not of the French and their Indian allies.[21]

On returning to Albany, Livingston drew up a report for the governor setting forth his own appraisal of the Indians' situation and recommending a future course of action.

I do find these Indians [he said] the same [as] I always tooke them to be, a subtle, designing people, and that there is nothing has the ascendant over them but fear and interest. The French they fear, having felt the smart of their blows often. Us they love because of the good that [they] daily receive frome us. They owne there is a God and as [sic] Devil. God is a good man they say, and lives above, Him they love because He never do's them any harm. The Devil they fear and are forc'd to bribe by offerings &c that he do them no harme. I take it that they compare the French to ye latter, and the English to the former.

Like Bellomont, Livingston attributed Iroquois unsteadiness first to their fear of the French and the inability of the English to protect them and second to the failure to send English missionaries among them. In order to meet these problems he urged that the Mohawk, Oneida, and Onondaga be persuaded to move their villages closer to Albany. All the tribes would welcome ministers, whose maintenance would be comparatively easy, the Indians providing them with neces-

[21] *CSP, 1700*, no. 345.XI–XIII; *NYCD*, IV, 647, 653–661.

sary supplies and services. "I do humbly offer," he continued, "that it is morally impossible to secure the 5 nations to the English interest any longer, without building Forts and securing the passes that lead to their Castles." However, he advised against a fort at the Onondaga village. That location, near the present site of Syracuse, was difficult of access for transporting supplies, yet relatively easy for the French to reach. Furthermore, it would defend only the Onondaga, and the other tribes would demand similar protection; a better site would be farther north, at the junction of the Seneca and Oswego Rivers, a few miles west of Lake Oneida. That spot was reasonably accessible by water from Albany; it would block a French thrust at any of the Five Nations by way of the Oswego River; and it lay near the rapids of that river, which the French would have to circumvent on foot. Livingston also recommended a more vigorous western policy. His suggestions, in fact, were similar to those which Bellomont, Governor Nicholson of Virginia, and even the Board of Trade in England had been urging upon one another for some time. Livingston's proposals included the recruitment of a corps of bushlopers like the Canadian *coureurs de bois* to extend English influence to the remoter tribes, the conclusion of peace between the Iroquois and these western Indians, and the construction of an English fort and trading post at Detroit. He also urged the construction of a fort and the establishment of a minister at the Scaticook village northeast of Albany, which might then serve as a point of attraction for more Indians from New England. "How contemptible soever they seem to be," he said, these unfortunate refugees had done useful service for New York in the recent war, and they might be expected to do the same in the future, particularly if augmented by further recruits.[22]

Bellomont promptly forwarded the Albanians' reports to England, and he subsequently fitted nearly all of Livingston's suggestions into his own policy. That the whole expense of retaining the Iroquois' allegiance should fall on New York when it was of utmost concern to all the colonies, he wrote the Board of Trade, was not only grossly unfair but an impossible burden for that province to carry. "I believe since my coming to the Government of New Yorke it has cost little less than 2000£, the presents to the Indians and the Messages to them, and to Canada on their behalf; and as the French apply them-

[22] *NYCD*, IV, 648–652.

selves to court them from us, our caresses must increase[;] . . . bare complements will not do with them, they must be furnished with that which is substantial and costly." He asked, therefore, that the other colonies again be required to contribute to New York's defenses and that 650 royal troops be sent to bring the present depleted garrisons up to a total of eight hundred. Such troops, he believed, might be made largely self-sufficient by putting them to work producing tar and other naval stores in the surrounding forests.[23] These proposals were constantly repeated and enlarged upon in the governor's subsequent letters home. Taken collectively, they comprised the most articulate and comprehensive frontier policy devised in New York since Dongan's day.

Colonial officials in America were always the victims of slow communication and transportation. Unknown to the New York authorities, the home government was now taking steps to answer their pleas for help; meanwhile it seemed to them as if the skein of Indian affairs were unraveling before their eyes while the government in England did nothing. In June 1700 the Albany interpreter Lawrence Claessen failed in an attempt to prevent Iroquois peace envoys from going to Canada. At the same time Iroquois negotiations with some of the Ottawa bands broke down, and the Seneca, complaining of the losses that they suffered from enemy forays, again demanded English action to stop them.[24] Actually the situation was both better and worse than the English imagined. Early in July, Onondaga and Seneca deputies exchanged pledges of peace with Callières at Montreal. They returned home in company with several Frenchmen who were sent to facilitate matters and bring the last prisoners back to Canada. Most of the remaining prisoners had been adopted into Iroquois families, and in many cases they were as reluctant to leave as the families were to let them depart. A few agreed to go, however, and in August they returned to Canada with the Frenchmen and an Iroquois peace delegation. At Montreal the Iroquois as well as the tribes in alliance with the French gave firmer pledges to restore all prisoners as a prerequisite to a lasting peace. Callières thereupon declared a truce and formally buried the hatchet. A grand conference was arranged for August 1701, by which time it was hoped that all captives could be rounded

[23] *Ibid.*, 644–646.
[24] *LIR*, 176–179; *NYCD*, IV, 684–685, 687–691, 693–695.

up and restored and the present agreement would be solemnly ratified by all parties. Should this plan succeed, it would constitute a signal triumph of French diplomacy and a setback to English hegemony over the Five Nations. But among Indians, who thought in terms of vengeance and atonement, a peace involving so many tribes with such long and bitter memories was a delicate matter to achieve. Furthermore, the English faction among the Iroquois kept Albany informed of most of these transactions, and the English continued their efforts to frustrate them.

Bellomont returned to New York in July 1700 in order to meet the colonial assembly before going to Albany for his conference with the Five Nations. He still had received no word that his appeals had been heeded in England and therefore called upon the legislature itself to appropriate money for the fort at Onondaga. This project, he thought, would require no more than £1,500. The representatives dragged their feet, however, pointing to the great distance involved and the cost of maintaining as well as constructing a fort there. Under considerable pressure they passed a bill to raise £1,000 through additional customs duties, stipulating that the house itself should retain control of the collection and disbursement of these funds. The governor and council were not very happy with this measure, but as it was the only bill that they were apt to get, they reluctantly approved it. Before proroguing the assembly, Bellomont signed another act requiring priests and Jesuits who had been among the Indians to depart the province by November 1.[25]

The governor had already received word that Frenchmen were in the Iroquois country and that Albany had sent again to frustrate their negotiations. This mission was no more successful than the previous ones, and Bellomont, who had to wait two weeks at Albany for the sachems' arrival, was convinced that the Iroquois were "entirely lost to us." He found, moreover, that his Onondaga project was questioned almost as much at Albany as in the colonial assembly. As he waited for the Indians, a number of local residents presented him with an address calling first for a stone fort with a proper garrison at Albany itself. If adequate safeguards were not taken for the city's protection, they threatened to abandon the place altogether should

[25] *Journal of the Legislative Council,* I, 144–149; *CSP, 1700,* nos. 687, 703; *NYCD,* IV, 712–713; *Colonial Laws,* I, 428–430, 432–434.

war break out again. Apart from strategic and financial considerations the objecters may well have feared that a fort at Onondaga would also become a trading post. Bellomont had set his heart on the Onondaga fort and regarded this criticism as frivolous and unwarranted. The whole issue, he reported in forwarding the address to England, had become entangled in political factionalism, with the Leislerians favoring the fort and the opposition against it. Neither Livingston nor Schuyler had signed the address, although a number of their relatives had done so in company with other prominent citizens. Nevertheless Bellomont later went so far as to accuse Livingston of having penned it himself, probably with Schuyler's backing.[26]

While waiting for the Indians, Bellomont also received an account of the Praying Iroquois in Canada from David Schuyler, who had just returned from Montreal. These Indians, Schuyler reported, had increased from 80 to 350 fighting men since the war, and more were arriving there all the time. There seemed to be no other reason for this exodus than "the ardent desire of the Indians of the Five Nations to be instructed in the Christian Faith; the want of Ministers to instruct them therein [at their own villages] being the apparent cause of their every day going over more and more to the French." Without such ministers, he said, "it will be absolutely impossible to keep the . . . Indians firm and steady to the Covenant Chain" with England.[27] Schuyler's appraisal reinforced the testimony of several of the tribesmen themselves, who had come to trade at Albany a little earlier. At that time the magistrates tried to persuade them to return by holding out the prospect of Protestant missionaries. The native spokesman replied that such persons should have been sent to the Iroquois sooner, in which case he doubted if any of them would have left their homes. "All the while I was here before I went to Canada I never heard any thing talked of religion or the least mention made of converting us to the Xtian faith, and we shall be glad to hear if at last you are so piously inclined [as] to . . . instruct your Indians in the Xtian Religion. I will not say but it may induce some to return to their native country." As it was, he concluded, "I am solely beholden to the French of Canada for the light I have rece[ive]d."[28]

Bellomont had hoped to recruit some missionaries in Boston after

---

[26] *CSP, 1700,* no. 668; *LIR,* 179–180; *NYCD,* IV, 716, 752–755, 783.
[27] *NYCD,* IV, 747–748. [28] *Ibid.,* 692–693.

the society in England had rebuffed his efforts. This attempt too had proved unsuccessful although the governor himself was at least partly to blame. He turned up his nose at Harvard-educated clergymen in favor of more orthodox divines, preferably of the Church of England. Such persons were few and far between in New England, and consequently his offer of an annual salary of £100 went begging. Returning to New York, he found the same situation; no one who in his estimation was qualified to perform this service was willing to live among the Indians. Bellomont renewed his appeals to England, asking for five sober young Anglican ministers, capable of learning the Indian language and willing to serve for £100 a year. If the Society for the Propagation of the Gospel would pay four-fifths of this sum, he promised to make up the rest out of the provincial revenue. After his previous disappointments Bellomont was gratified to find at Albany that Domine John Lydius was continuing Dellius' practice of inviting Indians to his house for daily prayer and singing. After attending one of these meetings, Bellomont ordered that Lydius be furnished an interpreter to help in the work.[29] The only other bright spot was the finding of a second Dutch minister, Bernardus Freeman, who was willing to devote part of his time to Indian work. Bellomont accordingly installed Freeman at Schenectady for this purpose.

When the Indians finally arrived at Albany, they stayed for more than a week. Bellomont described the ensuing conference as "the greatest fatigue I ever underwent in my whole life. I was shut up in a close chamber with 50 Sachems, who besides the stink of bear's grease with which they plentifully dawb'd themselves, were continually either smoking tobacco or drinking drams of rum." The number of sachems present was apparently unprecedented, and as they were accompanied by over two hundred women and children, the town's food supply was stretched to the limit. The sachems fully agreed with Bellomont's initial castigation of the Jesuits, but they refused to accept his offer of a hundred pieces of eight for each one that they brought to Albany. Instead they promised to send all French priests back to Canada if they attempted to resume their missionary work. The sachems were also willing to accept a Protestant missionary at Onondaga in addition to one stationed at Albany, but they were ob-

[29] *Ibid.*, 521, 690; *CSP, 1699*, no. 1011; Corwin, *Ecclesiastical Records of New York*, II, 1373–1374.

viously reluctant to see a series of missions dotting their countryside. As usual Bellomont voiced much greater optimism than he could actually have felt concerning the arrival of missionaries from England. In the meantime he promised the services of Lydius and Freeman, both of whom would take pains to learn their language. He assured the Indians that as soon as the missionaries arrived they would see "the vast difference" between Protestantism and "that which the Jesuits corruptly call the Christian Religion." He hoped that this knowledge would persuade them to recall the Praying Iroquois to their true homes and allegiance. Bellomont told the sachems that he would soon try to get the Bible translated into Iroquois and to have some of their children taught to read. Thus they would "have the comfort and edification of God's Word, which I am sure will be hugely pleasing to you when your children are able to read it to you." To this end he asked that two or three sachems' sons from each nation be sent to school at New York, where he would see that they learned to read and write both English and their own language. After three or four years they would be replaced by another group of boys, so that the Indians would always have persons among them who understood English. This plan might have been extremely useful to both peoples, but the sachems virtually ignored it. Their reply, that the women had sole custody of minor children, was true, but it was hardly a definitive answer to the proposal.

Moving to a subject about which he was much more concerned, Bellomont said that ministers were unwilling to serve as far away as Onondaga without adequate protection. For this reason he was sending an engineer to make plans for the fort there which he had previously mentioned. Bellomont called upon the sachems to agree with this officer regarding the proper location and to provide men to help in the construction. On this point too the sachems were not very communicative at first, but after some delay they agreed to the fort in principle and promised their co-operation in building it. Bellomont knew as well as they that continued warfare with the more numerous western tribes was disastrous to the fur trade and, more important, to the future of the confederacy itself. Therefore he urged the sachems to try to make peace with these tribes and divert their trade to Albany. What Bellomont did not know—and the Indians did not volunteer the information—was that the most fruitful negotiations of this sort in years were then taking place under French auspices and with the sachems' approbation. On this occasion the chiefs dutifully promised to continue their quest for peace, while expressing reluctance to offend the French until it was done. The governor accepted this reply, distributed his presents, and sent the Indians home, confident that he had regained their allegiance and foiled the French once more.[30]

Soon afterward Bellomont sent the engineer, Colonel Wolfgang Romer, together with Hendrick Hansen and Mayor Peter van Brugh of Albany, to select a site for the fort. Now the Indians were much less co-operative. Although they permitted the agents to explore the countryside, they tried to delay their proceedings in a number of ways and discouraged any further talk about the fort until the next spring. The sachems also persuaded an English trading party, which Bellomont had sent out, to turn back rather than proceed to the Ottawa country. In both cases the reasons given were flimsy; perhaps the Indians were afraid that haste in either venture might disrupt the pending treaty in Canada. Bellomont was chagrined beyond measure. To him the Indian and frontier problems were the main reason for his being in America, and his greatest ambition was to push his policies to a successful conclusion. Unaware of the Iroquois activities in Canada, he blamed his lack of success on those who had ventured to disagree with his policies or those whom he merely suspected of opposing them. He already believed that "Collonel Schuyler and his party" at Albany were guilty of currying favor with the Indians behind his back. The protest against the fort at Onondaga, which rightly or wrongly he associated with these men, had only confirmed that suspicion. This fresh delay he therefore attributed to the same source, and he wished heartily that he might dispense with their services by staying at Albany himself to supervise Indian affairs.[31] Although the assembly relented in October by appropriating a total of £1,500 for the fort, the approaching winter now made it impossible to pursue the project until spring. The Indians had won their point.

In renewing his appeal for missionaries after returning from Albany, Bellomont scaled down his request to two men for the present. They should be young, he told the Board of Trade, as they could never learn the Indian language otherwise, and they "must be men of sober and exemplary lives and good scholars, or they will not be fit to in-

[30] *NYCD*, IV, 714, 727–746. [31] *Ibid.*, 784, 798–807.

struct the Indians and encounter the Jesuits in point of argument."
Both ministers he proposed to settle at the Onondaga fort with a
salary of £150 apiece, at the same time dividing another £70 between
the two Dutch ministers at Albany and Schenectady. The Society for
the Propagation of the Gospel now offered to provide £80 apiece for
five missionaries for a period of three years, provided they be taken
from Harvard College. The last requirement was still odious to Bellomont, and he was dissatisfied with the time limitation. Nevertheless
he now was asking for less money and fewer men than they had offered, and the prospects of securing ministers seemed to be brighter
than ever before.[32]

The wheels of English government turned slowly in the seventeenth
and eighteenth centuries, and this was especially true with regard to
colonial affairs. Red tape and inefficiency, added to an ocean crossing
of one to four months, delayed effective action at the least and sometimes made it altogether impossible. The Board of Trade, as the
regular recipient of Bellomont's lengthy letters, was tolerably well informed of affairs in New York; but the same could not always be said
for the Board of Ordnance, the War, Admiralty, and Treasury offices,
Parliament, or the king and his principal secretaries, all of whom exercised varying degrees of control over the disbursement of goods
and services for the colonies. Bellomont had often mentioned the need
for more and better fortifications, troops, missionaries, and supplies,
but it was not until he had warned of a possible Indian uprising in
February 1700 that the home government took effective action on
most of these subjects. When it received this information in April, the
Board of Trade promptly requested royal appropriations of £500 for
the Onondaga fort and £800 for presents to the Five Nations and
asked for additional men for the Albany garrison. The king's approval
was forthcoming by the end of the month, but lack of co-operation
from the Ordnance officials delayed the shipment of these items and
men until the end of June.[33]

The Board of Trade was also in communication with the archbishop
of Canterbury, the bishop of London, and others in an effort to recruit
men and money for Iroquois missions. The bishop of London, whose

[32] *Ibid.*, 717, 766–767.
[33] *Ibid.*, 606–610, 639–642, 666; *CSP, 1700*, nos. 381, 387–388, 394, 531–532,
556, 559, 570, 579; *Calendar of Treasury Books*, XV, 74, 340–341, 385.

diocese embraced all the American colonies, regretted that Bellomont had seen fit to "banish" Dellius when the latter fell under his displeasure.[34] The controversial minister, now in Holland, was one of the first men to be approached by the Society for the Propagation of the Gospel. He refused their offer, however, although he promised his co-operation in finding other "Apostles" for the Five Nations. After Domine Freeman had similarly declined, the authorities turned to the Church of England, as Bellomont had requested in the first place.

Meanwhile Freeman continued his work at Schenectady and eventually became proficient in the Mohawk language. He translated the English Book of Common Prayer and parts of both Testaments into Mohawk and by January 1701 could report that ten out of a total of thirty-six Mohawk converts had been won over through his efforts. In that year the province granted him a salary of £60, plus £15 for expenses and the services of the official interpreter, Lawrence Claessen. The Mohawk at the same time requested that a full-sized church be built at their nearest village to replace the tiny bark chapel in which their services had hitherto been conducted.[35] Bellomont did not live to see it, but the Mohawk mission was becoming a reality, and the first Anglican minister arrived to take charge of it in 1704.

The ship carrying men, money, and presents from England did not reach New York until September 17, 1700, after Bellomont had already held his conference with the Indians. Instead of being grateful for this answer to his appeals, the governor immediately wrote back to complain that he lacked orders to refortify Albany and Schenectady. To no purpose had he advanced money for necessary equipment, he lamented, and he predicted that England was on the point of losing her American empire through ill-advised parsimony. The Board of Trade had already submitted another lengthy memorial to the king asking for further aid to New York, and Bellomont's latest communication evoked more anger than sympathy. The board replied in December that the Albany and Schenectady forts were indeed more important than that at Onondaga, as the Albanians had told him, and by implication at least it rebuked him for failing to use the funds at

[34] *CSP, 1700,* nos. 313, 328, 875; *NYCD,* IV, 707, 769–770, 774.

[35] David Humphreys, *An Historical Account of the Incorporated Society for the Propagation of the Gospel in Foreign Parts* (London, 1730), 285–287; Corwin, "Efforts of the Dutch-American Colonial Pastors for the Conversion of the Indians," 243; *NYCD,* IV, 774, 835, 906; *Colonial Laws,* I, 469–470.

his disposal where they were most needed. It repeated earlier advice to raise as much additional money as he could in America and at least to begin the work that he had talked so much about; meanwhile it continued its own efforts to reinforce him.[36] In response to the board's recommendations the king early in 1701 allowed Bellomont an additional £2,000 for refortifying Albany and Schenectady. He also revived the requisition system by calling upon the other colonies for money payments totaling £3,000 and by assigning them quotas of men in the event that New York should again be attacked.[37]

The quotas of 1701 were no more effective than the earlier ones, and for the same reasons. Furthermore, the money from England was largely diverted from its original purpose, and the fort at Onondaga was never built. It is impossible to blame any single individual or group for these failures. The home government was far more preoccupied with the Spanish-succession question which threatened to upset the European balance of power, and America remained very much at the edge of things. Bellomont must also share responsibility for not starting the fortifications on his own authority with the resources available to him in New York. The forts at Albany and Schenectady had legitimate priority over that at Onondaga, especially in view of the Indians' ambivalent attitude toward it, and these posts could have been rebuilt with much less effort and controversy than was expended on the Onondaga project.

Bellomont would probably have started the work at Albany and Schenectady in 1701 after hearing from the king and the Board of Trade, but death suddenly intervened on March 5. Lieutenant Governor Nanfan was on a leave of absence in the West Indies, and until his return in May the council was left in charge. This body, which Bellomont had more or less dominated for the past three years, immediately broke into Leislerian and anti-Leislerian factions. Both parties remained in essential agreement with Bellomont's Indian policies, however, save for the priority of the Onondaga fort. In this field the only immediate effect of Bellomont's death was the postponement of a scheduled conference with the Iroquois and of further steps toward fortification until the lieutenant governor's arrival.[38]

---

[36] *NYCD*, IV, 700–709, 717–718, 768, 818–820, 832.

[37] *CSP, 1700*, no. 1054; *1701*, nos. 16–23; *NYCD*, IV, 838–839, 842.

[38] *CSP, 1701*, nos. 351, 389.XI–XII; *NYCD*, IV, 867.

Livingston took this opportunity to send a lengthy memorial on Indian affairs to the Board of Trade. This statement was reminiscent of his and Bellomont's previous communications, but he now felt free to oppose the Onondaga fort more openly. The £2,000 so far allocated for its construction would hardly pay for the transportation of wheelbarrows there, he said. The project was entirely impractical, and the Indians had signified their disapproval of it by failing to cooperate with Colonel Romer. Needless to say, these arguments were considerably exaggerated. Livingston offered a program of his own which was, if anything, less likely to win approval in either England or America. He called for a consolidation of the mainland colonies into three large provinces and an annual appropriation of £15,000 for a series of forts and settlements at unspecified points in the Iroquois country to protect them against further French attack. On the other hand, his proposals for fortifications at Albany and Schenectady and for missionaries among the Iroquois were by now quite standard.[39]

Of the long succession of New York governors only three—Dongan, Bellomont, and William Burnet in the 1720's—sought actively to establish economic and political ties with the western Indians. As Arthur H. Buffinton has pointed out, Robert Livingston provided a connecting link between these governors, supporting and encouraging their expansionist policies over a period of forty years.[40] Although Bellomont may have gotten some of his ideas from Governor Francis Nicholson of Virginia, he unquestionably adopted many suggestions from Livingston. Bellomont was neither as energetic as Dongan nor as successful as Burnet in achieving an important position in the west, but his attempts in this direction formed a significant part of his over-all Indian policy.

The first evidence of Bellomont's interest in the west occurred in November 1698, when he wrote Nicholson encouraging the southern colonies to forestall the French by establishing a trade with the tribes behind them. Nicholson had already reported French intentions of settling the lower Mississippi region and asked the crown to encourage trade with the tribes in that direction. Bellomont's immediate concern was not so much with the French on the lower Mississippi as with the Ottawa, Miami, and other tribes in the western Great Lakes region

[39] *NYCD*, IV, 870–879.
[40] "The Policy of Albany and English Westward Expansion," 352 ff.

Iroquois Quest for Neutrality

—the perennial objects of New York and Iroquois attention. He labored under the geographical misapprehension, however, that these tribes lay closer to Virginia and the Carolinas than they did to New York. He wrote the Board of Trade to this effect in the spring of 1699 and gave it as the reason for his contact with Nicholson; otherwise he would have much preferred to draw the trade of these Indians to his own province. It was for imperial advantage, therefore, that he urged the crown and the southern colonies to push this project, promising at the same time to continue his own efforts.[41]

Bellomont had already sounded out a number of people in New York, including Livingston, who submitted a memorial strongly supporting the governor's views. Livingston urged a general Indian pacification, saying that the French had constantly fomented their western allies against the Iroquois. (There was considerable truth in this charge, although the French at that time were attempting to conclude just such a peace on their own terms.) To bring this about, Livingston said that two hundred New York frontiersmen should accompany three or four hundred Iroquois, together with their Indian prisoners, and build a fort at the site of Detroit. After an exchange of prisoners with the far Indians a peace settlement should be arranged. Then the far Indians ought to ratify the agreement at Albany and see for themselves the favorable trading conditions there. By this means, he concluded, the Albany fur trade would multiply ten times in value. Livingston spoke of Albany as the mart of this new western trade, but he failed to reconcile this assumption with the existence of a fort at Detroit. A year later, however, he accepted Bellomont's idea of a fort in the Onondaga country as well as his own at Detroit and envisioned both of them as trading posts for the western Indians. The English, moreover, could never hope to attract the bulk of this trade without a corps of bushlopers comparable to the French. To this end he advocated posting a hundred youths at the Onondaga fort to train for service farther afield. Livingston had nothing but scorn for the traditional policy of the Albany traders, whom he accused of "slothfulness and negligence" in letting the French monopolize the peltry of the far Indians. Later he accused them of stifling the colony's development by forbidding the expansion of settlement beyond the town.[42]

[41] CSP, 1697–1698, no. 961; 1699, no. 77.I; NYCD, IV, 488.
[42] NYCD, IV, 500–501, 650–651, 874.

Indian Affairs in Colonial New York

None of Livingston's suggestions was acted upon. The governor preferred his own projected fort at Onondaga to one even more remotely situated at Detroit. He nevertheless continued to press for action on the part of the crown and the southern colonies and in April 1700 proposed a governors' conference on the subject. The Board of Trade gave its guarded approval to trading operations in the south, so long as they did not threaten tobacco production, and got the king to approve the suggested meeting. Accordingly, in September, Nicholson and Governor Blakiston of Maryland set out for New York, picking up William Penn and Governor Hamilton of the Jerseys on the way. Blakiston was forced to turn back because of illness, however, and Nicholson arrived in not much better condition. As a result little business was transacted, and the governors' inconclusive talks on the Indian trade were never recorded. The conference broke up shortly, and another meeting was set for the following spring.[43]

New York made little if any effort to persuade the Iroquois to conclude peace with the western tribes until some Ottawa delegates came to Onondaga for that purpose in June 1700. These Indians, like the Shawnee in 1692, were interested in settling near the Five Nations and trading at Albany. Their intended home was on the north shore of Lake Ontario, in territory which the Iroquois had won by conquest many years before. They could have settled there only by invitation of the Iroquois and in return for submitting to a satellite position under the confederacy. For the moment, at least, the Iroquois were delighted at this prospect. When they informed Albany of their negotiations, they therefore added another plea for cheap goods in order to attract the Ottawa. The magistrates immediately sent Lawrence Claessen to second the Iroquois offer and bring the envoys to town, where they could sample Albany hospitality. The Indians did not come, but Bellomont was hopeful that a substantial number of the Ottawa might be won over anyway. According to the Iroquois' computation fully sixteen bands were involved. Unfortunately the prospects of an accommodation were dimmed as some of the Ottawa bands continued to make armed forays into the Iroquois country. Bellomont pointed out to the sachems at his conference in August that continual warfare with tribes far outnumbering them was likely to

⁴³ *CSP, 1699*, no. 579.XLIV; *1700*, nos. 8, 11, 315–316, 681; *1701*, no. 49; *NYCD*, IV, 590, 632, 724.

prove suicidal. He urged them to send some of the Ottawa to confer with him, in order that he might add his voice on behalf of the removal to Lake Ontario and the establishemnt of political and trade relations. The governor was also aware that Callières had decided to crack down on the activities of the *coureurs de bois* and that these traders, defying his orders to return to Montreal, were again interested in trading at Albany. Hoping to exploit this opportunity, Bellomont asked that the path to Albany be kept open for these persons too. The Indians readily agreed to both propositions and promised to give the Frenchmen "all the encouragement from us imaginable." [44]

Bellomont's information concerning the *coureurs de bois* had come in part from one Samuel York, a New Englander who had spent ten years in captivity in Canada and the Ottawa country. His escape to Albany occurred while the governor's conference was in progress. York confirmed the Indians' reports that the Ottawa were dissatisfied with trade conditions in Canada and that they as well as the Frenchmen with them were eager to make contact with Albany. When York offered to take a few traders and Indians to the Ottawa country to make this contact, Bellomont willingly agreed, although he recognized the danger of the French intercepting them. As a matter of fact, Bellomont put more faith in this project, and in establishing the Onondaga fort as a trading center for the western tribes, than he did in Iroquois readiness to let the Ottawa pass through to Albany. This reluctance, again, was less the result of a conscious middleman policy on the part of the Iroquois than of their inveterate hostility to those tribesmen, caused partly by the fact that they were competing for the same hunting lands in Ontario and Michigan. The Iroquois "are apt to be perfidious," Bellomont said, "and 'tis much to be fear'd they will as often as they meet those Indians, rob 'em of their peltry and then knock 'em in the head, that they may tell no tales." It never came to this because the Iroquois abruptly changed their minds. When York and his followers reached Onondaga, the Indians said that a recent Huron attack upon them made it too dangerous to continue farther. York therefore returned to Albany in defeat, as did Colonel Romer's party, which was there at the same time.

Two French *coureurs* appeared in New York shortly afterward, asking permission to settle and trade at Albany and offering to bring

"*LIR*, 176–178; *NYCD*, IV, 690–691, 693–695, 714, 732, 735–737, 739–741.

twenty or thirty others with their peltry if this request were granted. The English were perhaps overly cautious about dealing with these people, fearing a French trap; for this reason apparently nothing more was done in the matter.[45] As with Bellomont's other Indian policies, there was much more talk than action about improving contacts with the Ottawa and the French renegades. His successors seldom even referred to the subject, however. Even Robert Livingston, in his lengthy memorial of May 1701, scarcely mentioned western trade and proposed no forts beyond the Mohawk country. The French, on the other hand, established themselves at Detroit in that year. What success the English had in attracting Ottawa traders during the next few years was owing less to their own initiative than to that of the Indians, who began to enjoy a period of relaxed French control.

Comparatively less important after 1697 were relations with the River Indians nearer home. The Scaticook band had not been happy with its wartime residence just outside Albany. Drunkenness appears to have increased with closer proximity to the settlements, and the Indians were unable to resist the trading goods so close at hand. They were constantly in debt to the Albany traders, who did not hesitate to sell on credit what the natives could not presently afford. In order to recover their debts some traders resorted to violence and others confiscated the natives' corn, peltry, guns, and other property. In 1698 or 1699 the band returned to Scaticook, and it required considerable persuasion to keep them from going on to northern Vermont, where there was better hunting.[46] They appear to have flourished in the next two or three years, and in 1701 the river bands from Catskill to Scaticook could report a total of two hundred fighting men. They had grown so much, in fact, that they said they could no longer fit beneath the tree of welfare at Scaticook and asked Governor Nanfan to plant a second nearby. Bellomont may have been partly responsible for the increase in numbers; certainly he regarded their augmentation as desirable. Working through Captain John Schuyler, who appears to have had influence with these bands, he sent several messages inviting the ever-troublesome eastern Indians to settle at Scaticook. Livingston suggested a permanent fort and a Protestant mission here, which presumably would serve both to attract the Indians and to tame them

[45] *NYCD*, IV, 715–717, 748–750, 768, 782–784, 796–797, 800–807, 842.
[46] *Ibid.*, 575–577; *CSP, 1697–1698*, no. 822.I; *1699*, nos. 747, 773.

when they had once arrived.[47] Neither facility was provided, however. In June 1701 French envoys returned to the Iroquois country to make sure that the last year's promises were being kept and that all French and Indian prisoners would be returned at the final peace conference in August. Hearing of their mission in advance, the English sent Captain John Bleeker and David Schuyler to make as much trouble for them as possible. The Albanians were ordered to invite the sachems to a conference with Nanfan in July and until then to keep them from negotiating with the French or receiving Jesuit missionaries. As the French and English agents confronted each other at Onondaga and demanded opposite courses of action, the Indians were sorely torn. The sachems now heard definitely that Callières was on the point of building a fort and trading house at Detroit. From the reiterated French demands that the Indians remain neutral in case of another conflict between England and France, they also suspected, correctly, that war was about to break out anew. This news gave added emphasis to their fears of French power and the question of how best to meet it. Now more than ever they dared not break off the peace negotiations in Canada; but at the same time they could not lose the friendship and possibility of protection from Corlaer. Once again they chose to straddle, but in doing so they reasserted their independence. Decannisora, the shrewd and influential speaker of the confederacy, declared that they would receive a minister from the nation which sold them goods most cheaply, and meanwhile they would send sachems to Albany and Montreal simultaneously.[48]

Nowhere does the diplomacy of the Iroquois appear to better advantage than during these summer months of 1701. At Albany, Nanfan reminded them of the danger that Fort Frontenac had proved to be and warned that a similar garrison at Detroit would cut off their hunting lands and destroy their independence. He repeated the old promises of English protection and informed them that he was about to build stone forts at Albany and Schenectady—no mention was made of Onondaga. The sachems needed no reminder of the potentialities of a French post at Detroit. The "great King of England" must be acquainted with this invasion of their hunting lands and do all in his

[47] *NYCD*, IV, 380, 652, 715, 744–745, 834, 836, 902–903.
[48] Munsell, *Annals of Albany*, IV, 132–133, 135; *CSP, 1701*, nos. 494, 513; *NYCD*, IV, 889–895.

power to prevent it, they declared. To drive this point home they took the unprecedented action of deeding their western hunting lands to the king so "that he may be our protector and defender there." The sachems had not taken this step lightly, and to ensure that it had the intended effect they insisted that Robert Livingston be delegated to carry the deed and accompanying message to the king. The lands involved were those which the Iroquois claimed to have conquered from the Huron and other tribes fifty years before, extending from Lake Erie to Lake Huron and from Irondequoit Bay in the Seneca country to the southern end of Lake Michigan. Before leaving, they promised again not to receive Jesuit missionaries and welcomed the prospect, which Nanfan continued to hold out, of English ministers in their country.[49]

The governor was delighted at this turn of events, and although it was none of his doing, his happiness was partially justified. By this apparently unsolicited act of ceding their lands the Iroquois gave additional proof that their primary allegiance was to the English and that they still hoped for English protection in case of attack from the French and their Indian allies. The chief significance of the cession was symbolic, however. The French naturally refused to recognize it, and the English were no more able to exercise control in that vast area than before the deed was executed. The Indians, moreover, had no intention of opening it to English settlement or of surrendering their hunting rights there—far from it. They merely offered the king the dubious privilege of protecting it. Nanfan and his successors had ample opportunity to discover, as had Livingston and others already, that the Five Nations still regarded themselves as an independent entity.

Simultaneously with the conference at Albany a far greater assemblage gathered in Montreal under the auspices of Onontio. More than 1,300 Indians of thirty tribes—ranging from the Chippewa and Cree, the Miami and Ottawa, the Sauk and Fox and Illinois in the west to the Algonkin and Abnaki in the east—had responded to Callières's summons to bring their Iroquois prisoners and ratify the truce concluded a year before. These tribes, it appeared had done much more than the Iroquois to round up their captives, and they were more than a little aggrieved at the lack of reciprocity. Callières was unwilling, however, to cancel the result of more than two years' labor as long as the Iroquois had made at least a token compliance with his conditions. The peace was concluded, therefore, with all due solemnity. Looking toward the early resumption of war in Europe, Callières repeated his desire that the Iroquois remain neutral in such an eventuality. Another French delegation then followed the Iroquois sachems homeward, to be met again at Onondaga by Bleeker and Schuyler from Albany. The French failed once more to obtain their prisoners, and in a further assertion of independence the sachems declared that for the time being at least they would receive neither Jesuits nor Protestant missionaries.[50]

Both Callières and Nanfan were confident that they had won diplomatic victories with the Iroquois in 1701. The real victory, however, lay with the Indians themselves, who thus had managed to satisfy both parties while establishing their own independence to the greatest extent left them. Many details of the settlement of 1701 were modified in subsequent years; but the Five Nations were long able to maintain their close relationship with the English and at the same time to observe a relative neutrality in the latters' contest with the French, the next installment of which broke out in Europe this same year.[51] The Iroquois had seen their greatest days, and their history in the eighteenth century is one of gradual decline. But their policy of noninvolvement in colonial wars helped to preserve them as a major power in North America until the Revolutionary War.

[50] *Ibid.*, 917–920; IX, 722–725; *CSP, 1701*, no. 777; Parkman, *Count Frontenac and New France*, 442–452.

[51] For a fuller discussion of this settlement see Anthony F. C. Wallace, "Origins of Iroquois Neutrality: The Grand Settlement of 1701," *Pennsylvania History*, XXIV (1957), 223–235.

Bibliography

I. Manuscript Source Materials

"Moore–N.Y." Papers. New York Public Library.

New York Colonial Manuscripts, 1638–1800. 83 vols. New York State Library, Albany.

New York Council Minutes, 1668–1783. 28 vols. New York State Library, Albany.

"New York—MSS, Letters, and Docs." New York Public Library.

Nicasius de Sille to [Hans] Bontemantel, Oct. 27, 1655. In New Netherland Papers. New York Public Library.

Winthrop Papers. Connecticut State Library, Hartford.

Winthrop Papers, Alphabetical Volumes. 11 vols. Massachusetts Historical Society, Boston.

II. Published Source Materials

Acts of the Privy Council of England, Colonial Series, 1613–1783. 6 vols. London, 1908–1912.

Archives of Maryland. 65 vols. Baltimore, 1883–.

Bartlett, John Russell, ed. *Records of the Colony of Rhode Island and Providence Plantations in New England.* 10 vols. Providence, 1856–1865.

Calendar of State Papers, Colonial Series, America and the West Indies. 42 vols. London, 1860–.

Calendar of Treasury Books, 1685–. 26 vols. London, 1904–.

Champlain, Samuel de. *The Works of Samuel de Champlain.* Ed. by H. P. Biggar. 6 vols. Toronto, 1922–1933.

Bibliography

Collection de Manuscrits Relatifs à la Nouvelle-France. 4 vols. Quebec, 1883–1885.

Colonial Laws of New York from the Year 1664 to the Revolution. 5 vols. Albany, 1894–1896.

"Colonial Records; General Entries, 1664–65." (New York State Library Bulletin, History, no. 2.) Albany, 1899.

"Colonial Records of the State, [1664–1673]," Appendix G. In New York State Historian, *Annual Report, 1896* (Albany and New York, 1897), 133–369.

Corwin, Edward T., ed. *Ecclesiastical Records of the State of New York.* 7 vols. Albany, 1901–1916.

Danckaerts, Jasper. *Journal of Jasper Danckaerts, 1679–1680.* Ed. by Bartlett Burleigh James and J. Franklin Jameson. (Original Narratives of Early American History.) New York, 1913.

Davenport, Frances Gardiner, and Charles O. Paullin, eds. *European Treaties Bearing on the History of the United States and Its Dependencies.* 4 vols. Washington, 1917–1937.

Denton, Daniel. *A Brief Description of New-York* (1670). Ed. by Victor Hugo Paltsits. New York, 1937.

"Documents Relating to the Administration of Jacob Leisler." In New-York Historical Society, *Collections, 1868,* 241–428.

"The Dutch Records of Kingston, Ulster County, New York . . . May 31, 1658—November 18, 1664." In New York State Historical Association, *Proceedings,* XI (1912).

Fernow, Berthold, ed. *The Records of New Amsterdam from 1653 to 1674 Anno Domini.* 7 vols. New York, 1897.

Hazard, Ebenezer, ed. *Historical Collections Consisting of State Papers and Other Authentic Documents.* 2 vols. Philadelphia, 1792–1794.

Hazard, Samuel, et al., eds. *Pennsylvania Archives.* 9 series, 138 vols. Philadelphia and Harrisburg, 1852–1949.

Heckewelder, John. "Indian Tradition of the First Arrival of the Dutch at Manhattan Island, now New York." In New-York Historical Society, *Collections,* 2d ser., I (1841), 68–74.

Hicks, Benjamin D., ed. *Records of the Towns of North and South Hempstead, Long Island, New York.* 8 vols. Jamaica, N.Y., 1896–1904.

Hoadly, Charles J., ed. *Records of the Colony . . . of New Haven.* 2 vols. Hartford, 1857–1858.

Hutchinson, Thomas, ed. *Collection of Original Papers Relative to the History of the Colony of Massachusetts-Bay.* Boston, 1769.

Jameson, J. Franklin, ed. *Narratives of New Netherland, 1609–1664.* (Original Narratives of Early American History.) New York, 1909.

Bibliography

Johnson, Amandus, ed. and trans. *The Instruction for Johan Printz, Governor of New Sweden.* Philadelphia, 1930.

Journal of the Legislative Council of the Colony of New York (1691–1775). 2 vols. Albany, 1861.

Journal of the Votes and Proceedings of the General Assembly of the Colony of New York, 1691–1765. 2 vols. New York, 1764–1766.

Labaree, Leonard Woods, ed. *Royal Instructions to British Colonial Governors, 1670–1776.* 2 vols. New York and London, 1935.

Lahontan, Louis Armand, Baron de. *New Voyages to North America* (1703). Ed. by Reuben G. Thwaites. 2 vols. Chicago, 1905.

Leder, Lawrence H., ed. *The Livingston Indian Records, 1666–1723.* Gettysburg, Pa., 1956.

Letter from the Governor and Council of New York to the President and Council of Pennsylvania, April 15, 1687. In *Pennsylvania Magazine of History and Biography,* XI (1887–1888), 241–242.

Lincoln, Charles Henry, ed. *Narratives of the Indian Wars, 1675–1699.* (Original Narratives of Early American History.) New York, 1913.

Lindestrom, Peter M. *Geographia Americae with an Account of the Delaware Indians, Based on Surveys and Notes Made in 1654–1656.* Ed. by Amandus Johnson. Philadelphia, 1925.

McIlwaine, H. R., ed. *Executive Journals of the Council of Colonial Virginia, 1680–1739.* 4 vols. Richmond, 1925–1930.

McIlwaine, H. R., and J. P. Kennedy, eds. *Journals of the House of Burgesses of Virginia (1619–1776).* 13 vols. Richmond, 1905–1915.

Minutes of the Common Council of the City of New York, 1675–1776. 8 vols. New York, 1905.

Munsell, Joel, ed. *The Annals of Albany.* 10 vols. Albany, 1850–1859.

Myers, Albert Cook, ed. *Narratives of Early Pennsylvania, West New Jersey, and Delaware, 1630–1707.* (Original Narratives of Early Amercian History.) New York, 1912.

"New York's Colonial Archives; Transcriptions of the Records between the Years 1673 and 1675," Appendix L. In New York State Historian, *Annual Report, 1897* (New York and Albany, 1898), 157–436.

O'Callaghan, Edmund B., ed. *Calendar of Historical Manuscripts in the Office of the Secretary of State.* 2 vols. Albany, 1865–1866.

O'Callaghan, Edmund B., ed. *Documentary History of the State of New-York.* Octavo ed., 4 vols. Albany, 1849–1851.

O'Callaghan, Edmund B., comp. and trans. *Laws and Ordinances of New Netherlands, 1636–74.* Albany, 1868.

O'Callaghan, Edmund B., and Berthold Fernow, eds. *Documents Relative to the Colonial History of the State of New York.* 15 vols. Albany, 1856–1887.

Bibliography

Oyster Bay Town Records, 1653–1763. 6 vols. New York, 1916–1931.

Paltsits, Victor H., ed. *Minutes of the Executive Council of the Province of New York; Administration of Francis Lovelace, 1668–1673.* 2 vols. Albany, 1910.

Records of the Town of East-Hampton, Long Island. 5 vols. Sag Harbor, N.Y., 1887–1905.

Shurtleff, Nathaniel B., ed. *Records of the Governor and Company of the Massachusetts Bay, 1628–1686.* 5 vols. Boston, 1853–1854.

Shurtleff, Nathaniel B., and David Pulsifer, eds. *Records of the Colony of New Plymouth, in New England.* 12 vols. Boston, 1855–1861.

Street, Charles R., ed. *Huntington Town Records, Including Babylon, Long Island, N.Y., 1653 . . . 1873.* 3 vols. Huntington, 1887–1899.

Thwaites, Reuben Gold, ed. *The Jesuit Relations and Allied Documents . . . 1610–1791.* 73 vols. Cleveland, 1896–1901.

Toppan, Robert N., and Alfred T. S. Goodrick, eds. *Edward Randolph.* 7 vols. Boston, 1898–1909.

"Treaty between Col. Richard Nicolls, Governor of New York, and the Esopus Indians, 1665; Esopus Treaty, 1665." In Ulster County Historical Society, *Collections,* I (1860), 59–65.

Trumbull, James H., and C. J. Hoadly, comps. *Public Records of the Colony of Connecticut (1636–1776).* 15 vols. Hartford, 1850–1890.

Van der Donck, Adrian. "Description of the New Netherlands" (1655). In New-York Historical Society, *Collections,* 2d ser., I (1841), 125–242.

Van Laer, A. J. F., ed. "Albany Notarial Papers, 1666–1693." In Dutch Settlers Society of Albany, *Yearbook,* XIII (1937–1938), 1–18.

Van Laer, A. J. F., ed. "Arent van Curler and His Historic Letter to the Patroon." In Dutch Settlers Society of Albany, *Yearbook,* III (1927–1928), 11–29.

Van Laer, A. J. F., ed. "Documents Relating to Arent van Curler's Death." In Dutch Settlers Society of Albany, *Yearbook,* III (1927–1928), 30–34.

Van Laer, A. J. F., ed. *Documents Relating to New Netherland, 1624–1626, in the Henry E. Huntington Library.* San Marino, Calif., 1924.

Van Laer, A. J. F., ed. *Minutes of the Court of Albany, Rensselaerswyck and Schenectedy, 1668–1685.* 3 vols. Albany, 1926–1932.

Van Laer, A. J. F., ed. *Minutes of the Court of Fort Orange and Beverwyck, 1652–1660.* 2 vols. Albany, 1920–1923.

Van Laer, A. J. F., ed. *Minutes of the Court of Rensselaerswyck, 1648–1652.* Albany, 1922.

Van Laer, A. J. F., ed. *Van Rensselaer Bowier Manuscripts.* Albany, 1908.

Van Rensselaer, Jeremias. *Correspondence of Jeremias van Rensselaer, 1651–1674.* Ed. by A. J. F. Van Laer. Albany, 1932.

Winthrop, John. *Winthrop's Journal, 1630–1649.* Ed. by James Kendall

Bibliography

Hosmer. (Original Narratives of Early American History.) 2 vols. New York, 1908.

Winthrop Papers. 5 vols. Boston, 1929–1947.

Wraxall, Peter. *An Abridgement of the Indian Affairs . . . in the Colony of New York . . . 1678 to . . . 1751.* Ed. by C. H. McIlwain. Cambridge, Mass., 1915.

III. Unpublished Thesis

Buffinton, Arthur Howland. "The Policy of the Northern Colonies towards the French to the Peace of Utrecht." Ph.D. dissertation, Harvard University, 1925.

IV. Books

Adams, James Truslow. *History of the Town of Southampton.* Bridgehampton, N.Y., 1918.

Beauchamp, William M. *A History of the New York Iroquois.* (New York State Museum Bulletin no. 78.) 1905.

Brinton, Daniel G. *The Lenape and Their Legends.* Philadelphia, 1885.

Brodhead, John Romeyn. *History of the State of New York.* 2 vols. New York, 1853–1871.

Calder, Isabel MacBeath. *The New Haven Colony.* New Haven, 1934.

Charlevoix, Pierre François X. *History and General Description of New France.* Ed. by J. G. Shea. 6 vols. New York, 1868–1872.

Colden, Cadwallader. *The History of the Five Indian Nations of Canada.* 2 vols. New York, 1902.

Desrosiers, Léo Paul. *Iroquoisie.* (Etudes de l'Institut d'Histoire de l'Amérique Française, vol. I.) Montreal, 1947.

Duffy, John. *Epidemics in Colonial America.* Baton Rouge, La., 1953.

Ellis, George W., and John E. Morris. *King Philip's War.* New York, 1906.

Flick, Alexander C., ed. *History of the State of New York.* 10 vols. New York, 1933–1937.

Fox, Dixon Ryan. *Yankees and Yorkers.* New York, 1940.

Greene, Evarts B., and Virginia D. Harrington. *American Population before the Federal Census of 1790.* New York, 1932.

Greene, Nelson. *Fort Plain Nelliston History, 1580–1947.* Fort Plain, N.Y., 1947.

Hanna, Charles A. *The Wilderness Trail.* 2 vols. New York, 1911.

Higgins, Ruth L. *Expansion in New York with Especial Reference to the Eighteenth Century.* Columbus, Ohio, 1931.

Hodge, Frederick Webb, ed. *Handbook of American Indians, North of Mexico.* 2 vols. Washington, 1907–1910.

368

Bibliography

Humphreys, David. *An Historical Account of the Incorporated Society for the Propagation of the Gospel in Foreign Parts.* London, 1730.

Hunt, George T. *The Wars of the Iroquois: A Study in Intertribal Trade Relations.* Madison, 1940.

Innis, Harold A. *The Fur Trade in Canada.* New Haven, 1930.

Johnson, Amandus. *The Swedish Settlements on the Delaware: Their History and Relations to the Indians, Dutch, and English, 1638–1664.* 2 vols. Philadelphia, 1911.

Keith, Charles P. *Chronicles of Pennsylvania, 1688–1748.* 2 vols. Philadelphia, 1917.

Kennedy, John H. *Thomas Dongan, Governor of New York (1682–1688).* Washington, 1930.

Kessler, Henry H., and Eugene Rachlis. *Peter Stuyvesant and His New York.* New York, 1959.

Lauber, Almon Wheeler. *Indian Slavery in Colonial Times within the Present Limits of the United States.* New York, 1913.

Leach, Douglas Edward. *Flintlock and Tomahawk: New England in King Philip's War.* New York, 1958.

Merle-Smith, Van S. *The Village of Oyster Bay: Its Foundation and Growth from 1653 to 1700.* Garden City, 1953.

Morgan, Lewis H. *League of the Ho-De-No-Sau-Nee or Iroquois.* 2 vols. New York, 1901.

Nettels, Curtis Putnam. *The Money Supply of the American Colonies before 1720.* Madison, 1934.

Newcomb, William W., Jr. *The Culture and Acculturation of the Delaware Indians.* (University of Michigan, Museum of Anthropology, Anthropological Papers no. 10.) Ann Arbor, 1956.

Nissenson, S. G. *The Patroon's Domain.* New York, 1937.

Northrup, A. Judd. *Slavery in New York: A Historical Sketch.* (New York State Library Bulletin, History, no. 4.) Albany, 1900.

O'Callaghan, Edmund B. *History of New Netherland.* 2d ed., 2 vols. New York, 1855.

Onderdonk, Henry, Jr. *The Annals of Hempstead, 1643 to 1832.* Hempstead, 1878.

Onderdonk, Henry, Jr. *Queen's County in Olden Times.* Jamaica, N.Y., 1865.

Osgood, Herbert L. *The American Colonies in the Eighteenth Century.* 4 vols. New York, 1924.

Palfrey, John Gorham. *History of New England.* 5 vols. Boston, 1858–1890.

Parkman, Francis. *Count Frontenac and New France under Louis XIV.* 28th ed. Boston, 1893.

Parkman, Francis. *La Salle and the Discovery of the Great West.* 12th ed. Boston, 1892.

Bibliography

Parkman, Francis. *The Old Régime in Canada*. 27th ed. Boston, 1892.

Pearson, Jonathan, et al. *A History of the Schenectady Patent in the Dutch and English Times*. Ed. by J. W. MacMurray. Albany, 1883.

Raesly, Ellis Lawrence. *Portrait of New Netherland*. New York, 1945.

Reich, Jerome R. *Leisler's Rebellion: A Study of Democracy in New York, 1664–1720*. Chicago, 1953.

Ruttenber, Edward Manning. *History of the Indian Tribes of Hudson's River*. Albany, 1872.

Schultz, Bernice. *Colonial Hempstead*. Lynbrook, N.Y., 1937.

Schuyler, George W. *Colonial New York: Phillip Schuyler and His Family*. 2 vols. New York, 1885.

Severance, Frank H. *An Old Frontier of France: The Niagara Region and Adjacent Lakes under French Control*. 2 vols. New York, 1917.

Shea, John G. *History of the Catholic Missions among the Indian Tribes of the United States, 1529–1854*. New York, 1855.

Skinner, Alanson. *The Indians of Greater New York*. Cedar Rapids, 1915.

Smith, William. *The History of the Province of New York*. 2 vols. (New-York Historical Society, *Collections*, vols. IV–V.) New York, 1829–1830.

Stites, Sara Henry. *Economics of the Iroquois*. Lancaster, Pa., 1905.

Swanton, John R. *The Indian Tribes of North America*. (Smithsonian Institution, Bureau of American Ethnology Bulletin no. 145.) Washington, 1953.

Thompson, Benjamin F. *History of Long Island*. 3d ed., 3 vols. Ed. by Charles J. Werner. New York, 1918.

Van Rensselaer, Mrs. Schuyler (Mariana Griswold). *History of the City of New York in the Seventeenth Century*. 2 vols. New York, 1909.

Wallace, Anthony F. C. *King of the Delawares: Teedyuscung, 1700–1763*. Philadelphia, 1949.

Wallace, Paul A. W. *The White Roots of Peace*. Philadelphia, 1946.

Wilson, James Grant, ed. *Memorial History of the City of New York*. 4 vols. New York, 1892–1893.

Yates, John V. N., and Joseph W. Moulton. *History of the State of New-York*. Vol. I, pts. I and II. New York, 1824–1826.

Zwierlein, Frederick J. *Religion in New Netherland: A History of the Development of the Religious Conditions in the Province of New Netherland, 1623–1664*. Rochester, N.Y., 1910.

V. Articles

Bolton, Reginald P. "New York City in Indian Possession." In Heye Foundation, *Indian Notes and Monographs*, II (1920), 225–395.

Bibliography

Broshar, Helen. "First Push Westward of the Albany Traders," *Mississippi Valley Historical Review*, VII (1920), 228–241.

Buffinton, Arthur H. "The Policy of Albany and English Westward Expansion," *Mississippi Valley Historical Review*, VIII (1922), 327–366.

Cooper, John M. "Land Tenure among the Indians of Eastern and Northern North America," *Pennsylvania Archaeologist*, VIII (1938), 55–59.

Corwin, Charles E. "Efforts of the Dutch-American Colonial Pastors for the Conversion of the Indians." In Presbyterian Historical Society, *Journal*, XII (1925), 225–246.

Douglas, Frederic H. "Long Island Indian Cultures." (Denver Art Museum, Dept. of Indian Art, Leaflet no. 50.) Denver, 1932.

Douglas, Frederic H. "Long Island Indian Tribes." (Denver Art Museum, Dept. of Indian Art, Leaflet no. 49.) Denver, 1932.

Eccles, W. J. "Frontenac and the Iroquois, 1672–1682," *Canadian Historical Review*, XXXVI (1955), 1–16.

Eccles, W. J. "Frontenac's Military Policies, 1689–1698: A Reassessment," *Canadian Historical Review*, XXXVII (1956), 201–224.

Fenton, William N. "Locality as a Basic Factor in the Development of Iroquois Social Structure." (Bureau of American Ethnology Bulletin no. 149.) Washington, 1951. Pages 35–54.

Fenton, William N. "Problems Arising from the Historic Northeastern Position of the Iroquois." In Smithsonian Institution, *Essays in Historical Anthropology of North America, Published in Honor of John R. Swanton.* (Smithsonian Institution Miscellaneous Collections vol. C.) Washington, 1940. Pages 159–251.

Gardiner, John Lyon. "Notes and Observations on the Town of East Hampton" (1798). In New-York Historical Society, *Collections, 1869*, 225–260.

Gilmore, Melvin R. "Some Indian Ideas of Property." In Heye Foundation, *Indian Notes and Monographs*, V (1928), 137–144.

Hall, Edward Hagaman. "The New York Commercial Tercentenary, 1614–1914." In American Scenic and Historical Preservation Society, *Annual Report*, XIX (1914), 441–500.

Hewitt, J. N. B. "Era of the Formation of the Historic League of the Iroquois," *American Anthropologist*, VII (1894), 61–67.

Houghton, Frederick. "The Migrations of the Seneca Nation," *American Anthropologist*, n.s. XXIX (1927), 241–250.

Kroeber, A. L. "Nature of the Land-holding Group," *Ethnohistory*, II (1955), 303–314.

MacLeod, William C. "Family Hunting Territory and Lenápe Political Organization," *American Anthropologist*, XXIV (1922), 448–463.

Mooney, James. "The Aboriginal Population of America North of Mexico."

Bibliography

(Smithsonian Institution Miscellaneous Collections, LXXX, no. 7.) Washington, 1928.

Murray, Jean E. "The Early Fur Trade in New France and New Netherland," *Canadian Historical Review*, XIX (1938), 365–377.

Paltsits, Victor H. "Founding of New Amsterdam in 1626." In American Antiquarian Society, *Proceedings*, XXXIV (1924), 39–65.

Rankin, Edward S. "The Purchase of Newark from the Indians." In New Jersey Historical Society, *Proceedings*, n.s. XII (1927), 442–445.

Rife, Clarence White. "Land Tenure in New Netherland." In *Essays in Colonial History Presented to Charles McLean Andrews*. New Haven, 1931. Pages 41–73.

St. Paul, Henry Allain. "Governor Thomas Dongan's Expansion Policy," *Mid-America*, XVII (n.s. VI; 1935), 172–184, 236–272.

Scott, Kenneth, and Charles E. Baker. "Renewals of Governor Nicolls' Treaty of 1665 with the Esopus Indians." In New-York Historical Society, *Quarterly*, XXXVII (1953), 251–272.

Skinner, Alanson. "The Manhattan Indians." (New York State Museum Bulletin no. 158.) 1912. Pages 199–212.

Snyderman, George S. "Behind the Tree of Peace: A Sociological Analysis of Iroquois Warfare," *Pennsylvania Archaeologist*, XVIII (1948), 3–93.

Speck, Frank G. "The Wapanachki Delawares and the English: Their Past as Viewed by an Ethnologist," *Pennsylvania Magazine of History and Biography*, LXVII (1943), 319–344.

Sulte, Benjamin. "Le Commerce de France avec le Canada avant 1760." In Royal Society of Canada, *Proceedings and Transactions*, 2d ser., XII, sec. 1 (1906), 45–63.

Sulte, Benjamin. "Le Fort de Frontenac, 1668–1678." In Royal Society of Canada, *Proceedings and Transactions*, 2d ser., VII, sec. 1 (1901), 47–96.

Sulte, Benjamin. "Guerres des Iroquois, 1670–1673." In Royal Society of Canada, *Transactions*, 3d ser., XV, sec. 1 (1921), 85–95.

Wallace, Anthony F. C. "Origins of Iroquois Neutrality: The Grand Settlement of 1701," *Pennsylvania History*, XXIV (1957), 223–235.

Wallace, Anthony F. C. "Political Organization and Land Tenure among the Northeastern Indians, 1600–1830," *Southwestern Journal of Anthropology*, XIII (1957), 301–321.

Wallace, Anthony F. C. "Woman, Land, and Society: Three Aspects of Aboriginal Delaware Life," *Pennsylvania Archaeologist*, XVII (1947), 1–35.

Wallace, Paul A. W. "The Return of Hiawatha," *New York History*, XXIX (1948), 385–403.

Witthoft, John, and William A. Hunter. "The Seventeenth-Century Origins of the Shawnee," *Ethnohistory*, II (1955), 42–57.

Index

373

Index

Index

La Barre, Lefebvre de, 254, 260-261, 263-269, 271
Lachine massacre, 297-298
La Famine conference (1684), 266-267, 269
Lamberville, Father Jean de, 264, 272-273, 275-276, 282
La Montagne, Johannes, 65, 79, 85, 124, 129, 134, 144, 153-154, 157, 164
Land:
   acquisition from Indians:
      by Dutch, 36, 40-41, 43-45, 49, 58, 62-64, 91-93, 136, 150-151, 159, 168
      by English, 182-183, 193-199, 215, 329-331, 337-340, 361-362
   disputes over, 63, 91-92, 146, 148, 159-160, 173, 184, 195-199, 215, 330-331, 337-340
   tenure among Indians, 11-12, 17-18
Legal position of Indians, 64-65, 94, 184-186, 226
Leisler, Jacob, 177-178, 219, 295, 299, 302-303, 305
Le Moyne, Father Simon, 122-123
Liquor traffic, with Indians, 51, 70, 93-94, 125-126, 135, 149, 160, 168-169, 188-190, 223-225, 275
Livingston, Robert, 120n, 208-210, 212, 253, 295, 302-303, 306, 309-310, 338-339, 344-346, 349, 356-358, 360, 362
Lloyd, Col. Philemon, 240-241
Long Island Indians, 4-5, 8-12, 178-180
   in Esopus wars, 153, 162-166
   relations with New Netherland, 45, 62-64, 66-67, 75-77, 79-80, 82-83, 86-87, 89-93, 95, 97-98, 100-101, 103, 139-141, 145-146, 148, 151, 156, 159-160, 173
   relations with New York, 179-182, 185-188, 191-201
   see also individual bands
Loockermans, Govert, 98
Lovelace, Francis, 176, 180-183, 187-188, 190-191, 195, 199-201, 224n, 229, 241-242, 245
Luycasse, Gerrit, 210-211
Lydius, Domine John, 350-351

Magregory, Major Patrick, 270-271
Mahican tribe, 3-5, 8-12, 15, 27, 71n, 252, 323n
   relations with:
      Mohawk tribe, 32, 34, 46-48, 127, 129-130, 166, 228-230, 283, 326
      New Netherland, 32-34, 40, 46-49, 53, 83, 95, 115, 117, 129-130, 154, 157-158, 164, 166
      New York, 215, 224, 226, 228-231, 235-237, 253, 281, 283, 324-326
   see also Algonquian tribes and River Indians
Manhattan band, 8, 28
Manhattan Island, purchase of, 36, 40
Maryland, relations with New York, 239-241, 257-259, 288, 302, 308, 315
Massachusetts:
   relations with New Netherland, 105-108, 128
   relations with New York, 232-233, 235-238, 244, 299, 302-303, 315, 317
   see also Iroquois and New England
Massapequa band, 9, 63, 145
Matinecoc band, 9, 80, 82, 86
Mattabesec tribe, 42, 55
Matteno, Nyack sachem, 163, 166-169
May, Cornelis Jacobsen, 30, 35-36
Megapolensis, Domine Johannes, 169-172
Merric band, 9, 63
Miami tribe, 254, 260, 268-269, 277, 282-283, 325, 356, 362
Miantonomo, Narraganset sachem, 70n
Michaëlius, Domine Jonas, 39-40
Milborne, Jacob, 295, 299-300, 302-303
Millet, Father Pierre, 313-314
Minisink band, 7, 56, 164, 183, 190, 281, 289, 324-325
Minuit, Peter, 36, 48, 108-109
Miscegenation, among Indians and Dutch, 172
Missionaries, see Canadian Iroquois, Iroquois, Jesuits, and Religious conversion of Indians

Index

Pacham, Tankiteke sachem, 66, 76
Pauw, Michael, 45
Pavonia (patroonship), 45, 71-73, 77, 86, 139-141, 148
Pawling, Henry, 183-184
"Peach War," 138-148
Penhawitz, Canarsee sachem, 62-63, 79
Penn, William, 175, 254-257, 358
Pennacook tribe, 299, 326, 334
Pennsylvania, relations with New York, 254-257, 288, 308, 315
Pequot tribe, 55-56
Pinhorne, William, 330
Plymouth Colony:
　relations with New Netherland, 55, 105, 108
　relations with New York, 303
　see also New England
Poundridge, battle of (1644), 80
Printz, Johan, 98, 109-110

Raffeix, Father Pierre, 252
Raritan band, 7, 45-46, 65-67, 86, 159
Rechgawawanc band, see Manhattan band
Religious conversion of Indians, 38-40, 169-172, 200-202, 327-329, 350-351, 354
　see also Canadian Iroquois and Jesuits
Rensselaerswyck, Indian affairs at, 49-51, 96, 99, 101, 112-118, 124-125, 133, 135, 169-170, 172, 219, 224
Reynsen, Jacob, 97-98
Rhode Island:
　relations with New Netherland, 105
　see also New England
Rising, Johan, 110
River Indians, 323n, 326-327, 360
　relations with New York, 215, 221, 226, 283, 302, 306, 313-314, 322, 326-327, 360
　see also Catskill band, Mahican tribe, and Scaticook band
Rockaway band, 9, 62-63, 75, 80, 179n
Romer, Col. Wolfgang, 352, 356, 359
Roseboom, Johannes, 269-272

St. Francis Xavier des Près (mission), see Canadian Iroquois
Scaticook band, 235, 253, 281, 326-327, 330, 346, 360
　see also River Indians
Schaats, Domine Gideon, 170
Schenectady, 136, 205, 207, 215, 242-243, 284-285, 299, 303, 311-312, 343, 354-355, 361
　attack on (1690), 301
　Indian relations at, 215, 227, 281, 299, 301-302, 350, 354
　Indian trade at, 136-137, 218-219, 224
Schermerhorn, Jacob Jansen, 97-98
Schuyler, Arent, 325
Schuyler, David, 349, 361, 363
Schuyler, John, 304, 340-341, 360
Schuyler, Peter, 209-210, 219, 284, 295, 300, 306, 309-312, 315-316, 318-319, 322, 325, 330, 333-339, 344-345, 349, 352
Seneca tribe, 15-16, 18, 164, 323n
　relations with New Netherland, 127-128, 134
　relations with New York, 267
　see also Iroquois and Jesuits
Sequin tribe, see Mattabesec tribe
Shawnee tribe, 3, 324-325
Shinnecock band, 9, 181
Siwanoy band, 8, 80
Slavery, Indian, 81, 158-160, 202-203
Sloughter, Henry, 177-178, 184, 295, 305-306, 318, 327-329
Smallpox epidemic of 1690, 304-305, 324
Smith, Dirk, 150-152, 154, 157-158
Sokoki tribe, 129-130
Southampton, L.I., Indian relations at, 101, 198-200
Staten Island Indians, 7, 9-12
　relations with New Netherland, 63, 65-66, 68, 77-78, 86, 90, 139-141, 148, 156
　relations with New York, 182, 195, 197
　see also Canarsee band, Hackensack band, and Nyack band

Lightning Source UK Ltd.
Milton Keynes UK
UKOW01f1202190117
292402UK00001B/130/P